# The Jats

## Their Role and Contribution to the Socio-economic Life and Polity of North and North-west India

Volume 4

# *The Jats*

## Their Role and Contribution to the Socio-economic Life and Polity of North and North-west India

### Volume 4

*Edited by*

**Dr. Rajendra Kumar**

**Originals**

**Delhi**

First Published 2014



ISBN 10: 81-8454-138-4
ISBN 13: 978-81-8454-138-0

*Published by*
**Originals**
*(an imprint of Low Price Publications)*
A-6, 2nd Floor, Nimri Commercial Centre,
Ashok Vihar Phase 4, Delhi 110052 (INDIA)
tel.: +91.11.27302453 fax.: +91.11.47061936
url: www.LPPindia.com e-mail: info@LPPindia.com



*Printed at*
D.K. Fine Art Press Pvt. Ltd.
Delhi

PRINTED IN INDIA

# Contents

# Foreword

This volume, fourth in the series of 'Jats: Their Role and Contribution to the Socio-economic Life and Polity of North and North-West India' contains the papers presented in the National Seminar organized by the Maharaja Surajmal Centre for Research and Publication, New Delhi on 5th and 6th November 2011. Selected research papers arranged thematically present a wide range of topics under the variety of thought provocative themes, and this gives this collection such unity as it possesses to interpret the main currents of the history of the Jats from a standpoint which belongs to the new perception of historiography. The reader will find here newer subjects, newer interpretations, and newer academic vistas open before them to discuss the subject.

One can realize that the reader is not likely to be interested in the approach used by the scholars. What he may expect to be interested in is whether we can understand our past as a people better by giving more emphasis to the interaction of material conditions, ideas, struggles in actual work of description and analysis. And a serious reading would reveal the essential difference in the contents and treatment. Such kinds of interpretations can and do deviation from scholarly affairs adding to the problems that a historian generally faces while co-relating complex facts.

Question arises why the phenomenon of casteism, or consideration of a particular caste in modern society? Specialization in occupation or trade, and then its conversion into family business developed in every advanced society which changed it into class, caste or community. Today, though their descendants left those occupations, but they use these occupation as their surnames for their identity, for example in Britain we find

Smiths, Goldsmiths, Carpenters, Masons, Gardeners, Chaplains Fletchers (one who make arrows), Nailers, Procters, Thatchers, Wards, Carvers, etc. Indian Parsis still use the occupation of their ancestors as their surnames, Daruwa!as, Sutliwalas, Botliwalas, Zaveris (jewellers), Kesarwanis, Kaparias etc. though they are engaged in different occupations for a long time. Caste or community has been for many centuries a real and active part of Indian life and not just a self-serving orientalist fiction. Of all the topics that have fascinated and divided scholar-sociologists, caste (or community) is probably the most contentious. As a system of elaborately stratified social hierarchy that distinguishes India from all other societies, caste has achieved the same prominence in social, political and academic debates as race in United States, class in Britain and faction in Italy. It has been widely thought of as the most important fact of life in the subcontinent, and for some, as the very core or inherent characteristics of Indian civilization.

There is of course a huge body of academic writing on caste, both before, during and after colonial period. Since caste, which is best seen as a meeting ground between every day Indian life and thought and the strategies of rulers and other arbiters of moral and social order, tends to provoke more heated debate than almost everything else in the specialist literature. From the early nineteenth century British rule significantly expanded and sharpened the norms and conventions of race and community. However, the practices of representative government, served further to enhance the important of caste-affinities in the political arena. Both, for early participants in Electoral politics and to a significant extent in the period since independence, caste has been an effective tool and resource for creation of common interests across the boundaries of region, language, faith, and economic status. Even the government took decision to arrange caste statistics through census.

The subject of caste (or community) throws up some difficulties as well, to those unfamiliar with the field, especially in dealing with major historical events. For example as third battle of Panipat, the 1857 Rebellion and the freedom struggle, the literature often identifies groups of Indians by specific regional caste-title, often without making clear whether this kind of group-affinity truly overrides individual decision-making in times of crisis. Not surprisingly, many readers wish to understand more fully why the Jats withdrew themselves from Panipat and did not fight in alliance to Marathas against Abdali, what it meant when they read that, in 1857, there were areas where 'the Rajputs' remained loyal, while 'the Jats' and 'the Gujars' rebelled, or how Gandhiji and B.R. Ambedkar clashed in 1930 over the issue of how best to 'uplift' India's millions of so-called untouchables. Those to whom these terms and concepts are unfamiliar will rightly want to know what an endowment of Jats, Brahmins, Rajputs or untouchable caste identity actually entailed at these times. Furthermore, did such affinities change, or did they remain constant and immutable when so much else was changing in India's culture and material environment.

Our aim is certainly not to defend caste. Nor to uphold the kind of theory proposed by those social scientists whose goal is to identify single principle such as purity, power or orientalism with which to explain caste-experience regardless of regional or historical context.

Hence the Jats. It has been common since the days of British rule for both historians and anthropologists to refer to the Jats as important race of Indian 'caste-society' and as an all-permeating presence in North-west India. The Jats are a live community and as an economic entity (peasantry) were distinct and accordingly differently related to social and economic formation in North-west India. The relevancy of Jats history is an extent of the sequential development of Indian society.

Established in 1972, to provide educational facilities to the weaker section of the society, especially the rural youth, Surajmal Memorial Education Society has established three premier professional institutes in its campus at C- 4, Janakpuri, New Delhi and also two public schools, one each in U.P. and Rajasthan. It is in the process of establishing a new campus in Haryana also. One of the important organs of the society, Maharaja Surajmal Centre for Research and Publication has been undertaking the collection, preservation and publication of material on rural heritage, especially relating to the life and role of peasants in our national endeavours. The Centre has published 27 books which include research work of scholars, Hindi translation of the prominent works, reprinting of the famous works on peasants of North-west India, and the proceedings of National Seminars organized by the Society from time to time.

Through its endeavour, Maharaja Surajmal Centre for Research and Publication has attained the status of a premier Research institute and Indian Council of Historical Research, New Delhi has approved it in 2006 as a recognized institute for research projects in history. The Society is equipped with a good library and collection of manuscripts and also provides boarding and lodging facilities to the research scholars. The scholars can utilize the services of the Research Centre as institute of affiliation for their research projects submitted to ICHR.

Surajmal Memorial Education Society intends to explore and conduct research on different aspects of the Jat community. For our Centre for Research and Publication is continuing search for newer material on the history and contribution of the Jats therein. The critical insight to the prevalent material on the Jats led us to devise ways for associating larger number of scholars to carry out deep insight in the history of the Jats and to fill the gaps in it. In that attempt the society organizes National Seminars on various occasions. As a matter of fact, these seminars have become a regular feature of the activities of the Centre which are attended by eminent scholars from the every nook and corner of India to present their research findings.

In recent years historians have broken much new ground in the study of political and economic change in the subcontinent. We look forward to the scholars to undertake and promote research on several other topics in wider context in the light of new material in Indian and outside India sources and unearth fresh information.

For the burdensome work of organizing National Seminar, I take opportunity to appreciate the efforts of all the office-bearers of the Society and staff of the Centre for Research and Publication.

I wish to acknowledge the onerous efforts put in by our honorary Director Dr. Rajendra Kumar in compiling, editing and bringing out this prestigious volume.

**S.P. Singh**
President
Surajmal Memorial Education Society
New Delhi

# Introduction

Any serious student of the history of the Jats is faced with a paradox - there is 'much stated but little collated, much attested but little tested, much shown but little known'. The 'facts' have been displayed in an unending order of succession, but they are based on hearsay, or one sided account of matter from particular point of view of individuals and groups. Seminars give opportunities for making efforts to examine both sides of the coin and verify 'facts' against factual and circumstantial evidence, and focus the historian's torch on the facts and incidents wrapped in darkness. The research papers presented thus provide chance to the learned participants to share new facts and ideas on the specified themes through discussion. The benefit widens when these papers after critical examination and suggestions get published in the shape of a book and reach a wider readership.

Present volume is the compilation of the selected and in some cases revised papers presented in the XIIth National Seminar, 'The Jats : Their Role and Contribution to the Socio-economic Life and Polity of North and North-west India', organized by Maharaja Surajmal Centre for Research and Publication on 5th and 6th November 2011. The topic itself is very significant, especially when many debates are going on about the historiography and history-writing now-a-days. Many historians, particularly, foreign historians have written the history of India as accomplishment of their special purpose, to establish or forge a particular opinion and others rehashed the same. But now it is not a matter of concern, as new grounds are being dug, new vistas are being opened and fresh topics are being chosen. So is about the history of the Jats. It was time when we looked into the history of origin and antiquity of the Jats, based on Puranic and Arabic sources, or the history of their kings and warriors. But new horizons open a wide range of the methodology of historical research. When we go through the macro (detailed) study of the Indian history, we find that the Jats have been a distinct people in early as well as medieval period of our history. If we come up with the micro-methodology, we find that in pre-medieval times, some sources have been imposed upon us, as the *Chachnama* of the 8th century. Originally it was written in Arabic. Afterwards it was translated into Persian and still later in English. It has a large description of the Jats, which indicates that the term Jat was popularly applied to a 'low and servile creature, or to an impudent villain, tied to his community'. But a critical examination of this work is essential which has not been done so far. When we talk about the Greek sources of the Jats, difficulty arises that these sources have been translated by the British, and not by Indians. It is strikingly amazing that our intellectuals did not show any interest in translating even *Indica* of Megasthnese. Question arises whether the translation done by the English could be authentic because there has been always a technical terminology of dialect, customs and usages which can not be understood by any foreigner, the English, who have a different way of life. Only we can do this. Thus there is always a fair amount of difference in translation.

Studies of Greek sources in Multan and Pakistan tell us that Nebecus came with Yugander, who narrated the story of Alexander's last days, that when Alexander was going back to Greece, in a skirmish near Multan, one Jat stabbed him. Alexander died of these wounds within two-three months after reaching Athens, and nobody poisoned him as is generally said. If he would have died in India, in that case, it could be said that Alexander was defeated by Indians. Another description says that when Alexander was ascending on stairs, he was stabbed by a Jat and he fell down. His assailant was also killed immediately. It means that such references about the Jats require a thorough study.

Same thing is with Arabic sources, which tell us that the Jats were good sailors, who owned fleets of large boats. They used to cultivate the soil, as well as were engaged in trade. Sometimes they showed highhandedness. This highhandedness was termed as plunder, and the Jats were called plunderers and dacoits. They even did not leave Mahmud of Ghazni. According to *Tabqat-i-Akbari,* Mahmud of Ghazni attacked India seventeen times. He undertook his seventeenth expedition in 1027 for chastising the Jats who inhabited at the hills of Jud and had appropriated money from his people and molested his army on its return from Somnath. Mahmud is said to have organized a fleet of 1,400 boats, while the Jats had 4,000. A naval fight ensued between them at Multan, in which most of the Jat army was drowned. The rest were slain.

Moreover, it is mentioned in *Tarikh-us-Subuktgin,* that two or three thousand mounted Jats attacked the Ghaznavid commander Tilak (1034 AD), 'chiefly for the purpose of seizing his property and money', when he was pursuing the rebel Governor of Lahore, Ahmad Nialtgin in the lower Punjab. They carried away his son with them and subsequently killed Nialtgin too. The Jats returned Governor's son and the head of the deceased only after getting a handsome portion of the promised 'reward'. Due to these and other acts, early historical accounts of Sind indicate that the term Jat was 'synonymous with thief and scoundrel' as Richard Burton wrote on page 247 in *Sindh and the Races that Inhabit the Valley of the Indus.* The Afghans and the Persians resented this 'degraded' group which eked a poor living out of agriculture and moved about the barren plains tending and breeding camels.' Early 18th century accounts described the non-Sikh Jats, who were dominant in the regions south and east of Delhi as plunderers and bandits prying on the imperial lines of communication. Not only the Jats, but also the Marathas and all others were engaged in such plundering. The Jats plundered Sikandara, Akbar's tomb near Fatehpur Sikri, Red Fort of Agra and Delhi. But according to the norms of time, it was not considered a wrong practice. What does it mean to plunder the wealth of enemy? If one would not have the sources of enemy reduced, how could he adhere to establish his own authority over the opponents?

In medieval period, in 17th century, we find the Jats struggling against the Mughal empire. Gokula or Raja Ram or Badan Singh did not revolt merely against the said bigotry of Aurangzeb, the main reason of hostility was the question of identity or recognition. The spirit of independence among Sinsinwar Jats was not a 'Hindu reaction' to the political upheaval during the eighteenth century. We should look those incidents with reference to the development of the era. With Akbar, the Great, the Mughals started a new practice of aliening wealthy sections of the society with the rulers. So the important Rajput kings were granted high military titles--Mansabs. Some of the Maratha Sardars also received such titles, but such tradition could not be maintained during seventeenth century, and those cultivators, who were called *khudkasht* by medieval administrative units, and who were owners of their land, and were thought to be of lower status than the zamindars, could not be given neither any title, nor any importance they deserved.

The British had a clear understanding on this matter. William Hunter writes, 'The *khudkasht* right was a valued right not only because it implied an economic advantage, but because it conferred a certain social status. The resident cultivators for the governing body of village communities *bhadralok* or a respected class, as such they not only had a good standing and power of borrowing from the moneylender but also had a number of communal privileges in regard to their homes and plots and to the pastured and forest land, to the service of the village-servants and officials and to the prick of the field left occupied.' In Maharashtra we find the term *merasi* and in Rajasthan *dharuhala* for Khudkasht. Question arises who belonged to this Khudkasht class in North-west India. Clearly they were the Jats. That is why the progressive, wealthy, communities of the Khudkasht, the Jats became hostile and disputes arose between them and the zamindars, whose patron were the Mughal authority. The Rajputs, being the mansabdars and zamindars, tried to crush the Jats. But the Jats, who were progressing and willing to go ahead to fetch power and become the zamindars, came in open revolt against the former. The Rajputs had alliance with the Mughals, therefore the Mughals stood with them against the Jats. The critical point reached for these peasants in general, when the land revenue imposed on them had attained an intolerably heavy magnitude. The first to be hurt by such an increase in land revenue were the small khudkasht, the *reza riaya,* on to whose shoulders the upper class peasants tended to transfer their own burden. Under the circumstances, the peasants were hit very hard. Its sharp reaction amongst the Jats, culminating into a rebellion, appears to have been because of their adventurous disposition and martial character. This explains the cause and course of the characteristic medieval uprising. Tuzuk-i-Jahangiri describes that 'Jahangir received a report that the Jat ganwaran and muzarian of the eastern side of river Jamuna constantly engage in loot and take shelter behind dense jungles and fastnesses, difficult of access, pass their days in rebellion and defiance, not paying the land-revenue to the Jagirdars'. An army was thereupon dispatched to suppress the revolt 'with slaughter, enslavement and rapine'. The revolt of 1633 against Emperor Shahjahan, of 1669 against Aurangzeb and of 1830 against Begum Sumru were of the same character. Paradoxical though it might appear and strange though it seem, these uprisings occurred at times when the Mughal government was by no means weak or imbecile, and though the Jats counted for majority and provided leadership to them, it consisted of other local people such as Mev, Gujar, Ahir, Meena and others. Historians generally viewed that the Jats were not willing to accept the revenue laws of the Mughal administration or the Mughals adopted oppressive measures to extract revenue from the Jats. But it is not so. This was actually the struggle for progress, recognition, empowerment, identity and authority. The Jat community was advancing and wanted a justifiable place and a status. However the endogenous Jat cultural identity has been largely neglected by many historians, who focus on changes in political institutions, administration and the economy as crucial determinants in the formation of identities among the rural communities and underline the decisive influence of colonial conceptions of community. This focus has been inadequate in many respects in explaining the formation of a localized identity.

A distinct feature of Jat community in pre-colonial period was the absence of a political authority or monarchical form in East Punjab and the Doab of West Uttar Pradesh, but it was not so in the Jat states of Jind and Patiala in Punjab and Bharatpur state in South. The reason was that the Haryanavi and the Doab Jats with their distaste for headmen and chiefs, had their villages managed by their *panch* and *mukhias*. However, after colonial period this panchayat system could not play important role, due to various misunderstandings and misconceptions.

This collection of papers gives consideration to all the above ideas, as it is exhorting to note that as many as thirty one papers find place here alongwith the valuable contributions in the shape of the inaugural address by Dr. Yoganand Shastri, Speaker, Delhi Vidhan Sabha and keynote address by Doctor P.K. Shukla, former Secretary, Indian Council of Historical Research. The papers brought together here show an attempt to discuss the background to various segments of Jat history, indicating the kinds of evidence available and the doubts and theories that are under discussion among scholars. A universally acceptable narration of incidents would be hard to understand as some of the evidence is tentative and can change with new findings. But through discussion attempts can be made to get more facts known, and to explain the kinds of problems involved. It should be noted that many of these papers open new horizons of research in Jat history.

Much has been written about mythological or real descriptions of the Jats regarding their origin, religion, social set-up, livelihood patterns, stereotypes and perceptions of historians about them. Platitudes, preferences and prejudices are bound to be there in ethnic narratives. So far many Jat historians have tried to trace the antiquity of the term Jat through the antiquity of their clan names, emphasizing the word Jat presuming to be of Vedic origin. S. S. Rana closely examines this concept and in accordance with linguistic and grammatical reasons concludes that the term 'Jat' is not Sanskritic in origin. He pleads for a more dispassionate and deeper study of the issue in truly historical context. Professor Khajan Singh Sangwan presents a critical study of the traditional system of dispute resolution by the Khap Panchayats, and justifies their relevance by comparing the dispute ascertainment by the Court and the Panchayats. M. S. Rana discusses the gotra system among the Jats and critically appraises the intra-village and intra-gotra marriage. Niti Singh discusses the social and political dimensions of the Jat insurgency during the Mughal period and successfully proves that the Jat revolts would not have been possible without the help given by the peasantry to the rebels. Mamta

Tyagi attempts to highlight the nature and intensity of military confrontation between the Jats and the Kachhwahas in Braj region in the last half of the 17th century. Manisha Choudhary explores the Jat rebels' attitude and conduct in course of their struggle against the Mughals and their agents during late seventeenth and early eighteenth century, and the role of alliances and leadership, mobilization and rebellious 'repertoires' in medieval country side. Farha Adeeba gives useful information using the Persian sources in original about Maulvi Fazl-e-Azim Khairabadi, a noted poet, scholar and historiographer of early 19th century, and his work *Afsana-e-Jang-e-Bharatpur,* a brief history of Bharatpur and an eye-witness account of the British operation against Raja Durjansal of Bharatpur. Zakir Husain makes a thorough study of the participation of the Jats, specially the Raja of Ballabhgarh in the great uprising of 1857 on the basis of the documentary survey of the Mutiny collection records available with the National Archives of India. N. S. Alam makes a brief survey of the role of the Sikhs in 1857, their heroic deeds, bravery and military strategy against the British, which indicates that if such documents of the Sikhs and the Jats are carefully collected, edited and translated in English with the original text of the contemporary records, it would be of utmost significance for the historians of the Great Revolt of 1857. Mahender Singh Baghi gives us useful information based on primary sources from National Archives of India, and on his field work about what actually happened in Ballabhgarh after the uprising of 1857 was crushed.

Rajesh Kumar gives a brief account of the Loharu's Peasant Unrest of 1835, the famous Singhani tragedy, its reasons-the atrocities of the Nawab of Loharu, through revenue settlement of 1923, high rate of taxes, brutal suppression of the unrest by mercilessly killing of the scores of agitating peasants. Surprisingly enough that this heinous barbarity perpetrated by the Nawab has not received the attention it deserves. K. S. Bajwa describes the western understanding of the Jat Sikhs of Punjab in 19th century in detail. Manveer Kaur presents a demographic study of the Jats of Punjab during the colonial period. R. L. Kundu and S. L. Kundu have gone through the promotion of unopposed elections in Haryana from Panchayat to Lok Sabha elections, viewing it the reflection of matured democratic trend and positivism in the present political scenario. Nirmal Kumar tells some significant ideas and activities of Sir Chhotu Ram, and analyzes some of his ideas on peasant problems in Punjab during his time. Eṭee Bahadur presents her paper on Ch. Charaṇ Singh's views on co-operative farming at the historical Nagpur Session of Congress. In the 64th annual session of the Indian National Congress held at Nagpur from 9 to 11 January 1959, the Congress adopted a resolution in favour of the introduction of a joint co-operative farming, which in fact was the idea of Jawaharlal Nehru. Charan Singh, being the spokesman of the peasantry, emphatically and logically opposed the policy and proposed policies that would strengthen the existing system of proprietorship and would sustain rural democracy.

Our Hindi papers enriched with serious studies about foundation and primary sources have been presented by various scholars. Manohar Singh Ranawat describes about Persian sources of Jat studies available at Shri Natnagar Shodh Sansthan, Sitamau, district Mandsaur, Madhya Pradesh. Mahendra Singh Khargawat describes availability of chain of historical epigraphy in shape of Rampuria Records as paper notebooks, kept at Rajasthan State Archive at Bikaner, date back from 1642 to 1942. Both of these sources are of historical significance for the research scholars on Jat history. Malika Bohra presents the life and acts of Sardar Gokula Jat, the founder of Peasant Revolt, while S. L. Ware discusses the influence of Jat Peasants' Revolt of 17th century on Malwa. Rakesh Kumar Sharma tells about Maharani Kishori of Bharatpur. Pranav Dev has shown the architecture of Bharatpur forts. Shiv Kumar Bhanot studies the role of Community Panchayats of the Jats of Western Rajasthan during 18th and 19th century. Brahma Ram Chaudhary, Jaswant Singh Khichar, Kalpana Chaudhary and Arti Chaudhary discuss the social, economic and political participation of the Jats in North-West India with special reference to Bikaner and Jodhpur divisions. Joga Ram Saran traces facts of the movement of the Jats against Jagirdari system in Barmer. Sumesta describes the endeavours of Community Reform Societies for transformation in the social, educational and peasantry life of the Jats of Rajputana estates in the first half of the 20th century, while F. K. Kapil pays attention on the role of Jat leadership in the Rajasthan politics during 1949-54. Ram Swarup Dhengula presents a brief survey of the social and economic lives of the Jats of Jatwara region of Bundelkhand, and Dharmendra Pare tells us about the social, economic and political conditions of the Jats of Harda district of Madhya Pradesh. Jaswant Singh Khichar highlights the personality of Swami Keshavanand and his attempts to popularize education in North-west Rajasthan and Tejpal Singh describes about Dharma Jat, one of the Panjpyare of Guru Gobind Singh.

Collection of these papers are the result of sustained efforts of late Dr. Vir Singh, the former Director of Maharaja Surajmal Centre for Research and Publication, who organized the Seminar efficiently, but due to his ill-health and advancing age, the proceedings could not be published earlier, and I was entrusted the responsibility of editing this volume. It is at this stage that this volume is being published.

I am deeply indebted to Shri S. P. Singh, the popular and progress-minded President of the Surajmal Memorial Education Society, who is the originator and patron of this volume, and without whose constant and active inspiration this book would not have seen the light of the day. I tender my grateful thanks to esteemed collaborators for their valuable contributions. To me the task was not an easy one, as I had to call several papers again, which were misplaced, revised them and cut short some of them to make precise. I think the authors would not mind it.

I express my gratitude to Shri Ajit Singh Chaudhary, Secretary, Surajmal Memorial Education Society, Dr. S. S. Rana, Shri Jaipal Vidyalankar and Shri Kaptan Singh for their help and cooperation as they all sincerely encouraged me in my academic pursuits.

In the end, I acknowledge the hard work of my Research Associate, Miss Monika Kajla in publication of this work. I would not forget to thank Shri Pradeep Mittal for printing the proceedings neatly and publishing it in record time.

**Dr. Rajendra Kumar**
Director
Maharaja Surajmal Centre for
Research & Publications

# जाट इतिहास में यौधेय गणराज्य की प्रासंगिकता

**डॉ. योगानन्द शास्त्री**

आज के सेमिनार का विषय बहुत गम्भीर है और उस पर बहुत अधिक कार्य नहीं हुआ है। अभी मैंने डॉक्टर एस.एस. राणा साहब से पुछवाया कि जाट शब्द का प्रयोग सबसे पहले कब हुआ है? तो उनका उत्तर था कि सातवीं-आठवीं शताब्दी से पूर्व जाट शब्द का प्रयोग नहीं हुआ है।

लेकिन मेरी मान्यता है कि सातवीं-आठवीं शताब्दी से पहले यौधेयों के रूप में जाटों की पहचान थी और वे उसी प्रदेश में रहते थे जहां वर्तमान में जाट रहते हैं। रोहतक उनका मुख्य नगर था। महाभारत काल से भी पहले उनकी अवस्थिति हम पाते हैं। उशीनगर के पुत्र निद्य और माता युधा से उनकी उत्पत्ति हुई। हालाँकि निद्य सम्राट थे, राजतांत्रिक प्रणाली के पोषक थे लेकिन उनके पुत्र यौधेयों ने उस एकतन्त्र प्रणाली को बदलकर गणतंत्र, प्रजातंत्र प्रणाली में प्रवृत्त किया तथा सदा उसके पक्षधर रहे। यौधेयगण प्रभावशाली गण था। महाभारत में लिखा है-'यौधेयाश्च ललि त्याश्चक्षुद्राश्चाप्युशीनराः'-उशीनर के पुत्र होने की बात भी है।

महाभारत काल में यौधेय कौरवों की तरफ से लड़े। अब यह नया और उद्वेलित करने वाला विषय है कि ऐसा क्यों था? यौधेय उस समय शक्तिशाली गण था। उसके आस-पास दूसरे गणराज्य थे-काकभ्र, औदुम्बर, कुणिंद, मालव, अम्बष्ठ, त्रिगण आदि। सबने मिलकर पाण्डवों का विरोध किया व सभी कौरवों की तरफ़ से लड़े थे। महाभारत के समय के बाद भी यौधेय अपनी मजबूत स्थिति को बनाये रख सके।

महाभारत काल में इनके प्रदेश का नाम बहुधान्यक था। वह यौधेयों की मुद्राओं पर अंकित होने से यौधेयों के इस प्रदेश का स्वामी होना सिद्ध करता है। बाद में तीसरी-चौथी शताब्दी ई. पूर्व में जो सिक्के इस गण ने चलाये उनपर भी 'बहुधान्यक' लिखा गया- योधेयानां बहुधान्यके। इन सिक्कों पर ब्राह्मी लिपि है और भाषा संस्कृत है।

बहुधान्यक का अर्थ है जो बहुत धान्य अर्थात अन्न उत्पन्न करने वाला क्षेत्र हो। जिस समय युधिष्ठिर ने राजसूय यज्ञ किया तो चारों भाइयों को विजय के लिये चारों दिशाओं में भेजा। नकुल को पश्चिम दिशा में विजय के लिये भेजा। महाभारत के सभापर्व में वर्णन है 'नकुलस्य तु वक्ष्यामि कर्माणि विजयं तथा। वासुदेव जितामाशा यथासवजयत प्रभुः।' नकुल इन्द्रप्रस्थ से निकलकर खाण्डवप्रस्थ, खाण्डवप्रस्थ से निकलकर रोहिदकारण्य में गये, 'निर्याय खाण्डवप्रस्थात्'। आज जिसको हम रोहतक कहते हैं पुराने जमाने में इसका नाम रोहितक था। थोड़ा ही भेद हुआ। रुहेड़े का जंगल था। रुहेड़े को संस्कृत में रोहितक कहा जाता है। रुहेड़े के जंगल को काटकर रोहितक बसाया गया। नकुल के आक्रमण की जो बात थी महाभारत काल में उसका उल्लेख हुआ है। नकुल धन-धान्य से पूर्ण ऐसे रोहतक पर आक्रमण करता है जो धन-धान्य ही नहीं, गऊओं का भी खजाना और कार्तिकेय का जो निवास स्थान है। महाभारत में भी आया है-'ततो बहुधनं रम्यं गवाढ्यं धनधान्यवत्। कार्तिकेयस्य दयितं रोहितकमुपाद्रवत्।'

यह रोहतक बहुत धनी, गऊओं से भरपूर, अनेक प्रकार के अन्नों से परिपूरित नगर था-'तत्र युद्धं महच्चासीत् शूरैर्मत्तमयूरकैः। मरुभूमीं च कात्स्र्त्येन तथैव बहुधान्यकम्।' यहाँ मत्तमयूरक, मोर का ध्वज धारण करने वाले यौधेयों से नकुल का संग्राम हुआ। इसमें जीत नकुल की हुई—'तान दशार्णान् जित्वा स प्रतस्थ पाण्डुनन्दनः।' कार्तिकेय रोहतक के नगर देवता थे। रोहतक शिवपुत्रों की राजधानी थी। यौधेय शैव थे। वे शिवजी और कार्तिकेय की उपासना करते थे। और उनके वाहनों की उपासना करते थे। मोर कार्तिकेय का ध्वज था। यौधेयों की तांबे तथा चांदी की भी मुद्राएँ कनिंघम को मिली थी, उन पर एक ओर छः मुख वाला कार्तिकेय हाथ में भाला लिये खड़ा है। यह भाला शक्ति का प्रतीक है। इस पर ब्राह्मी में 'भागवतस्वामिनो ब्रह्मण्य यौधेय' लिखा है। दूसरी ओर देवी का चित्र है जिस के बांये हाथ में कमल का फूल है। कुषाणों को जब यौधेयों ने हराया और अपनी विजय के सिक्के प्रचलित किये तो उन पर 'यौधेय गणस्य जयः' के साथ-साथ मध्य में शक्ति लिये, यानि भाला लिये कार्तिकेय की प्रतिमा भी है और दूसरी ओर सृष्टि या पार्वती की प्रतिमा दी गई है। कार्तिकेय के पैर के पास मोर का चित्र है। मोर कार्तिकेय का वाहन था। पूरे इलाके में आज भी मोर बहुतायत में मिलते हैं। जाटों में मोर गोत्र भी पाया जाता है। उत्तर प्रदेश और हरियाणा में नगरों-ग्रामों के नाम मुर्थल अर्थात् मयूरथल, मोरवाना, मोरकुक्का आदि अभी भी पाये जाते हैं।

दसवीं शताब्दी में एक शासक रुद्रदामन के साथ जब राजपूताना में यौधेयों का युद्ध हुआ तो उसमें यौधेय हार गये। रुद्रदामन ने कितने अभिमान के साथ संस्कृत भाषा में ब्राह्मी लिपि में अभिलेख लिखवाया : सर्वदाना स्कृता विधेयानां यौधेयानां प्रसयोदतात उत्सादकेन्। उन्होंने उन यौधेयों को हराया वीर शब्द जिनका पर्याय बन गया था। खाली

एक टुकड़ी को हराया था सबको नहीं हराया था। बाद में इनका कुषाणों के साथ युद्ध हुआ। कुषाणों के दो राजा विम केडिफिसिस और कुजुल केडिफिसिस हुए जिन्होंने वाह्लीक, बुखारा तक अपने राज्य का विस्तार किया। इनके बाद के राजा कनिष्क व हुविष्क ने मथुरा और नेपाल की तराई तक अपना राज्य स्थापित किया। इनके साथ युद्ध में यौधेय हार गये और यहां से स्थानांतरण करके चकरौता के पहाड़ों में चले गये।

वहां उन्होंने नये सिक्के चलाये। वहां पर यौधेयों ने शक्ति संचय करने के बाद एक नई नीति अपनाई। उस समय के जो दूसरे गण कुणिन्द, अर्जुनायन, आग्रेय आदि थे उनके साथ मिलकर यौधेयों ने एक संघ बनाया। जाट शब्द भी इसी प्रकार एक संघ का द्योतक है-'जट झट संघाते।'

मैं यह सिद्ध करना चाहता हूँ कि जाट शब्द संघात्मक है। संघ यौधेयों को भी बहुत अधिक प्रिय था। दूसरे गणराज्यों के साथ भी यौधेयों ने संघ बनाया। यह संघ इसलिये बनाया कि देश पर विदेशी आक्रमणकारियों ने जो जीत हासिल की है, अपना सिक्का जमाया है, उनको देश से निकालकर बाहर किया जाये। इनमें अर्जुनायन, कुणिंद, आग्रेय तीन गणराज्य थे।

लेकिन तीसरी शताब्दी ई. के बाद इनका अस्तित्व नहीं मिलता। इन तीनों गणों ने यौधेयों में अपने आपको समाहित कर लिया। इसलिये यौधेयों के सिक्कों पर इन तीनों गणों के लक्षण मिलते हैं। यौधेयों के अनेक प्रकार के सिक्के मिलते हैं, सम्भवतः पन्द्रह प्रकार के सिक्के मिलते हैं। इनकी रोहतक में भी एक टकसाल मिली है। लखनऊ विश्वविद्यालय में आर्कियोलोजी के प्रोफेसर बीरबल साहनी ने 1937 में रोहतक में जो खुदाई कराई उसमें रोहतक में एक टकसाल मिली। इसमें 'यौधेयानाम् बहुधान्यक' लेख वाले सिक्के मिले। दूसरी टकसाल जो स्वामी आत्मानन्द ने खोजी वह भिवानी के पास मिली। उसमें एक आश्चर्य की बात थी कि यौधेयों ने एक जैसे तीस-तीस सिक्के ढाले। कुषाणों ने बाद में उसी प्रक्रिया को अपनाकर सिक्के ढालने की दूसरी प्रक्रिया को अपनाया। सबसे बाद में जो इनके राजा वासुदेव प्रथम व कनिष्क तृतीय हुए जिनको यौधेयों ने हराया, उन्होंने एक बार जिस सिक्के को जिस सांचे में ढाला उस सांचे को बाद में बदल दिया। इस प्रकार कुषाणों ने एक बार में एक सांचे में एक ही सिक्का ढाला।

यौधेय देश की ख्याति बहुधान्यक के रूप में और अन्न और धनयुक्त देश के रूप में ईसापूर्व तीसरी व चौथी शताब्दी में थी। ईसा पश्चात दसवीं शताब्दी तक वही ख्याति रही। 'यशतिलक' नाम का एक नाटक है जो सोमदेव सूरी ने लिखा है उसमें यौधेयों व उनके देश की बहुत प्रशंसा की गई है। 'स यौधेयो इति ख्यातो देशः क्षेत्रोऽस्ति भारते।'

उसने लिखा-'यौधेयों के क्षेत्र में इतना अनाज पैदा होता है कि बोये हुए खेत को काटने में असमर्थ होते हैं, काटे हुये धान्य को खलिहान तक लाने में असमर्थ होते हैं, लाने के बाद उसे गाहने में असमर्थ होते हैं, गाहकर निकाल भी लिया तो घर ले जाने में असमर्थ होते हैं। यह सब इसलिये होता है कि उस समय तक बारिश का मौसम आ जाता है।' इससे अंदाजा लगाया जा सकता है कि यौधेय कितने समृद्ध थे।

इतना निश्चित है कि जाटों के जो भी पूर्वज थे वह बहुत महान थे। बाद में यौधेयों से जाटों में कैसे परिवर्तन हुआ इसकी जानकारी हमारे पास उपलब्ध नहीं है। इस पर अनुसंधान की आवश्यकता है। कनिंघम ने उनको अस्त्र-शस्त्र के सहारे जीवन चलाने वाला लिखा है। पाणिनी ने भी प्राचीन समय में चार प्रकार के गणों का उल्लेख किया है : पहले आयुधजीवी—हथियार के सहारे जीवन चलाने वाले। दूसरे वार्तोपजीवी—कृषि एवं व्यापार के द्वारा जीवन चलाने वाले। तीसरे वार्ताशस्त्रोपजीवी—जिनमें आग्रेय गण आता है। जो व्यापार भी करते थे, व समय आने पर हथियार भी उठाते थे; तथा चौथे प्राणउत्सेधजीवी—जो लूटमार से जीविका चलाते थे।

ये चार प्रकार के लोग थे। यौधेय आयुधजीवी थे। उनके सिक्के, साहित्य व उनके क्रिया-कलाप भी इस बात को सिद्ध करते हैं।

मैं चाहूंगा कि आप लोगों में कोई इस दिशा में कार्य करें तो मुझे बहुत प्रसन्नता होगी ताकि अनछुए पहलुओं पर अध्ययन हो सके।

*Keynote Address*

# Some Aspects of the Social Base of the Peasantry of North-west India with Special Reference to the Jats of Punjab during Colonial Rule

**Dr. P.K. Shukla**

This paper discusses how the social base of the landowning castes of the Punjab, specially the Jats, was strengthened during the colonial rule to the neglect of low caste poor peasants. An attempt is made to examine the complex agrarian changes brought about both in the irrigated and non-irrigated areas of the province that resulted in the appropriation of the surplus produced by the peasantry. Such accumulation of surplus in the form of rent and land revenue demand failed to generate the capitalist relations in agriculture. This paper will also throw some light on the peasant uprisings caused by excessive land revenue demand by the ruling class.

In a major work B.B. Chaudhuri[1] has recently argued that all sections of the 'peasant' did not qualify for the state-owned crown land in the Punjab. The focus of the colonial state was restricted to only 'resourceful' peasants who were required to make considerable investment for the cultivation of virgin land. In such a situation the enterprising agricultural castes constituting the landholding peasantry were favoured. These were regarded 'as the backbone of Punjab Society'. The peasant grantees were largely *the Jats*, *the Arains*, *the Kambohs*, *the Sainis* and *the Gurjars*. Among all the landowning castes, the *Jats* were the biggest beneficiaries. Other notable grantees included large and small landlords, and the members of urban bourgeoisie, such as the merchants, contractors, lawyers, doctors and retired public servants, belonging mostly to non-agricultural castes – the *Khatris*, the *Aroras*, the *Khojas*, and the *Banias*.

Thus the colonial government wholly excluded the vast landless stratum of the rural population, especially the village menials *(Kamins)*, service groups and artisans, in spite of the fact that the the *Chamars* (leather workers), the *Churhas* (low caste sweepers) and the members of artisan classes formed sixty per cent of the total agricultural labourers in the canal colonies. Such a discriminatory attitude of the colonial government clearly shows that they used the existing caste-hierarchies in India to portray their rule as more benign than that of their predecessors. The involvement of such castes in agricultural work clearly indicates that the landless labourers, who are generally not considered as peasants in the theoretical framework of the system, were and probably still continue to be peasants in so far as their working relationship with the landlords is considered[2].

Though the Arya Samaj movement started by Swami Dayanand Saraswati (1824-1883) ultimately turned into a revivalist movement and also contributed to the assertion of an aggressive Hindu indentity[3], Dayanand Saraswati's sharp criticism of many existing Hindu practices, such as idolatry, polytheism, and child marriage did not affect the existing social composition of caste in relation to peasant-landlord-cultivator relationships. As far as the comparative position between peasant grantees and labourers was concerned, not much change was noticeable in terms of the land-ownership pattern. The 'peasant colonizers', the largest single group of grantees of land in Punjab, were all drawn from the traditional 'agricultural castes'. The fact is that for the sake of homogeneity and social harmony grantees of the same caste were settled in the same village. Imran Ali's[4] analysis of the distribution of the land by castes shows a virtual monopoly over colony land of castes that ranked high in economic position and social status. He says:

> "Landless workers, whether agricultural labourers, sub-tenants, or caste survivors… still fulfilled roles similar to the ones they had taken

> confined to their home villages.... These groups often moved their colony villages with the grantees from their home districts, thus continuing their old *sipidari* relationships".

In some areas the condition of labourers slightly improved. The Sikh-Maratha conflict, the period of 'Maratha anarchy', and the dreadful famine of 1783 resulted in a scarcity of labour in both southeast and southwest Punjab. In such situation a labourers became settled peasants, which was useful for the proprietors. The position of some of them had become so strong that a distinction between the labour and the owners was obliterated. But the enterprising agriculturists such as the *Jats* and the *Arains* gradually replaced the non-cultivating 'proprietors' and land-controllers.

It has been held that due to high-caste taboos the position of the *Rajputs* as landlords or proprietors diminished. They were considered the worst cultivators in the Punjab. By contrast, the *Jats*, irrespective of whether they were Hindus, Sikhs or Muslim, had greater skills in farming which made them the best cultivator in India'. The *Rajputs* were mostly part-time agriculturists, representing the gentry of the province and thus constituted the aristocracy of the countryside. Proud of their birth and traditions, they did not relish the hard-work of an agriculturist. It has been argued that caste-status, a disdainful attitude to agriculture and sensitivity to *ijjat* (social respectability) forbade *Rajputs* to take help from women of the family for agricultural[5]. On the other hand, the *Jats* were influenced by the new social order of *Nanakpanthis* (the followers of the Sikh Guru Nanak). However, if we analyse the social composition of the *Jats*, the *Sainis* and the *Arains* in relation to the distribution of the land we find that the *Kamins* were not the beneficiaries of the changes brought about by the colonial government — be it canal-irrigated or non-irrigated areas of the Punjab — although they were considered indispensable associates of the zamindars in their agricultural operations[6]. Among the lower castes, those at the lowest rung such as the *Chuhras*, the *Chamars* and the *Dhanaks* performed the largest and the most difficult kind of agricultural work, including collecting the refuse and scattering it over the fields. The other non-landholding castes such as the

*Lohars*, the *Tarkhans*, the *Telis*, the *Nais*, the *Kumhars* and the *Julahas* also helped in agricultural work at peak seasons such as sowing and harvesting.

The caste-system continued and the lower caste people constituting one-eighth of the entire population suffered a lot. In spite of philanthropic organizations such as the Arya Samaj, the Christian missionaries, and the Ahmadiyah charities, the literacy rate as a whole was as low as 7% and it was lowest among the lower castes, around 2%. Moreover, the landless cultivators far more numerous as compared to landlords. 22.5 per cent cultivators owned just 1.5 per cent of the cultivated areas, while 4.2 per cent cultivators possessed 18.5 per cent of the cultivated area. Less than one per cent (0.9 per cent) landlords had 7.9 per cent of cultivated areas. The poor peasants had to look after the needs of the government officials. The *Banias* and the *Sahukars* sucked their blood by charging interest on loans at exorbitant rates[8]. The colonial government, on the other hand, gave concession only to the landlords. In this way the big landlords prospered at the cost of the poor peasants who were actually engaged in extending the cultivated areas for the production of commercial crops. This shows how the surplus generated by the poor peasants was usurped by the rich landlords.

Mridula Mukherjee informs us that in Punjab 'the extent of differentiation and depeasantization was comparatively less than in many other regions because of tenurial structure, relatively late integration into the colonial system, etc. Also the depeasantization had not reached the extent it had in other regions because of the comparatively much greater extension of cultivation via canal irrigation… Employment opportunities outside agriculture were comparatively much greater here [Punjab] than in many other regions because of internal migration and major recruitment base in the army'. Therefore, she concludes, 'there was relative stability of the small peasants in the Punjab'. 0.1 million non-combatants in the army were from Punjab in the First Word War. The non-combatants in the army were the *Syces*, *Bhistis*, *Sweepers*, *Craftsmen*, etc. who belonged to traditional non-land holding castes. But it may be noted that their number in the army was much less in proportion to their population. Moreover, the recruitment to the army was an economic necessity for the small yeoman farmer families. They were not in the strict sense of the word, mercenaries[9]. By helping the British to suppress the Revolt of 1857, the Punjab chiefs and soldiers had saved the empire. It was felt by the colonial authority that 'the best Indian material for the recruitment in the army had been ultimately discovered'.[10]

Though differentiation among the *Kamin* castes was not prevalent throughout the Punjab province, there were broadly two groups according to the nature of their function. The labour of *Vadee Kamins* or *Kamin* was intimately connected with agriculture. The services of the *Khangi Kamins* or house menials were utilized by the zamindars. There were *Kamins* like *Tarkhans* (carpenter), *Lohars* (black smith), the *Chamars* (leather workers), the *Churhas* (sweepers), the *Dhobis* (washermen) and the *Nais* (the barbers). They were highly skilled but they represented heterogeneous caste groups.

Although the zamindars appreciated the significant role of the *Kamins* in the village organization and accepted them as integral part of the village society, there were differences in the wage rates of the *Kamins*. The *Lohars* received lower rates of wages than the *Tarkhans*. Prior to colonial rule a small partition of whole produce was set apart for the *Kamins* but during the colonial period the custom disappeared when there was a demand for cash. *Kamins* now received only their allowances from the cultivating proprietors in lump sum at each harvesting season. The *Kumhars* were paid very little in non-irrigated regions. The same was the position of the *Chamars* who often organised caste *panchayats* as a token of protest against the highhandedness of the village proprietors. The tenants had to give to the *Kamins* not a share of the whole produce but a fixed amount of produce. There economic condition deteriorated so much that they started migrating to other regions of the province. A large number of artisans were also indebted to the village *sahukars*. The Land Alienation Act (1901) was also a deterrent for them. The Act denied the status of agricultural tribes to the village artisans and menials and hence they were automatically debarred from acquiring land. This legal disability implied in the Act affected the *Ramgarhias* and the *Bagri Kumhars* of south-eastern Punjab districts. Exclusion from the land market came to them as a sharp blow[11].

There was a steady rise in the wages for agricultural labourers in some districts but in the districts of Peshawar, Amritsar, Ludhiana and Delhi there was steady decline in real wage rates towards the close of nineteenth century. It was found that many of the labourers continued to suffer from a daily insufficiency of food. They were deeply indebted to their employers and remained almost in a state of debt slavery. In the south-eastern districts their condition was equally miserable. They were frequently called upon to render *begar* and they practically constituted the poorest section of the village social order. The situation was even more critical in Delhi. As early as 1879 it was found that their financial condition in the average years was so precarious that they were not commonly trusted by the village *sahukars.* In Rohtak their condition was equally miserable, while in Hoshiarpur even in average years they had very little surplus of their own and they were deeply involved in debt. Similarly in Peshawar many of them were after tied to their creditors in debt slavery. Even more miserable was the fate of the *halis* of Hazara. The *halis* were generally agriculturists who owned land but they lost it to the creditors. They were no longer required to keep plough of their own and they ultimately became farm servants of the rich agriculturists. They were unable to repay loans to the creditors in their life time which was to be repaid by the heirs of deceased *halis.*

From a brief description of the conditions of the peasantry there emerges a picture of an immense complexity of the agrarian changes occurring in the Punjab in the second half of the nineteenth century. These changes were far from uniform in type and nature. It appears that the old agrarian structure was modified in some places to suit the interests of the colonial state. But we do not find fundamental structural changes particularly from the point of view of 'the existence of capitalist relations in agriculture'[12]. Neither was there an investment of capital nor an increase in productivity. The extension of cultivation did take place as a result of the canal colonies but the extension of cultivation was accompanied by an increase in the rural population. It may be noted that during the period from 1891 to 1931 the areas under cultivation expanded by 16 per cent, while the rural population increased by 23.2 per cent. Moreover, the size of the total available workforce in agriculture expanded much more than the extension of cultivation. This shows the 'myth' of capitalist farming in the Punjab during the colonial rule. Although colonialism integrated the Punjab into the international capitalist economy, this integration was based upon a distorted pattern of modernization. The requirements of British imperialism made Punjab a reservoir for military recruitment while at the same time intensifying the class differentiation and exploitation of the lower castes. This created conditions for the appropriation of the surplus of the region to serve the interests of the British empire.

The Peasant uprisings can be traced back to medieval India and the reasons behind such provocation was the demand for payment of land revenue. For example, a widespread rebellion occurred in the Doab in 1330 during the reign of Muhammad Tughlaq when demand for land revenue was increased. In 1622 during the reign of Jahangir the peasant rose in revolt against the Jagirdars. But the Jat peasant uprising under the leadership of zamindars in the Doab area is important because it resulted in a very great expansion of Jat zamindari in the Doab at the expense of other zamindar clans.[13] It seems that a number of upper Jab peasants moved into the ranks of zamindars. Here again, the ordinary peasants who actively participated in the revolt were not the beneficiaries. It may be noted that menial Caste Hindus from different villages guarded the ditch at Bharatpur against the rebels but got no reward.

Even the Maratha power in its formation in the seventeenth century fed on peasant unrest. The Maratha Chiefs were of zamindar origins. Their army consists mostly of low-born people like peasants, shepherds, carpenters and cobblers. But the conditions of the peasants did not improve upon the success of the Maratha Chiefs. The position of the Kunbis, the inferior peasants, was as miserable as before.

The peasant revolts which combined with religions movements associated with Kabir, Nanak, Raidas and other teachers deserve our due attention. These preachers employed the language of the people chiefly to propagate submission to God. Their teachings tended towards social egalitarianism because they condemned ritual and caste observance.[14] Most of the teachers belong to the low *Jatis* – Namdev, a calico-printer, Kabir, a weaver, Raidas, a scavenger, Sain, a barber, Dadu, a cotton-carder, Dhanna, a Jat peasant. Guru Arjun has praised Dhanna Jat in beautiful verses composed in Braj language. He has asserted that God could be acquired by men of such low birth. In the verses of Kabir and Arjun, God's faithful worshipper appears as a peasant as well as village headman.[15] Such preachings of the great saints represented the urge of a number of low-ranking classes to rise in the social scale. Its openness to the menial casts is in itself an outstanding achievement which requires an urgent attention in the context of Brahminical social order engineered and strengthened during the colonial rule.

The peasant society in the Punjab or elsewhere directly involved in the production processes of foodstuff has immense potentiality for bringing out social and political Change. Qualitative changes in the agriculture technology could be brought about either by the large proprietors with sizable surplus or by state apparatus. But it was done by colonial regime only in some parts of canal areas – which benefitted only a handful of prosperous peasants. The early nineteenth century Punjab was primarily the land of small cultivators – constituting about 90% of the landed groups. Outside the eastern plains, most of them were engaged in subsistence cultivation with traditional techniques and implements. The most effective means of irrigation in the Punjab were wells with the Persian wheel. In the eastern plains, the requirement of capital and artisanal skill for counteraction restricted the use of Persian wheel by the small cultivators who constituted the bulk of population. At the same time there was a fairly high revenue demand which ruined even the peasant proprietors. The limited surplus available with large proprietors was channelled into the colonization of waste lands which received active encouragement from the colonial state.

It has been estimated that out of over 34,722 villages in the Punjab in the nineteenth century, 33,020 were owned by the cultivating proprietors and only 1707 by the non-cultivating proprietor i.e. the zamindars of one or more villages.[16] Numerically, and in terms of area cultivated, the self-cultivating proprietors who used family labour and the means of cultivation by themselves constituted the most agrarian group in the Punjab. It clearly shows that there existed a gulf between the ordinary peasants and the landlords. In such a situation the agrarian tension was inevitable and the colonial authorities by the large took help of landlords in maintaining the *raj*.

In spite of huge numerical strength the peasantry was divided on the basis of caste and community and therefore there was comparatively backward level of class consciousness. Thus the Indian peasant revolts exhibit a remarkable deficiency. They rose in revolt in a locality (the Doab), or as a caste (Jats), or as a sect (Satnamis, Sikh), but they fail to attain recognition of any common objective that transcended parochial limits. Be it the Punjab or any other part of India, the caste divisions in Indian society, the immense gulf between the peasantry and 'menial' proletariat are big hindrance for establishing an egalitarian social order. Despite such drawbacks the peasantry's attempt towards the attainment of self-awareness is an achievement of the national movement. But many of the burdensome vestiges of the past and the division and superstitions are still prevalent in the peasant society.

## References

1. B.B. Chaudhuri : *Peasant History of the late Pre-Colonial and Colonial India*, vol. III, Part 2, published under a series of vol. with the general editorship of D.P. Chattopadhayaya, *History of Sciences, Philosophy and Culture in Indian Civilization*, HSPCIC, New Delhi, 2008, p. 362.
2. For a detailed analysis see Irfan Habib : *Essay in Indian History: Towards Marxist Perception*, New Delhi, 1995, pp. 107-160 under the caption "The Peasant in Indian History".
3. Sumit Sarkar : *Modern India,* (1885-1947), Delhi, 1983, p. 75.
4. *The Punjab under Imperialism,* Delhi 1989, by Imran Ali quoted in B.B. Chaudhuri, *Op.cit*, p. 364.
5. B.B. Chaudhuri : *Op.cit.* p. 193.

6. Himadri Banerjee : *Agrarian Society of the Punjab (1849-1901)*, Delhi, 1982, p. 175.
7. Mridula Mukherjee : *Colonizing Agriculture: The Myth of Punjab Exceptionalism*, New Delhi, 2005, p. 131. It is one of the best books on Punjab peasantry which deals with all aspects of the peasants, such as the peasant as tax-payers, peasants as debtors, peasants in the market, peasants as classes, etc. Based on district-wised statistical data on landholding this study does not find 'proof of the existence of capitalist agrarian relations or the growth of capitalism in agriculture' in the Punjab, p. 137.
8. S. Gajrani : *Peasant Movement in Punjab*, Delhi, 1987, pp. 4-8.
9. Elliott, J.G. : *A Roll of Honour: the Story of Indian Army* (1939-45) quoted in Bhagwan Josh : *Communist Movement in Punjab,* Delhi, 1979, p. 17.
10. O.' Dwyer M. : *India I know It,* 1885-1922, quoted in Bhagwan Josh, *op.cit.*, pp. 17-18.
11. Himadri Banerjee : *Op.cit.*, p. 184.
12. Mridula Mukherjee : *Op.cit.*, p. 131.
13. Irfan Habib : "The Peasants in Indian History" in *Irfan Habib Essays in Indian History: Towards Marxist Perception*, New Delhi, Third Reprint 2000, p. 156.
14. *Ibid.*, p. 157.
15. Irfan Habib : "Evidence for Sixteenth Century Agrarian Conditions in the Guru Granth Sahib", *The Indian Economic and Social History Review* (*IESHR*) 1, 1964, quoted in op. cit. p. 157.
16. *Punjab Famine Commission Enquiries Report*, 1878-79, Vol. II, pp. 559-568 quoted in Indu Banga, "Landed Rights in Medieval Punjab: An Ecological Perspective" in *Peasants in Indian History I: Theoretical Issues and Structural Enquiries* ed. Jointly by V.K. Thakur and Ashok Aounshuman, Patna, 1996, p. 239.

# 1

# Is the term 'Jat' Sanskritic in Origin?

*Dr. S.S. Rana*

The people who are called, and call themselves Jats today are, no doubt, the most ancient Aryans, generally settled in north and north-west India. Many writers[1] have tried to prove their antiquity through the antiquity of their clan names, inseparably from the label Jat. In most cases the emphasis has been on the label, 'Jat' presuming it to be of sanskritic origin. It is not necessary that if the people are ancient, their current label should also be equally ancient. But the temptation of tracing the label in sources, where it does not exist on the part of several amateur Jat historians, has led to great amount of confusion. The confusion has got worse confounded, especially at the hands of those who overtaken by their caste (label) patriotism have thrown to winds the regard for authentic historical facts and sound principles of research and linguistic investigation. In the case of several of such writers the label became more important than the people themselves. For them, ancient Sanskrit texts, particularly those of uncertain authenticity[2] came handy to yield, mixed with some imagination, the desired crop. The most favourite and sought after ally in the otherwise very uncertain field has continued to be the Paninian text *jaṭa*, *jhaṭa sangháte.* The text has been erroneously described as- *sútra* of *ashṭádhyáyí* or a *shloka* or a phrase in the *ashṭádhyáyí,* by most of such writers (who do not seem to do any thing with Sanskrit), with generally faulty Roman transliteration, giving scope for miscarriage of intent. The effort of some writers in claiming to be precise by citing the reference number (3.3.19) of the text sought to be quoted from the *ashṭádhyáyí,* leaves one looking for the originally cited text only to land into an enigma, since the text at 3.3.19 is entirely different viz. *akartari cha kárake sanjnáyám.* Let us explain things:

The *ashṭádhyáyí* is a work of eight chapters, each having four quarters, where each quarter contains a number of *sútras* arranged in a linguistically systematic and meaningful manner. The *sútras,* individually and many a times in combination of several *sútras* by inference order, explain the formation of words of the Sanskrit language, as it was in Panini's time. The sútras deal with the raw material in the form of verbal roots *(dhátus)* by adding suffixes to obtain nominal and verbal forms of words. Panini has identified and after appropriate classification put the verbal roots *(dhátus)* in a separate compilation, called the *dhátupáṭha.* Our two *dhátus* are listed at serial numbers 305 *(jaṭa)* and 306 *(jhaṭa-sangháte)* in the *dhátupáṭha* with the simple meaning that each of the two is used in the sense of a cluster or a heap. The *sútra* in the *ashtádhyáyì* at 3.3.19 says that the suffix *ghañ* (having net value of 'a') comes after verbal stems when the sense of the root is denoted as having attained the completed state, e.g. *prásah, áhárah* etc. However, the condition is that the (noun) word thus formed shall not be the one which can be used as an agent in the nominative case (in *kartá káraka). But* our term *jáṭa* (if we take it as a Sanskrit term) can not be explained by the *sútra* under reference, as it is very much used in the nominative case *(kartá káraka).* Though words like jaṭá (hair locks), *jaṭah* (one having *jaṭá*) or *jaṭila* (one having intertwined hair) can be explained by other *sútras,* the fact remains that Panini has nowhere in his works mentioned the word *jáṭa* as such. If we wish to manufacture it retrospectively as a Sanskrit word of ancient ages Panini's *sútras* do not warrant it, the ancient Sanskrit literature does not reflect it. It is a pity that even some people, well versed in Paninian grammar have failed to notice the true meanings of the references made. Bhim Singh Dahiya and Hukam Singh Pawar sound parochial in insisting that the term *jáṭa* has been deliberately obliterated from the ancient Sanskrit literature by the canny brahmanas for ulterior motives. Do they mean to say that the whole of sanskrit literature has come from brahmana pen? And if one were to accept Dahiya's thesis that almost all ancient rulers of India were Jats, how come that they as patrons of learning could have been so ignored by their court poets and other contemporary writers. Paradoxically both of them go on tracing the term *jáṭa* in various ancient Sanskrit texts where it does not exist.

Further, it may be pointed out that Panini leaves little scope for mixing up of the meaning of the words *'sangha* and *'sangháta'*, the former meaning an association of persons working for a common purpose, a corporation, a political unit or a group of living beings *(práñi samúha)*, while the latter standing for a heap, cluster, accumulation, grouping, collection etc., generally of inanimate things, and of living entities, only when they give a monolithic appearance *(aprasřitávayavah samúha, sanğhátah)* like a herd of sheep *(avikatah)*. It may also be mentioned here that Panini has listed as many as twenty *dhátus* meaning *sangháta,* all of which lead to the formation of nominal stems which convey the meaning of group, heap, combination or cluster of inanimate things.[3]

We also have a long history of the use of the two words i.e. *sangha* and *sangháta* in ancient sanskrit literature, giving two distinct meanings as explained above.[4] Kautilya in his Arthashástra makes the same distinction between the meaning of *sangha* and *sangháta*.[5] Therefore, the attempt on the part of several writers in first assuming the term *jáṭa* to be of sanskritic origin and then trying to derive the same from the root *(dhátu) jaṭa* meaning *sangháta,* and there after proceeding to construe it to convey the meaning of a political republic *(sangha)* is far fetched and untenable. B.S. Dahiya and Hukam Singh Pawar have imagined the term *jáṭa* in the word *jáṭya* listed by Yaska (of the 8 th century C.E.) in his etymological treatise *Nirukta* (1.14) among terms which had become obsure in their meaning with the passage of time. Explaining the term under reference Yaska states: *"jáṭya átñáro bhavati"* i.e. the term *jáṭya means* a wanderer (mendicant, presumably having matted hair). Both the above referred writers have gone far beyond this simple meaning, giving unbridled flight to their imagination. Dahiya has (hopefully, inadvertantly!) altered the very text *átñáro* into *jáṭañáro* to instantly obtain the desired result, i.e. *jáṭa.* This kind of argumentation is unacceptable. Hukam Singh on his part labouriously wades through a wide period of history, offering arbitrary and weird etymologies of the term, getting amusing at times. For sample, consider this: "*jáṭa* is called *átňára* because he has blister folds *(átaňa* in modern Khadi Boli) on his feet." This is neither good linguistics nor good history. Hukam Singh's suggestion that the *jaṭá-pátha* of the vedic mantras could very well be taken as *jáṭa-pátha* (i.e. a recitation arrangement done by Jats) surely will send any one having an idea of the vedic recitation system, into splits. Dahiya's penchant for marshalling Sanskrit and Prakrit texts, especially inscriptions in support of his thesis only reveals the inadequacy of his competencies in truly interpreting them. No right thinking person would like to go with him in tracing the Jats from demons like Jatásura and báňásura mentioned in the Brihatsamhita of Varahamihira.

Another favourite text of the proponants of sanskritic connection of the term *játa* is the disputable reading '*ajayajjarto húňán*' in the sanskrit grammar of Chandragomin of the 6th century C.E. in the context of illustrating the use of *Lang Lakára* to denote an incident pertaining to immediate past. The alternative reading *ajayat gupto húñán* is supported by majority of scholars. However, even if we accept the former reading it does not help as the arguments advanced are based on assumptions. It is proposed by a section of scholars like K.P. Jayaswal (on whom Dahiya and Hukam Singh rely) that the *jartah* (=*játa*) here refers to Yashodharman, the Aulikara king who is referred to have defeated the *húňas* in his Mandasor Pillar Inscription. But this suggestion comes under cloud with the discovery, in 1983, of the Risthal (near Mandasor) Inscription (of 476 M.S.= 515 C.E.) of his father (?) Prakashadharman. The inscription clearly states that the latter defeated the *húñas* led by Toramana (Mihirkula's father). In any case the grammarian Chandragomin of 5th century C.E. could not have referred to a posterior event in the life of Yashodharman of the 6th century C.E.(vide his Mandasor Stone Inscription of Malaya Samvat 589 (=532 C. E.). Moreover, deriving the term *játa* from *jarta* arbitrarily, without putting the same in a chronological frame work remains merely a wild guess. We may also refer here to the futile suggestion of some writers who try to connect the vedic term *jaritá* with *jarta,* since the former simply means the singer of praise (of a deity). Equally untenable is the perambulatary derivation of the *term játa* from *jnáti* via *jnáta* and *jata* offered by Thakur Deshraj in his painstaking work Jat Itihas. Mere incidence of the letters 'j' and 'ṭ' (no matter hard or soft) falling together in a term have led many a novices to jump to unwarranted conclusions, and ironically, welcomed in certain circles only offer examples of caste patriotism. But it becomes difficult even for a layman to stomach the assertion (as we find in the Devasamhita) that the Jats owe their origin from the locks of hair of the mythical god Shiva, or for that matter the hair tuft of Virabhadra was the source of the Jats. Mythology should not be mixed with historical investigation. The domains of the two are entirely different.

So we have to reconcile and look for the antiquity of the people we are talking about on the strength of their clan names which occur in abundance in ancient sanskrit sources including Inscriptions, and for the moment, delink the label *játa* for its own history and provenance to be researched separately. Panini can be of great help as he has supplied us with a big list of *gotras* (clan names) in his *gaña-pátha* and also the sútras dealing with *taddhita* suffixes in the *apatyádhikára.* Having no success in tracing the term 'Játa' in the sanskritic or Indic sources, we should proceed to explore the possibility of the term having something to do with the Arabic/Persian connections of a much later period than hitherto believed. We should also ponder over the question why the term *játa* has continued to carry a pejorative sense since the times we have noticed it being used for (or restricted to) a community which has ever stood for justice and truth as the saying goes, as also the fact that the term Jat transcends the meaning of a caste and is used in a general sense for describing people, language, food, colour or things, albeit in a pejorative sense.

## References

1. Thakur, Desh Raj (Jat Itihas-in Hindi, 1934); Joon, Ram Swarup (History of Jats, Urdu/Hindi- 1938, English-1967); Dahiya, B.S.(Jats:The Ancient Rulers-1980); Pawar, Hukam Singh (The Jats: their Origin, Antiquity and Migrations,1993).
2. *Devašamhita*-in Sanskrit, written 18th/19th century, most likely commissioned to spread the absurd theory of the origin of Jats from the hair locks of Shiva.
3. Such dhátus are: *gošṭa; lošṭa; jaṭa; jhaṭa; piṭa; piḍdi; púla; mřikša;*

*vakša: Súla; Sroñřì; Slokřì; styai; sṭyai; huḍi (of bhvádi gaňa);* and *musta; púla;piḍi; Ḍapa; Ḍipa; ghaṭa (of churádi gaňa,) ašúnga; aša (of divádi gaňa).* Many words coming from these *dhátús* conveying the meaning of cluster, heap or a monolithic combination can be observed in the modern Indian languages, e.g. *gošá* or *gošṭá;lothá; piṭaka; pinḍi; púlì* or *púlá* etc.

4. Use of *sangha* for animates in the *Bhagvadgita:bhutavišeša-sanghán* (11.15); *mahrši- siddha-sangháh* (11 .21); *gandharva-yakšásura-siddha—sangháh* (11.22 );*avanipálasanghaih* (11 .26); *siddha-sangháh* (11.36)

   Panini's: references to *Sangha* can be seen in the *sutras:* 1.2.13; 3.3.42; 3.3.86; 4.1.1 and 5.1 .58. We get a sense from Panini that *sangha* and *gaňa* were synonymous terms. Yaudheya *gaňa* is counted among *Ayudha-jìvi-sanghas.*

   The use of the term sangháta for inanimates may be seen below: *upáya-sangháta iva pravṛiddha*-Raghuvansha, 14.11;*kshata-setu-bandhano jalasangháta ivási vidrutah*-Kumarasambhava, 4.6; *tušára-sangháta-shilátalešhvapi*-Kumarasambhava, 5.55; ....*toyaugha-nikara-vrátavára-saugháta-sanchayáh*-Amarakosha- 5.39

   Also see Mahabharata (XII.298.17) for use of *sangháta* for a heap or cluster:

   *sanghátaván martyalokah parasparamášhritah*

5. i) Kautilya uses the term *sangha* in the sense of a corporation (*sajátádnyah sanghah*-2.1.32; *dešhasya-Játyáh-sanghasya dharmo-grámasya vá mithah*-3.7.40; *tena jnáti-kula-sanghánám*-3.10.45; *játi-sanghášchhidrešu prahareyuh*-9. 6.72; *dešha-gráma-játi-sangha-mukhyešu*-13.5.9 and in the sense of a union of labourers (*tena sangha-bhṛitá vyákhyátáh*-3.14.12.; and in the sense of a confedertacy of princes (*mitrasanghasya vá yo antastháyí tam labhet*-9.6.16; and in the sense of an oligarchy (*sangha- lábho danda-mitra-lábhanáamuttamah*-11.1.1; *višhiṣta-balábháve sama-balaistulya- bala-sanghairvá balavatah sambhúya tišthet*-7.15.3; *višhešatašcha sanghánám sangha-dharminám cha rájakulánám dyúta-nimitto bhedastannimitto vinášah..*-8.3.64

   ii) Examples of *sangháta* used in the sense of cluster, heap or combination or group inanimates in the Arthashastra : *pratisargamekártha - charyám sanghátam cha varjayet* - 5.4.10; *ašṭaproti sanghátya... iti naipálakam*-2.11.100 and also 2.14.17, 26, 30. *sanghátaván martyalokah parasparamásritah* (Mahabharata. XII.298.17)

2

# Traditional System of Dispute Resolution: A Critical Study of Khap Panchayats in India

*Prof. Khazan Singh Sangwan*

Khap panchayats are historically very old but attracted the attention of the scholars, when electronic media highlighted certain decisions of the Khap panchayats, which were violative of human rights of the individual. These decisions were mainly related to marriages which violated the traditional moral code of conduct especially, the concept of village *bhaichara,* gotra[1] *bhaichara* or Khap *bhaichara* which forms the basis of community harmony in Indian village especially in northern India.

Khap panchayat, like caste system and joint family systems, is traditional institution which have been helping in dispute resolution and in regulating the behaviour of individual or group(s) in rural India. These Khap panchayats are mainly confined in resolving disputes of wider concern within its territory whereas the smaller issues are taken up by the village panchayats. Sometime these Khap panchayats have been active in political sphere also, but mainly confined only to social issues. After independence, the authority of these Khap panchayats have been challenged by modern institutions of justice like court which function on the principle of rule of law, whereas the Khap panchayats function on the basis of concept of *bhaichara* customs, traditions and moral values prevailing in the area of their jurisdiction.

But still the Khap panchayats are popular among common masses because they do not involve any money, less time consuming, face to face arguments by both parties before the large audience including influential person of the Khap panchayat. People feel that decision by panchayat is impartial. It helps in maintaining peace and harmony among the people of different caste and therefore acts as agency of social control. These factors have been responsible for its survival over such a long period of time. The state and especially the local administration normally do not interfere in the functioning of these Khap panchayats. The decisions passed by Court against these Khap panchayats are not implemented by the local administration with the same spirit as the court have asked them to implement. Even the state try to avoid any confrontation with these Khap panchayats.

This shows the popularity of the Khap panchayat among rural masses. But sometime the decisions of the Khap panchayats though goes well with the old established tradition but are not in tune with modern law of the land, and therefore, violates human rights. This creates a situation of contradiction between traditional system of dispute resolution and modern institutions like judiciary and administration. In this paper, I would like to focus on the traditional system of dispute resolution i.e., the Khap panchayat, its brief history, structure and functioning by analyzing its various decisions taken over a period of time and how these decisions at times are in contradiction with modern laws.

**Brief History of Khap Panchayat:**

There is lack of literature on the origin of the Khap panchayat as such but there are certain references in some of the studies, which talks about the existence of multi-village organization, which are structurally similar to Khap panchayats. There are records which provide evidence of existence of certain villages or cluster of villages as one unit. Some of these multi-village units were based on *gotra* (clan) or caste. The very organization of villages on the basis of geographical area for administrative purpose or revenue purpose or providing military support to the king shows that these villages might have also constituted a political entity.

Thapar[2] in her book *From Lineage to State* has discussed multi-village organization. She points out that a clan constitutes a Jana and the territory on which they settled was called the Janapada i.e., where the tribe places its feet. The actual control over territory was limited to smaller areas of cultivated land. As long as the settlements were comparatively small, lineage authority was a sufficient mechanism of social control. It was not necessary that a lineage group settled at one particular place would continue to stick on. There is evidence of a fairly widespread movement of people not only from western India to the Ganga Valley but also into the Vindhya region. The assimilation of local population must certainly have been one of the reason for the frequent breaking away or fissing off from the main lineage. In one sense migrations were also a form of easing tension and establishing new settlements.[3] Such migration by any section of the lineage led to the mixing of population belonging to different lineages.

The organization of a lineage claiming common ancestor but belonging to different villages was also known as *gana*. The term *Sabha* and *Samiti* occur more frequently in the later Vedic literature.[4] In the *Atharvaveda* they are often mentioned together. The *Samiti* appears to have been a more open assembly than the *Sabha*.[5] These *Sabhas* and *Samitis* use to decide the social, political and economic issues of the people belonging to the same lineage.

Sharma in his seminal work on Indian feudalism maintains that villages in the Rastrakuta empire were grounded mainly in the unit of ten and its multiples for revenue purposes. In the case of the Gurjara branches of the Rastrakutas, within their domain a unique mixture co-existed simultaneously.[6] While the Gurjara branch followed the decimal pattern, the Rajput system consisted of units of 12 and 84 villages. Units of 12 villages or their multiples also prevailed elsewhere in the Rastrakutas empire outside Gujarat.[7]

The Sanjan plates of Amoghavars-1 mentions a group of 24 villages and under Govinda III, the Pratisthanabhukti contained several groups of 12 villages. All these were obviously fiscal units and they were given as fiefs to vassals or officials who were responsible for the administration.[8]

Gurjaras who came to India as a conquering minority from outside imposed themselves as a dominant clan on settled villages. The tribal practice of sharing the spoils among the members of the tribal led to the allotment of villages among the conquering chiefs, some of whom received them in the units of eighty four. Thus units of 12 and 84 villages which are found in Gujarat under the Rastrakutas may have originated as a result of Gurjara settlement in that area.

In countries other than India also, we came across the existence of such territorial units. For example when the Yue-ches conquered Ta-hia (Tokharestan) in the 2nd Century B.C., they distributed the whole areas among five chiefs.[10] But in the early middle ages, the central Asian Tribes preferred to have units of twenty four. The earliest indication of such units is found in Tokharestan in the middle of seventh century A.D., when the Turkish ruler of that region divided the area into twenty four districts with the help of the Chinese.[11]

Similar practices were also observed by the tribe of Oghuz, i.e., Turkish people of central Asia. In the beginning the Oghuz were a group of nine tribes,[12] but as they gradually incorporated defeated people into their fold, the number rose to twenty-two in the eleventh century.[13] Slowly their number went upto twenty four.

Ghosal noted that the entire territories of each kingdom were further sub-divided into 'clan monarchies' or the proto Rajput kingdoms, specially under the Gurjara-Pratiharas in the 8th-l0th centuries. Here the territory was parcelled out by the ruler after regaining his own share among his kinsmen and clan chiefs.[14] Each of the latter than set about dividing his territory among his own clansmen while retaining, his own share, until by this process of 'sub-infudation' every village was assigned to a particular man in return for supply of troops when needed by the assigner.[15] He further observed that the existence of these territories down the centuries indicate the sweeping and indeed the lasting nature of the territorial distribution that took place among the dominant clans at that time.

Irfan Habib[16] while describing social distribution of landed property mentioned that it is between 8th and 10th centuries that the new territorial units comprising groups of villages, specified on numbers that were all multiple of 6, *viz*. 12, 42 and

84 were established. These units were mentioned in the records of Pratiharas and the succeeding dynasties of Cahamans, Gahadvolas, Paramaras and Chalukyas.

Baden-Powell maintains that pre-Aryan races had established villages and permanent cultivation in ancient times.[17] Therefore, it can safely be concluded that clan settlement took place under purely tribal conditions of life. He further added that we cannot expect to find that all the villages resulting from Aryan, Jat and other later races are connected with the tribe. For one thing, it was only a limited number of Aryan clans who never developed monarchial ideas, and who settled without Raja's or chief's of territories. Most other seems to have become monarchial very readily. The boundaries of these clan areas were fixed and respect thereof would invariably have to be enforced.

He further noted that all over northern India, there was clear indication of clan areas under the name of *taluqa*, *ilaqa* or *tappa* or *thapa*.[18] Such division being the national consequence of tribal life appears all over India and especially in the tribal belts. In regions like the plains of undivided Punjab and north-west provinces the *ilaqa* or *tappa* was still occupied by a number of villages, all belonging to the same clan. This territorial unit was utilized as the basis of surveys and records of casual right during the British period. In nearly all cases, it is found that old clan areas have ultimately formed the basis of the administrative and land revenue sub-division of district; and that is why the *pargana*; and *taluqa*; and other such ancient sub-divisions are in use till today.

But pre-British clan territories clearly lead us to believe that these were not unorganized hoards or collection of individuals, instead they were invariably organized on some principles. It is possible that a sense of clan union which might have lingered on among the twice-born classes found its echo in the joint family system.

In Ludhiana Settlement Report[19] Gordon Walker writes that in the Samrala tehsil, the multiplicity of *got* (clan) among the Hindu Jats is a remarkable feature. Here the adjoining villages not only belong to different *gotras* (clan) but inside each village, we generally find two or three sections (*patti*) of distinct. In their appearance, the village founders came from different parts of the country and belonged to different *got* (clan). The basis of unity was perhaps a sense of belonging to the same general tribe. In the south-west of the district, the Jats on the other hand in some cases settled in large but homogenous bodies. The existence of small villages in the eastern parts was due to the protection provided by the imperial authority which was strong enough to protect its subjects. On the other hand, no such protection was felt and people of one tribe had to collect in large contiguous villages for protection. The Grewal and Gill Jats had a cluster of fifty villages, each near Ludhiana town and in Jagraon tehsil respectively and perhaps they would not have needed any kind of protection. The villages of the Jats and other show a sense of clan organization. They tend to aggregate for social comfort and defence.

The existence and role of Khap panchayats were recognized during the Mughal period in a much more clear terms. Emperor Akbar granted freedom to Khaps in religious matters and internal administration. Taxes were exempted and were allowed to carry its internal function with full freedom.[20] In another mandate issued by emperor Akbar 'every community and the Khap of the Doab have the freedom to carry out their functions according to their old custom and laws within their respective Khaps.' He further stated that these different Khaps may unite in one group and live in peace with each other (Mandate of 8th Ramzan 987 Hizri [A.D. 1578] of emperor Akbar). Such royal mandates were issued by various Mughal emperors from time to time. In one of the last mandates issued in 1157 Hijri (A.D. 1748) to the Khap *Wazir*, was regarding raising military force to help the emperor for maintaining peace in the area but simultaneously he warned the Khap *Wazir* that if any section revolted against him will be dealt with strict action.

The *Wazir* of the Khap Balyan, in Muzaffarnagar, district in U.P., recognized as the leader of the Khap through a mandate issued by emperor Akbar. In another mandate issued by Bahadur Shah on 13th Rajab 1116 Hijri (A. D. 1707) stated that the *Wazir* of the Khap Balyan was given the right to fix and collect the land revenue from the Khap villages, on behalf of the government.[21] On certain occasions emperor used to invite chaudharys of various

Khaps to visit him and use to offer feast and gifts so that the mutual trust can be created between emperor and chaudharys of the Khap by assuring them about non-interference in the internal affairs of the Khap.

This kind of dependency by the Mughal emperor on Khap and Sarva Khap panchayat provided legitimacy to the Khaps in protecting religious faith of the Hindu caste falling under the jurisdiction of various Khaps. This also enabled the Khap panchayat to raise large armies to defend the area by putting resistance to Mughal rulers.

The above mentioned historical records and studies indicate that territorial units of certain villages are very old and can be traced to the vedic and post-vedic period. Whenever a large tract of land was available, the tribe immigrated into it enblock and occupied that territory. As a result of this some tribes established their dominance over others in particular areas. The subsequent change in the composition of such sedentrised groups seem to be motivated by demographic and political factors. The emergence of multi-clan, multi-caste units like *Chaubisi* (Twenty Four), *Baawani* (Fifty two) and *Chaurasi* (Eighty four), should be seen in this context only. The Mughals and Britishers instead of interfering in the functioning of such organization, choose to use them to sub-serve their own interests. Simultaneously these organizations continued to provide common platform to its constituents in order to discuss or thresh out their various problems.

These above studies also shows that in India there existed organizations of villages which were organised in one unit on the basis of one of the following criteria:

1. The villages were united on the basis of *gotra* (clan) being descendent of one common ancestor e.g., Dahiya Khap, Sangwan Khap, Sheoran Khap, Dalal and Hooda Khap etc.
2. The village were also organised on the basis of single caste dominance but with multi-*gotra* (multi-clan) e.g., *Chaubisi* of Meham, *Chaurasi* of Bawal etc.
3. Group of villages based on different caste and clan were combined in one unit for revenue purposes and also for

supplying persons for defence purposes to the ruler or the revenue in-charge of these villages.

Though, the villages have existed as self-sufficient and autonomous bodies in the past, it does not mean that they existed in complete isolation from one another. Different villages belonging to the same clan or different clan but living in a particular geographical area use to hold assembly in the form of panchayat, and decide the issues related to them. There were officials of the King (ruler) who use to collect revenue from village or group of villages forming a particular geographical area based on clan (*gotra*) unity or other criteria depending upon the grouping of the villages discussed above. Malvia while commenting on the relationship between the state and village community points out that villages in ancient India were important in the administrative machinery mainly because of the close unity in which they were knit through the institution of panchayat. It is through this institution that the populace exercised its rights and duties. The panchayats were expected to ensure high level of justice, fair play and efficiency, in the absence of all these the panchayats could not get respect and inspire the villagers. This, in turn, could be possible because the state gave the village body complete authority and rights over all affairs relating to the village.[22]

**Review of Literature:**

There is not much literature available on Khap panchayat as such but I would like to make a brief review of studies which have examined traditional method of dispute resolution in various communities located in different parts of the country. The dispute resolution by multi-village panchayat in other parts of the country can be equated with the Khap panchayats of northern India.

Lewis[23] found the existence of multi-village panchayat of twenty villages popularly known as Bisgama, which is further divided into smaller units of two, three and four villages popularly known as Dugama, Tigama and Chaugama. These villages are dominated by people of Dabas *gotra*.[24] He also noted that similarly other castes also had their caste organizations on the pattern of the Dabas. He observed that this multi-village panchayat is still active but its effectiveness had declined due to the emergence of new institutions of dispute resolution.

Chauhan in his study of a Rajasthan village have tried to analyze a multi-village panchayat popularly known as *chokhla*.[25] He has discussed the nature and working of the *chokhla* of different castes and found that *chokhla* was helpful in maintaining some control over its members through collective action.

Sachchidananda[26] has discussed about the multi-village panchayat among the Mundas. He has found two important institutions which are *Hatu* panchayat and *Parha* panchayat of the Munda polity. The former functions at the village level and the later is the regional council of a group of villages. The Munda panchayat consist of the influential and elderly persons of the villages. *Parha* organization was found to be concerned with the members of Munda tribe living in the *Parha* area. The members of the other clan residing in the *Parha* area also supposed to abide by the decisions of their territorial *Parha*. He further observed that with the introduction of statutory panchayat and courts of law, these panchayats are in the process of decay but still the influence of the Munda society try to revive it by changing their composition and functions to meet the challenges of the situation.

Murti has tried to analyse the traditional panchayat system of the Badagas of the Nilgiris and found the existence of panchayat based on four tier system. At the apex it was Four-Nad panchayat (Maklu-Bitta), next lower level was called Nad Panchayat than at third level it was village panchayat and the hamlet panchayat at the base.[27]

Fox has examined the historical structure of local political groups and their interaction with state government machinery and noted that in northern India, caste and unilineal kinship were major determinants of the structure of state hinterland interaction.[28] The compact lineage might be designated as a *tappa* and be incorporated with other kin defined *tappas* into a *pargana*. These groups claiming to be Kshatriya status performed many political and military functions.

Aggarwal while studying the relationship between the caste, religion and power noted the existence of multi-village panchayat among the Meos of Haryana and adjoining Rajasthan.[29] The hierarchy of traditional Meo panchayat was *pal, thamba* and at the village level. The jurisdiction of the panchayat at *pal* level was multi-village and over all castes in the area. It was found that the position of the *Ćhaudhary* at *pal* level was hereditary. Ranking below the *Ćhaudhary* were *dhings*. *Dhings* were wealthy men who controlled large factions. The *dhings* and *Ćhaudhary* together with the leaders of the various *thambas* within the *pal* constituted the *pal* panchayat which could be convened by any member of the *pal*. Below the *pal* panchayat were the *thamba* panchayats.

The panchayat was affective in settling the inter and intra caste disputes. Members from other well to do castes were also included if they were wealthy and exceptionally capable. However, this privilege was not extended to the lower castes. The introduction of statutory panchayat administration and courts have diluted the effectiveness of the traditional panchayat.

Baljit Singh observed that in an Uttar Pradesh village when a village caste panchayat fails to satisfy a faction, the aggrieved party may call a bigger caste panchayat may be of seven villages, twelve villages, twenty-four villages, forty-two villages or even eighty-four villages. He quoted a case of factional split among *Julahas* (weavers) over the question of dowry for which a caste panchayat of 84 villages was called and matter was resolved.[30]

Mayer[31] has tried to see the relationship between caste and kinship in central India and observed the existence of multi-village panchayat which he terms as Council. The Council of five neighbouring villages was known as *Pankhera* (group of five villages) or circle council. The third type of council at higher level was known as provincial council. He observed that the main function of all these councils was to have social control over the people of its caste and sub-castes. The lack of kinship relations and geographical compactness of the lineage has made this institution of Council less effective over a period of time and mainly under the impact of modern forces.

Hayden[32] has tried to analyse the traditional mode of dispute resolution among the nomads i.e., a non-literate Telugu speaking caste of Maharastra. He noted that caste councils (panchayats) were among the most important traditional legal institution in rural India. He found that as long as caste was the primary social group in India, caste panchayat were common feature. However, when caste lost its salience as a primary source of identity and social ties, the importance of caste panchayat also declined.

Miller[33] while studying the changing patterns of social inequality in a village of Rohtak district have made mention of the khap panchayat of Chahar (Jat) *gotra*. He noted that the caste group elders continue to deal with intra-caste matters but their influence has become weak over a period of time.

M.C. Pradhan[34] has studied Khap panchayat of Balyan *gotra* (clan) consisting of *Chaurasi* (Eighty four) villages in western U.P. The focus of the study was to know the political system of the Jats of Northern India. Because in this region Khap panchayats are the major source of dispute resolution. The author has tried to analyse the structure and functioning of Khap panchayats based on single clan (*gotra*) with the help of the concept of *bhaichara* (brotherhood) from village to multi-village level. He found that the concept of *bhaichara* helps the Jats in the organization of their social and political life under the changing conditions. He also noted that how the Jats are moving from traditional, homogeneous, non-contractual society to modem, contractual and heterogeneous society. But still the Jats are highly traditional and membership is still defined by descent groups which are homogenous in customs and beliefs and are guided by these in their social behaviour.

It was also noted that the participation by other caste into political system of the Jats is on contractual and voluntary basis, without the use of coercion. The acceptance of decision of a Khap council used to be obligatory and not optional as it is now. The contractual associations are being formed within the clan as well as between the Jats and other castes at the village level. The factional affiliation has given way to the emergence of contractual type of behaviour. All this and other modem forces i.e. education, adult franchise, political parties bureaucracy and modem legal system have diluted the effectiveness of the Khap panchayat.

On the basis of above studies it can be concluded that the multi-village panchayat system which can be equated with Khap panchayat of northern India have existed in other parts of the country which use to act as a source of dispute resolution in rural India. The basis of these panchayats were either *gotra*, caste, tribe, or geographical area, which confined to certain limited villages. These panchayats decide intra and inter-caste issues to maintain peace and harmony in the area of the panchayat. These panchayats were open to all but only the influential persons use to decide the issues keeping in view the facts placed before the general assembly of the panchayat. The decision of the panchayat was supposed to be acceptable to all. If matter is not resolved at village level than it is taken to higher level panchayat. The traditional system of dispute resolution also shows the existence of higher bodies of the panchayat which consist of group of villages and can be equated with Khap and Sarv-Khap panchayats of northern India.

**Khap Panchayat**

Before, I discuss the structure and functioning of the Khap panchayats it will be better we understand the meaning and nature of the Khap.

**The Khap :** The concept of Khap is very popular in northern India, but we find the existence of similar type of multi-village organizations in other parts of the country which provide basis of unity among the people of a particular geographical area. This organization of people at multi-village level is known by different names in different areas but in northern India it is popularly by the name of Khap. Therefore, in this section I would like to discuss the meaning and nature of the Khap.

According to Pradhan (1966)[35] the Khap can be defined as a unit of a number of villages organized into a political council for the purpose of social control. The Khap area may be inhabited either by a dominant caste having control over most of its agricultural land or by single clan or by more than one clan, each having a number of villages to itself and being predominant in them. In a situation when a single clan has only few villages say four or five, few other clans also join into a common Khap for the purpose of their defence and control over its people. When a Khap is dominated by single clan its headship lies within the same clan. When the number of clan is more, headship in that situation goes to that clan which has more number of villages.

The Khaps can be classified into following types:

1. Khap which are based on single caste and single clan. It this category a particular geographical area is dominated by a single *gotra* (clan) of a particular caste and the *gotra* has a sizeable number of villages in that area for example Dahiya Khap, Hooda Khap, Malik Khap, Sangwan Khap, Sheoran Khap etc. all located in Sonepat, Rohtak, Bhiwani districts of Haryana, and Balyan Khap in Muzaffarnager district of U.P. These Khaps have about 40 villages to eighty four villages. The people of other *gotra* also live in these villages but their number is very less. The major landholding in these villages is owned by majority *gotra* (clan), other castes like scheduled caste and backward castes also reside in these villages but power lies with the majority *gotra* (clan).
2. Second type of Khaps are based on single caste but multi *gotra* (clan). Such types of Khaps are having villages which are dominated by single caste but some of the villages are dominated by various *gotras*. *Chaubisi* organization of twenty four villages of Meham in district Rohtak (Haryana) is example of such Khaps.
3. The third type of Khaps are consisting of multi caste and multi *gotras*. Such Khaps have villages in a particular geographical area out of which some villages are dominated by a particular caste and other villages are dominated by other castes or with different *gotras*. These different castes which dominate such Khap enjoy more or less equal status in caste hierarchy and own major land holding of these villages. Bawal Khap of *Chaurasi* (eighty four villages) in Rewari district is an example of such Khap.

**Structure of the Khap Panchayat :**

The structure of the Khap panchayat can be divided into four categories. These are - Sarv-Khap panchayat, Khap panchayat, *tappa* or *kanni* panchayat and village panchayat.

**Sarv-Khap :**

Sarv-Khap is the combination of many Khaps of the neighbouring area, but sometime representatives of other Khaps from larger distances also participate in it. The size of the Sarv-Khap depends upon the nature and seriousness of the issue involved. The participation in Sarv-Khap by representatives of other Khap is voluntary but only on invitation. Women are not allowed to participate in panchayats at any level whether it is Sarv-Khap, Khap (*tappa*) or even village panchayat. Women are not even allowed to put their views in the panchayat even in the case of under consideration is related to the women. Similarly lower caste and schedule caste do not participate in these panchayats. Sarv-Khap panchayats are held only when some serious issues are discussed. The panchayats are held very rarely. Such panchayats can be called by separate caste also which is known as Sarv-Khap panchayat of such and such caste.

**Khap Panchayat :**

The Khap is normally named after the dominant *gotra* (clan) e.g. Sheoran Khap, Sangwan Khap etc. or in the name of number of villages e.g. *Chaubisi* of Meham in Rohtak district or *Chaurasi* of Bawal in Rewari district. For dominant clan or caste, Khap includes all caste falling under its jurisdiction. Each Khap has a *pradhan*, sometime hereditary, and in some cases, the *pradhan* is nominated on the basis of his reputation of fair play, power to argue and socio-economic position in the area. Economic condition cannot be the sole criteria for achieving the position of *pradhan*. The decision are binding on other caste also if it is of wider significance, otherwise different caste can also hold its separate panchayat on the pattern of upper caste. Each caste can call the meeting of its caste members falling under the jurisdiction of a particular Khap. Such panchayats are known as 'Khap Panchayat' of such and such caste. If the dispute is inter-caster, than it is decided by the Khap Panchayat of the upper caste or clan in which other caste people also participate. The other caste also follows the norms and tradition of the upper caste falling under the jurisdiction of the Khap e.g. the minority caste will also follow the principle of Khap *bhaichara* or *gotra bhaichara* and therefore rule of exogamy will also apply in case of marriage among these castes also. These minority castes also have the feeling of Khap belongingness, though it is declining over a period of time.

**Tappa or Kanni Panchayat**

The Khap is sub-divided into sub-units consisting of minimum two to ten or twelve villages depending upon the size of the Khap. This group of villages is known as *tappa* or *kanni* or *ganwand* (Pradhan, 1966) and is based on the principal of local contiguity, kinship proximity and ties of economic and social interaction between the villagers. Out of these villages one village is normally bigger than other villages. It is because some time certain families from this village migrate to new place due to social or economic reasons and settle down there and with the passage of time it takes the form of a village. Therefore, the *tappa* villages have some feeling of commonness which binds them in one unit.

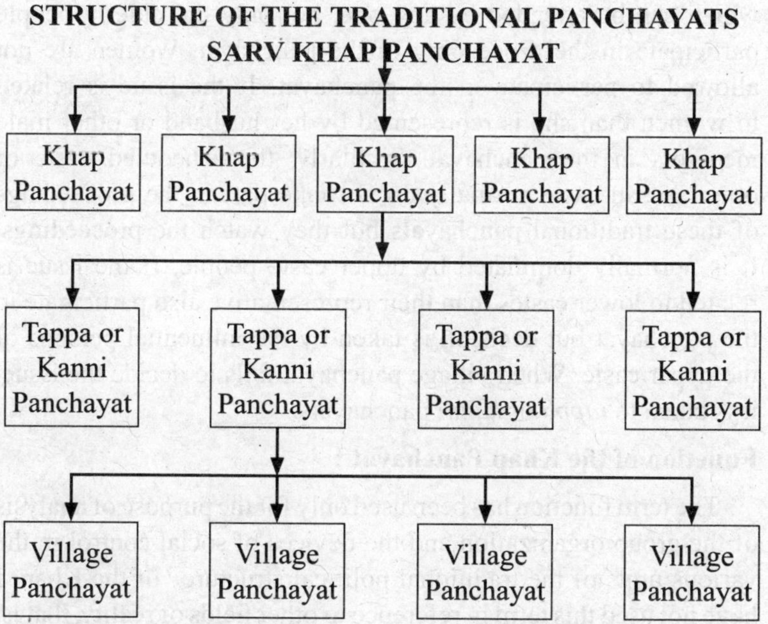


These villages can organize a panchayat which is known as *tappa* or *kanni* panchayat. If this panchayat fail to resolve the issue only than the matter is taken up at Khap level. There is no hereditary *pradhan* at *tappa* or *kanni* level. Only the influential person who is considered as man of integrity alongwith the capacity to argue, normally influence the decision and nominated as *pradhan* for a particular panchayats. These panchayats are open for participation and discussion irrespective of caste. Different caste can organize there separate panchayats. Sometime lower caste people also invite influential person from upper castes in their panchayat which helps them to resolve the issue and also helps in the wider acceptance of their decision.

**Village Panchayat**

Village is the smallest unit in the Khap panchayat. The village panchayat is represented by the influential of the village belonging to various *thok*.[36]

Issues related to village are discussed in village panchayat which can be attended by any one, but only the elderly people participate in the proceeding of the panchayat. Women are not allowed to participate in the panchayat. If the issue is related to women than she is represented by her husband or other male members in the panchayat. Similarly, the scheduled caste or other artisan caste normally do not take part in the proceedings of these traditional panchayats but they watch the proceedings. It is normally dominated by upper caste people. If the issue is related to lower castes than their representative also participate in the panchayat but decision is taken by the influential persons of the upper caste. When village panchayat fails to decide the issue, it is taken to *tappa* or *kanni* panchayats.

**Function of the Khap Panchayat :**

The term function has been used only for the purpose of analysis of the group organization and the devices of social control in the various units of the traditional political structure[37] of the Khap. I have not used this term in reference to other fields of reality, that is, social roles, institutional pattern, social processes or social norms. Further I have not tried to distinguish between the manifest and latent functions of the Khap panchayat and, therefore, our focus is to describe the function of the various units of Khap and their consequences.

When I deal with the functions of the various Khap councils my focus centres on how these councils are helpful in maintaining the social order by controlling the fissile tendencies or managing the conflict within the jurisdiction of various councils. These councils functions towards the establishment and maintenance of internal cooperation and external independence.[38] The Khap and Sarva Khap councils had some executive and administrative functions during the medieval period, such as land revenue collection and the general administration of the Khap area. These panchayats have also worked for the social welfare of the people falling under its jurisdiction. These functions, had legitimacy in the traditional role of the Khap panchayat.

**Functions of the Panchayats at Various Levels :**

Sarv-Khap panchayat consists of neighbouring Khaps of the area. There is no fixed number of Khaps in the meeting of Sarv-Khap panchayat. It all depends upon the seriousness of the issue and the invitation to Khap *pradhan*. The number of Khaps taking part in Sarv-Khap may go from 8-10 Khaps to even upto 50 Khaps or more. It is not only the *pradhan* of the Khap who participate in the Sarv-Khap but it is open for every one. It is the *pradhan* of a Khap who calls the meeting of the Sarv-Khap with agenda, date, time and venue of the meeting. The meeting of the Sarv-Khap is called only when the issue between two Khaps is not resolved or the issue is of serious nature. Informally the Khap *pradhan* discuss the issue in hand with other *pradhans* before participating in the Sarv-Khap just to mobilize the opinion in such a manner which can appeal the larger section of the community as per the past practice or norms of the moral code of conduct.

The host Khap makes arrangement for the Khap *pradhans* and other participants for their tea, meal and *huqqa* (Smoking pipe). The president or secretary welcomes the delegates. Since there is no hereditary *pradhan* of the Sarv-Khap, therefore, one of the senior persons among the Khap *pradhans* is nominated as the *pradhan* of the meeting of the Sarv-Khap for that day. The nominated *pradhan* controls the proceedings of the Khap panchayat till the decision is arrived. The Sarv-Khap *pradhan* asks the host Khap to present the issue before the gatherings of the Khap *pradhans* and other participants.

After explaining the detailed history of the case, other Khap *pradhans* are invited to put their views in the meeting. After listening to all the speakers, a smaller committee of 10-15 Khap *pradhans* is constituted to reach a consensus keeping in view the opinion and discussions of the proceedings. Before announcing the decision, opinion of the participants is taken by raising their hands that the decision of the Sarv-Khap panchayat, would be acceptable to all. It is the duty of the different khaps to implement the decision in their respective Khap, if issue is related to all Khaps. But if the issue is related to a particular Khap than the concerned Khap is supposed to abide by the decision of the Sarv-Khap. These decisions are informal but announced in the gathering so that it is accepted and conveyed in all Khaps. If the decision is not implemented by the Khap than the meeting of the Sarv-Khap involving more Khaps is called again so that the earlier decision can be reinforced.

The effectiveness of the Sarv-Khap decision depends upon the type of issue, nature of the decision, community feelings and unity and solidarity between different Khaps. The sense of community feeling, cooperation, traditional value system and feeling of *bhaichara* provide main strength to the institution of Sarv-Khap panchayat. The main role of the Sarv-Khap is to maintain peace and harmony between various Khaps by settling disputes between Khaps or by passing resolutions related to social welfare of the people like education of the girls, ban on female foeticide, ban on dowry, limited expenditure in marriages etc.

The Khap panchayat is still considered as a powerful institution for resolving disputes or in reinforcing the traditional norms and value system within its jurisdiction. The Khap panchayat acts as sole-adjudicative, rule-making and rule-application body, but after independence due to loss of legal power it acts as an institution of adjudicating disputes between the members of clan and other castes of falling under its jurisdiction. When the decision of the Khap is violated by any individual, group or family or village, Khap tries to act as an executive body. It also acts as legislative body when issues are related to the welfare of the people by passing resolution such as ban on dowry, alcoholism, female foetiable and infanticide, expenditure in marriage, etc.

The main function of the Khap panchayat is to resolve issues between its clan members or castes so that the peace and harmony can be maintained under its jurisdiction. If the *tappa* or *kanni* fails to decide the dispute, matter is referred to the Khap. The complaint is sent to the Khap *chaudhary* who calls the meeting of the representatives of the *tappa* or *kanni pradhans*, alongwith other influential persons of the Khap, who can also participate in its proceedings. If the Khap is of single clan (*gotra*) than most of the participants are from the same *gotra* but if Khap is consisted of multi-*gotra* (multi-clan) than representatives of different *gotras* take part in it. Similarly in case of multi-caste Khap, representatives of various castes take part in its proceedings. Once the decision is taken by the Khap with the consensus of its constituents, than it becomes the duty of its clan or caste representatives of various *tappa* or *kanni* to see to it that the decision of the Khap is implemented. If somebody found of violating the decision of the Khap, sanctions are imposed by the Khap so that the sanctity of the Khap decision is maintained. Though the importance of the Khap is declining, but still Khap is one of the most effective institution of social control at least in northern India.

*Tappa* or *kanni* which forms the third layer of the Khap panchayat is next to village level panchayat. Normally the *tappa* or *kanni* panchayat consists of two to eight, ten or twelve villages depending upon the size of the Khap. At *tappa* level there is no hereditary *pradhan* and is normally elected or nominated depending upon the skill of oratory, reputation in the area and socio-economic condition of the person. Once elected, he can continue for a longer period or till he survives. The issues which cannot be resolved by the village panchayat are taken to the *tappa* panchayat. All the influential persons of the *tappa* take part in this panchayat. Common people can also express their views. This gives an opportunity to the young people to show their capabilities of leadership. The procedure of decision making is similar to Khap panchayat.

The village panchayat decides day-to-day issues by calling the meeting of the village influentials. When issue comes to the village *pradhan* he asks the village *chowkidar* to announce the assembly of the panchayat along with date and time. Most of the village elders assemble normally in the center of the village and express their opinion freely. People from neighbouring villages do not participate in village panchayats. Both the parties are invited to put their views in the assembly. Sometime this has hot exchanges while arguing their case. The village elders regulate the discussion by not allowing direct accusation by either party. The discussion helps in letting off steam and also helps in providing solution to the problem. After listening to both parties the *panchs* discuss the issue away from the main sight of the panchayat. Before announcing the decision the consent of both parties is taken that they will abide by the decision of the panchayat. After taking the consensus, decision is announced which act as binding on both the parties. The decision of the panchayat in majority cases is such that no party feels defeated and therefore decision is readily accepted by both parties.

**Sanctions**

Social sanctions help the panchayat in the implementation of the decision taken by the panchayats. The fear of social sanction acts as deterrent action on the minds of individual or family who violates the traditional norms. Sanctions are the most important aspect of traditional mode of dispute resolution. The panchayats from village to Sarv-Khap level has their own method of giving punishment to its members depending upon the type of deviation from the norms of the village, caste or Khap or the type of crime, one commits. Most of the punishments are in the form of fine, for acts like theft, fraud, blackmail, physical violence etc. In case of serious crime like murder, incest, inter-caste marriages, the punishment is also of severe nature like expulsion from the village or caste, stopping of sharing *huqqa* (smoking), water or meal i.e. excommunication or outcasting from the caste or group or even from the village or Khap.[39] Ex-communication or outcasting is considered as the extreme form of sanction available to the panchayat. Another extreme form of punishment is that a person or family is asked to leave the village or Khap territory. This kind of punishment is very rare and is announced only in extreme form of cases like incest or rape, inter-caste marriage. Inter-caste marriage is also considered as serious crime, only when a girl from upper caste marry a boy of lower caste especially the scheduled caste.

## The Concept of *Bhaichara* and Khap

The concept of *bhaichara* (brotherhood) means generation-wise brotherhood, i.e., members are classificatory 'brother' and 'sister' (*Bhai-Behan*) to one another and as such cannot inter-marry.[41] This idea of *bhaichara* starts from village level and continue upto Khap level. There exists three types of *bhaichara* (i) village *bhaichara,* i.e., members of one generation are treated as brothers and sisters irrespective of their origin from one common ancestor and therefore related to one blood; (ii) *Gotra* or clan *bhaichara* i.e. all members belonging to the same *gotra* are treated as brothers and sisters even if they belong to different villages of their caste, or even if they belong to scheduled caste; and (iii) Khap *bhaichara*. But there are certain Khaps which are multi-*gotra* and multi-caste where the people can marry within the Khap. Therefore, the idea of *bhaichara* is not only restricted to kinship system but it applied to social and political field also.

To make it more clear the concept of *bhaichara* at village level means all people living in the village and belonging to one generation are treated as brothers and sisters, irrespective of *gotra* or caste and therefore cannot inter-marry within the village. Even the scheduled castes also enjoy the same relationship of *bhaichara*. The village is a exogamous community. This idea of *bhaichara* extends upto the neighbouring villages which share geographical boundary and therefore marriage cannot take place in adjoining villages.

### Khap *Bhaichara* :

The Khap belonging to one *gotra* such as Sangwan Khap, Dahiya Khap, Hooda Khap etc. enjoy *bhaichara* on the basis of common lineage. The families belonging to the same caste but with different *gotra* also do not marry in the villages of the single *gotra* Khap, because such Khaps are numerically dominated by single *gotra*. All other persons living in a Khap area irrespective of their caste or *gotra* treat each other as brothers and sisters in such Khaps. This gives the feeling of brotherhood.

There are other Khaps which are multi-*gotra* and multi-caste, such as, *Chaubisi* of Meham in Rohtak district, *Chaurasi* of Bawal in Rewari district and *Satrol* (Seventy villages) of Hansi in Hisar districts in Haryana. In these Khaps people belonging to the same caste can marry in another villages belonging to different *gotra* but excluding adjoining villages.

Similarly, the villages falling under one *tappa* or *kanni* also has the same practice of not marrying within the *tappa*. Though marriage can take place in another *tappa* if the Khap consists of multi-*gotra*. The concept of *bhaichara* exists in these Khaps at social and political level i.e. the belongingness to a particular Khap with the idea of egalitarianism. But in real sense this idea of egalitarianism exists only among the people of dominant caste but to maintain peace, harmony and unity in the Khap, the leaders of Khap extend this idea of equality (*bhaichara*) to the people of other caste also.

**Khap, Panchayat and Modern Law : A Contradiction**

The traditional panchayats from Sarv-Khap panchayat to village level panchayats have existed in India from the time immemorial. The importance of these panchayats have been recognized by various rulers especially the Mughals and Britishers (Pradhan, 1966: 96-97). Britishers though tried to create modem legal system of dispute resolution by creating court of law but rarely interfered in the functioning of the traditional panchayats. Before independence, these traditional panchayats have acted as unified force in favour or against the then rulers from time to time. The major basis of their strength was the concept of *bhaichara* either on *gotra* (clan), caste or territorial basis. This system believed in *gotra*, village and Khap exogamy but caste endogamy. In addition to this, the belief in the *panchs* i.e., five judges sitting in the panchayat was considered as five gods and their integrity was never doubted by any one. The basis of this legitimacy for the *panchs* was drawn on their fair play, democratic functioning through face to face dialogue by both the parties. In addition to this, these panchayats decide the issues within a very short span of time without spending any money. The decision of the panchayat is always of such a nature where both parties use to reconcile in such a manner that neither of the party use to feel defeated. Since the decision was taken by their own people among whom they have to live therefore, the dispute resolved by panchayat was always welcomed. There was no feeling of defeat or victory by any party. Therefore the panchayat decision use to help in maintaining *bhaichara* at all levels.

These panchayats have not only acted as agencies of dispute resolution at community level but also helped in maintaining peace and harmony between different castes or communities living in the jurisdiction. Therefore, these traditional panchayats were considered as supreme authority by the people in rural areas. Mughals recognized the popularity and authority of these Khap panchayats and therefore emperors like Akbar, Bahadur Shah etc. gave full freedom to the Khap panchayats. While writing a letter to the *pradhan* of Khap Balyan, Akbar went to the extent. 'Every community and the Khaps of the Jats of the Doab have the freedom to carry out their function according to their ancient customs and laws within their respective councils'.[42]

The introduction of Modern law and creation of courts by Britishers for resolving dispute affected the functioning of the Khap panchayats. After independence education, recognition of individual rights, adult franchise, introduction of panchayati raj institutions at village, block and district level, state and parliamentary elections, urbanization, economic independence and other such factors have provided opportunities to the individual to come out of traditional system or moral ideology of *bhaichara*. Now individual has other options to pursue his goal which was earlier confined to family, village or Khap.

Now question arises that even after the introduction of modern legal system and other democratic institution, where individual can express his or her desire, can get dispute resolved without the pressure of the *gotra*, caste or community, then why and how the Khap panchayats are still maintaining their existence?

While analysing the support base of Khap panchayats, the *pradhans* of the different Khaps and the common masses at large feel that these panchayats take decision on the basis of common moral values, old traditions and customs prevailing in the society. The concept of *bhaichara* at village and Khap level is another factor for maintaining solidarity in the community. The decisions of the Khap panchayats are quick, does not involve any expenditure and are not based on false evidences. Since the panchayats are held in open and people from different walks of life can participate in it, therefore, the issue is debated at length and consensus is brought before pronouncing the decision. Khap *pradhans* are of the opinion that these Khap panchayats do justice and does not pronounce decisions which is not done in the court of law. Since these decisions does not involve any victory or defeat for either of the party, therefore, there is scope for both the parties for consenting to the decision of the Khap panchayat without continuing further hostility.

These *pradhans* justify the relevance of the Khap panchayats by comparing the dispute resolution by the court and Khap panchayats. They say that in court of law to get justice is beyond the reach of a common person. It is very time consuming, involves huge money, many times evidences are destroyed, changed or mobilized by other or are not allowed to appear before the court or even if appear many do not stick to the truth. Common people are not familiar with functioning of the legal institutions. Even if the decision is announced by the trial court, it can be taken to higher court by other party. Therefore it consumes lot of time and resources and ultimately people are not satisfied with that decision. Even after coming victorious, the hostility between the two parties continues for many years.[43] The impact of western culture through mass media and electronic media which is mainly in contrast to Indian culture and value system further makes the Khap panchayat more relevant especially on issues related to inter-caste marriages, love marriage which normally violates village, *gotra* and Khap *bhaichara*.[44]

Since modern law recognizes the individual and his rights and is based on rational legal system therefore undermines the importance of traditional concept of *bhaichara* and especially the traditional marriage norms like village, *gotra* or Khap exogamy, and caste endogamy. The moral ideology which was the basis of all these and other behaviour pattern looses its force before the modern law. In addition to above factors, the individualistic approach to achieve one's goal have further affected the importance of Khap panchayats in modern time.

Modern Legal Institutions though are based on law and evidence but has many flaws. It is very costly and time-consuming process. There are chances of manipulation of evidence or sometime due to fear or allurement people do not gather courage to act as witness and therefore the culprits go scot-free. The decision of the court is either in favour or against one of the contending party therefore it gives a sense of victory or defeat which creates rift between the parties. If the parties are from the same village then it creates a feeling of jealously and disturbs the harmony and peace, whereas in the decision of the Khap panchayats, a consensus is created which minimize the differences between both parties and therefore peace and harmony is maintained.

The major contradictions which the Khap panchayats are facing is that these panchayats still hold old tradition and ideology of morality at very high level.

On one side the Khap leaders have to behave according to the will of the larger population, which is based on traditional norms and customs, from where they draw their support whereas on the other side the modern law goes against these traditional ethos of the society and therefore it is said that it violates human rights of the individuals which are based on modern laws.

These situations have in some cases attracted the criticism of certain decisions of the Khap panchayats. Recently Punjab, Haryana High Court has asked the State Government about the functioning of the Khap panchayats which at times take law into their own hands and pronounce decisions that are violative of human rights. The state and political parties do not want to come out openly against the Khap panchayats because these Khap panchayats enjoy popularity among the rural folk. On the other hand, Khap panchayats also do not want to come out openly against the verdict of the court. Now people have alternative methods of dispute resolution to make use of panchayat as well as legal course and try to get benefit from both sources. If traditional source is not favourable then a person approaches the court of law.

**Conclusion**

The existence of Khap panchayats goes back to Vedic period and its historical role by opposing Mughals and Britishers provided legitimacy in the mind of the people towards its functioning for the cause of the common people. Khap panchayats have functioned in tune with the ethos of the traditional society. The concept of *bhaichara* and social harmony enjoyed the highest preference in the minds of the people and their leaders and therefore, this concept of *bhaichara* alongwith prevailing custom, tradition and moral ideology emphasized on the importance of collectivity rather than individualism.

The introduction of modern legal system i.e., courts and other agencies dealing with the dispute resolution are based on the importance of individual rather than collectivity. Education, provision of voting right, urbanization, mass media and the factors have helped in bringing awareness about individual rights. On the other hand certain modern forces like statutory panchayats, and elections and courts have disturbed the social harmony of the society. Mahatma Gandhi himself wrote that the traditional panchayat system promoted social harmony, while the courts disrupted social relations.[45]

Further, the new legal system has its own weaknesses and have not came upto the expectation of the masses because of its complicated procedure, cost involved, time consumed and manipulation of evidence by the powerful or rich, whereas on the other hand traditional panchayat use to decide the matter within no time, without spending any money and without manipulation of evidence. This dissatisfaction with Indian Legal System has further helped in the survival of the Khap panchayats even after about 65 years of independence.

The major weakness of these Khap panchayats lies in the fact that its leaders still decide issues on the basis of old tradition, moral ideology and keeping in view the collective will of the masses. The recent decision of the Khap panchayats have come under attack because its decisions were not in tune with the modern legal system and rule of law. The issues like inter-caste marriages, rape, incest, village and *gotra* exogamy, are still treated as heinous crime, for which punishment is very strong because it disturbs the social harmony. Many times in such cases the decision of the Khap panchayats goes against the rights of the individual and, therefore, Khap panchayats attract criticism.

If we want to make the dispute resolution system more rational we have to involve the local leaders in such a manner that they also had some legal knowledge and dispute is resolved in a face-to-face situation by which social harmony can be maintained and justice is delivered in a short span of time. The increasing importance of Lok Adalat is an example before us. The recent idea of government of India to create informal system of justice can be successful only by involving local leaders for the purpose of fast delivery of justice, can be a blend of modern legal system and old tradition value system and moral ideology for maintaining social harmony in the society. In many cases the disputes are resolved in rural areas by the traditional justice delivery systems. We should not reject anything which traditional without going into the pros and cons of the existing system. All which is modern may not fit in the Indian situation because of our culture and traditions, which are surviving for the last so many centuries.

## References


1. I have used *gotra* synonym to clan-meaning thereby that all those who claim to be descendent of one common ancestor is known as gotra or clan. I have used gotra or clan interchangeably.
2. Romila Thapar: *From Lineage to State,* Bombay, Oxford University Press (1984), p. 34.
3. *Ibid*., p. 46.
4. *Ibid*., p. 56.

5. *Ibid*., p. 57.
6. R.S. Sharma: *Indian Feudalism*, Calcutta (1965), p. 77.
7. R.S. Sharma: *Op cit*., p.77.
8. Altekar: *The Rastrakutas and their times,* Poona (1967) quoted in R.S.Sharma: *Op cit*., p. 86.
9. R.S. Sharma, *Op. cit*., p.107.
10. P.C. Bagchi: *India and Central Asia*, quoted in R.S. Sharma: *Indian Feudalism*, *Op cit.,* p. 108.
11. *Ibid*., p. 198.
12. C.E. Boshosth: *The Later Ghaznavis*, Edinburgh, Edinburgh Univ. Press, (1977) quoted in R.S. Sharma, *ibid.,* p. 109
13. *Ibid*., pp. 210-11.
14. U.N. Ghosal: *Hindu Revenue System*, p. 36, quoted in R.S. Sharma, *ibid*., p. 99.
15. R.S. Sharma, *Op cit*., pp. 96-98.
16. Irfan Habib, "Social Distribution of Landed Property" in *Enquiry* New Series, Vol. II, No. 3 Winter (1965), p. 42.
17. Baden-Powell: *Land Systems of British India*, Delhi, Oriental Publishers (1974), p. 117.
18. *Ibid*., p. 179.
19. Gordon Walker: *Ludhiana Settlement Report* (1884), pp. 45, 79.
20. The text of emperor mandate has been quoted by M.C. Pradhan: *The Political System of the Jats of Northern India*, Oxford University Press, (1966), p. 97. 'By the present *firman* (Mandate), certain community councils in India which during the reign of the Muslim Sultans, before my reign, were charged certain taxes, are now being excused. Each community council has my permission and is free to carry on its traditional functions in my reign. Both Hindus and Muslims are one in my eyes, so I give freedom, [of action) to these councils they are exempt from the payment of *Jazia* (religious tax) and other royal taxes. (Issued by emperor Akbar on 11th Ramzan, 989 Hijri [A.D. 1580]. Mandate issued by grand Wazirs Abul Fazal and Raja Todar Mal.
21. The record is available with Pradhan of Khap Balyan in Shoram village in UP. with the seal of emperor Akbar quoted in M.C. Pradhan's book, *Op cit.,* p. 98.

22. Malvia: *Op. cit*., p. 46.

23. Oscar Lewis: *Village Life in Northern India (A village near Delhi),* (1965), p. 29.

24. According to Lewis: *Op cit.,* p. 23, the word Dabas refers to *gotra* (clan) belonging to Jat caste which is non-localized, exogamous, patrilineal.

25. B.R. Chauhan: *A Rajasthan Village*, New Delhi, Vir Publishing House (1967), to him *Chokla* is a word of regional usage which is used in place of panchayat and is a unit of caste (sub-caste) spread over a number of contiguous villages binding the members of the caste (sub-caste) to certain codes and regulations falling under the jurisdiction of the caste (sub-caste) organization in that area.

26. Sachchidananda: *The Changing Munda*, Concept Publishing Co., New Delhi (1979).

27. Mantra Murti: Traditional Panchayat System of the Budagas of the Nilgiris, *Indian Journal of Political Science*, Vol. XIII, No. 3, July-Sept., 1982, pp. 48-61.

28. Richard, G. Fox: *Kin, Clan, Raja and Rule : State Hinterland Relations in Pre-Industrial India*, California, University of California Press (1971).

29. Partap C. Aggarwal: *Caste, Religion and Power: An Indian Case Study*, New Delhi: Shri Ram Centre for Industrial Relations (1971).

30. Baljit Singh: *Next Step in Village India: A Study of Land Reform and group Dynamics*, Delhi, Asia Publishing House.

31. Adrian C. Mayer: *Caste and Kinship in Central India: A Village and its Region*, London, Routledge and Kegan Paul (1965).

32. Robert M. Hayden: *Disputes and Arguments among Nomads: A Caste Council in India*, New Delhi, Oxford University Press, (1999).

33. D.E. Miller: From Hierarchy to Stratification: Changing Pattern of Social Inequality in a North India Village, Delhi, Oxford University Press (1975).

34. M.C. Pradhan: *Op. cit.*

35. M.C. Pradhan: *Op cit*., pp. 114-115.

36. Thok is a maximal lineage. i.e., a group of families having a common ancestor settled in a compact geographical area in the village.

37. M.C. Pradhan: *Op. cit.*, p. 122.
38. I. Sehepara: *Government and Politics in Tribal Societies* (C.A. Watts and Co., London, 1956), pp. 123.
39. M.C. Pradhan: *Op. cit.*, p. 105; Hyden: *Op. cit.*, p. 49.
40. David, G. Mandlebaum: *Society in India*, Barkeley, University of California Press (1972), pp. 295-99; Lewis Dermont: *Homo Hierarchicus*: *An Issue on the Caste System*, Chicago, University of Chicago Press (1970), pp. 177-79.
41. Lewis Dermont: *Homo Hierarchicus: The Caste System and its implications* (2nd ed.), Chicago, University of Chicago Press (1980).
42. M.C. Pradhan, *Op. cit.*, p. 97.
43. These views were expressed by Khap *pradhans* in a Seminar organized by Department of Sociology, Maharshi Dayanad University, in March 2005 in which in addition to Khap *pradhans*, affected parties, social activists and lawyers participated. See *Frontline*, May 6, 2005, pp. 51-52.
44. Preeti Chaudhary in her keynote address in the Seminar quoted above made this observation.
45. M.K. Gandhi: *Hind Swaraj or Indian Home Rule,* Allahabad, Navjivan Publishing House (1939), pp. 54-57.

3

# Intra-Village, Intra-Gotra Marriage : A Critical Appraisal

*Dr. M. S. Rana*

Village is cornerstone of Indian rural society, be it in north or south, east or west. It is not just a cluster of mud houses inhabited by SOME people. It is a socially congenial unit of agnate groups, self-sustaining economy, social-network of contacts and ethnology continuing and flowering since ages. 'From time immemorial the village has been a basic and important unit in the organization of Indian social polity. It finds prominent mention in the classical texts of the land. For example, according to the *Rig-Veda* (generally dated in the latter half of the 2nd millennium B.C.) society developed in a series of ascending formations, starting from the family (*griha* or *kula*) and gradually extending to the village (*grama*), the clan (*vis*) the people (*jana*) and the country (*rashtra*). The term *grama,* still largely used in India for village, denoted an aggregate of several families sharing the same habitation.'[1] An old adage goes that, 'god made the country [village] and man made the town.' God's creation is ageless and infalliable. Its indigenous organisation is based on time-tested age old values and customs that have weathered all sorts of assaults on its primeval character.

A village is inhabited by people of diverse castes and classes who earn their bread by working on farming and agri-related cottage workshops. Besides, its generic name, a village is also known after the name of the numerically, economically and politically dominant caste; for example, if Jats are a dominant caste in a village, it would also be known as a Jat village, and if there is some other dominant caste, it would be known by the name of that caste. Dominant caste status is not necessarily on the basis of traditional caste ranking. Though statutory panchayat system is available in all villages, but it is the dominant caste's writ that winds through the village. Observance of established social and cultural norms, customs and conventions and public morals by its inhabitants is a customary responsibility of the dominant caste. Its hereditary head enjoys intervening authority so that social harmony prevails in the village. Non-dominant communities *suo motu* approach the *pradhan/chaudhary* to resolve their discords.

Besides, the landowning communities, village is also inhabited by numerous other communities-such as farm labour, carpenters, blacksmiths, weavers, potters, barbers, scavengers and other sundry communities who practise various types of trades. We may broadly bracket them as agri-tagged service class. These communities retain their traditional bonds with their patron farming families, who by way of return for their services in farm operations, receive a lot many freebies known as *jajmanies* round the year and on special occasions such as birth of a child or marriage in the family of their *jajman.* 'A patron [*jajman*] family, in its turn, need not attend the wedding of a child of their sweeper's family, but that wedding elicits some gifts from every patron of the sweeper family.'[2] *Jajmani* system was a hereditary socio-economic relationship among the landowning and service class in a village. The *jajmani* service scale was measured for every plough owned by the *jajman.*[3]

An all pervasive feature of village socio-cultural environment is kinship-based relationship. It transcends all economic, caste and community barriers. Social network of intercourse is determined by age and kin-based mode of calling. Each and every inhabitant expresses his/her social respect in the course of Interlocution with each other. Every aged is addressed as *dada/dadi, tau/tai, chacha/chachi, bhai/behan, bhai/bhai bua* and so on. This mode of interlocution is an indication of social solidarity and cohesiveness among them. It also instills in them a sense of morality and they hardly think of its transgression in their daily dealings. It softens caste feelings and an informal bond of brotherhood *(bhaichara)* becomes a motivational force among them.

Besides, kinship-based mode of calling among its inhabitants, all families in the settlement are known as 'linked families'. This close affiness transcends all formal divide based on castes, *gotras,* trade and vocations. 'The village is a unity, yet half of its adult population, the women come from outside communities with which the village is linked by complicated marriage relations.' This corporate identity finds mention in the classical texts of the land. The family-like spirit has nurtured the village since time immemorial.

The locational element in rural settlements has also contributed towards an inter-caste unity and security among its inhabitants. They stand united to face man-made or natural calamity. In such unforeseen situation, 'first-aid' is self-provided. Village-centred social and cultural occasions strengthen the feeling of village 'ness'. 'It is normally not visible, but some incident suddenly and strikingly reveals its existence. When the village is threatened with an epidemic or draught or flood or fire or when the government passes an order which the villagers regard as unjust, or on certain religious occasions or in a fight with a neighbouring village, the unity of the village reveals itself in an unmistakable manner.[4]

## Gotra

Like caste and ritual, the origin of *gotra* is also densely covered by cobwebs of a plethora of theories enumerated in the scriptures beginning with the Vedas.

'The sociological sense of the term *gotra* has been derived from the Vedic usage ('cow-stall') as follows. In ancient times the Indian family, even when–in consequence of its numerical increase–is property had been greatly subdivided, would still continue to use and occupy jointly the land reserved for grazing cattle; and we may therefore conclude, it is said, that the Brahmanical *gotra* was in its origin simply a community of this kind, i.e. a family whose members enjoyed joint rights in a particular pasturage. But this hypothesis does not in any degree account for the most characteristic features of the *gotra*, which, in fact, can be explained only by comparison with the *gots* of the aboriginal tribes of India.'[5] The Vedic genesis of *gotras* had its nucleus around clusters of families. This concept has been further supported by ancient grammarian, Amar Sinha, a classical Sanskrit scholar and lexicographer and one of the nine gems in the court of king Vikramaditya of Ujjayini whose era Samvat begins in 56 B.C. In his *Amarakosa* he 'explain *gotra* as synonymous with *santati* ('lineage'), *janana* ('race'), *kula* ('family'), *abhijana* ('descent'), *anvaya* ('progeny'), *vamsa* ('race'), *anvavaya* ('lineage'), *asantana* ('family, offspring'), *(Amarakosa,* 2.7.1). The meaning *akhya* ('name') has apparently been developed from that of 'family', family name.'[6]

It has been found that like the Brahmanical *gotras,* the aboriginal tribes and the Dravidians, south of the Narmada have had their own share of *gotras*. The Dravidian *gotras* are very much like the Brahmanical *gotra.* The Brahmanical hypothesis about the origin of *gotra* is not in juxtaposition with the *gotras* of aboriginal tribes. The *gotras* of the aboriginals are intimately related to totemism (named after plants, trees and animals). It appears something akin to caste also determined the social status of *gotras.* The *dwijs* take their *gotras* name after the *rishis* to whose linkage they belonged to; while the aboriginals assign their *gotra* names to natural objects. 'These groups are distinguished from the *gotras* of the higher castes, however, by their undisguised adherence to totemism. Each of the exogamous clans bears the name of an animal, tree, plant, or some other natural or artificial object, and the member of the clan are not allowed to eat, to cultivate, to burn, to carry, or in any other way to make use of that particular object. Thus, to give a few specially characteristic examples, all the Bhils venerate totems, and avoid injuring or using them, and, when they pass their totem, they make a ceremonious bow, while the women veil their face.'[7]

Both kinds of *gotras* recognize that children belong to fathers' *gotra*, not of the mothers' and intra-*gotra* marriage is prohibited.

*Gotra* is not particular to Hindus. It also finds reference in the Pali canons of the Buddhists and the Jaina scriptures. Indian and

European oriental scholars have concluded that *gotras* have divine origin and have been a part and parcel of Indic society since ages. Legend has it that Lord Brahma blessed the *gotras* in the form of seven *rishis* Bhrigu, Angiras, Marichi, Atri, Pulaha, Pulastya and Vasistha. In the *Satapatha Brahmanas,* the modified list of seven *rishis* included Gautama, Bharadvaja, Vishvamitra, Vasistha, Kasyapa, Atri and Agastya. These *rishis* are called *gotrakarnis*– the founder of numerous *gotra* families. The number of families remained in a state of flux. According to *Asvalayana Sruta Sutra,* the total number of families was forty-nine. But Hindu society has a baffling number of *gotras.* The Jats who are hypersensitive about *gotras,* have more than 300-some *gotras.* Similary, the Rajputs, Brahmins and others have long lists of *gotras.* The branching and sub-branching of *gotra* is attributed to the acquired factor. Some families named their *gotra* after the name of their *purohits,* astronomical figures, minor deities and geographical landmarks. The incursions by the Yavanas and later by the Muslims also made assaults on Hindus society and its socio-religious structures. It devalued and defiled some of its life sustaining streams. The society had to bear, their presence without sacrificing its pristine socio-cultural institutions. For our purpose more names were acquired and added to the family of *gotras.* Some *gotra* names got desanskritised. The foreign impact on assuming *neogotra* names remained confined to the north of the Narmada.

The observance of *gotra* related rites is mandatory through all four *asramas*-the *brahmcharya, grihastha, Vanaprastha* and *sanyasa* and the 16 *samaskaras*. It formally begins with the *Namakarana Samaskara* and continue through *Shradha Samaskara.*

'In the *ekoddistasradhda,* the funeral rite performed on behalf of a single individual, according to the *Sraddhavidhi*, a foodball *(pinda)* was offered to the departed, and his personal and *gotra* names were uttered along with the words, 'This food for thee!' According to the *Vishnu-Purana,* the food offered by the proper persons to forefathers, with utterance of their names and *gotra,* became a meal for the *manes.* [L-*gotra*] Similarly, in the *Udakakarman* ('libation of water') for the deceased, a handful of water was poured out, and his personal and *gotra,* this is thy water.[8]

**Marriage**

Hindu marriage is not a social formality or a play thing. It is a sacrament as defined in the *Grahyasutras.* It is one of the four *asramas* one has to live through–*brahmcharya* (the student's life), *grihastha* (the householder's life) *vanaprastha* (the hermit's life) and *sanyasa* (the ascetic's life). The concept of *asramas* is only provided in Vedic religion. No other religion provides for such a disciplined way of living (life cycle). American sociologist Andrew Coilver points out that 'The characteristic stages of family cycle in village India are less clearly demarcated than they generally are in urbanized, industrialized societies. In a demographic comparison of family cycle in India and in the United States, Andrew Coilver points out that the stages in America are quite distinct. The American cycle begins with two relatively short phases, one from marriage to first birth and the second comprising the child-bearing period. Then follows a longer period, mainly of child-rearing and a shorter one during which the children marry and leave the parental home. Next is a long period in which the parents live alone, often followed by several years of widowhood.'[9]

What is true of American married life cycle is also true of other western marriage systems. We find no meeting points between the Hindu and western marriage ways. The Hindu marriage filiality is not confined between the would be husband and wife; it is an inalienable particle of patriarchal family. It overflows and nurtures all the four *asrama's* and even after death as provided in the *Shradhavidhi.*

The aims of Hindu marriage are said to be *dharma, praja* (progeny) and *rati* (pleasure). Though sex is one of the functions of marriage, it is assigned third place, indicating thereby that it is the least desirable aim of marriage. *Praja* (procreations) implied flowering of the family tree, it grows further. The offsprings (both male and female) carry forward the family lineage and perform essential rites and rituals towards their ancestors in this and the other world. Since a girl is married away from one family to another her pre-marriage *samskaras* are per performed in her parents' family and post marriage *samskaras* in her in-laws' family. *Dharma* is a very comprehensive and all pervasive term. For our purpose it amounts that a new family should abide by the tenets prescribed in the *dharmasastras*.

In the *smriti* literature eight forms of marriages are recognised and prescribed. These are: *brahma, daivya, arsa, prajapatya, gandharva, raksasa, paisacha* and *asura*. The first four forms were recognised to be *dharmya*, i.e. according to *dharma* and the remaining four *non-dharmya*. In the case of Brahmans, Manu recognizes the first four forms of marriages. He condemns the last four forms as improper. The *smrities* do not recognize a form of marriage which plays a great part in the epic-the *svayamvara* or self-choice, a ceremony at which a princess chooses for herself, a suitor at a great assembly held for the purpose.

The *gandharva* form of marriagc transgresses all marriage norms laid down in the *Dharmasastras* and it falls in the category of *adharmya* mode of marriage. Manu, the Hindu law giver condemns it as it is altogether improper.

'The *gandharva* rite, which some authorities recognize as applicable to all classes, and which the *Kamasutra* eulogizes as the best form of all, is described as a mutual union by desire, the classical example of which is that of king Dusyanta and Sakuntala. The *Kamasutra* recommends that its performance should be accompanied by the usual offerings in the fire and the circumambulation of the fire by the wedded pair, on the ground that the observance of these formalities would compel the parents of the bride to recognize the validity of the marriage.'[10]

The attitude of the Brahmanic writers towards this mode of marriage was not very favourable, and even Kalidasa has shown his disapproval by referring to Sakuntala's marriage with Dusyanta in a satirical tone, when through the curse of Durvasa she found herself in trouble.

Regarding *dharmya* and *adharmya* mode of marriage Kautilya summed up discussion of the different modes of marriages by saying that 'any kind of marriage is approvable provided pleases all concerned' (marriage by mutual consent and parental arrangement).

The *Grahyasutras* and *Dharmasutras* prescribed a number of bars and qualities to be looked into before a marriage is sanctified. The five generation bar is important of them all. Prior to tieing of nuptial knot the bride and the bridegroom families, with the assistance of family *purohits* have to examine the compatibility status of the families and of the prospective couple. Compatibility warrants that the two families do not violate the *sapinda* exogamy, *gotra* exogamy and exogamy by locality. According to *Sankhyayana Grihya Sutra*, i. 6.4, the deputy suitors when proposing marriage to a girl announced the *gotra* names of bridegroom and bride-obviously in order to show that there was no legal obstacle to the proposed union. The exogamy bar in respect of *sapinda* extends upto three to five circles on the parents side and *gotra* exogamy extends to *sagotra*. Some *gotras* are known by more than one name; these are sub-branches of the principal *gotra* and legally have *sagotra* status. For example 'the Deswal, Maan, Dalal and Siwal *gentes* [L. *gotra*] of the Jats are of common descent, and must not inter-marry.' Such *gotras* are also known as *sahodar gotras*.

Hindu marriage is a sacrament and not a way-side dating arrangement. The approved mode of marriage is one in which the girl and the boy families unanimously consent to the matrimonial alliance. Towards its fulfillment, the scriptures provide a series of rites. The main rites are: *homa, panigrahana* and *satpadi*. 'They are necessary for marriage to be complete, because they or any of them are not properly performed, the marriage may be legally questioned.

With the ushering in of industrialization, urbanization and economic liberalization, the observance of exogamy factors either have been diluted or thrown to winds. The family's role in celebrating marriage in accordance with the classical system laid-down in *Dharmasastras* has been given a goodbye by the modernite couples. These have been replaced by quick-fix temple marriage. Such self-made marriages do not fall under the first four modes of Hindu marriage. The readers may classify them in the last four forms of marriages. 'The approved modes, on the other hand, were those in which a girl was decorated and was given over by her father to a suitable partner. The main idea in each of these approved modes was that the bride was given as a gift. In other words, it meant that the dominion which the father exercised over a female child from the day of her birth was now transferred to the person who was selected as her husband. This theory of marriage was first discussed in the *Dharmasutras* when every opportunity was sought to restrict the freedom of woman. It may consequently be interpreted to suggest that marriage being primarily a gift from the father, it was he who decided to whom the gift should be given. In this idea of marriage as a gift, therefore, there was little scope for woman's voice to prevail in the selection of her spouse. This then was the second harrier in the free choice of a marriage partner.'[11]

Irawati Karve in her *Kinship Organization in India* also states that, 'a *vadhu* is always taken from her father's house (where the marriage ceremony takes place) to her husband's house. So she is a *vadhu* as against *kanya* who is living in a house.'

**Intra-gotra Marriage**

In the domain of marriage, Hindu law givers have prescribed certain bars and restrictions which should be observed in letter and spirit. These exogamies are in consonance with the Hindu marriage *dharma* prescribed in *Grihyasutras.* The *sapinda* and *gotra* exogamies are intertwined. *Sapinda* exogamy prohibits marriage between persons related to each other within certain generations on the parents side. The generation bar is not uniform for all caste groups and sub-groups and regions. For our purpose the Narmada is taken as a benchmark i.e., the Hindus of the south of the Narmada follow a different sets of exogamic traditions and the Hindus of the north have a different sets of exogamies. Baudhayana, a *sutra* writer has dwelled upon marriage practices observed by the Dravidians and other communities in the south and the Aryans in the north. We may assign them to the caste and cultural composition of the people inhabiting these regions. His view is that 'he who follows these practices in any other country [north of the Narmada] commits a sin. He concludes that such marriage relations are peculiar cultural traits of the people of that region.

'The prohibition of marriage within one's own *gotra* had manifestly become the rule by the time of the *Dharmasutras*: thus, in the code of Manu we find that a maiden who is not related by blood on her mother's side, and does not belong to the same *gotra* on her father's, is recommended to the twice-born as eligible for marriage and the community of the household ceremonies; Apastamba forbids a father to give his daughter to a man of the same *gotra* as himself, while Gautama and Vasistha permit marriage only between those who have not the same *pravara.*'[13]

The *Smrti* writers such as Yajnavalkya, Narada, Vasistha, Gautama and Paithinasi prescribe exogamous restrictions ranging from three to five generations. Gautama prescribes that 'one marrying a *sapinda* relation of the father and the mother becomes an outcaste.' Gautama is thus ahead of his contemporaries both in widening the scope of exogamy and in penalizing its breach.

The *Smrti* writers prescribed penance of a very serious nature for any breach of the rule of *gotra* exogamy. The commentators were even more strict: they not merely condemned *sagotra* marriage but degraded the status of woman in such a marriage and at times even of the children born of such a marriage. If a twice-born marries a girl of the same *gotra* or reciting the same *pravara,* he shall renounce her and perform the lunar penance. If the breach is intentional the husband becomes an outcaste and so does his son. The woman in such a marriage is *candali* [chandali]. If one unintentionally cohabits with a *candali* he becomes an outcaste and he has to observe a penance for 12 years. If he intentionally lives in the company of a *candali* for a long time he actually turns himself into a *candala.* If he cohabits with her even for a single night he must observe three years' penance. Thus the commentators of the tenth to the twelfth century A.D. recommended the social boycott of partners in marriage and of their issues too, and prescribed severe penance for them before being taken back into their own social group. And the writers of the digests followed in their footsteps.[14]

The concept of *sapinda* and *gotra* exogamy was not the figment of imagination of some person or persons. A good thought must have been given in prescribing some restrictions or bars in establishing marital relations within a caste group. The *rishis* and *sutradhars* might have evolved these exogamies on the basis of divinely virtues. They also might have relied upon research methodology of observation which even today is an important research method for social sciences; nature, plants and animal might have served as their research tools in arriving at some valid conclusions. The *Grahyasutras* and the *Dharmasutra,* codified their finding in prescribing that 'marriage should not take place between a man and a woman of the same *gotra.*'

Modern genetics is an eighteenth century scientific development. Gregor Mendel (1822-84) set the ball rolling in the area of genetical researches. Plant sciences have been its great beneficiaries.

Human genetics in its rudimentary form was known to the Hindus as early as 56 B.C. Amar Sinha, a Sanskrit scholar and a lexicographer and one of the *navaratnas* in the court of king Vikramaditya, in his classical dictionary *Amarakosa* has defined human genetical terms such as *santati* ('lineage'), *janana* ('race'), *kula* ('family') *abhijana* ('descent'). *anvaya* ('progeny'), *vamsa* ('race'), *anvavaya* ('lineage'), *asantana* ('family, offspring') and many such others terms. How far our *rishis* and *sutradhars* had been benefited by the Hindu genetical knowledge in the process of codifying them in the *Grahyasutras* is yet a virgin research areas.

**Intra-Village Marriage**

A village is generally peopled by several castes and communities. A caste may have more than one *gotra* families in the same village. Overall, it is taken as a composite social unit and irrespective of castes and *gotras* there runs a thread of familial relationship (brotherhood, *bhaichara*) among its inhabitants. All boys and girls are brothers and sisters to each other. They intermingle and share moments of joyous and sad happenings. The kinship mode of personal locution is a distinctive feature of village culture.

'In the village one may use kinship terms towards anyone with whom one has personal contact, regardless of caste or economic status. Consideration is taken only of the person's age, and young children are especially taught this habit. Brahman or Kayastha boys and girls will call the Muchi or Bagdi maidservant "father's sister" *[Buwa]*. The latter in turn may call the children in terms of *tui* (language used for junior members by elders of the house). Not only children but adults also may call people of lower castes by kin terms.'[15]

Agri-based working relationship provides a cementing force among its inhabitants. A family-akin social environment flows through its lanes and by–lanes. 'Since all persons born into the village are considered to be connected by a fiction of common descent, and since most persons address each other–even across caste lines–by kinship term appropriate to their generation in the scheme of common descent, a marriage between a boy and of girl of Kishan Garhi [a village near Agra] would constitute incest'.[16] The savillage marriage injunction also overflows to other agnate villages in the vicinity. The cluster of such villages is called *gawand* in local parlance. Like the village panchayat we have *gawand* panchayat which may be activated to resolve unforseen issues. Such agnate village area is named after the number of villages, such as *dassi* (a group of ten agnate villages), *bissi* (a group of twenty agnate villages), *pachchisi* (a group of twenty-five agnate villages) and so on. McKim Marriott in his essay *Social Structure and Change in a U.P. Village* finds that inter-village marriage distance extends to twelve miles [beyond agnate villages]. The inter-villages marriage distance normally extends upto 60-80 kms.

Exogamy by locality is observed in a large part of northern India. This means that the people belonging to one caste living in a village behave as if they were descendants of one common ancestor. Social scientists have given more cogent reasons against savillage marriage:

1. Such marriages conflict with the proper relationship between spouse and between affinally related families. [children who played together and called each-other brother and sister become husband and wife one fine morning are more likely to have tension-ridden marital life. 2. Morton Klass is his account of marriage in a 'West Bengal Village' states that: 'For a number of reasons, which he assesses quite correctly, such conflicts are more likely between

families of the same village and less likely between families of different village.'[17] 3. T N Madan in his study of a Kashmir village says that savillage marriages: 'Not only is the assimilation of a bride to her husband's family impeded if her natal family is in the same village but also the proper superiority of her conjugal over her natal family is awkwardly disarranged if the two are fellow villagers.[18]

Village spatiality angle has been further sharpened by Iravati Karve in her *Kinship Organisation of the Northern Zone*, by classifying the villages as 'daughter-receiving villages' and 'daughter-giving villages'. This is like one way traffic. This practice is respected by villagers at their end. The distance between the villages may vary with every new marriage. It should be noted the exogamy is not confined to various *gotra* families in a village but it applies to all *jatis* in a village. David G Mandelbaum adds that: 'There, if any family of Village A has taken a bride from Village B, a girl of Village A of any *jati,* must never be given in marriage to Village B.' As between any two villages, all in one must be the marital superiors to their respective *jati* fellows in the other (Karve 1965, p. 125).[19]

Regarding spatial exogamy, the Rajputs, who are spread over the entire northern India, established their marital relation in far off places. 'In the Gangetic plain it is, therefore customary for eastern brides to seek western grooms. This rule of marriage is given as a saying, 'the girl from the east, the boy from the west.' (*Purab Ki Beti, Pacchim Ka Beta*).

There are three other familial factors which prohibit savillage marriage. First, that all families irrespective of *gotras* and castes are linked together by day-to-day mundane matters and they automatically acquire linked family status. They behave like unifamily members overriding all sorts of barriers even of caste and religion. The nasty idea of savillage marriage is a taboo to them. Second, a village observes kin-based lineal calling system, such as *dada-dadi, maa-bapu, tau-tai, chacha-chachi, devar-bhabhi and bhai-behan.* In case, two sisters from village B are married in a family of village A, their offsprings will not address them as *mausi* but by kinship terms *tai* or *chachi. Mausi* is an acquired personal calling terms and it is used along with *mausi-mausa,* by the brother or nephew of the girls' *saas* and *sasur* when they visit her in-laws village. Conversely, the calling terms *nana-nani, mama-mami* are used by the off–springs when they visit their mother's village. Both modes of personal calling terms–kin–based and acquired ones cannot go together in a village as its inhabitants are considered descendants of one common ancester.

Savillage marriage will open Pandora's box of social evils, so far unconceived by a sane mind. A village girl turning into the village *vadhu* militates against the canons of *Grihyasutras.* Among the eight forms of Hindu marriage even the lowest three forms–*raksasa, paisacha* and *asura* preclude savillage marriage. It would dismentle the established social structure of the village and eliminate the concept of kinship which has been a hallmark of Indian rural societies.

## References


1. S.C. Dubey : 'Introduction', *Indian Village,* London, Kegan Paul (1955), p. I.
2. David G. Mandelbaum : *Society in India* [2 volumes in one], Bombay: Popular (l972), p. 98.
3. William Henricks Wiser : *The Hindu Jajmani System,* Lucknow: Lucknow Publishing House (1936).
4. M.N. Srinivas : 'Introduction'. *India's Villages,* Bombay : Asia (1955), p. 8.
5. Subodh Kapoor (ed.) : *The Hindus : Encyclopaedia of Hinduism, 5* vols., New Delhi : Cosmo (2000), p. 771.
6. *Ibid.*, p. 772.
7. *Ibid.*, p. 771.
8. *Ibid.*, p. 768.
9. David G. Mandelbaum : *Society in India,* Bombay : Popular (1972), p. 95.
10. Subodh Kapoor (ed.) : *Op. cit.*, New Delhi, Cosmo (2000), p. 1181.
11. K.M. Kapadia : *Marriage and Family in India,* London : OUP, (1966), p. 136.

12. Irawati Karve : *Kinship Organization in India*, Ed. 2, Delhi, Munshiram Manoharlal (1990).
13. Subodh Kapoor : *Op. cit.*, p. 768.
14. K. M. Kapadia : *Op. cit.*, p. 128.
15. M.N. Srinivas : *Op. cit.*, pp. 194-95.
16. *Ibid.*, p. 111.
17. Morton Klass : Marriage Rule in Bengal, *American Anthropologist*, 68 (1966), pp. 951-70.
18. T. N. Madan : *Family and Kinship : A Study of Pandits of Rural Kashmir*, NY : Asia, (1965), pp. 111-12.
19. David G. Mandelbaum : *Society in India,* Bombay : Popular (1972), p. 103.

# 4

# Social and Political Dimensions of the Jat Insurgency[1]

*Niti Singh*

During the late seventeenth and eighteenth century large part of India witnessed agrarian revolts led by the *zamindars* or by some sect leaders. Prominent among these revolts were Jat, Maratha, Satnami and Sikh uprising. The Jat and Maratha revolts were led by *zamindars* but the Satnami and Sikh revolts were led by their sect leaders. In case of Jat and Maratha revolts caste became a uniting factor whereas in case of the Satnami and Sikh revolts sect appeal was a rallying point.[2] These revolts have been differently understood by scholars. William Irvine and Jadunath Sarkar considered these revolts to be 'Hindu reaction' to orthodox religious policies of Aurangzeb.[3] Subsequently, this thesis was also upheld by K.R.Qanungo.[4] However, in his book published in 1963, Irfan Habib challenges the view of Irvine, Sarkar and Qanungo.[5] He studied these revolts afresh and came to the conclusion that administrative and economic factors were behind the occurrence of these uprisings. He characterized these revolts as agrarian revolts resulting from increasing exploitation and pauperization of peasantry. Thus, Habib highlighted the economic dimension of these revolts. According to him, the *zamindar* leadership converted these revolts caused by economic factors into political revolts. Recently, some historians labeled as 'revisionists' have questioned Habib's thesis on these revolts. They are of the view that these revolts were not result of pauperization of peasantry.[6] Though these historians have eschewed from propounding an alternative thesis about these revolts, they have succeeded in questioning the theory of Irfan Habib whose argument is centered on the economic factors.

Somehow both the Aligarh and 'revisionist historians' have failed to pay attention to the social and political thrust of Jat insurgency. I have come across, some information available in Rajasthan States Archives at Bikaner in the form of *arsatthas* (revenue records) and *arzdashts* (supplications) which throws considerable light on the social and political dimensions of Jat insurgency. The Jat *zamindars* who emerged as powerful rural gentry could not achieve political and social ambitions due to the existing powerful Mughal-Rajput political alliance which left no avenue for the Jats to join 'high politics'. In this paper I am arguing, that it is the social and political ambitions of the Jats which collided with the Mughal Empire, forcing the Jats to revolt against the Mughals and their allies. Clearly, the 'religious' and economic factors were not the sole factors behind the Jat uprising. My study shows that there were bold social and political undertones to these rebellions.

## I

In the *Ain-i-Akbari,* compiled in 1595, Jats have been clearly recorded as *zamindars* in the *subas* of Multan, Lahore, Agra and Delhi. The *Ain-i-Akbari* also mentions Jat *zamindars* as owners of considerable land and military power.[8] The tables I and II on proceeding page show the armed power of the Jats.

During the 17th century we can see that the landscape of the Jat Zamindari undergoes a massive transformation and expansion. At the beginning of the seventeenth century, for instance six out of 32 parganas in *sarkar* Agra, two out of 16 in Narnaul and five out of 7 in Saher have entered Jats as *zamindars*.[11] But by late seventeenth century Jats emerged and replaced prominent Rajput *zamindars.* Table III shows this change.

Table I. Armed Power of Jats in *Sarkar* Agra[9]

| Pargana | Cavalry | Infantry | Elephants | Castes |
|---|---|---|---|---|
| Agra with sub urban district | 3000 | 15000 | … | Gaur, Jat, Lodh. etc. |
| Bianah with sub urban district has a stone fort | 50 | 100 | … | Ahir, Jat |
| Chausath | 50 | 1000 | … | Rajput, Brahman, Jat, Ahir |
| Khanwah | 30 | 4000 | … | Rajput, Jat |
| Kotumber | 50 | 300 | … | Rajput, Jat |
| Hindaun | 100 | 1000 | … | Rajput, Brahman, Jat |

Table II. Armed Power of Jats in *Sarkar* Sahar[10]

| Pargana | Cavalry | Infantry | Elephants | Castes |
|---|---|---|---|---|
| Bandhauli | 10 | 300 | … | Jats etc. |
| Sahar has a fort | 200 | 7000 | … | Bachhal, Gujar, Jat, Kuchhwaha |
| Kamah | 10 | 300 | … | Meo, Jat, Ahir |
| Koh Mujahid | 4 | 200 | … | Meo, Jat |
| Hodal | 10 | 200 | … | Jats etc. |

Table III. Shows Emergence of Jats as Zamindars[12]

| Parganas | Sarkar | Caste of Zamindars in Ain i Akbari | Caste of *Zamindars* under the reign of Aurangzeb |
|---|---|---|---|
| Ao | Agra | Rajput | Jat |
| Sonkhar-Sanokhari | Agra | Rajput | Jat |
| Bhusawar | Agra | Rajput | Jat |
| Kuthumbhar | Agra | Rajput, Jat | Jat |
| Khori | Alwar | Khanzada of Mewat | Kuchhwaha, Jat |

The Kuchhwaha Rajas of Amber state were the first to accept Mughal sovereignty in Rajasthan. Through this alliance the Mughals were able to extend their control over the region through the house of Amber. On the other hand, it made the Kuchhwahas key players in the political management of the region. This Mughal-Rajput alliance discouraged upward social and political mobility of the non-Rajput *zamindars* of the region. It appears that the Kuchhwahas very early realized the fact that the rise of any other group might compromise their relations with the Mughal authority. Their alliance with the Mughals helped them to continue their dominance in the area, preserve their territories from any invasion and share the privileges received by them in the form of honors' titles and *jagirs*. Apart from it, the Kuchhwahas left no opportunity to expand their share in land. This brought the Kuchhwahas and other *zamindars* specially the Jats in direct conflict with each other. There are several ways through which the Kuchhwahas tried to expand their rights over land. The Kuchhwaha rulers began to claim *bhom* rights on large number of parganas outside their hereditary *watan*. They further imposed a *bhom* tax ranging between 2 and 3 per cent of the land revenue.[13] Many soldiers (particularly the Narukas) of the Amber ruler turned themselves as bhomias. These Narukas converted the villages of their *chakari* (sub assignment) into their *bhom*. Such instances brought the *chakar* turned bhomias in direct conflict with the traditional *zamindars*. And lastly the Kuchhwahas patronized the Vaishnavite sect in the form of huge land grants. These land grants were seen by the Jat rebels as a disguised attempt to fulfill the territorial ambitions of Kuchhwaha rulers. Hence, the *zamindars* of various castes, among which Jats were in large numbers, established a united front against the imperial *jagirdars* for the preservation and expansion of their *zamindari* rights. Their ambitions clashed with the interests of the Amber rulers who in turn were eager to take advantage of the disturbed conditions to expand their *watan* (hereditary domain). Therefore, the *zamindars* clashed with the Mughals and Amber rulers at the same time.

The Jat revolts would not have been possible without the help given by the peasantry to the rebels. It is interesting to note that the Jats were supported by other low caste elements such as Gujars, Ahirs, and Meos. Surprisingly, they also found a strong support from the Naruka Kuchhwahas who were considered by other Kuchhwaha clans as undesirable elements. While reading the documents, it appears that during the rebelling years the Jats and the *zamindars* had a symbiotic relationship with each other. On one hand without the support of the Jats, the revolt of other *zamindars* would have been suppressed easily whereas on the other hand the absence of solidarity expressed by the rebel *zamindars* of other caste it would have been difficult for the Jats to sustain the rebellion for such a long time.

The Jat rebellion spread across the *suba* Agra and Delhi of the Mughal Empire. For instance the Jats led these revolts on both sides of river Jamuna between Delhi and Agra. The rebellion in the Braj region was a powerful assertion by those groups which did not find further avenues of fulfilling their political ambitions. Here the rebels established a strong coalition of *zamindars* against the Amber state and Mughals. The Narukas and the Jats together revolted in many parganas of Mewat region.

The information recorded in the contemporary revenue records written by various officials also proves that the Jats had acquired considerable fiscal power. For instance in 1694, the total assessed amount of revenue in pargana Kol (Aligarh) was Rs. 4,09,917 of which Rs. 2,41,610 have been shown as arrears pending with various Jat *zamindars*.[14] Similarly in pargana Udai Rs. 40,514 have been shown pending with the Jat *zamindars*. Interestingly, in Tappa Khair of pargana Kol (Aligarh) Amar Singh Jat has been shown a *zamindar* of 250 villages.[16] Clearly, he was a man of considerable economic substance and political clout. The information pertaining to pargana Khori which had 336 villages also indicates the fiscal clout of the Jat rebels. In this pargana, the rebels had collected Rs. 1,55,380 out of which Churaman Jat got Rs. 90,000.[17] This information also helps us to understand why Churaman Jat was taking so much interest in pargana Khori. A similar trend can be noticed in pargana Nagar from where the Jats and the Naruka rebels got Rs. 1,80,000.[18] This pargana was *jagir* of Nawab Mukhtiar Khan. In some parganas of Mewat, Naruka, rebels had collected Rs. 4 lakhs.[19] Apart from availability of wealth with rebels, they also possessed huge stocks of grains to sustain themselves during the rebellion. For instance, from pargana Punkhar the Jats had collected 20,000 *mans* of grains.[20]

The Jats also held strongholds–*garhis*. For instace Raja Ram Jat held a fort at Sonkh. Bukhna Jat held a fort at Kasot, and Sukha Jat held a fort at Chhaiya. These *garhis* were strong symbol of Jat power and status. During the revolting years, these *garhis* acted as centres of planning the strategies of attack. Many of the Jat strongholds were strategically located in forests, which proved to the benefit of the Jat rebels. For instance Churaman constructed a fort at Thoon which he made into the headquarters of the rebellion. The geographical location of Thoon helped the Jats in organizing their rebellion. The impenetrable swampy forests at the outskirts of Thoon became an important reason for Churaman's success during the rebellious years. The accumulated wealth, *garhis* and military power of the Jats is indicative of their prosperity and not poverty as has been suggested by Habib and others. This power and prosperity is the outcome of a centuries old struggle of the Jats.

## II

If we look at the history of the Jats during the preceding ten centuries, it appears that the Jats were struggling to acquire better social and economic status in medieval society.[21] They have been described in the *Chachnama* as lower caste people with lots of pejorative adjectives used against them.[22] By the twelfth and the thirteenth centuries, the Jats had been recorded as migrating cultivating community still struggling for the betterment of their status. Richard Eaton highlighted that many Jat clans came to be associated with the shrine of Baba Farid in Pak Pattan from the late fourteen century onwards. The simple religious of *adab* of the shrine not only integrated the Jats with the ritual and religious practices of the shrine, but also provided a 'universal cultural system'. Thus, a close look at their history during the preceding ten centuries and the available revenue records of the sixteenth and seventeenth century would suggest that the Jats were still in the process of upward social mobility.

Inspite of the Jats being recorded as *zamindars* they were not given high respect in society and entry in contemporary politics. Hence, one of the major reasons for the Jats to rebel was their social status. In a traditional society, social mobility could take place when (a) the individual families or group could change their traditional occupation, (b) acquire wealth and control over land, (c) acquire social and political power. It appears that the Jats had acquired the first two conditions and were struggling to acquire the third. Through these revolts the Jats were not only challenging the authority of the Mughals and Kuchhwahas in the region but also subtly negotiating possibilities of moving upward in the social hierarchy.

Since Brahmanism and Vaishnavism were patronized by the Mughals and Kuchhwahas, there appeared a division between the elite culture and popular culture. The Jats believed in the veneration of the *lok devis* and worshipped the *prakriti* (nature). This division resulted in the low status being ascribed to the Jats in the Brahmanical order. Therefore, an urge for upgraded social status emerged as another reason for the Jats to rebel against the state which had foreclosed all political avenues for the Jats.

Being owners of considerable land, military and fiscal strength, and forts Jats' rebellion showed signs of being a product of more than mere religious and economic discontentment. The reasons for the rebellion along with other reasons were dormant for long. They needed upward social mobility and political representation. Due to the strong Mughal-Rajput alliance, the Jats could not participate in the high politics of the times. Mughals saw Rajputs as ruling elite and worthy of being incorporated in their administration. On the other hand, Rajputs took the benefit of the situation as bringing any other claimant in to power would compromise on the fiscal and administrative benefits given by the Mughals. The Jats were broadly described by the Rajputs as an intermediate rebelling section of the society as they formed the dominant category of peasants who rebelled against the state.

As there was no dearth of wealth with the rebels they could easily manage to mobilize huge military power to fulfill their political ambitions. In the light of this information, it is difficult for us to accept the suggestion made by Irfan Habib and R.P. Rana that these revolts were predicated upon increasing poverty of the peasantry.[23] Thus, it can safely be argued that it was substantial fiscal and military power of the Jats which was propelling them to clear the hurdles in the way of their social aspirations and political ambitions. It is interesting to note that, the Jat revolts started from a very narrow geographical base. It started from *tappa* Jataat of pargana Sahar in suba Agra.[24] Pargana Sahar had 250 villages out of which *tappa* Jataat consisted of 51 villages.[25] If we compare these numbers of villages initially under the control of the rebels with the total number of villages of the Bharatpur State in 1906, it shows considerable expansion. The total number of villages in the State of Bharatpur are given below.[26] Clearly, the Jats of Braj region succeeded to a great extent in not only enhancing their social status but also in capturing political power. Subsequently, the rise of Bharatpur had a salutary impact on the Jats of other regions of India.

Table IV. Total Villages of Bharatpur State in 1906

| S. No. | Name of Tehsil | Total number of Villages |
|---|---|---|
| 1. | Pahari | 134 |
| 2. | Dig | 129 |
| 3. | Weir | 147 |
| 4. | Biana | 168 |
| 5. | Kamah | 122 |
| 6. | Bharatpur | 145 |
| 7 | Rupbas | 148 |
| 8. | Kumber | 115 |
| 9. | Akheirgarh | 112 |
| 10. | Nagar | 172 |

## References

1. I would like to thank my supervisor Prof. R.P.Rana for encouraging me to write this paper. I would also like to thank the staff and members of Rajasthan State Archives at Bikaner for their help.

2. Habib, Irfan : *The Agrarian Systems of Mughal India 1556-1707*, 2nd revd. Edn., Delhi, Oxford University Press, 1999, pp. 365-389.

3. Sarkar, Jadunath : *History of Aurangzeb, Vol. III* 3rd edn., Calcutta, Orient Longman, 1926, (rpt., Bombay, Orient Longman,1974), see Chapter XXXV.

4. Qanungo, K.R. : *History of the Jats,* Delhi, Sunita Publications, 1925, rpt. 1987.

5. Habib, Irfan : *The Agrarian Systems of Mughal India 1556-1707,* 1st edn. Asia Publishing House, 1963, see chapter 2 and 3.

6. Alam, Muzaffar : *The Crisis of Empire in the Mughal North India: Awadh and the Punjab, 1707-1748*, Delhi, Oxford University Press, 1986. See the Introduction.

7. Eaton. M. Richard : The Political and Religious Authority of the Shrine of Baba Farid, in Barbara Daly Metcalf (ed.) *Moral Conduct and Authority: The Place of Adab in South Asian Islam,* University of California Press, 1984, p. 342.

8. Fazl, Abul : *Ain-i-Akbari,* ed. H. Blockmann, Calcutta; Asiatic

Society of Bengal, 1867-77 (first volume translated by H. Blockmann and revised by D.C. Phillot, second and third volumes translated by H.S Jarret and revised by Sir Jadunath Sarkar, Calcutta: Asiatic Society of Bengal, 2nd edition,1927-49) (rpt., New Delhi, Low Price Publications, 1994). See description of Suba Agra.

9. *Ibid.*, p. 192.
10. *Ibid.*, p. 206
11. *Ain-i-Akbari*, Low Price Publications, Vols. II-III, pp. 193-94, 197 and 205-06.
12. Cf., R.P Rana, *Rulers to Rebels*, p. 113.
13. Arsatthas, Pargana Banawar vs. 1748/1691; Maujpur vs 1771/1714; Dausa vs 1722/1665; Malarna vs 1722/1665; Tonk vs 1765/1708; Fagi vs 1754/1697; Chatsu vs 1721/ 1664; Hindaun vs 1764/1712 and Jalalpur vs 1723/1666.
14. Arzdashts, dt. Chait Sudi 7, VS 1751/1694 and Asadh Vadi 2, VS 1752/1695.
15. Arzdasht, dt. Asadh Sudi 13, 1740/1683.
16. Sharma, U.N., *A New History of the Jats*, Jaipur, Mangal Prakashan, 1977, p. 176.
17. *Arsattha*, Pargana Khori VS 1770/1713 (rabi).
18. Arzdasht, dt. Asadh Sudi 14, VS 1760/1703. The parganas were Sonkhar (under Jats, Narukas, Kalyanots and Chauhans), Kuthumbar (under Jats), Banawar, Mandawar, and Toda Thek (under Narukas).
19. Arzdasht, dt. Asadh Vadi 5, VS 1742/1685.
20. Arzdasht, dt. Kati Vadi 13, VS 1741/ 1684.
21. Rana, R.P. : *Rebels to Rulers, The Rise of Jat Power in Medieval India c1665-1735,* Manohar Publication, New Delhi, 2006, see chapter Agrarian Revolts.
22. *The Chachnama: An Ancient History of Sindh,* by Mirza Kalichbeg Fredenbegi, Delhi, Idarah –i-Adabiyat-i-Delhi, 1900 (rep.1979), p. 37.
23. Irfan Habib : *The Agrarian Systems of Mughal India 1556-1707*, see chapter The Agrarian Crisis of the Mughal Empire; Rana, R.P. *Rebels to Rulers, The Rise of Jat Power in Medieval India c1665-1735*, see chapter Agrarian Revolts.
24. Saher ceased to be a *sarkar* at some stage and was merged into a

new *sarkar* called Islamabad (Mathura). See, Irfan Habib, *The Atlas of the Mughal Empire,* Delhi, Oxford University Press, 1982, p. 19.

25. Arsattha, dt VS 1746/1686. Paragana Saher consisted of 250 villages out of which in *tappa* Jataat the first Jat revolt happened. Other *tappas* were, *tappa* Hathiya which consisted of 14 villages, *tappa* Taroli consisted of 54 villages, *tappa* Haveli consisted of 33 villages, *tappa* Jasawal consisted of 22 villages, *tappa* Kahaha consisted of 19 villages, *tappa* Bahuki consisted of 7 villages, *tappa* Mehta consisted of 12 villages, *tappa* Kharoh consisted of 23 villages, and *tappa* Sergath consisted of 22 villages.

26. State Council Bharatpur, File no. (XI-3-1906).

## 5

# The Jat Resistance against Kachhwaha Pacification Campaigns in Braj Region* (1688-1694)

***Mamta Tyagi***

The rise of the Jat power is an important event in the history of medieval India. The first Jat revolt occurred under the leadership of Gokula Jat in Talpat.[1] Soon it was suppressed by the Mughal armies albeit resulting in heavy mortality on both sides. However, the Jats burst into revolts in 1680 and these revolts lingered on for many decades to come. This time the area of Jat uprising was quite widespread. Many parganas of *sarkars* Sahar, Agra and Alwar were affected.[2] The ebb and flow of these revolts spreading from decades to decades kept fluctuating. By 1688 the Jat revolt had acquired a threatening military dimension for the Mughals in *suba* Agra. Therefore, emperor Aurangzeb was forced to pay special attention to the Jat revolts. He directed the Amber ruler, Raja Bishan Singh Kachhwaha to organize pacification campaigns against the Jat rebels. In bargaining Raja Bishan Singh demanded lots of concessions from Mughal emperor who willingly obliged the Amber Raja.[3] Raja Bishan Singh ordered Hari Singh Khangarot, who was a powerful chieftain of Diggi *thikana* to suppress the Jat uprising. In this paper an attempt has been made to highlight

* I would like to thank my supervisor Prof. R.P. Rana for helping me to write this paper. I would also like to thank staff members of Bikaner State Archives for their support and assistance.

the nature and intensity of military confrontation between the Jats and Kachhwahas. As the Jats organized a guerilla warfare against the Kachhwaha commander, their military tactics has also been discussed in this paper. The strategy followed by Hari Singh Khangarot against scattered Jat fortresses located in the center of thick forest is also being analysed. In nutshell, the paper deals with the Jat rebellion spread on both sides of river Jamuna and Hari Singh's attempt to contain and suppress them. In this paper an attempt has also been made to highlight Hari Singh's negotiations with the Narukas (Kachhwaha) in order to detach them from the Jats and come over to the side of Kachhwaha army. My paper is based on some archival material available in the Rajasthan State Archives at Bikaner as well as relevant records of the khangarot *thikana* of Diggi. Usually scholars have empasized economic and religious causes behind these revolts and ignored everyday forms of military warfare between the contending parties. This paper will discuss the politico-military history of the fights between the Jats and Kachhwah a in the Braj region.

The Jats rose in revolt in 1668 A. D. under Gokula Jat and fought with the Mughal general Hasan Ali Khan. In this battle the Mughals lost four thousand soldiers while they killed three thousand rebel Jats. The number of Mughal soldiers killed in this battle showed that this revolt was carried by the Jats who were expert in fighting skills and not by ordinary peasants. After each defeat the Jats rose again and fought back with more numbers and with greater intensity causing more damage to the imperial army. The magnitude of damage to the imperial army shows that Jats were powerful, brave and fierce in their military operations. Later on this revolt shifted from the Doab to Sinsini which was located in pargana Ao of Sahar.[4]

After fifteen years of Gokula's death[5] Rajaram Jat[6] declared an open war against the Mughals. They built *garhis* and *naglas* (fortified block-houses) which were scattered in the *sarkars* of Agra and Mathura. For instance, the forts of Sinsini, Sogor, Sonkh, Abair, Kher, Jawar, Dig, Hathras and Musran. *Garhis* played an important role in the military and conflicts. The possession of a *garhi* or fortress was as important hallmark of the power of a *zamindar*.[7] The bhomias preferred to construct their *garhis* on hilltops (*dungar*). This gave them a geographical advantage over their enemy at the time of war. *Garhis* are also located in the capital city of the chief and therefore its capture by the enemy of rival party symbolized the end of the rule of the chief in his region. Rajaram took the advantage of the absence of Mughal Emperor from North India. This revolt was spread on either side of Jamuna and covered a wide tract between Delhi, Dholpur and Agra.

Once being expelled from their home territory the Jats did not fight openly in the fields. They were ferocious and followed the strategy of guerilla warfare. They attacked in groups, killed and plundered and disappeared in the jungles. In this way they sacked and ravaged the Mughal capital of Agra and the imperial highway between Delhi and Agra.

To suppress Rajaram Jat, Aurangzeb sent his general Khan-i-Jahan Kokaltash Jafar Jangh in May 1685, but he did not achieve success in subduing the Jats. Then Aurangzeb sent his grandson Bedar Bakht, son of Azam. Bedar Bakht and Khan-i-Jahan opened a front against Rajaram Jat. But things were still getting out of hand. Thus, Aurangzeb decided to hand over the job of suppressing the Jats to the Kachhwahas.

Raja Bishan Singh of Amber in April, 1688 A.D., received order to serve under prince Bedar Bakht against the Jats.[8] Raja Bishan Singh appointed Hari Singh Khangarot as Commander-in-chief of Kachhwaha army and joined the imperial army at Mathura and initiated a series of pacification campaigns against the Jats.[9] The first assignment the Kachhwaha army received was, a) to provide regular supplies to the army of Bedar Bakht who had laid siege to the fort of Sonkh (16 miles south-west of Mathura) after the death of Rajaram Jat,[10]; b) to guard the imperial highway from Hodal southward to pargana Farrah that shares its boundary with Agra; c) to keep an eye on the movements of the Jats of Mahaban who threatened to create diversions in favour of the besiegers of the *garhi* of Sonkh. The Jats already had a face to lace combat with Hari Singh when he was carrying a convoy to Sonkh. Hari Singh killed the rebels mercilessly and hung their bodies on the trees in order to spread terror among the rebels.

To defeat the rebels in Sonkh, prince Bedar Bakht brought all the artillery of warfare and placed them on the wall of the fort. Soon the fort of Sonkh fell. Prince Bedar Bakht marched with the main army from Sonkh to Sinsini and sent back his artillery to Mathura under Khan-i-Jahan. Meanwhile Hari Singh Khangorat commander of the Kachhwaha army attacked the Jats of pargana Mahaban on the other side of the Jamuna. The Jats faced a severe defeat with a heavy loss of soldiers. Soon after this battle Hari Singh Khangorat was called back to Mathura to safeguard the journey of Khan-i-Jahan Kokaltash to Delhi through imperial highway, as during those days the Jats kept on attacking the convoys that passed through the imperial highways. Though Hari Singh achieved success in this task but he faced innumerable battles between the Kachhwaha army and Jats as far as Kotban, midway between Kosi and Hodal.

In the beginning of the year 1689 prince Bedar Bakht marched in the direction of Rajaram's capital fortress of Sinsini. The fort of Sinsini was surrounded by a thick forest and a ring of other torts in various Jat villages Ranghar, Kasot, Soghar, Rarh, Pingora, Sonkh, Sakora, Raisis, Bhattawali, Chakora, Gaddo, and Sonkhar-Sonkhari. These *garhis* and *naglas* (fortified block houses) existed within a radius of 25 to 30 miles.[11] This time Jats made a plan to defeat the Kachhwaha army. They provided them an undisputed passage so that they could surround and attack them from all sides. They cut the shortest supply route from Mathura via Sonkh-Kumher road, while the Jats started revolts from Kama and Pahari parganas. At this point of time Hari Singh was busy in providing protection to the treasure convoy on the way of Delhi-Ajmer under the leadership of Sipahdar Khan, *faujdar* of Mathura. Hari Singh escorted this convoy from Hodal to Agra.[12] When Emperor Aurangzeb felt that the situation was deteriorating he asked the Kachhwaha ruler to suppress it as soon as possible and promised him Sinsini after its fall. This offer propelled the Kacchwahas to pay more attention to capture Sinsini and subdue the Jat revolt. The campaign to capture Sinsini fort continued for fourteen months (December 1688 to January 1690). The Kachhwaha army broke the ring of forts mentioned above to conquer Sinsini.[13]

After the fall of Sinsini Kachhwahas focused their attention towards the other forts in Braj region. This time they have to deal with the impenetrable forests that provided safe cover to the Jat rebels. The existence of thick forest frustrated the Mughal generals engaged in counter-insurgency campaigns.[14]

The intervening countryside between Govardhan and Sinsini was held in strength by the rebels. It was very difficult for a convoy to pass through this place to Sinsini because the rebels usually came out from their secret places, attacked the convoy and disappeared in the thick forests. In order to defeat the Jat rebels of Sinsini it became important for Kachhwahas to transfer the convoys of treasure and gun-powder safely. This job was personally done either by Hari Singh or by the Amber Raja himself. For instance, on 29th June, 1689, the first convoy of corn and horses and a royal tent for the Prince was transported under the supervision of Hari Singh. When Hari Singh reached the western skirts of Govardhan[15] (12 miles west of Mathura), bands (*dhar*) of rebels attacked them in the jungle between the hills. Hari Singh killed the brother of Bukna Jat, *zamindar* of Kasot along with thirty men and wounded others. However, several of his own men were also killed and wounded. In this way, he succeeded in the safe transportation of convoy and thwarted the Jats in their attempts. After this, in September 1689, Hari Singh along with Bakhtawar Bhadauriya escorted a large convoy from Aring (45 miles west of Mathura) via Govardhan. This time also the Jat rebels were hiding in the jungles near Gantholi (3 miles west of Govardhan). They attacked Hari Singh but got defeated.[16] Hari Singh killed twenty of their men and wounded many more with few casualties on his side. It was a stiff job to disperse the Jats as they were brilliant in their fighting skills and it was equally difficult to identify them from the common peasantry because they were getting full support from the local peasantry and these rebels mixed up with them in the village. They used to hide in thick forest and always attacked suddenly.

Prince Bedar Bakht gifted a special *Khilat* (robe of honour) and a horse and an elephant to Hari Singh to honour his bravery. Eventually, the situation became more intense for the Kachhwahas.

They entered into the heart of the Jat country to besiege Sinsini but now practically they were being besieged by the Jats from all the sides. Even after the beginning of the war between the two, the villages within six or seven miles from Sinsini were being held strongly by the Jat rebels. The Kachhwaha army was not getting any success in subduing them. In fact, the Mughal officers would not venture beyond the shelter of the camp, and the Rajputs in the siege camp lacked initiative and leadership. Thus, the whole burden of dislodging the Jats from their fortified villages fell on the shoulders of Hari Singh Khangarot. His effective leadership, warfare skills and strategies led to the destruction of Sabora (Sabora, 6 miles s.w. of Sinsini) and other *mauzas*, 'which nobody had attacked before.'[17] Then he planned a surprise attack on the *garhi* of Kasot (8 miles east of Sinsini), which served as a connecting link between Sinsini and the forts of Sogor, Abair and Pingora, which were surrounded by thick forest and it was extremely difficult to access them.[18] Hari Singh started for Sinsini at night with a light cavalry. He crossed the jungle overnight and attacked the Jats in early morning. He did not give them a chance to retaliate. They fought till noon. Though the Jats received severe losses and fled but this battle also left the Kachhwaha army totally exhausted. Therefore, when Kachhwaha army moved back to Mathura via Sonkh, they were hardly left with energy to handle the fresh attacks of the Jats. However, the Kachhwahas showed their bravery and made supreme exertions. They killed eight hundred rebels and odd enemies and obtained a great victory.[19]

Hari Singh following orders of Prince Bedar Bakht carried with him *Rahagadahs* and *Dhunsas* and a mechanic *(Karigar)* to erect them. He also collected revenue from *chakla* Islamabad (Mathura), so that the honour of the prince could be saved.[20] Emperor Aurangzeb realized that Hari Singh was the right man to deal with the rebellious Jats and therefore he offered him the *mahals* of the *sarkars* of Mathura and Kol plus zamindari of the pargana Mathura. He also rewarded Raja Bishan Singh of Amber with the faujdari of Mathura and also accepted their request of the Chancery to farm out the revenue of eighteen *mahals* of the district of Mathura and Kol (Aligarh) with total revenue of about one lakh of rupees.[21]

Hari Singh had to personally provide protection to each convoy passing through the imperial highway. This assignment kept him away from the happenings in the Doab region where Amar Singh Jat of Kher was making revenue officials as prisoners. Prince Kambakhsh sought the help from Bedar Bakht who reached Sinsini with Hari Singh. Hari Singh had to deal with the Jat rebels on both east and west side of the Jamuna. On the other hand, Pratap Singh Naruka joined hands with the Jats and was creating disturbances in Kuma and Pahari. To wrest Mathura from Jat rebels and to disconnect them from the local people, Hari Singh carried out some administrative changes which proved to be very beneficial. He appointed many *thanedars* (police officers) in every affected pargana and for every *sarai* on the imperial highway. Competent revenue collectors were appointed in the ijara *mahals*. Grievances of the people were redressed carefully. Thus, Hari Singh was able to win the support of the countryside. This strategy weakened the roots of the Jats in the region and provided a golden opportunity to the Kachhwahas to widen their principality.[22] Hari Singh made gifts of honour to *chaudharis* and *muqaddams* to pull them on his side against the Jats.

In June, 1689 Hari Singh and Raja Bishan Singh of Amber were asked to subdue the Jat rebels in pargana Kama. This time again they crossed the entire path in night and fell upon the Jats of Kama at midnight. Hari Singh made a systematic clearing of rebels. In course of which some villages belonging to the grand-children of late Kirat Singh, second son of Raja Jai Singh, were also raided. The reason behind this raid was that the villages of Kirat Singh's grand-children used to serve as hiding place for Jat rebels. However, this instance was misrepresented in front of the Emperor. It was alleged that Raja Bishan Singh and his commander-in-chief, Hari Singh were planning to kill descendants of Kirat Singh[23] and for this they were driving out loyal and inoffensive peasants front villages and resettling them with those devoted to their own interests. This misconception led to the loss *of mansab* of Raja Bishan Singh.

The Emperor began to realize that the Jat revolt posed a serious military threat. Jats had entered into a sort of understanding with the local *zamindars* who provided a protective shield to them. Many other groups joined this revolt. The other allied groups were Ahirs, Gujars, Narukas and the Gaur Rajputs. All these groups defied imperial power and they had an urge for upward social mobility.[24] Apart from this they all had independent reasons to join this revolt. Thakur Hari Singh was employed against this confederacy of rebels but with the coming of many powerful groups together the power of the Jat revolt increased. Now they organised more attacks from all the sides and it became difficult to handle them through military power. Therefore, Hari Singh adopted the path of selective negotiation in order to establish peace in Mathura. He started negotiations with the Gaur Rajputs who held many villages in the Mathura district and also with Pratap Singh Naruka in order to detach them from the Jats and come over to the side of the Kachhwaha army. This policy of Hari Singh bore immediate fruit. After the coming over of the Narukas to the imperial side, Jats lost control over Sinsini. Their villages were plundered and people were killed mercilessly. However, prince Bedar Bakht and emperor both doubted Hari Singh's attempt to bring Narukas on their side. They did not trust on Narukas and thus donated their loyalty towards the imperial cause. But Hari Singh tried to prove their loyalty by showing some documents signed by the *Qazi* and *Chaudharis* of villages who testified the fact that parganas Pahari and Kama were cleared of rebels and their lands were given to the loyal *zamindars* by the Amber raja. He also explained his motive behind taking Narukas into his service.[25]

In 1689, Hari Singh attacked Amar Singh Jat of Kher in Doab. He made a bridge of boats to cross the Jamuna. He crossed the river but before he could transfer the artillery the bridge was swept away. Without the artillery Hari Singh could only push up to Tappal (12 miles west of modern Aligarh) chasing scattered bands of the Jats. But it became difficult for him to move further without artillery and attack Amar Singh's forts of Kher and Rath.[26] On the other hand, Jats again started troubling in the neighbourhood of Mathura. So Raja Bishan Singh moved to Sinsini. Raja Bishan Singh summoned Hari Singh to come back to Mathura to subdue Jat rebels and escort supplies to Sinsini. Hari Singh left a portion of army in his base camp at Tappal and crossed back the river secretly. Amar Singh was not aware of the absence of Hari Singh from Tappal and thus he was busy in guarding his fort. After reaching Mathura, Hari Singh rebuilt the bridge and crossed the river with a stronger army. His army consisted five thousand horse, five thousand foot and heavy imperial artillery. He attacked Amar Singh's capital fortress of Kher. Amar Singh was prepared to defend himself. He also built another fort, Rath (Rait) to serve as a link of communication with the rebel Jat *zamindars* of Khurja and Chandausi. Rath was considered as the 'gateway' of Kher by the Jats. Hari Singh studied the geography of the region around Rath and Kher. He first attacked Rath and gave a surprise to Amar Singh. Amar Singh left there a garrison of 2000 skilled soldiers under the command of Peshkar Birju. The Jat rebels had an advantage over the Kachhwahas because they were fighting from the top of the fort whereas the Kachhwaha army was fighting from the lower terrain. This resulted in a pitched battle of hacking and hustling on the plain below and of arrow and bullet above from the fort. But even then Kachhwaha army stormed the fort and they were lying the scattered dead bodies of the rebels. Birju himself managed to escape with few hundred men and joined Amar Singh. This victory boosted the morale of the Kachhwaha army.[27]

About a month later, Hari Singh attacked Kher in April, 1690. In this fight Amar Singh was severely wounded. Amar Singh fled to southward to join his allies Nanda Jat[28] and others in the neighbourhood of Mursan whereas his lieutenants Birju and Taula Jat fled to Khurja. Soon, Hari Singh caught both of them. Arrest of Taula and Birju Jat and wounding of Amar Singh's broke the morale of Jat rebels and they handed over the command of the Fort of Kher to Hari Singh without any resistance. In order to establish peace in Kher, Hari Singh confirmed the parganas to the Jat peasantry after taking their chief men as hostages. For the next four years there was peace in this region. Thus Hari Singh's strategies were justified. Hari Singh was busy in suppressing the rebels on the other side of the Jamuna river. On the other hand, Prince Bedar Bakht tried to discredit Raja Bishan Singh for the fall of Sinsini and accused him of disloyalty. This resulted in the reduction of his *mansab* by 500 zat and 1000 sawar and the charge of Sinsini was handed over to Rao Ugarsen Kachhwaha. Hari

Singh was given a cash reward of one lakh and twenty thousand rupees as *inam* for equipping his army for a fresh campaign against the Jats. Hari Singh Khangarot recruited 1200 sawars and two thousand footmen in twenty days from Agra and Bayana at the rate of a daily pay of four annas per sawar and one anna per footman. He raised a full new army of Kachhwahas.[29] On the other hand all available men from Amber territory and especially the Khangarots were also summoned for immediate service. By the end of October, 1690 an army of fifty two thousand horse and foot including the imperial artillery assembled under the flag of Kachhwaha ruler. Of these troops Khangarot cavaliers and their retainers numbered ten thousand stood behind the chief of Lamba, who never led his followers but to booty and victory. They began a fresh campaign against the Jats of Kumher and Bharatpur. This time their target was three forts: Kasot (8 miles of Sinsini), Abair (6 miles south-east of Kasot and 7 miles west of Kumher), and Sogor (4 miles south of Abair). These three forts were within a distance of ten miles. These were concealed in the midst of a dense forest. Jat rebels used it as a defence for themselves. In the east of Abair was the fortified *garhi* of Rara, the home of Rauriya Jats, who in alliance with the Sogoria Jats of Sogor held in strength the whole country as far as Pingora. In the west of Abair the Jats built a triangular line of defence with the newly built *garhi* of Sonkh, a line from Pingora to Bhatauli forming its base; and a line from Sonkh via Raisis to Pingora indicating its eastern side. The Kachhwaha army was divided into three parts. One part was watching the Jats of Kama and Pahari, who recently threatened the region of Sinsini from North; Second part was stationed at Mathura for guarding the imperial highway so that the supplies of the commodities to the army station of Sogor and Ahair should not be disturbed; and third part was with the commander in chief of the Kachhwaha army. To bring out the Jats from their den the Khangarot chief began a devastating drive through the enemy country. During this process Jats came out suddenly and attacked the army and then disappeared. Finally, to provoke them Hari Singh killed one Jat chief, wounded a brother of Bukna Jat of Kasot and inflicted heavy casualities on the rebels.[30]

Further in December, 1690 the Kachhwaha army chief left the Raja in the main camp near Abair and went to raid Jat villages with 3000 horse and one thousand foot to a distance. They burnt eight *Naglas* (fortified block houses) and four *mauzas* within the jurisdiction of Sogor, Pingora and Helak.[31] Wherever the army devastated a village they carry their food stock along with them. Perhaps the Kachhwaha army wanted to keep a regular supply of food and on the other hand they want to cut the supply of food to the survivors. But at some places before the army attacked the villages, villagers left for jungle along with their families and cattle. The peasants of four villages such as Sewar (two miles of south-west of Bharatpur) came and told Kachhwaha chief that they are humble raiyats, and that out of fear of the Jat rebels they dared not show their loyalty. The Kachhwaha chief forbade the plunder of their villages and assured them of providing protection and favour.

The Kachhwaha army was attacked by the Jat rebels who were hiding in the forest. The Jats attacked them suddenly and cause severe damage of men and then they disappeared in the forest again. When the Kachhwaha army reached the jungle in between of Abair and Sogor they were attacked by the rebels from both the sides. The Kachhwaha defeated the enemy with their light artillery *(gaj-nals)* and *shutar-nals* (swivels mounted on elephants and camels).

On the other hand Kachhwaha ruler along with the imperial *mansabdar* Aqa Ali went to raid Mahaban (7 miles south-west of Bharatpur). But there they were informed that the Jats expected them hence they prepared a battle field for the welcoming of the imperial army. They had dug a trench at the very spot where the Raja was standing, filled it up with the gun-powder to be fired by a device, and concealed the whole thing by light cover of earth and *khasgrass*. Similarly, they contrived in fire the Khera (high village mound) where Aqa Ali was then standing. Knowing about this Raja and the imperial *mansabdar* returned to their camp and waited for Hari Singh Khangarot. At that time he was busy in clearing the forest and bringing out the Jat rebels from the forest.

Without Hari Singh the camp was not safe because the Jats kept on attacking it and run away killing and carrying off camp followers during his absence. After that the Khangarot chief started clearing the forest and fighting minor battles with the Jats. It became a problem to protect the forest-cutters from the match-lock fire of the Jats concealed in the jungle. So the Kachhwaha chief placed artillery in the jungle to tackle the enemy ambushes. But the officers of the artillery raised objection on this saying that the artillery was for use against the fort-walls only, and not for wasting shell in the jungle. But the Kachhwaha army chief gave them orders in written and asked them to follow it without any confusion.[32]

It is impossible to starve the inhabitants of Abair and Sogor to surrender because of secret supplies by unknown ways through the jungle with which only the Jats were familiar. So Kachhwaha planned a strategy to take such a party by surprise. For the next six months they stopped all their activities related to digging, clearing and shelling of forests. Soon they found the secret ways via the forest to the fort of Sogor thus the Kachhwahas entered the fort and attacked the Jats.

Capturing the fort of Abair did not prove an easy task for the Kachhwahas. The Jats gave stiff resistance to the Kachhwaha army. The Mughal Emperor was unhappy because of delay in the reduction of Abair. There were two main reasons behind this delay. First, in 1691 Jat rebels in other regions began plundering the imperial territory to take revenge of the Kachhwaha army attacks. Situation became more difficult when the Meos and Narukas joined the revolt and this extended its wings further in south, west and north of the modern Bharatpur territory. To the north of Sinsini, Pratap Singh a *zamindar* of Balahi, Sabal Singh of Indrauli and rebel Meos of Sikar and Badipur were active in Kama and Pahari. Fatehram, son of Rajaram Jat and Churaman Jat, nephew of Rajaram Jat, were moving in Jat country with their roving bands. On the other hand in Agra, Sipahdar Khan, *subadar* of Agra did not cooperate with the Kachhwaha Raja as he was not powerful enough to prevent the revolt. The result was that the Jats from Bayana and Bhusawar began concentrating in the region in the west of Pingora, and their large concentration in Bhatauli (18 miles of south west) threatened the Kachhwaha army in the south-west. Similarly, Churaman Jat[33] with his Naruka allies Kanha and Devi Singh gathered a strong force at Sonkh (8 miles west of Sinsini and 18 miles north-west of Abair). Whereas, Ram Singh and Sheo Singh with Shafi Khan, subahdar of Ajmer, began plundering the home-territory of the Kachhwahas (Amber). With the joining of hands of different caste the nature of this revolt changed from a peasant resistance to a political and social upheaval. It was not like the Meo revolt which was easily subdued by the Kachhwaha rulers because in that revolt only two Meo pals participated. But Jat revolt was a coalition of multi-caste and every caste had its own reason to join it. And that's why it became difficult to suppress it. In this revolt the rebels firmly established themselves in every pargana.

Hari Singh had to carry out a double fight with the Jats besieged in their forts as well as those who were attacking the imperial army and diverting them from siege operations. In the last week of March, 1692 Abair fell. The Raja got back his original *mansab* with a head to foot dress of honour. The capture of Abair was hailed everywhere as a great victory.[34] The Khangarot chief tightened his grip on Kasot and Pingora in 1692. Pingora offered a stiff resistance and the Jats from Bhatauli attempted a diversion to drive the imperialists from the siege. Hari Singh marched towards Bhatauli and subdued the rebels. The rebels of Pingora were also defeated and its fort was dismantled like other Jat strongholds. The Raja of Amber appointed Gaj Singh, eldest son of Hari Singh Khangarot, as *thanedar* of the fort of Pingora.

From 1690 to the end of the year 1694 A.D. the Khangarot chief suppressed the Jat, Naruka and Panwar rebels of Mathura, Agra, Hindaun, Bayana, and Alwar. The third phase begins with a campaign in Doab and closed with the death of Hari Singh Khangarot in Jawar on April 5, 1695 A.D.

To conclude, emphasizing the climatic and geographical factor of this region Abul Fazl noted that "owing to the peculiarity of its climate the peasant masses *(umum-i-riaya)* of that territory are notorious throughout the vast country of Hindustan for rebelliousness, bravery and courage.[35] On both the sides of river Jamuna constant military operations were conducted against the rebels.

To discuss the politico-military history of the battles between Jats and Kachhwahas it is important to study the geography of the Braj region. Military operations are drastically affected by the geography of a region and it also had a huge impact on the political history. Thus the geography of an area widens our understanding of history. The terrain of Braj region had affected the battles between Jats and Kachhwahas. The impenetrable forests and other physical features were an advantage for the Jats. But the military strategies adopted by the Kachhwahas led them to overcome this natural weakness and suppressed the rebels. The outcome had changed if the commanders had treated the geography differently. But their familiarities of the region led them to won these battles. Another important aspect of these battles was the network of communication among the rebels. They contacted each other through secret letters, planned their strategies and held secret conferences because of which they were able to give tough fight to the imperial army. Another important aspect of these battles was the skilful use of fortresses (*garhis*) by the rebels as bases of resistance. These *garhis* were strategically located and were an object of display of power. These *garhis* were well equipped with armed persons and other necessities of life.

Last but not the least these battles showed that though the Jats were pacified but every time they came with more power and force to attack the imperialists. They caused heavy damage to the imperial campaigners and inflicted heavy mortality on them. Therefore, it can be claimed that the Kachhwahas were successful in suppressing the Jats but temporarily. Apart from terrain and *garhis*, the Jats ultimately succeeded due to their undiminishing combativity.

## References

1. Qanungo, K.R.: *History of the Jats*, Sunita Publications, Delhi, (1925,) rpt., 1987, p. 21.

2. A Descriptive List of the Vakil Reports Addressed to the rulers of Jaipur, Vol. 1 (Persian), published by the Rajasthan State Archives, Rajasthan, Bikaner, (1967).
3. *Ibid*.
4. The Jats have maximum number of their zamindaris in *sarkar* Sahar, see *Ain-i-Akbari,* tr. Colonel H.S. Jarrett, Vols. II-III, Low Price Publications (LPP), Delhi, rpt. (1997), p. 206.
5. Irfan Habib : *Agrarian System of Mughal India 1556-1707*, Oxford University Press, Delhi (1999), p. 392.
6. Rajaram Jat owns a large area of land in Sinsini.
7. R.P Rana : *Rebel to Rulers*, Manohar Publications, New Delhi, (2006), pp. 117-118. He gave reference of Krishna Naruka, a rebel *bhomia*, who built his *garhi* on the dung of village Kot of *pargana* Banawar, Arzdasht, dt. posh Sudi 15,VS 1761/1704.
8. Maharaja Bishan Singh accepted the order of suppressing the Jats but in return he demanded extensive powers, adequate finances and the *jagirdari* and zamindari rights of various parganas, Vakil Reports, *Kesho Rai to Bishan Singh,* dt. 13 Rajab 1099 AH/ May 4, 1688; 4 Sabban 1099 AH/ 25 May 1688 and 24 Ramajan, 1099 AH/ July 18, 1688. A Jagir worth 20,000 dams was granted to him in Kama, Vakil Reports, *Kesho Rai to Bishan Singh*, dt. 13 Zilkada, 1099 AH/ August 21, 1688. He was accorded the zamindari of the Jat villages in pargana Ao and Sonkh, *Vakil Reports*, Kesho Rai to Bishan Singh, dt. 11 Zilkada, 1100 AH/ August 17, 1689 and Safar, 1101 AH/ November 23, 1689.
9. *Vakil Report,* Kesho Rai to Bishan Singh, dt. 28 Jammadal Akhir, 1099/ AH 1688.
10. *Vakil Report,* Kesho Rai to Bishan Singh, dt.11 Shawwal, 1099 AH/ July 30, 1688.
11. Qanungo, K.R. : *Op. cit*., p. 63.
12. *The Diggi Thikana papers* available in the Centre of Rajasthan, Jaipur. Document No. 147, February, 1689.
13. *Vakil Reports*, *Op. cit*., dt. 8 Jamadal akhir, 1101 AH/ March 9, 1690.
14. Qanungo : *Op. cit*., p. 96.
15. Govardhan mountain occupies a central place in the mythical landscape of Braj. The cult of mountain and cattle i.e. govardhan

puja is quite popular in the Braj region. It's a way to protect the jungles which became an abode of unrestricted freedom of Jats. For further details on Govardhan cult see, Charlotte Vaudeville, 'The Govardhan Myth in Northern India', in her, *Myths, Saints and Legends in Medieval India*, pp. 113-117.

16. The Jats actually attacked Hari Singh's convoy at Ao, 16 miles west of Govardhan and 7 miles north-east of Sinsini.
17. *The Diggi Thikana papers*, Document No. 63, November, 1689.
18. See Appendix 2 in R.P. Rana : *Op. cit.,* pp. 204-206.
19. Qanungo : *Op. cit*., p. 68.
20. *Ibid.*, p. 69.
21. *Farman*, No. 33 dated 22 Shadab 36 regnal year of Alamgir (April 8, 1694) rewarding the *faujdar* of Islamabad (Mathura) at the parganas of Hindaun and Bayana to the Maharaja (Bishan Singh) with an increase of 3 hazari zat, 3000 sawars (do aspa) and *inam* of 65 lakh dams, *Catalogue of Historical Documents in Kapad-dwara*, Jaipur, Pt. I, p. 4.
22. The soldiers of the Amber Raja took advantage of the increased disturbances of the Jats of Braj. They began *to* embezzle the entire *hasil* (collected revenue) of such villages. See Arzdasht, dt Maha Vadi 5 and 7, VS 1746/19; Arzdasht, dt. Bhadwa Vadi 5, VS 1749/1692.
23. *The Diggi Thikana papers*, Document No. 61.
24. The Narukas and Kalyanots who had been acting as a buffer between the Jats and the Amber Raja, joined the Jats after the failure of the campaigns of Nawab Khan Bahadur, Arzdasht, dt. Mangsir Vadi 2, VS 1744/1687. The Narukas and other Rajput bhumias had a conflict with the Amber Raja over the zamindari right. Therefore, the Jats and Rajputs became allies in their struggle against the Mughals and Kachhwaha ruler see R.P. Rana : *Op. cit.*, p. 146.
25. He wanted to keep Naruka away from helping Jats of Sinsini and then to destroy the Narukas from root (Sheet no. 61).
26. Amar Singh was the *zamindar* of Khair (village) of pargana Kol (tappa Khair), *Arzdashts*, Vaisakh Vadi 11, VS 1749/1694.
27. *The Diggi Thikana papers,* Document No. 65.
28. In tappa Lagasma of Kol Nanda Jat and eleven other *zamindars* revolted. The Jats had already brought pargana Antrauli under their

control. R.P. Rana : *Op. cit.,* p. 149.

29. *The Diggi Thikana papers*, Document No 84.

30. *Ibid*., Document No. 59

31. Qanungo : *Op. cit.,* p.80.

32. *The Diggi Thikana papers,* Document No. 68, 29 December, 1690.

33. Churaman Jat had a strong foothold in Agra, Delhi and Thoon. For further details see Tapan Raychaudri and Irfan (eds.), *The Cambridge Economic History of India,* Vol. 1, 1200-1750, Orient Longman, Cambridge, (1982), p. 376.

34. *The Diggi Thikana papers,* Document No. 97 and 120.

35. A.N. III p. 231, cited from Irfan Habib : *Agrarian Crisis of Mughal Empire*, Asia Publishing House Bombay, (1963).

6

# Contesting and Negotiating Power : The multi-faceted dynamics of the Jat Uprising during late 17th and early 18th century

*Manisha Choudhary*

During the late seventeenth and early eighteenth centuries the Jat revolts in Mughal suba of Agra left a lasting impact on the polity, society and economy of the region and played a decisive role in limiting fortunes of the mother empire. As Jats were the principal leaders and provided major support of these revolts, their multifaceted strategies need to be highlighted. Nearly 200 years ago a French Jesuit F.X. Wendel said '...the jats have...... hurt so many people that no one can be persuaded that they are capable of doing good or even worth being praised.'[1] This popular conception persisted and for a long time the Jat history was ignored by historians. The role of Jats is not only limited to regional histories. Their activities affected Mughals, Kachhwaha and the various invaders time and again. Jats presented themselves as the warriors who fought to save honour and respect of their lands. Many narratives in the Persian sources like *Roznamcha* present a judicious picture of the Jats. They have transformed from nomadic pastoralists to settled agriculturalists. Their transformation from a pastoral to an agricultural economy was also occurring, parallel to their sedentration between eleventh and the sixteenth century and it continued even after that.[2] Sir William Irvine while writing about the later Mughals made occasional significant references about the Jats whereas focus of his work was Maratha history.[3] Jadunath Sarkar highlighted the Sikh, Jat and Maratha revolts of the late seventeenth century as 'the Hindu-Reaction' against Aurangzeb.[4] The pioneer and extensive work on the Jats was done by Prof. K.R. Qanungo, whose scholarship drew attention of scholars to the history of Jats which was ignored for long. Qanungo, followed the same theme of historiography and tried to re-inforce that the Jat revolts in medieval India were part of 'Hindu Reaction'.[5]

Prof. R.P. Rana, challenges the existing historiographical notion associated with work of Jadunath Sarkar. He argues that 'the Jats did not belong to any particular religious tradition, they could not be freely clubbed with high caste Hindus. In fact from the seventh to the seventeenth century they were at the receiving end of the Brahmanical social order'.[6] During late seventeenth century the Mughal authority was limited to a restricted area around Delhi. Over that the fierce factionalism at court, the foreign invasion, self-aggrandizement of officials and rise of indigenous powers further complicated the situation.

In post-Aurangzeb period the powerful elements at the court found it expedient to conciliate the Jats in order to retain power and rejuvenate the declining empire.[7] The later readily accepted their role. They no longer remained plebian rebels perpetually fighting against the imperialists but became allies of one or the other court faction. Being conscious of their strength the Jats availed the opportunities for expansion also. With stabilization of Jat power and position the dependence of Mughal grandees increased on them. So much so, that the imperial *wazir* Safdar Jung went more than half way to seek their ready cooperation in the imperial affairs.[8] This dependence of imperial forces on the Jats clearly indicates to the power and prestige the Jats enjoyed at this time. Earlier the Jats were 'not remarkable in Hindustan' and by seventeen sixties they earned for themselves 'a reputation never seen outside'.[9] As the Jats were Martial by character, their ability to fight and warrior-ship increased their involvement in the imperial affairs. This contributed for steady growth of Jats and placed them in hostility with Marathas and the invaders. When the imperial wars were fought outside the regions of Jat villages, Jats played the role of faithful feudatories to Mughals.

Most of our information about the activities of the Jats is collected from Persian sources such as the Mughal official documents, the court histories, general and provincial histories, biographical sketches written by Mughal private servants. Of these sources *Roznamcha, Iqbalnama* take a judicious view of the Jats. Till date the historians have looked on to the Jat history as the rebellious history. Here an attempt has been made to look into the Jat history from a different perspective. The sources provide an insight into a different state of affairs wherein the Jats were not only revolting against the state but they were constantly contesting and negotiating power, and this negation of power was very much present in the post-Aurangzeb times. In July, 1780, Jai Singh has occupied Amber and expelled the local faujdar, Sayyid Hussain Khan. The Mughal Emperor Bahadur Shah sent re-inforcement to him for recovering the place. To recover the same Hussain Khan sought help from Churaman and sent him money to recruit troops. In response, the Jat leader collected a big force and reached Narnaul where Khan was living ever since his expulsion. Jai Singh also approached Churaman with an appeal that he (Churaman) should detach himself from Sayyid Hussain Khan and co-operate with him against the Mughals. Jai Singh assured Churaman that in response to it he will expel Churaman's opponent (Jaitar Singh) from pargana of Kaithwada. This made Churaman to desert Sayyid. As Churaman was able to carve out a big force from the Mughal resources he also decided to stay away from both the powers and later took service under Jai Singh to do needful in Mathura region.[10] There are many such incidents which depict the strong say of Jat leaders. The Jat leaders not only enjoyed support of their community but other deprived communities also took their side to fight against the exploitative state. The skills to negotiate power helped the Jat leader Churaman to gain support from Sanyasis and many other fighter professionals. In 1716, when Jai Singh decided to destroy fort of Thune and suppress Jat revolt, Churaman had nearly 12,000 professional sanyasis fighters in his stronghold. He also employed Afghans from Shahjahanpur and Bareilly on a payment of three rupees per day and had support of Mewatis.[11] The expedition of Jai Singh brought Churaman closer to Saiyyed brothers. Later this hostility of Amber Raja made Churaman to develop close relations with Raja Ajit Singh, who assured him security.

The consistent negotiation and contestation of power with the Imperial and Rajput authorities by powerful Jat leaders made the presence of Jat visible. The authority of Raja Ram raised so much around Agra that 'no one could pass without paying a fee to Raja Ram, who was bent upon avenging the execution of Gokula.'[12] If the fluctuating balance of power inclined too sharply to one or few groups, others who lacked access to power turned political challengers. The Jats of Braj who were at sharp end of politics organized a series of revolts against the Mughal-Kachhwaha alliance.

The Jats created a rebellious dynamic by constructing alliances with other challengers. The first recorded description of the Jats with considerable detail is in the *Chachnama* (an account of Arab conquest of Sindh A.D 710-14). Besides teaming cattle they were soldiers, sailors and guides. In *Al-Hind,* Alberuni described the Jats as 'cattle owners and low shudra people'.[13] They transformed from pastoral to an agrarian economy in between eleven to sixteenth century.

The peasantry constituted by far the most numerous classes in 17th century India. However, the material position of peasantry was under increasing threat. So far most of the studies about Jat revolts have suggested that the Jat rebels from Gokula Jat to Surajmal were mere *zamindars* challenging the power of the Mughal state. However, there is one important source, which reveals diverse strategies adopted by the Jats such as negotiating with rulers to share political power both at local level and imperial level. This source is known as *Dastur Komwar* Jat preserved in the Jaipur Historical Section of the Rajasthan State Archives at Bikaner. This paper is largely based on the information recorded in the *Dastur Komwar Jat.*

The source *(Dastur Komwar)* throws light on the cordial relations of Jaipur State with the Jat leaders like Surajmal, Badan Singh, Partap Singh, Khema Jat etc. The exchange of various objects, gifts, *nazars* and ceremonial receptions with elabourate rituals and gestures of respect depicts the elite noble treatment meted out to the Jat elites. Naval Singh, son of Surajmal came to Jaipur in V.S.1812/1755 A.D., there he was received extensively by Jaipur Raja and was presented 2 *siropaos,* 1 *sirpeach* and a string of real pearls.[14] The ceremonial reception was also extended towards the ladies who accompanied the Jat ruler.[15] Many such instances clearly indicate the relations of Jat Rulers with the Raja of Jaipur. Numerous gifts were presented to Jat leaders and their ladies on various festive occasions, state ceremonies and social ceremonies. The Jaipur state invited these rulers to celebrate the festivals like *Dussehra, Holi, Teej, Bhaiduj* etc. and showered on them valuables gifts with respect. For instance in V.S. 1827/1770 A.D., Kesari Singh received a *than* from Jaipur Raja along with a *sirpeach* (decorative piece for head gear) which amounted Rs. 352 in connection with his coronation.[16] In V.S.1813/1756 A.D., Kishor Singh Jat of Mahawa visited the *Huzuri* (Jaipur Raja) and for his welcome he was presented a *siropao*.[17]

Clearly, the cordial relations of the Jat rebel rulers with the Jaipur rajas were the main arm of the Mughals in the midst of contest indicates Jats' efforts to negotiate political power with their rivals. Sir Jadunath Sarkar has described the Jats as 'the most important racial element in the vast tract of land that stretches from the bank of the Indus, through the Punjab, the northern state of Rajputana and the upper Jamuna Valley, down to Gwalior, beyond the Chambal'.[18] Prof. Qanungo singles out the inbred democratic strain in the Jat. The Jat community has been within historic times, the great refuge of the victims of Hindu social tyranny, and the uplifter of the depressed and untouchables to a more respectable status, transforming all recruits to a homogenous Aryan mould..... in physical features, language, character, sentiments, ideas of government and social institutions, the present day Jat is undeniably a better representative of the ancient Vedic Aryan than any member of the three castes of the Hindus.[19]

The decline of empire became turning point in the fortunes of many nobles, local *zamindars* and the rural communities.[20] Its collapse pushed India into a prolonged period of political turmoil, agrarian dislocation and contraction of commerce.[21] There are plenty of evidences which depict the chaos and corruption at all levels of Mughal administration. The various military uprisings of Jats, Sikhs and Marathas during seventeenth and eighteenth century clearly indicate to the inability of Mughal warfare. Historians of different persuasions have divided the Jat revolts into two distinct phases. In the first phase we are told, prominent Jat leaders like Gokula, Raja Ram Jat, Ram Chander Sogharia and Churaman Jat expressed their anger through the barrel of the gun. They organized a series of armed revolts against different Mughal generals who were sent against them. These leaders constructed *garhis* (mini-fortresses) and manufactured muskets to fight the Mughals and their allies. This phase of Jat revolts has been characterized as a 'large plundering movement' by Irfan Habib.[22] K.R. Qanungo characterized Churaman Jat as a 'wolf' and later termed him a 'poacher'.[23] The title of R.P. Rana's book suggests that this phase of the Jat revolts was marked by the presence of 'rebels'.[24] Clearly, all these scholars have profiled all the Jat leaders of this phase as uncompromising armed victories over the Mughals, which laid the foundation of the Jat power.

The second phase belonged to Badan Singh and Surajmal who co-operated with the Jaipur Raja and gave proper administration to the Braj region. Writing about Badan Singh, Satish Chandra says, 'he was a good administrator and under his watchful stewardship the Jat house of Bharatpur gained in power silently and steadily'. Badan Singh possessed the qualities which were required to deal with the multifaceted problems. He had uncommon skill, tireless patience, force and power of pursuance. Every method was employed by him to destroy his enemy like rewarding friends, enriching kingdom, bribing freely and marriage alliances. With the immense weakening of the Mughal Empire and the rise of Jaipur state as a powerful entity, these Jat leaders felt it wiser to have cordial relations with the Kachhwaha rulers. Raja Sawai Jai Singh of Jaipur showed uncommon foresight when he placed Badan Singh on *Gaddi,* vacated by Churaman. This act kept Jats associated with the Jaipur State and in reward the Jat kingdom enjoyed the authority, influence, prestige, territory and wealth. In response to all these rewards the Jaipur State enjoyed military services of Jats. Though, these Jat rulers had many victories to their credit, their emphasis was more on negotiating power.

Churaman died in V.S. 1778/1721 A.D., prior to this also many of the Jat leaders are negotiating power with the Rajas of Jaipur. Many Jat leaders were associated with Jaipur State and they are important for the Jaipur Rajas to balance their power relations. For instance Udiya Jat came to Jaipur in V.S. 1774/1717A.D. In the same year, Chintamani (vakil of churaman), Kheta Jat, Urd Ram, Savant Singh also visited Jaipur Raja.[25] In V.S.1775/1718 A.D,, Khema Jat, Savant Singh (nephew of Khema Jat), Man Ram (son of Kheta Jat) came to Jaipur and were received with grand welcome.[26] Umaid Singh, son of Rao Badan Singh, Roopa Jat and Veer Bhan made a visit to Jaipur.[27] Various other Jat leaders also had say in the affairs of State but many a times servicemen *(chakers)* and *vakils* operated on behalf of the Jat leader. These *chakers* and *vakils* were learned people who had the understanding of power relations. In V.S. 1778/1721 A.D., Muhkum Singh's *Chaker* and *Vakil* Brindaban visited Jaipur on their masters behalf and performed the due ceremonies and also received *siropao* for their master.[28] Many a times these visit were under guidance of some favorite or a close confident of Raja.

However, thc evidence available in *Dastur Komwar Jat* shows that even during the first phase of the Jat revolts, Churaman and other rebels also practiced the art of diplomacy with their rivals. For instance, in V.S.1777/1720A.D., Raja Ram came to meet *Hazuri* (Raja of Jaipur) along with Tularam.[29] In the same year many other Jat leaders who are labelled as the rebellions to the State, also visited to the Raja of Jaipur. Such as, Duda Ram, Jagram Jat, Devkaran Jat, Bhaju Ram s/o Gokula, Ramdas Jat, Khema Jat and Bhika Ram brother of Khema Jat.[30]

A deep insight of the document, *Dastur Komwar* gives a clear idea that there was no fixed time of the Jat rebellion. During the time of early rebellions also the Jat leaders were in constant association with the Rajas of Jaipur. The diplomacy to balance the power kept them in constant flux. As per the requirement of the State the Jat leaders also negotiated power. Various instances prove that there was never a permanency in the relations of Jat leaders with the Rajas of Jaipur. Efforts of Badan Singh acquired authority, title, and territory which no other Jat chief possessed.

However, the prosperity came to the Jat Rulers only after efforts of Maharaja Surajmal, who provided proper administration to the Jat kingdom. Surajmal started his carrier by defeating *meos* who lived in the hilly northern parts of Bharatpur. After this particular event Surajmal emerged out as an able general of headed conduct and courage. Peshwa Baji Rao visited Jaipur in 1736, to honour him Jai Singh made arrangements to hold a big Darbar. Badan Singh was also invited but due to his inability to attend Darbar he asked Surajmal to represent him. He was received well in Darbar by Jai Singh as a prince of humble origin. While introducing Surajmal to Peshwa, Jai Singh made remarks about humble origin of Surajmal. The high virtue of courage, good character and honour added to Surajmal's profile. The sad sunset of Mughal Empire coincided with the dawn of Maratha, Jat and Sikh power. The emerging power holders and game changers were mainly controlling the military power. There martial character kept them in centre of power. There military skills and their ability to fight made them associates of kingdom. The ever changing position of power kept these forces in flex and they associated with whom, they got elevation in their status and position.

The change and elevation in the status of Jat leaders throw light on how the plebian leaders were able to carve out space for themselves. Further, the exchange of gestures associated with respect, symbols of royalty and honour in the court depict the powerful status enjoyed by the Jat leaders. The court rituals were markers of respect in Jaipur State and the above discussed cases stress that the Jat leaders were always received in Jaipur court with a grand welcome ceremony and proper Protocol was followed to mark their presence. The reception ceremonies which were attended by king (*Shree jee*) and mother queen (*Majee Sahib*) were of immense importance, as their presence was exclusive for the special guests of state. The presents were made to guest in accordance with his status and power he enjoyed at the Jaipur Court. The narratives related to Jat leaders in *Dastur Komwar* are very elabourate. The extensive reception ceremonies organized to welcome the Jat leaders put light on the prestige enjoyed by them at Jaipur Court.

## References


1. F.X. Wendel : *Memoires de l'origine accroisement etat present de puissance des jats dans l' Indostan II de Partie, suite des Memoires des Pattans,* cited from Girish Chandra Dwivedi, *The Jats : Their Role in the Mughal Empire,* Arnold Publisher, (1989), p. 9.
2. R.P. Rana : 'Change, Protest and Politics: Situating the Jat Revolts of the Late Seventeenth and Early Eighteenth Century', *Social Science Probings,* December 2004, 53-73, p. 57.
3. William Irvin : *The Later Mughals,* cf. Girish Chandra Dwivedi, *The Jats: Their Role in the Mughal Empire,* Arnold Publishers, New Delhi, 1989, p. 9.
4. Jadunath Sarkar : *History of Aurangzeb,* vol. III, 3rd edition, Calcutta, (1996) chapter xxxv.
5. K.R. Qanungo : *History of Jats,* reprint, 1987, p. 19.
6. R.P. Rana : *Op. cit.,* p. 54.
7. Girish Chandra Dwivedi : *The Jats : Their role in the Mughal Empire,* Arnold Publishers, New Delhi (1989), p. 10.
8. *Ibid.,* p. 10.
9. *Memoircs des Jats, op. cit.,* p.29.
10. Girish Chandra Dwivedi : *op. cit.,* p. 56.
11. *Ibid.,* p. 63 refer foot note 57.
12. K. Natwar Singh : *Maharaja Surajmal 1707-1763*, Rupa & co., New Delhi, (2001), pp. 9-10.
13. Cf., R.P. Rana : *Rebels to Rulers, the Rise of Jat power in Medieval India c.1665-1735*, Manohar, (2006), p. 123.
14. *Dastur Komwar Jat :* pp. 399-400. Hereafter *D.K.*
15. *D.K.,* In V.S. 1782/ 1725 A.D., Fuda Ram Jat came to Jaipur with his wife and daughter. Both of them were presented gifts and were received in royal apartments.
16. *D.K. Jat,* Register no. 7, p. 326.
17. *D.K. Jat,* Register no. 7, p. 325.
18. K. Natwar Singh: *op. cit.,* p. 1.
19. *Ibid.*, p. 2.
20. R.P. Rana : *op. cit.*, p. 11.

21. Irfan Habib : *Agrarian System of Mughal India 1556-1707,* 2nd revised edition, Oxford University Press, Delhi, 1999, p. 405.
22. *Ibid.,* p. 393.
23. K. Natwar Singh : *op. cit.,* p. 16.
24. R.P., Rana : *Rebels to Rulers, the Rise of Jat Power in Medieval India c.1665-1735,* Manohar, 2006.
25. *D.K. Jat,* pp. 310-329.
26. *D.K. Jat,* pp.315-335.
27. *D.K. Jat,* pp. 317-385.
28. *D.K. Jat,* pp. 352-55.
29. *D.K. Jat,* pp. 333-34.
30. *D.K. Jat,* pp. 317-34.

# 7

# Afsana-e-Jung-e-Bharatpur or Waqa-e-Jung-e-Bharatpur by Maulavi Fazl-e-Azim

***Farha Adeeba***

Maulavi Fazl-e-Azim son of the Maulana Fazl-e-Imam Khairabadi and the elder brother of Maulavi Fazl-e-Haq Khairabadi (1212-1276 A.H./1797-1861 A.D.) who was the Chief Judge (Sadar-us-Sudur) in Akbar Shah's time, was a really gifted *allama* and doctor of law and literature; he was also a thinker or philosopher who believed strongly in the need of the time the Hindu Muslim alliance in order to drive away the English from India.[1]

Maulavi Fazl-e-Azim originally belonged to Badaun.[2] One of the forefathers migrated from there to Khairabad and settled there.[3] 'Azim born at Khairabad'[4] was taught rational and traditional sciences by his learned father.[5]

Azim was a noted poet, scholar and historiographer of early 19th century. He has left behind some works mainly on the regional histories like *Jungnamah-e-Rajghan-e-Almora*, *and Raja Nepal,* also referred *Tarikh-e-Kuhistan*. When the English army invaded Kurkh, he was with the same English gentlemen who participated in this war, which took place in 1813-14 A.D. He indicated some account of this war in his another history *Afsana-e-Jung-e-Bharatpur* composed in 1240-41 A.H. /1825-26 A.D.[6]

It means he was an eye witness of Nepalese war and compiled a short but very important history of the British victory on the Nepal which took place in 1814-16 A.D.[7]

Fazl-e-Azim also gives some account of his life in the beginning of *Waqa-e-Jung-e-Bharatpur*, that he was separated from his family in his boyhood and was employed under William Fraser, the collector of Delhi, as a secretary.

زایام طفلی من خستہ جان جدا گشتہ از پہر واز خانمان
رسیدم بدہلی ونوکر شدم نمکخوار ولیم فریزر شدم

He remained with him for twenty years. He accompanied William Fraser in all of his journeys and sojourns. After the Nepalese war Azim reached Delhi and got service under Patodad.

Unfortunately the employment proved disappointing for the Chief, who continually found fault with him, so he resigned. Consequently he was left jobless, after which it was difficult for him even to earn his livelihood.

In the meantime his earlier patron Fraser, who had accompanied General Martindell's army as a political agent in his Nepalese war, returned to Delhi and Azim was again attached to his former master.

There broke out a war at Bharatpur again and the author accompanied his patron in this war.[8] He was in close contact with Ghalib who composed a *Qita*[9] (fragment) for his mathnavi *Afsana-e-Bharatpur* and Fazl-e-Azim composed a *Qasida* (Ode) in the praise of Ghalib.[10]

Subsequently he was appointed as a Deputy Collector in the Saharanpur District.[11] During the mutiny of 1857 A.D. he was arrested and sent to Rangoon, where he died. Azim was also a good poet. His Diwan, collection of verses containing nearly two thousand verses *Ishqi* described in his Tazkirah *Nashtar-e-Ishq* that Azim had his own style, he used very simple language and composed sweet and romantic verses applying unique ideas.

His works enumerated by Story are :[12]

1. *Afsana-e-Bharatpur* or *Waqa-e-Jung-e-Bharatpur*[13]
2. *Waqa-e-Kuhistan*[14]
3. *Sham-e-Shabistan*, a romantic mathnavi.[15]
4. *Tarikh-e-Bharatpur*[16] or *Zafar Namah*, a political account of the siege of Bharatpur by Lord Lake, based on a prose narration by Brahman called Shambhu.

*Afsana-e-Bharatpur* :

It is a mathnavi on the operations against Raja Durjan Sal of Bharatpur (1240-41 A.H./1825-26 A.D.) It begins with Hamd (Praise of the God) :

بنام خداوند خلاّقِ جان          که بنده نواز است و روزی رسان

خدای که کون و مکان آفرید          زمین و زمان تو امان آفرید

(In the name of Allah. He is the creator, who has given us food and who has created the world).[17]

Giving the reason of composing this Mathnavi the poet says that once he was too gloomy and mentally disturbed, in such a case he heard the voice from the heavens inviting him to compose the Mathnavi, *Afsana-e-Bharatpur*, dealing with the battle to which he was an eye witness. He completed these works as the following chronogram contains in 1241 A.H./1826 A.D.)

بگفتا به من هاتف ذی شعور          بگردید وا عقده بهرت پور

He gives a short account about himself as reproduced earlier, praises William Fraser and the ruling king Akbar Shah II, and gives also a scanty historical background of Badan Singh Jat, a Zamindar. He comes to the actual subject like collection and proper equipment of the army, siege of the fort by the British army and Major Fraser's march etc. Finally the fort was conquered and the ruling Raja was imprisoned. The victorious army entered the fort and found it filled so well with equipments and such other amenities that the English army had not witnessed earlier.

Later Madho Singh created a war atmosphere at the time of Balwant Singh's accession to the throne but the later ascended the throne with the help of the Britishers peacefully.

The Mathanavi is composed very skillfully. The continuity and the force of diction required for the expression of such narrations remain alive through out. Eye witness account narrated in simple language has added the importance of that work. The work has been authenticated by the renowned poet Mirza Ghalib, who composed a *Qita* (Fragment) for the Mathnavi.

A short sketch of Alwar city is written under a separate title.[18]

## References


1. Mehdi Hasan : *Bahadur Shah II and the War of 1857,* p. 389.
2. *Sham-e-Anjuman*, p. 288.
3. *Subh-e-Gulshan*, p. 288.
4. *Nashtar-e-Ishq*, p. 370.
5. *Nashtar-e-Ishq*, p.288.
6. *Afsana-e-Jung-e-Bharatpur*, fol. 7-a.
7. *Afsana-e-Bharatpur*, fol. 8-a.
8. *Afsana-e-Bharatpur*, fol. 6a to 8a.
9. *Afsana-e-Bharatpur*, fol. 60b, and 61a.
10. Story Vol. 1, p. 646.
11. In *Nashtar-e-Ishq*, his poetic genius is very much applauded, fol. 370b.
12. Story I. p. 646.
13. Aug. *Salam*, MS No.540 but the author himself name it as *Afsana-e-Bharatpur*.
14. *Waqa-e-Kuhistan*.
15. A.S.B. MS No. 886, and Rieu, MS No.1054.
16. *Afsana-e-Bharatpur*, fol. l.a
17. *Ibid.*, fol. 54b.
18. *Ibid.*, [illegible] 7b.

## 8

# New Light on the Great Revolt of 1857 with Special Reference to the Jats

*Zakir Husain*

Notwithstanding the destructive role played against the Mughal empire by the Afghans, Marathas, Nizam, Sikhs, Nawabs of Bengal and Awadh, Rajputs and Jats that gradually splintered it into independent states and principalities of the Nawabs and the Rajas. Though this also led to the emergence of the regional forces of Meos, Gujars and Ahirs, yet the emergence of thc menace of the English East India Company resulted into the unification of all the above mentioned centrifugal powers for the liberation of the country in the name of the so-called last Mughal sovereign. Since each and every caste and community played a dominant role in their respective areas of influence the concept of an independent India against the Company's hegemony developed at a magnificent scale. The 24 Rajputana princely states unanimously decided to vehemently resist any British policy of annexing their principalities unlike the people of Awadh which also caused great uprising and disturbance.

Delhi and the neighboring territories mainly abound with Jats are also significantly inhabited with pockets of Meo population as well as scarcely scattered with Gujars and Ahirs. Since our focus of study is fundamentally the evaluation of the role of the Jat Raja of Ballabhgarh and the Jat freedom fighters along with their supporters of other communities particularly the Meos, we have also taken into consideration the role of Nahar Singh, the

Raja of Ballabhgarh, because the Jat were staunchly supported by the Meo community.

The situation was so much critical in the great saga of 1857 that Shahmal Jat who rose into rebellion was eliminated with his 600 supporters by the British. In view of his utmost influence Shahmal's relatives also supported his cause in a befitting manner. Since a thorough study of the documentary evidence of Raja Nahar Singh of Ballabhgarh, another Jat stalwart of freedom has already been made on the basis of the documentary survey of the Persian records available with the National Archives of India by my colleague Ms N.S. Alam, a careful study of numerous papers of the Sikh majority of whom are also the offshoots of the Jats need to be studied separately in the light of the Persian/Urdu records of the National Archives and elsewhere as they played a prominent role as well in 1857. Contrary to the well-established notion of their espousing the British cause, which in fact, has been proved wrong at least owing to the availability of Persian/Urdu records which is also firmly proving their loyalty to the country. The interesting details furnished about them are of unique historical significance as no such endeavor has so far been made concerning them because after all they were Indians in the first instance, which fact has even escaped the attention of a renowned historian of Ganda Singh's stature.

The British spies, aired the rumour of the so-called allegation of the freedom fighters that since the Raja of Ballabhgarh was allegedly supporting the British cause they were bent upon penalizing him.[1] Such an unsubstantiated allegation led Megh Raj, the British spy, on 15th July 1857, to report that 100 cavalry and 550 sepoys of the army were dispatched either to collect Rs. 2,00,000/- or to arrest[2] the Raja. This misunderstanding was so much deep rooted that a contingent of the army was sent accompanied with two cannons to advise the Raja of Ballabhgarh owing to his alleged friendship with the British while 12 of his horsemen were seized.[3]

These misconceived notions were shattered when it was reported that the Nawab of Jhajjar and the Raja of Ballabhgarh and some other chiefs were collecting money for the freedom fighters.[4]

When the chief of Ballabhgarh was enquired about his contribution to the first War of Indian Independence, he immediately retorted that since Abdul Haque, his plenipotentiary, by seizing his treasury, was staying in Delhi, either he would be sent back or the money could be recovered from him.[5] Since the men of the Raja of Ballabhgarh had arrived in Delhi whose credentials could not be ascertained, the Raja had made their arrangements.[6] Although the situation in Ballabhgarh was reported to be under control yet the prisoners were freed and the Raja of Ballabhgarh was alleged to engage in plundering with the Gujars.[7] The aforesaid Abdul Haque was appointed the administrator of Gurgaon, where from he returned with pomp and show.

How much cunning were the British spies who alleged that there was an imperial spy in the court of the Raja of Ballabhgarh who intimated the Mughal Emperor about the news. It was said that he had furnished details of a letter of the Lieutenant Governor of Agra, to Raja of Ballabhgarh asking him to furnish provisions to the English army. The informer was named Bal Mukund, who resided near Sarai and as per the English spy he was also required to be expelled from Ballabhgarh.[8] Since the Raja of Ballabhgarh was sincere enough to the Mughal emperor he sent Rs. 10,000/- and a horse as expenses for the army through Fateh Ali, the Superintendent to the emperor.[9] Furthermore, his sincerity was so much well established that he had sent to Kale Khan (Miyan Nasiruddin), the spiritual mentor of the emperor, a sum of Rs. 10,000/- through Nizamuddin which was seized by Queen Zeenat Mahal.[10]

The loyalty of the Raja of Ballabhgarh was not skin deep as he not only enthusiastically celebrated the Muharram but was very much anxious to embrace Islam and support the emperor wholeheartedly.[11] (This fact cannot be substantiated because this was merely a British propaganda aimed at misguiding the Jat community).

This newly found information about the Raja of Ballabhgarh slightly corroborated by his correspondence with Bahadur Shah can yield dividends of utmost significance as his loyalty is further established beyond any doubt by different sources of historical significance. The sufferer was not only the Raja of

Ballabhgarh but the inhabitants of the Ballabhgarh region who faced numerous difficulties. This is also confirmed from *Subedar* Ramdhan Singh's letter to Commander-in-Chief as he solicited his instructions regarding the disposal of the collapsed houses of the house owners of Ballabhgarh to remove their wooden furniture and other articles.[12] Such complaints against the Jats were extremely rare. The Jats were never alleged for any uncalled-for activities.[13] The Raja of Ballabhgarh even pleaded the emperor to stop Hakim Abdul Haque, his plenipotentiary from proceeding to Delhi.[14] Since Nahar Singh was sincere enough, his appeal to the Mughal emperor about Ahmad Ali, agent of the Raja of Ballabhgarh, praying that Raja's men proceeding with him with the articles belonging to the Raja which were left at Delhi be granted a passport that was acceded to them accordingly.[15]

The Jats were not only active in Haryana but they also played a crucial role in U.P. as well as Maulvi Rajab Ali reported on 21 July 1857 that Shahmal Jat caused a great loss to the British in Meerut owing to his freedom struggle against the British and he was killed there during the course of an attack upon him along with his 600 colleagues.[16] It was also communicated that Shahmal Jat was assassinated during his confrontation with Meerut Volunteer Force. Thereafter his son proceeded to Delhi where the freedom fighters were planning to dispatch two infantry battalions along with 8 cannons to Baghpat.[17]

Dilsukh, a Jat who was the *Lumbardar* of the city (of Delhi) and was the owner of a large portion of the city came out of the city accompanied with his men and assured Captain Hudson of his loyalty and made arrangement for the dinner of the English army.[18] The English were intelligent enough even to engage Jat spies like Dhanna Jat, resident of Nangli, who reported on 20 August 1857 about the activities of the freedom fighters.[19] But in spite of such incidences the Jats remained steadfast in their loyalty to the Mughal emperor as Shahmal's relatives again rose into rebellion in Meerut and they began to realize 4 annas per rupee as revenue collection in this region.[20] There were some other problems being faced by the Jats *viz.* Sinhi Jat pleaded to the Commander-in-Chief for protection against violence being perpetuated by Gujars.

Since the Jat freedom fighters actively participated in the great war of Indian Independence in 1857, Kunwar Jat and others solicited the personal intervention of the Commander-in-Chief for the recovery of a horse seized by the *Tilangas*.[21] This was the position of the ruling class as well as the gentry where no one remained backward in advancing the cause of liberation of the country from the British yoke.

The Jat Raja of Ballabgarh was also invited to enthusiastically support the cause of liberation by the Mughal emperor. However, the Mughal emperor wrote to *Diwan* Bhola Nath of Bharatpur state directing him to kill two Englishmen who were in the service of Bharatpur State.[22] However in Alwar, apparently the Meo freedom fighters closed the gates of Alwar and the English agent could not enter there.[23] The situation had become so much disturbed that the Political Agent at Bharatpur sent thc *Tehsildar* of Gopalgarh to enquire into the causes of disturbance in Alwar.[24] Even the English Officers became so much alert that they began to keep themselves informed of the state of affairs at Alwar and Jaipur.[25] The people of Alwar became apprehended at the arrival of freedom fighters there.[26]

The information coming from Ballabhgarh, Meerut, Baghpat, Delhi, Alwar and Bharatpur concerning the activity of Jat ruler of Ballabgarh and the gentry from the above regions is quite significant if it is also coupled with detailed news about the active participation of the Sikh freedom fighters who came forward in making utmost endeavors in liberating especially the National Capital Region from the British yoke, which was tremendously supported by the Meo freedom fighters, independent of any support or opposition to their cause for freedom struggle in the country.

## References

* However a brief survey of the documents has been made by my colleague N.S. Alam whose pioneering effort needs to be strengthened by others who are interested in this field by undertaking similar studies on the basis of Persian/Urdu documents from other regions by searching, transcribing, translating and editing with copious footnotes etc. for a better understanding of their role.

1. Anonymous, 5th July 1857, M.C., OBL, (OR) MSS-EUR-C124, p. 192.
2. Mutiny collection 199, pp. 215-16.
3. Gopal Shoky and others, 16 July 1857, M.C., p. 216.
4. M.C., 123, p. 245 of 18 July 1857.
5. R.C. Majumdar: *The Sepoy Mutiny and the Revolt of 1857,* Calcutta, vol. III, p. 172, 19th July 1877.
6. *Ibid.*, p. 176.
7. *Ibid.*, 24 July 1857, p. 179.
8. The informer of Col. Bajor, 18 Aug. 1857, M.C. 157, pp. 382-383.
9. R.C. Majumdar, vol. III, pp. 172, 192.
10. Gauri Shankar, M.C., vol. II, No. 170, pp. 7-8.
11. M.C., vol. II, No. 174, pp. 15-16, Gauri Shankar 2nd Sept. 1857.
12. *Mutiny Papers*, NAI, Coll. No. 112, S.No. 50, dated 25 July 1857.
13. Cf. C-in-C to Mubarak Khan, *Kotwal*, in regard to a complaint against Kallu Jat vs Bhota, *Mutiny Papers*, Coll. No. 122, S. No. 76, 20 Aug. 1857.
14. *Mutiny Papers*, Coll. No. 143, S. No. 2 of 17 June 1857.
15. *Mutiny Papers*, Coll. No. 146, S. No. 25-26, undated.
16. R.C. Majumdar, Vol. III, p. 175.
17. M.C., 161, p. 419.
18. R.C. Majumdar, vol. III, p. 190, Captain Hudson's *Munshi* from Khorkhuda front 19 Aug. 1857.
19. M.K., 159, pp. 406-407.
20. M.C., 167, p. 445.
21. *Mutiny Papers*, Coll. No. 67, S. No. 135, dated 6th October 1857.
22. *Mutiny Papers*, Coll. No. 151, S. No. 17, undated.
23. *Cf., Mutiny Papers*, Coll. No. 199, S. No. 261,7 08 Aug. 1857.
24. *Mutiny Papers,* Coll. No. 199, S. No. 282-283, 16 Aug. 1857.
25. *Mutiny Papers,* Coll. No. 199, S. No. 286-289.
26. *Mutiny Papers,* Coll. No. 199, S. No. 290, 17 Aug. 1857.

## 9

# Paradox of Great Uprising of 1857 – Role of Sikhs : A Second Reconnaissance

*N.S. Alam*

The annexation of Punjab in 1849 had far reaching repercussions on the Sikh community. Notwithstanding the wrongly established notion that it did not affect their loyalty to the British, the fact remains that it had tremendously created feelings of hatred against the British onslaught. Furthermore, this martial race gave vent to their pent up feelings in 1857 because due to such tragic event of the annexation of Punjab in 1849 they could not remain steadfast in their loyalty to the British. Furthermore, only the Sikh chieftains were siding with the British while the Sikh masses were opposing them. Even numerous Sikh sepoys were siding with the freedom struggle in 1857.

When the great saga of Indian independence in 1857 commenced then numerous Sikh sepoys did not remain backward in expressing their solidarity with the common Indian masses owing to their loyalty to the country. Despite the endeavor of the English East India Company for marshalling this offshoot of the Jats in their favour, we find numerous instances that they were basically anti-British. There are several instances that consequent upon the break-up of the great uprising of 1857 they, as Indians, espoused the cause of Indian freedom struggle. The Sikhs, as a community, most often sided with the freedom fighters and they strenuously attempted to establish an independent Sikh Regiment in 1857, a demand which was initially accepted. However, during the last days of freedom struggle of 1857 in Delhi, they were scattered in different regiments. But it does not speak of the fate of the Sikh community, majority of whom were siding with the freedom fighters in Delhi. Whether they were killed with the freedom lovers or the Sikh forces allying with the British succeeded in saving them.

How much gallantly they fought against the British is known from a number of instances, *viz.,* a Sikh accompanied with three horsemen was imprisoned on the charge of spying against the British. If we thoroughly examine the brilliant role of the Sikh freedom fighters then we can easily rely on a report about the Sikhs who boasted that they would defeat the English, if they could get a regiment or two of their own people to fight against the British army.[1] Their claims began to be translated into action as they started deserting the English army in small and large numbers true to their reputation of being sincere to the Indian War of Independence in 1857. We are first of all informed about the arrival of Sikh deserters to Delhi in 1857 itself.[2]

Interestingly enough, this was not limited to the desertion of the Sikhs from the English forces but they used to remain in direct contact with the freedom fighters. We come to know the fact that a large number of Sikhs at the English camp used to remain busy in communicating with those who were with the so-called mutineers (in fact freedom fighters).[3] Since the Mughal Commander-in-Chief was very much acquainted with their sincere efforts of remaining busy in striving for the liberation of the country, he issued orders to the officers to direct the Sikh soldiers under them to assemble outside the Ajmeri Gate.[4]

Since the Mughal Emperor was well aware of their meritorious services, he began to utilize their potentialities for the liberation of the country. The Sikh regiment came into existence since the very inception as the Mughal Commander-in-Chief began to issue orders to them to commence hostilities against the English at Alipur.[5] The Mughal emperor not only greatly exercised their fighting spirit but also used to provide them requisite facilities. We come to know about the specific order that the Mughal Commander-in-Chief had issued to the officers of the Sikh Regiment about their proper accommodation.[6] This was not in isolation as the services of a renowned general of Bakht Khan's stature were also used in their favour. That is the reason of Bakht Khan's acknowledging the receipt of orders from the Commander-in-Chief regarding the transfer of Sikh Regiment from the trenches of Idgah.[7]

In view of the mutual hatred of those engaged in fighting the war of independence it was reported by Hasti Singh regarding a Sikh sepoy, who was in communication with the English.[8] Similar allegation was levelled by Mohammad Shafi to the Commander-in-Chief pleading his helplessness in ejecting the Sikh soldiers from a house occupied by them, as in using force he apprehended the danger.[9] However, it was but natural that in any uprising of unmanageable magnitude, such incidences happen because after all the soldiers coming from outside Delhi had to stay probably in vacant houses, as is evident in the above case.

Since the Sikh Regiment was raised separately which was merged due to unknown circumstances, it became an assiduous cause of their grievances. Accordingly, they represented to Mirza Mughal for redressing their problems and he directed the court (of freedom fighters) to attend prayers of the Sikhs who solicited either (permanently) to be separated from the rest of the army or disbanded.[10] However, it seems that they were not separated under such critical circumstances as their help was must in the war of independence without any discrimination. But their opponents like Bullan Singh, Commander of the 10th Regiment suggested that since the Sikh Regiment was suspected of being in league with the English, their dispatch to Bahadurgarh would be injurious.[11]

Since General Bakht Khan was very much aware of such dirty mechanizations especially in such a crisis where distinction of foes and friends was blurred as he recommended to Shah Alam, the prince (probably the temporary Commander-in-Chief) to send the Sikh Regiment as per the directions.[12] The Commander-in-Chief directed Gauri Shankar Shuki to relieve the Sikh guards,[13] probably to give them temporary relief. However, if it was a conspiracy of some vested interests, then the Mughal emperor adopted certain remedial measures by directing the Commander-in-Chief for the reconciliation of the sepoys[14] because he was quite confident of their military strategy. Quite possibly the correction of the information furnished by the Sikh sepoys about the arrival of the English at Karnal became the subject of confirmation.[15] Mohammad Khizr Sultan communicated to the Commander-in-Chief his request for recovering two pairs of silver bangles seized by certain Sikhs from two sepoys of Bareilly Regiment and to restore them to the owners.[16] Such was a common complaint which one could encounter in the great uprising of 1857.

The Sikhs were, however, well acquainted with their tacit opposition by their enemies. Kar Singh, Colonel of the Sikh Regiment informed the Commander-in-Chief that all the Sikh sepoys were faithful to the Mughal emperor.[17] The Mughal emperor, in view of their loyalty, ordered the officers of Sikh Regiment, to send 5 companies to the trenches of Shamagarh. This was such an open secret that the Mughal emperor fully utilized the services of the Sikh Regiment. The Sikhs also enthusiastically served the Mughal cause in an excellent manner as the reports of their deserting the English force had become a recurring phenomenon. An unknown spy reported that 200 Sikhs moved to Delhi where they stayed in Sabzi Mandi and their food arrangements were used to be made as well.[18]

We also find such examples of *en mass* desertion of the Sikhs to the Mughal emperor *viz.,* 280 or 300 Sikhs met the emperor through Mirza Mughal.[19] Some of the Sikh sepoys of the English camp communicated a message to the rebel Sikh sepoys in Delhi that they were also quite sympathetic to the Mughal emperor. If the Sikh freedom fighters were pressing for their separation from the other freedom fighters' army then they visualized that consequent upon the breaking of hostilities with the English, the Sikh sepoys of the English force would join the Sikhs as 125 Sikh horsemen of the English camp and 30 to 40 Afghans could join the camp of the freedom fighters.[20] Perhaps due to a disinformation and misunderstanding the Sikhs were again merged with miscellaneous regiments. The reporter Turab Ali was bold enough to admit that the sepoys of the Sikh Regiment were much brave as compared to other Indians.[21]

Although numerous Sikhs were with the English yet a large number of them were with the freedom fighters who were tremendously siding with Mughal emperor as some of the Sikh freedom fighters reported to the Mughal emperor that they had seized 12 cannons of the enemy and they had also entreated for the help of the imperial regiment which was allowed to them.[22] Ten-twelve Sikh Platoons also came from Rurkee.[23]

Such a brief survey of the heroic deeds of the Sikhs does entails the necessary details of their bravery and military strategy which indicates that if such documents of the Sikhs along with many other documents of the Jats are carefully collected, edited and translated into English with the original text of the contemporary records then it would be of utmost significance for the historians of the Great Revolution of 1857. This is still a desideratum which requires extraordinary dedication, labour of love and utmost attention of scholars who are well versed not only in the intricacies of the documentation practices of the Mughals but also of the Jat Raja of Ballabhgarh whose role can be highlighted with detailed documentary evidences. We can visualize that any brilliant scholar having command over the linguistic apparatus would accomplish this uphill task without caring for any restraint involving even financial expenditure because this phase of their history is also equally replete with Persian/Urdu documentation scattered at several places for which an incomplete outline has been drawn.

**Appendix**

Letter from Gauri Shankar, a spy to the English officials:

Today 80 persons of Sikh Community deserting the official battlements of the (English Camp) have come to Delhi. The Telangas assert that 300 Sikhs have arrived. But the writer has witnessed the arrival of 80 Sikhs who had gone to Mirza Mughal Beg inside the (Red) Fort. The Motive of their visit is either practical or just for the sake of the guardianship which has not been divulged as yet.

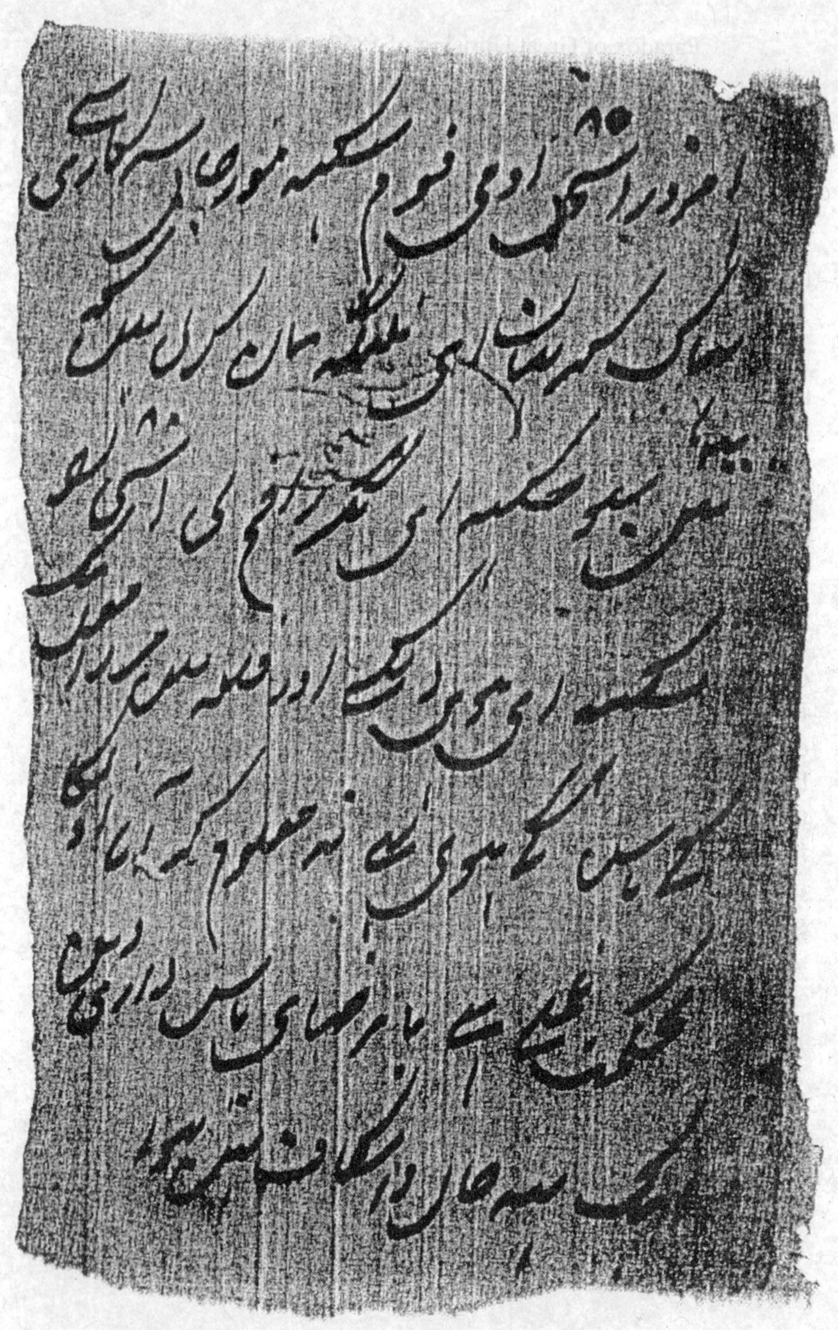

Letter from Gauri Shankar, a spy, to English Officials, that some Sikh deserters from the English camp have come to Delhi.

–NAI, Collection No. 19, Serial No. 11, Dated 28 August, 1857.

## References


1. *Press List of Mutiny Papers 1857-Being a Collection of the Correspondence of the Mutineers at Delhi, Reports of the Spies to English Officials and Other Miscellaneous Papers,* Calcutta, 1921, Coll. No. 19, S. No. 3 of 4 Aug. 1857.
2. *Mutiny Papers,* Coll. No. 19, S. No. 11, dated 28 Aug. 1857.
3. *Mutiny Papers,* Coll. No. 20, S. No. 6, dated 3 Sept. 1857.
4. *Mutiny Papers,* Coll. No. 57, S. No. 370, dated 25 Aug. 1857 (Urdu).
5. *Mutiny Papers,* Coll. No. 57, S. No. 370, dated 25 Aug. 1857.
6. *Mutiny Papers,* Coll. No. 60, S. No. 253, dated 1 July 1857.
7. *Mutiny Papers,* Coll. No. 60, S. No. 640, dated 2 Sept. 1857.
8. *Mutiny Papers,* Coll. No. 60, S. No. 715, dated 12 Sept. 1857.
9. *Mutiny Papers,* Coll. No. 60, S. No. 820, undated.
10. *Mutiny Papers,* Coll. No.70, S. No. 224, dated 21 May 1857.
11. *Mutiny Papers,* Coll. No. 70, S. No. 240, dated 29 Aug. 1857. This was perhaps the personal vengeance of complainant which was made in the garb of the un-called-for recommendation.
12. *Mutiny Papers,* Coll. No. 70, S. No. 243, dated 1 Sept. 1857.
13. *Mutiny Papers,* Coll. No. 70, S. No. 254, dated 4 Sept. 1857.
14. *Mutiny Papers,* Coll. No. 73, S. No. 146, dated 22 Aug. 1857.
15. *Cf., Mutiny Papers,* Coll. No. 83, S. No. 12, dated 26 June 1857.
16. *Mutiny Papers,* Coll. No. 101, S. No. 13, dated 5 Sept. 1857.
17. *Mutiny Papers,* Coll. No. 150, S. No. 11, undated.
18. M.K., pp. 417-19, dated 16 August 1857.
19. *Mutiny Papers,* coll.
20. News from col. Major's spy dated 15 Aug. 1857, R.C. Majumdar, III, pp. 382-83.
21. *Ibid.,* vol. II note 185, p. 547.
22. M.K., vol. II, N 185, pp. 54-55.
23. R.M., vol. III, p. 201.

# 10

# Aftermath of the Uprising of 1857 in Ballabhgarh

*Dr. Mahendra Singh Bagi*

The main aim of this paper is to see that what actually happened after the uprising was crushed in 1857 in Ballabhgarh. The present research paper is based mainly on primary sources from National Archives of India, New Delhi and the 'field'. Some contemporary newspaper sources have also been relied upon. Some persons related to Raja Nahar Singh directly or indirectly were interviewed. Besides, some secondary sources have also been used to complete this research work.

Nahar Singh, the Raja of Ballabhgarh was arrested for his deeds against the British. Charges were levied against him that he supported the revolt from its very beginning i.e., 10th May 1857 to 1st December 1857; and that he made correspondence with rebels; and that he sent troops to Palwal for the help of the rebellions; and that he used unlawful authority and openly waged war against the British. It was considered a heinous offence under the provision of Act No. XVI of 1857 of the Legislative Council in India.[1] European Military Commission headed by Brigadier General Chamberlain sentenced Raja Nahar Singh for transportation of life. On 9th January 1858, Raja Nahar Singh was hanged at *Kotwali* in Chandni Chowk, Delhi.[2]

As far as the uprising of 1857's crushing is concerned the British adopted the policy of 'Suppression and Reward'. Rebels were crushed and loyalists were rewarded. Hence Nahar Singh, the Raja of Ballabhgarh was executed for his deeds against the British.

Soon after the execution was over, the British Government searched the house of Raja Nahar Singh for property concealed therein. It was also decided that the whole of moveable property belonging to Raja Nahar Singh, which was captured by the troops, although without resistance, was to be considered a prize.[3]

Unfortunate incidents happened in the princely state of Ballabhgarh. The troops entered the inner portion of the Ballabhgarh palace where the ladies lived. The troops not only snatched cash and jewels but even clothes were not spared. A large number of the Raja's horses, bullocks and *rathas* were carried off and appropriated by the British army.[4]

The most common of articles from the palace such as *qalamdan* (pen-case) (1), *Sanduq-i-tin* (box of tin) (1), plate of copper (4), plate (small) (15), plate (large) (8), *nishter* (lancet) (14), carpet (1), brokencot (1), cot (2), pillow (4), quilt (2), chair (17), table (3), coach (4), bottle (1), table (small) (1), *chilman* (2), *modha* (3), sword (4), painting (4), *gulli* (1), *lota* (1), plate (china) (7), *sandasi* (2), *aari* with top cover (1), *kashti* (China) big (2), *kashti* (China) (3), *katora* (bowl) (1), *chowkichirag* (1), *chadar* (2) and *basta* of paper (1) were confiscated.[5]

In this palace nobody was allowed to reside. Later, Rani Kishan Kaur was permitted to reside there. The palace consisted of several houses. Actually, this is a square, two-storey building built of white sand stone, with carved doors and a courtyard in the centre. On one side is the *tehsil* with treasury, and on the other the *munsif's* court, and above this the police post house. Outside this is a building now used as *thana*. The fort is surrounded by stonewall about thirty feet high.[6]

These high stone walls were strengthened with a deep ditch and high mud bastions. Within it was a small crowded, but tolerably well-built town, with narrow streets, tall houses and many temples.[7] This palace was renovated in the last decade of the twentieth century by Ballabhgarh Development and Beautification Committee under the supervision of Deputy Commissioner of Faridabad.[8]

Soon after the confiscation, some property of Nahar Singh was sold.[9] Jewellery, guns, swords etc. were sold at the Magistrate's office. Some valuable swords were sold very cheap, while surprisingly the inferior weapons fetched high prices.[10] Actually manipulations took place there and no Indian objected it.

Raja Nahar Singh's estate was also attached.[11] The British Government confiscated the property of 37 villages including Tuglakabad, Rajpur Kala, Mulhaida, Alipur, Raipur Kala, Kheri Khurd, Badauli, Faujpur, Ninha, Garhi Begampur, Korali, Gadkhera, Dayalpur, Manaru, Jharsaitely, Badkhal, Dungarpur, Sadholi, Ballabhgarh, Chandawali, Tilori Banger, Chirsi, Sagarpur, Sihi, Sikargarh, Mewla Maharajpur, Faridpur, Shahpur Kala, Piyala, Sarurpur, Saran, Kabulpur, Manjauli, Maujpur, Ranhera, Shahpura and Daultabad of Raja Nahar Singh.[12]

In 1878, four of the villages were sold by auction.[13] The auction held, managed a huge amount of Rs. 64,500 and was bought by Rani Kishan Kaur. The amount was given to the trustees of the building.[14]

The family members of Raja Nahar Singh were treated liberally[15] except Mohan Singh, brother-in-law of Raja Nahar Singh. The Commissioner of Delhi sentenced Mohan Singh to transportation for life on 20th April 1858. The charges[16] leveled against him that he was a *mukhtar* in the employment of late Raja Nahar Singh, that he presented a petition to the late King of Delhi, on behalf of the late Raja of Ballabhgarh and that he had a hand in the murder of late Munro. Mohan Singh's appeal was rejected by the British.[17]

Nahar Singh's family and relatives were brought to Delhi in the first week of June, 1858 and were lodged in a confiscated house near the Delhi gate in the city where they stayed for long. The Chief Commissioner ordered that the late Raja's family should be given a moderate maintenance.[18]

The expenditure was paid out of the public treasury. C.B. Saunders, the Commissioner of Delhi directed that an advance of six months pension as proposed by Egerton should be made to several members of Nahar Singh's family. Some family members refused to take the advance of pension. Arrangements were made for the family and orders were issued for preparing pensions and grants of land to several members of the family.[19]

The Governor General appointed Lala Hargobind to be an extra Assistant Commissioner of the second grade in Delhi territory from 23rd November 1857. The Chief Commissioner in Awadh was authorized to disburse the arrears of his salary from 1st June to 23rd November 1857 after that his salary could be charged in the accounts of Punjab territory.[20]

There is a source lying at National Archives of India, New Delhi which shows a list of 43 members including Rani Kishan Kaur (34) (wife), Balwant Kaur (16) (daughter), Kunwar Khushal Singh (15) (nephew), Kunwar Ranjit Singh (32) father of Khushal Singh, Shama Kaur (wife of Ranjit Singh), Kawal Kaur (41) (widow of Dharam Singh, uncle of Nahar Singh), Novidh Kaur (19) (widow of Nihal Singh, son of Dharam Singh), Indu Kaur (65) (maternal grandmother of Nahar Singh), Kunwar Baldev Singh (54) (grandfather of Raja), Kunwar Gurpreet Singh (34) (uncle of Raja), Kunwar Oudh Singh (42), Khushal Singh (20), Fateh Kunwar (80), Umrao Kunwar (16) (descedents of Kunwar Raj Singh, brother of the grandfather of Raja Nahar Singh), Ali Bux (55), Bijay Singh (45), Hansa Bahadur (35), Azizudin (16), Zulfa (20), Wumshat Bahadur (78), Ghani Bahadur (30) (distant relatives of Raja Nahar Singh), Kunwar Balmukund (50), Khushal (50), Maya Kaur (60), Pato (60), Purval Singh (30), Madho Singh (56), Khushali Ram (40), Chandan Singh (12), Mohan Singh (10), Fateh Singh (30), Pritam Singh (18) (these 11 persons were heirs of Med Singh), Dalip Singh (12), Akhil Singh (32), Kewal Singh (28), Balwant Singh (22) (descendents of Bhopal Singh, brother of Med Singh), Achal Singh (60), Baldev Singh (80), Churaman (22), Harbux Singh (20), Burkat Singh (18), Maharaj Singh (16), Ganga Prasad (25) (descendents of Raja of Ballabhgarh) who had close and distant relationship with Nahar Singh, Raja of Ballabgarh.[21]

The detail of each individual has been given with the allowances they enjoyed during the late Raja's life, and also other information regarding their means of support as could be ascertained from the local enquiries. The amount of the pension proposed for each individual by Egerton was also shown. Most of these were not commensurate with the former means and position of the family members, and were also not according to the liberal spirit in which the government wanted them to be treated. This arrangement was open to being decreased if the Raja's relatives allowed retaining their grants with an assessment of revenue. Names of these persons might be struck of from the list of pensioners. The sanction of pensions and grants in land recommended for the several members of the family of late Raja Nahar Singh was also revised by the Lieutenant Governor of Punjab. The Chief Commissioner also allowed pensions to relatives of Nahar Singh.[22]

As is clear from the above fact that the British were very liberal with late Raja Nahar Singh's family. In fact, they needed the help of these 'political elite' after the end of the uprising.

Rani Kishan Kaur later petitioned before the British Government for three considerations:

1. Firstly, that Kunwar Khushal Singh, her nephew and adopted son of the late Raja may be placed upon the *gaddi* (throne) of Raja Nahar Singh.
2. Secondly, that she may receive a grant of all crowned lands, gardens and buildings lately rested in Raja's possession.
3. Thirdly, that a large marriage donation may be allotted to her marriage celebrations.[23]

After that, several members of Raja Nahar Singh's family had also petitioned before the British. One of them was Ranjit Singh (Nahar Singh's brother) proclaimed himself as the Raja. Later, Baldev Singh (grand-father of Raja Nahar Singh) sent a petition on 1st January 1860 to the British. Then there was Khushal Singh (adopted son of Raja Nahar Singh) who sent a petition to the British Government on 17th January 1860.[24] But the British Government did not accept none of these petitions.

Some persons claimed against the estates of Raja Nahar Singh before the British Government.[25] One of them was Van Menon, a bandmaster who had ordered certain instruments from England at the request of Nahar Singh. These instruments had not been delivered to the Raja when the uprising broke out in the Native Army. Saunders considered that the bandmaster should not be held responsible for their cost. He ordered the amount of rupees 2,289 were paid to him from the treasury and he also ordered that instruments could be at the disposal of Government.[26]

Two more creditors Ilahi Bux, merchant of Meerut and J.D. Lyre, late Commissioner Agent Delhi, whose claims amounted to approximately Rs. 1 lac on accounts of articles purchased from them by Raja Nahar Singh. The Chief Commissioner recommended that these claims should be paid by a payment from the Government treasury in consideration of the territorial revenues of the late chief having been confiscated to the state.[27]

## References

1. *Foreign Department Proceedings,* Nos. 51-55, F.C., N.A.I., New Delhi, 4 March 1859, pp. 1-4.
2. *Political Department,* Delhi Division. No.11, File No.7, Haryana State Archives, Panchkula, 11 November, 1857/*Mutiny Records*, Part II, Correspondence, Lahore, Haryana State Archives, Panchkula, 1911.
3. *Foreign Political Consultation,* Nos. 56-59, F.C., N.A.I., New Delhi, 11 June 1858/*Political Department,* Delhi Division, File No. 8, Haryana State Archives, Panchkula, 1858.
4. *Political Department,* Delhi Division, File No. 7, Letter No. 11, Haryana State Archives, Panchkula, 11 November 1857.
5. *Mutiny Papers,* Bundle No. 61, No. 170, N.A.I., New Delhi, 1857.
6. *Delhi District Gazetteer, 1883-1884*, pp . 212-214.
7. Walter Hamilton : *The East India Gazetteer,* Vol. I, Delhi, p. 294, 1828.
8. *Dainik Jagran,* 15-11-1999.
9. *The Englishman and Military Chronicle,* 3 March 1858.
10. *Bombay Times and Journal of Commerce,* Vol. IX, No. 3, 8 February, 1858, p. 7.
11. *Foreign Political Consultation,* Nos. 1919-1922, N.A.I., New Delhi, 30 December 1859.

12. Ranjit Singh Saini : *Raja Nahar Singh Ka Balidan,* Delhi, 2000, pp. 178-79.
13. *Ibid.,* p. 3.,
14. *Delhi District Gazetteer,* 1883-84, p. 180.
15. *Foreign Political Consultation,* Nos. 1919-1922, NA.I., New Delhi, 30 December 1859.
16. *Foreign Political Consultation,* Nos. 3288-3301, N.A.I., New Delhi, 31 December 1858.
17. *Ibid.*
18. *Foreign Secret Consultation,* Nos. 123-25, F.C., N.A.I., New Delhi, 8 April 1859.
19. *Ibid.*
20. *Foreign Department Proceedings,* Dispatch to Secretary of State, No. 24, N.A.I., New Delhi, 8 March 1859.
21. *Foreign Secret Consultation*, Nos.123-125, F. C., N.A.I., New Delhi, 8 April, 1859.
22. *Ibid.*
23. *Ibid.*
24. Ranjit Singh Saini : *Op. cit.*, pp. 150-152.
25. *Foreign Political Consultation,* Nos. 571-72, F.C., N.A.I., New Delhi, 6 August 1858.
26. *Foreign Department Proceedings,* Dispatch to Secretary of State, No. 24, N.A.I., New Delhi, 8 March 1859.
27. *Ibid., Foreign Political Consultation,* Nos. 299-300, F.C., N.A.I., New Delhi, 23 July 1858.

# 11

# Peasants' Unrest in Loharu State : Singhani Tragedy, 1935

*Dr. Rajesh Kumar*

Loharu was a small state in the Punjab States,[1] with an area of 222 square miles and population of 24 thousand souls. The unrest started among the kisans of this tiny state in 1931 itself, but the real struggle against the atrocities of the Nawab started in February 1935. As a result on 8th August 1935 the Nawab's troops opened fire on the assemblage of kisans at Singhani (a small village about seven miles in the south east of Loharu). The ruthless repression by the Nawab with the help of British-led troops is an unforgettable incident in the history of Loharu State. Many peasants were killed in this firing with many more wounded.

The main plank of the dissatisfaction had apparently been the revenue settlement (especially the camel tax) of 1923 by the Nawab. The *lagan* was raised from Rs. 2-5 to Rs. 3 and above all, the Nawab introduced a new cess called camel tax (Rs. 2-8 per camel annually).[2] The kisans held a number of meetings and decided that they will not pay their dues under the new settlement of 1923, and will force the Nawabi administration to revert to the previous settlement of 1909.[3]

The kisans started organizing the people of the region, formed a Panchayat (Loharu Jat Panchayat), and invited the Jats of the neighboring territories to attend the annual session of the Jat Sabha at Barwas[4] on 24th February 1935. One thousand kisans from the Shekhawati region (nearby villages of Jaipur state), Jind and Patiala states came to attend the Jat Sabha meeting. But, the Nawabi rule showed strong opposition to hold such meetings and refused to allow any outsider from entering the state boundaries. The visitors melted away without holding any meeting.[5]

At this juncture in March 1935, a large number of kisans from Loharu and from the neighboring villages of Shekhawati attended a joint meeting of local Jat Panchayat and Arya Samaj held at Kaloth village (within the Surajgarh jurisdiction, in Jaipur state) where the Nawabi rule in Loharu was criticized and the photographs of the Nawab were insulted. The Loharu administration could not tolerate such kind of activities of the people, and sent a police party to Surajgarh to prevent such meetings with the help of Jaipur police.[6] The Nawab had the suspicion that the roots of the *kisan* agitation in Loharu were in the nearby Shekhawati region, and he wrote a letter to the Vice-President Council of State, Jaipur on 6th March 1935.[7] The Nawab also met with the Agent to the Governor General of Punjab States, and made a complaint against the Shekhawati kisans, who were threatening to invade his (Nawab Loharu's) little state and to create trouble there by the Birla's concern.[8]

On the other side the kisans (of Loharu state) were petitioning, wiring and using all sorts of constitutional methods for the removal of the unbearable land revenue, camel tax, and marriage tax.[9] But when the administration did not pay attention to them, then the poor 'Riaya' (farmers), refused to pay all sort of cesses to the state. In these circumstances, the Nawab pretended to resolve the tension and invited the kisan leaders to attend a meeting at Loharu, on 15th July 1935 where the AGG, Punjab States was also present.[10] The kisan representatives submitted the following grievances and demands to the AGG :

1. Land revenue should be assessed and collected according to the rules made in the 1909 settlement.
2. People should not be burdened with the cess collected at the time of the marriage of a family member of His Highness the Nawab Sahib, and also with the tax which was levied on 'Kareva' (widow re-marriage) of subjects.

3. The tax levied on animals should be removed, especially the camel tax of Rs. 2-8 per head.
4. Occupancy rights to land used to belong to the state's subjects. But His Highness the Nawab has sold the rights and taken possession of the land. The occupancy rights should be restored to the subjects.
5. The post of *lamburdar* [Lambardar] is hereditary and on the death of a Lambardar the post should go to the son without charges.
6. There should not be any interference on the part of the state in the matter of re-marriage.
7. The inhabitants should be given their due share in the state services.
8. Income-tax should be levied in accordance with the rules made by the British Government.
9. The legal and other assets of issueless deceased state subject should go to collaterals.
10. Land revenue should be collected twice a year and in times of bad harvest, remission should bc granted in land revenue.
11. Subjects of the state should not be forced to contribute towards the state debts. The debts of the state should be cleared off by reducing state expenditure.[11]
12. The prohibition of widow re-marriage without the permission of the Nawab which was given on the payment of a fairly large fee should be discontinued.
13. The claim of the Nawab as owner of the Nazul land of the village 'shamlat' and its sale on various occasions should be turned down.[12]

The Nawab agreed on few of these complaints and announced some relief, but he refused to accept the 1909 settlement and to remove the camel tax on the ground that the demands to return to the previous settlement was unreasonable and could not be complied with.[13]

The kisans held a meeting at Dobra (another nearby village in Shekhawati), where it decided to set up a parallel Government at Chahar Kalan, a village 20 miles away from the Loharu State headquarters. A confrontation soon started between the Nawab and kisans, where the parallel Government opposed all Nawabi atrocities and refused to pay taxes (especially the camel tax) to the state.[14] Some Mahajans (who paid their dues to the state and asked for police protection in their villages) were punished by the parallel government.[15] In the second half of July 1935 a large number (three to four thousand) of kisans were gathered at Chahar Kalan and announced not to pay the taxes. The ring leaders of the agitation made preparations for a resistance to the collection of taxation in the state, and proceeded to arm themselves and to assemble at certain places.[16] On 30th July 1935, a police party marched to Chahar Kalan to assist the revenue staff.[17] The villagers refused to pay the taxes, mercilessly beaten up two policemen, and rescued two of their leaders (who had been arrested by the police).

On lst August 1935, the AGG–Punjab States was informed that the demonstration at Chahar Kalan had assumed a serious turn. The following day he proceeded to Loharu to discuss the situation with the Nawab, and he was told that a large number of peasants with axes, *gandasas* and *lathis* had assembled at Chahar Kalan on 30th July 1935, and threatened to attack the state police. The AGG after having consultation with the Nawab decided that further military reinforcement was necessary.[18] With the help of British-led troops the Nawab retaliated through armed action against the kisans by beating them and burning their houses.[19] The people deserted the village[20] and took refuge in the nearby villages of British territory and Jind State. A large number of kisans including five ring leaders were arrested by the Nawab's troops and detained in the Loharu Fort. During the detention the Jail authorities tortured them cruelly and some of them died in jail.[21]

Some of the armed kisans, who had dispersed from Chahar Kalan on the midnight of 5th August 1935, assembled again in a village called Singhani on 8th of August 1935 to discuss the further policies and programme to deal with the atrocities of the Nawabi rule. Suddenly, the Nawabi troops led by Bhure Miyan (brother of Loharu Nawab) arrived at the scene and tried to disperse the crowd. But, he (Bhure Miyan) was failed to do so. Irritated, he ordered the troops to open fire on the mob. Some of the participants (kisans) including few women received deep bullet wounds in the indiscriminate firing and died on the spot. Sixty to seventy people injured severely and were taken to the hospital at Bhiwani, where some of them died two or three days later.[22]

The firing on kisan agitators at Singhani had became a serious issue in the Punjab Politics. Chaudhary Chhoturam presided a mass meeting at Bhiwani and appointed a Relief Committee to work for the Loharu sufferers.[23] Ultimately, the Nawab of Loharu conducted a magisterial enquiry of Singhani firing and those who had descried were advised to return to their villages.[24] A proclamation issued by the Loharu Nawab on 16 August 1935 said that all the cesses except the camel tax had been cancelled and insistence put on the collection of revenue was fixed as in 1923. He also threatened that if the villagers will not return, their land would be forfeited.[25]

Jai Narain Vyas, the General Secretary, All India States' People's Conference, said that he had the occasion to see the Loharu refugees, who were lying homeless in the jungles exposed to rain and sun. He also came to know from the refugees that raids were made in Kasni, Mandholi, and Gokalpura villages by the Nawab's troops. Vyas was also told that cattle were being snatched, kisans were frightened and were wandering outside the state and that was the reason that great resentment had been aroused among the people.[26] On the appeal of Pandit Nekiram Sharma, Loharu sufferers Day was observed at many places, Bhiwani, Shimla, Delhi, Jodhpur, etc., and resolutions were passed urging for an independent enquiry into the happenings of Loharu.[27] On the other side Ratan Singh, President of the Rajputana Jat Sabha, requested the Paramount power to enquire into the charges and counter-charges about high taxation, arson, loot, molestation of women and firing as well as into the grievances of the peasants of Loharu.[28]

The atrocities of the Nawabi rule at Chahar Kalan and firing on the peasants' meeting at Singhani were heavily criticized.

On 7 October 1935, on the occasion of 'Dushehra Darbar', The Nawab said "...The Loharu agitation was actually started on 24th February 1935.... Since then I have personally watched and controlled the situation. Now I would advise you to forget as past what has happened. You have received liberal concessions from the state and you should feel satisfied with them. For my part, I declare that I forgive you all, except those few absconding offenders who are alleged to have been the real cause of troubles to you and to myself alike."[29]

It could have been easier for the Nawab to forget the past, but it was not so easy for those who had lost their near-dears in the firing, who were victims of loot and arson by the Nawabi aliments and took refuge in the neighbouring states or in the villages of British-India territory.

To conclude the peasants' unrest in Loharu–the Chahar Kalan incident and firing by the Nawabi troops on the kisan meeting at Singhani, it may be said that it was the most serious incident in the history of Loharu. The Nawab's authorities in association with the colonial troops had ruthlessly suppressed the kisan unrest in the state and a large number of peasants lost their lives.

Note : The Appendix gives the names of persons who were martyred in Singhani on 8 August 1935.

## References

1. Loharu State was in the Punjab States during the colonial rule; after independence it became a part of the Patiala and East Punjab States Union (PEPSU); after the submission of the report of the State Reorganization Commission, Loharu was merged into the Punjab. On 1st of November 1966 after the creation of Haryana, it became a Legislative Assembly Constituency and tehsil in the present Haryana State.
2. *Jaipur Judicial Records*, File No. 4327 Part-II of 1935, D.O. No. 775 dated 7th August 1935, from Young, I.G.P., Jaipur to Vice President, Council of State, Jaipur, Rajasthan State Archives, Bikaner [hereafter referred as RSABI].
3. *Times of India*, 9th August 1935.
4. A village five miles away, in the east of Loharu.

5. *Jaipur Judicial Records,* File No. 4327 Part-I of 1935, confidential copy of Memo No. 73, dated 04.03.1935, from Diwan of Loharu State to I.G.P. Jaipur, RSAB.
6. *Ibid.*, Telegram dated 5th March 1935 from Diwan of Loharu State to Vice President, Council of State, Jaipur, RSAB.
7. *Ibid.*, Confidential D.O. No. 45 dated 6th March 1935, from Nawab of Loharu to Vice President, Council of State, Jaipur, RSAB.
8. *Ibid.,* D.O. No. 120-C dated 8th March 1935, from A.G.G. Punjab States to Vice President, Council of State, Jaipur, RSAB.
9. *Bombay Chronicle,* 11th August 1935.
10. *Civil and Military Gazette,* 9th October 1935.
11. Foreign and Political [hereafter F/Poll], File No. 243-P(S), National Archives of India [hereafter NAI]; F/Poll, File No.464-P, 1935, NAI : *Hindustan Times*, 10th August 1935.
12. *Hindustan Times*, New Delhi, 13th August 1935.
13. F/Poll, File No. 243-P(S), NAI; *Times of India*, 9th August 1935.
14. F/Poll, File No. 243-P(S), NAI.
15. *The Statesman*, 21st August 1935.
16. *Ibid.,* 26th August 1935.
17. F/Poll, File No. 243-P(S), NAI; Jaipur Judicial Records, File No. 4327 Part-II of 1935, D.O. No. 271-C dated 4th August 1935, from Superintendent of Police, Shekhawati, to IGP, Jaipur, RSAB.
18. *The Statesman*, 26th August 1935.
19. F/Poll, File No. 243-P(S), NAI; *The Statesman*, 15th August 1935.
20. F/Pol1, File No. 243-P(S), NAI; *Times of India*, 9th August 1935.
21. F/Poll, File No. 243-P(S); NAI; F/Poll, File No. 464-P, and 674-P. 1935, NAI.
22. *Ibid.*; *The Tribune*, 11,12,14,15,18 August 1935.
23. *The Tribune,* 14th August 1935.
24. *National Call*, 15th August 1935.
25. *Ibid.*, 20th August 1935; *Hindustan Times*, 21st August 1935.
26. *The Tribune*, 26th August 1935.
27. *Hindustan Times,* 10 & 11 September 1935.
28. *Ibid,* 24 August 1935.
29. *Civil and Military Gazette,* 9 October 1935.

## Appendix (Pages 126-130)

### List of persons who were killed in firing in Singhani on 8 August 1935 and those who died in detention

| Sr. No. | Name | Parent / W/o, etc. | Resident of | Caste/ Occupation | Participated In | Died | Remarks |
|---|---|---|---|---|---|---|---|
| 1. | Amar Chand | Udmi Ram | village Singhani | Jat (Sheoran), cultivator | attended the kisan meeting at Singhani on 08.08.1935 | killed in firing on 08.08.1935 | |
| 2. | Ameelal | Sardara Ram | -do- | -do- | -do- | -do- | |
| 3. | Arjun Ram | Dharmpal | village Chahar Kalan | -do- | attended the kisan meeting at Chahar Kalan; arrested and detained in Loharu Fort | died in detention in Loharu Fort due to torture by the Jail authorities in 1937 | |
| 4. | Bhani Ram | Nemchand | village Singhani | Jat (Kadiyan), cultivator | see Amar Chand, sr. no. 1 | see Amar Chand, sr. no. 1 | |
| 5. | Bhola Ram | Bhadur | -do- | Jat (Sheoran), cultivator | -do- | -do- | |
| 6. | Chuni Lal | Sohan Lal | village Gothra | -do- | -do- | -do- | |

| Sr. No. | Name | Parent / W/o, etc. | Resident of | Caste/ Occupation | Participated In | Died | Remarks |
|---|---|---|---|---|---|---|---|
| 7. | Daulat Ram | Basti Ram | village Singhani | -do- | -do- | -do- | |
| 8. | Dhana Ram | Gordhan | village Gothra | Jat (Rao), cultivator | -do- | -do- | |
| 9. | Gharsi | Ramnath | village Singhani | Jat (Sheoran), cultivator | -do- | -do- | |
| 10. | Gutiram | Mohara Ram | -do- | Jat (Rao), cultivator | -do- | -do- | |
| 11. | Heera | Nanak Ram | village Gignaoo | Jat (Punia), cultivator | -do- | -do- | |
| 12. | Kumbhla *alias* Kamla | Gomma Ram | -do- | Jat (Khedar), cultivator | -do- | -do- | |
| 13. | Lalji | Kamla | village Singhani | Agarwal, piece-goods merchant | -do- | -do- | economically supported the rebel kisans. |
| 14. | Mallaha Ram | Jharu Ram | -do- | Jat (Sheoran), cultivator | -do- | -do- | |
| 15. | Mam Chand | Godha Ram | -do- | Tarkhan (carpenter) | -do- | -do- | |

| Sr. No. | Name | Parent / W/o, etc. | Resident of | Caste/ Occupation | Participated In | Died | Remarks |
|---|---|---|---|---|---|---|---|
| 16. | Noopa | Udmi Ram | -do- | Jat (Meichu), cultivator | -do- | severely injured in the firing on 8.8.1935 in Singhani and died in hospital at Bhiwani on 12 August 1935 | |
| 17. | Peeru | Jay Ram | -do- | Jat (Sheoran), cultivator | -do- | killed in firing on 8.8.1935 | |
| 18. | Puran Ram | Pema Ram | village Gignaoo | Jat (Bassera), cultivator | -do- | -do- | |
| 19. | Ram Lal | Maya Ram | village Pipli in Shekhawati Region of Jaipur State (now in Rajasthan) | Jat, cultivator | -do- | -do- | |
| 20. | Ram Nath | Basti Ram | village Singhani | Jat (Sheoran), cultivator | -do- | -do- | |

| Sr. No. | Name | Parent / W/o, etc. | Resident of | Caste/ Occupation | Participated In | Died | Remarks |
|---|---|---|---|---|---|---|---|
| 21. | Shiv Baksh | Dharma | -do- | Agarwal, piece-goods merchant | -do- | -do- | economically supported the rebel kisans. |
| 22. | Shyochand | Khubi Ram | -do- | Dhanak, shoe-maker | -do- | -do- | |
| 23. | Shyo chand *alias* Shiv chand | Ram Lal | -do- | Jat (Rao), cultivator | -do- | | |
| 24. | Shyochand | Ramrakh | village Obra | Jat (Sheoran), cultivator | see Arjun Ram, sr. no. 3 | see Arjun Ram, sr. no. 3 | |
| 25. | Sukh Ram | Parsaram | Village Sirsi | Jat (Punia), cultivator | attended the kisan meeting at Chahar Kalan in 1935 and arrested | died in Chahar Kalan police station in 1935 due to torture | |
| 26. | Sultan Singh | Nekki Ram | village Chandwas | Jat (Sheoran), cultivator | coming back from his in-laws' place with his wife and passing near by the kisan meeting at Singhani on 8.8.1935 | killed in firing on 8.8.1935 in Singhani | |

| Sr. No. | Name | Parent / W/o, etc. | Resident of | Caste/ Occupation | Participated In | Died | Remarks |
|---|---|---|---|---|---|---|---|
| 27. | Sundari Devi | w/o Jhandu Ram (Lambardar) | village Singhani | -do- | see Amar Chand, sr. no. 1 | -do- | |

Sources:- Foreign and Political, File Nos. 243-P (S), 464-P, and 674-P, 1935; *The Tribune*, 11-12, 14-15 & 18 August 1935; Sheoran, C.B. Singh, *Sheoran Bawani (Loharu) Ka Hairatangej Itihas*, Modern Publishers, Hisar (Haryana), 2008, pp.230-60.

## 12

# Western Understanding of the Jat Sikhs of Punjab : 19th Century Perspective

**Dr. K.S. Bajwa**

It is generally conceded by the modern historians of the Sikhs that thc British had started taking interest in the Sikhs and their past from the times of Warren Hastings, the first British Governor-General (1772-1785) in India.[1] But there are sufficient evidence to suggest that Lord Clive, the first Governor of East India Company in Bengal began to show concern with Sikh affairs, though at diplomatic level. For instance, in a letter addressed to Nawab Shuja-Ud-daulah on February 19, 1767, he expressed satisfaction and delight that Ahmadshah Abdali had suffered defeat from the Sikhs. In another letter written to Shah Vali Khan, Prime Minister of Abdali, he offered congratulations on the Shah's victory over the Sikhs, and thus 'freeing humanity from their tyranny.'[2] However, political ascendancy of the Sikhs in the north-western region of the Indian sub-continent necessitated for Warren Hastings to have a detailed and authentic information about the Sikhs.[3] Besides the British, three other powers, the Afghans, the Marathas and the Sikhs were in the field to contest for political hegemony in this region. In 1761, crushing defeat of the Marathas at the hands of Ahmad Shah Abdali, the Afghan king, removed the Marathas from this contest and their desire to establish *Hindu-pad-Patshahi* in Hindustan turned into a sweet dream. On the other hand, the Sikhs through hard fought battles got liberated their homeland, the land of the five rivers from the Afghans. Nonetheless, British authorities at

Fort William were closely watching the scramble for power in this region. They were hoping that the struggle between these powers would ultimately ruin their resources and they would automatically emerge stronger. But the ascendancy of the Sikhs dismayed them. Since they considered themselves as the legitimate political successor of the Mughals, therefore, rise of the Sikhs on the political scene was viewed as a great threat to British plans to be a paramount power in India. Hence, to form a definite, long term policy against the Sikhs required specific and comprehensive information about their past and present. Their past was meant to elucidate their present for sound political action in the near or distant future. This practical interest was supported and supplemented by the intellectual curiosity of the few who were interested in universal history or the history of religion. More candidly, the British imperialists were in quest for the real basis of inspiration behind startling political ascendancy of the Sikhs. As a corollary by the last quarter of 18th century onward, travellers, diplomats, administrators and scholars had written about the Sikh history and religion.[4] However, presently, I propose to analyze and understand the Jat Sikhs society during the 19th century as reflected in the European Travel Literature.

In 1830s, Alexander Burnes, a British diplomat while travelling in the Kingdom of Lahore enumerated the population of Punjab as 30,00,000 in all. Out of these about 5,00,000 were the *Khalsa.* Burnes does not make it clear what he meant by the term *Khalsa*? Does it include the whole Sikh population professing the Sikh faith or the *Singhs* of Guru Gobind Singh alone?[5] Even if, it includes the whole Sikh population, the proportion of the Sikh population does not seem to be satisfactory in the light of his own observations. For example, he observed that 'the paucity of the Sikhs was so striking in some areas that their number was confined to garrison alone which did not exceed 500 men in the city like Multan.'[6] There were very few Sikhs beyond the river Jehlum. Even to the east of Lahore, where there was a concentration of Sikh population, there proportion in the total population was not more than one third. However, they were predominantly Jats.[7]

These travellers were exceptionally interested in the Jat Sikhs. Burnes observed them as a 'robust and athletic race of sinew limbs and tall stature'. In his estimation they were the most rising people of modern India.[8] To Jacquoment they were unsophisticated but simple and honest in manners, which made them 'a good sort of people'.[9] Hugel viewed them as 'strongly built' people.[10] Masson describes them as 'frank generous, social and lively', which certainly made them fine race of men.[11]

Though, Sikhism does not exhort to adopt a particular profession for its votaries, yet the Jat Sikhs precisely due to their aptitude were exclusively a military and agricultural people.[12] Their love for horses and arms knew no bond. There was scarcely a Sikh who did not have one or more brood mares.[13] A large portion of the Jat population was serving either in the army of Maharaja Ranjit Singh or under different chiefs and they were not 'the worst clothed and worst fed.'[14] Nonetheless, they made a good soldier and were incurred to long marches and every fatigue. Their 'coolness and courage' surpassed belief.[15] The tract of *Majha* was celebrated for the bravery of its soldiers as it was for the breed of good horses.[16] Commenting upon their bravery, Victor Jacquoment observed, 'they are like hunting leopard which are taken out for hunting in an iron cage and only released when the game is insight.'[17]

Political ascendancy of the Jat Sikhs in the land of the five rivers resulting in the establishment of Sikh rule under Maharaja Ranjit Singh caused a considerable change in their habits and attitude towards other communities of Punjab. However, in Alexander Burnes' opinion, this change was not for the better. To him, 'the peculiar tenants of Sikh religion made them distinct people from the Hindus and the Muslims, but the change might affect the energies of the community adversely'. Here, Burnes had in mind the suspension of bi-annual meetings of the Khalsa brotherhood at Amritsar, where decisions were taken by general consent through the institution of *Gurmatta* about the issues of utmost importance relating to the Sikh community. He observed that so entirely had the Sikh nation altered its constitution under Maharaja Ranjit Singh that within a period of twenty years, it had passed from 'apure republic' to 'an absolute monarchy'.[18]

Change in his political sphere from 'democracy' to 'monarchy' which Burnes noted in the 1830s, did have social implication on the Jat Sikhs. For instance, to consolidate his rule, it is imperative for the ruler to enlist the support of every section of his subject. Thus, in the process of acquisition of political power and its exercise, there started a process of wooing the other communities. In this process several Hindu beliefs and practices entered the Sikh way of life implicitly or explicitly. As a corollary of this, almost every Sikh chief have had a *pandit* in his establishment. Godfrey Thomas Vigne found, for instance, Raja Suchet Singh consulting his *Pandit*, who also happened to be an astrologer, even going out for hunting. Sardar Thakur Singh Sandhanwalia, for example, was found repeating some prayer over a basin of warmed *ghee*, produced by the Brahmin, who alike mumbled something and at conclusion of the ceremony dropped into the fluid some copper coins.[19] It is significant to note that *Kashmiri Pandits* were held in such an estimation that the Sikhs thought it repugnant to take any part in their punishment. In this regards, Jacquoment observed that to 'kill a *pandit* was nearly as bad as to kill a bullock.'[20]

Many kinds of superstitions were prevalent amongst the rulers as well as the common Jat Sikhs found mention in their travelogues. For example, Maharaja Ranjit Singh sent Pandit Radha Krishan to Jwalamukhi to offer prayers for his speedy recovery from illness. A sum of rupees fifteen thousand was given to him to purchase *ghee* to be consumed by sacred flames of *Jwalaji*.[21] During one of his visit to the Maharaja, Vigne presented a bottle of water denoting it from the *Ganga Jal*; the Maharaja was much pleased and Kanwar Naunihal Singh dipped his finger into it and reverently moistered his forehead.[22] Furthermore, cow was sacred to them and its slaughter was forbidden. If any one found guilty of slaughtering the cow, was beaten up by the Sikh peasants even along with the seller of the beef. Caste prejudice amongst the Jat Sikhs too was not less strong than the Hindus. Their priests, for example, were of high castes.[23] However in an ordinary interaction with Hindus, the *banias* did not receive much courtesy.[24]

Life styles of the Jat aristocracy were not different from the life style of the Maharaja. One may find a difference of degree but certainly not of kind they went about attended by large retinue. Their apparel was gorgeous, and residences like mansion. They kept, though small *Zanana*, consumed much spirituous liquor, and listened to the *nach* girls.[25]

Their apparel consisted of *Pagri*, a Jacket and large bulky trouser terminating at the knee, the legs from the knee onward generally remained naked. The chiefs occasionally wore full trouser, which was of a latter introduction. A scarf was usually kept over the shoulders. It was usually trimmed with a coloured border. Sometimes, scarlet shawls or other showy fabrics were used for this purpose. The chiefs and wealthy people wore *angarkha* (coat), tied over the chest and reaching to the knee. Occasionally, a mantle lined with skin was put over the whole apparel. Not only the Maharaja, even his attendants used to clad splendidly and displayed a profusion of gold and jewelled ornaments. Generally, the Sikh dress was of white colour, except on the day of *Basant* when everybody wore yellow coloured garments.[26]

Dwellings of the upper classes were good enough to suit their status. Tranquility which followed the establishment of Sikh rule made the aristocracy to think of improving their places of residence. Consequently, the aristocracy built and inhabited in the houses which corresponded to 'baronial castle'. A family mansion of a chief named Jawala Singh has been described by Burnes as, 'it stood in the centre, surrounded by a village, peopled by retainers, the whole being enclosed by a mud wall and out ditch. Within the space was to be found a bazar, extensive stable which were built on a plan of great regularity.'[27] Though the houses of the Sikh chiefs were 'the best', and had at a distance an 'imposing and reputable appearance', yet they were inferior to the fortified dwellings of the Rajput chiefs of Mewar.[28] Jacquoment found their houses at Amritsar 'much inferior in design and construction to those at Benares.'[29] The peasantry of course, mostly lived in *Kachcha* houses, made of sun-dried bricks.[30] However, it was common amongst the wealthy as well as the poor to whiten their houses and cover the front with 'coarse mythological pictures'.[31]

Not much information is available in this literature about the food habits of the commoner as well as the wealthy. It may be pointed out here, that the Sikhs, like the Hindus, were not-restricted to certain foods and drinks, but they were forbidden to eat beef. Common food items were however, *chapattis* made of wheat flour, varieties of boiled rice, pulses, meat, chicken, eggs, milk, butter, *ghee*, fruits, *sarbats* and varieties of other dishes adorned the dinning tables of the upper classes.[32] In fact, sumptuous meals were taken by the aristocracy.[33] Nonetheless, 'the thumb and fingers, used while eating, appeared to Burnes' poor substitute for knife and fork'.[34]

Main intoxicants in vogue were : opium, *bhang* and liquor. Opium was largely consumed by the rich section of the society particularly the aristocracy. A narcotic preparation by the juice of hemp or infusion of poppy heads and hemp was mostly used by the poor. In spite of the prohibition of liquor in Sikhism, the Jat Sikhs used it indiscriminately. The Maharaja himself was very fond of liquor and the Sikh aristocracy and peasantry made no exception. No social gathering, celebration of an event or a festival could pass without the introduction of a bout.[35] In this regard, Vigne observed that, 'the Orientals have no idea of drinking unless they can drink too much'.[36]

There is enough evidence in this literature to mark the position of Jat Sikh women which happened to be better than that of the women amongst the Muslim and Hindu society. For instance, the Sikh women were not strictly confined to their houses as it was the case with Muslim and Hindu ladies.[37] However, polyandry was prevalent among the Jat Sikhs of Punjab also. For example, Masson tells us that it was common among the Sikhs to have a wife shared between real brothers. He further exhorted, that this rude practice was not imputable to them as Sikhs, for 'they were the remains of the ancient and rude state of society'.[38] It may be noted that such a wife in accordance with Masson was considered to be an impure creature for her husband. She was hardly considered as being of the same species with himself. He further asserts that should the Sikhs continue to grow as an independent nation, it might be hoped that increased civilization would gradually remove these traces of barbarism. Ultimately, the Jat Sikhs would grew as enlightened human beings.[39] While dealing with the women, the western writers were particularly conscious about the evil practice of *sati* that was not approved by Sikhism. Notwithstanding this, *sati* was, however, prevalent in the Punjab in the royalty and nobility.[40]

Festivals had an important role in the emotional life of the Jat Sikhs as it was the case with other communities of Punjab. *Dussehra, Diwali, Lohri, Basant, Holi* etc. were celebrated with great fervors. The Maharaja himself used to celebrate these festivals with great enthusiasm.[41] He used to hold annual review of his forces on that day.[42] Both *Diwali* and *Lohri* were celebrated with greater splendor. On the occasion of *Diwali Harmander Sahib* (Golden Temple) was lighted with lamps.[43]

Besides celebration of festivals, they were very fond of watching and listening to cers. Dancing was a popular means of recreation. Amongst the royalty and nobility, irrespective of their means, it was the general practice to have the dancing girls. Reception of a guest to the court was considered improper without performing dance before him/her. For this purpose, the Maharaja have had the 'rarest beauties in his court'.[44] As profession, dance was in vogue in the Punjab. But it was looked down upon as the dancers were called *Kanjri* by the rustic. However, polite person preferred to call them as *nachwali*.[45]

Gossip was another amusement. Baron Charles Hugel has underlined the strong passion of Jats to listen gossip. He found much truth in the proverb that 'you can take away the wife and children of a Sikh while he is listening to the adventures of Rustam and Sohrab and he would not miss them'.[46]

Idea of educating their children was not relished by the peasants. For instance, while travelling in the *Rachna Doab,* when Burnes suggested to an agriculturist to send his boy to school, he replied that education was useless to a cultivator of the soil.[47] With few exceptions, this notion did prevail in the higher starta of the Jat Sikh society too.[48]

In retrospect, study of the evidence on Jat Sikh society in the Punjab does not reflect serious concern of the travellers. No doubt the Sikhs are discussed in detail, but the description lacks depth. For instance, only those aspects have been discussed which come under direct observation like: dress, dwellings festivals, amusements etc. They fail to understand the Sikh society and its social dynamism; social order and social institutions. Above all forces of change too have not been taken up adequately. Furthermore, in the name of the Sikh society, only the aristocracy is discussed. However, the information provided in this literature on the early 19th century Sikh society is not without significance. For example, these travellers have noted the change which political ascendancy had brought about in the Sikh way of life. It is significant to note that, being brought up in a particular socio-cultural set up, they observed those social institutions and practices which appeared to them peculiar and which were generally over looked by the native chroniclers.

## References

1. Fauja Singh (ed.) : *Historians and Historiography of the Sikhs,* Oriental, New Delhi (1978), pp. 1-2.
2. C.P.C. II, pp. 52, 145, 327, Quoted in *History of the Sikhs* by H.R. Gupta, Vol. III, pp. 341-42.
3. For instance, James Browne was nominated as British Agent and the Minister at the Court of Delhi on August 20, 1782. His object was to organize a confederacy against the threatening attitude of the Sikhs. Before he left Calcutta for Delhi, Warren Hastings instructed him, "You must study the character, connection, influence and power of the several competitors for the possession of the King's favour or the exercise of his authority, the state, views and relations of the independent chiefs and states whose territory borders on his. However, this period mark the beginning of regular Anglo-Sikh relations. Also this is the period when a first regular treatise on the Sikhs; *History of the Origin and Progress of the Sikhs,* was written by James Browne which subsequently became the very basis of Westem Historical Writings on the Sikhs: C.R.C. William, 'The Sikhs in the upper Doab', *Calcutta Review,* LXI, 1875, p. 40; Hari Ram Gupta, *History of the Sikhs,* Munshiram Manoharlal, New Delhi 1980, Vol. III, pp. 171-215; Ganda Singh (ed.) *Early European Accounts of the Sikhs,* Indian Studies Past and Present, Calcutta, 1962, pp. 1-7. It may be pertinent to note here that two

months before the appointment of Brown, Hastings had deputed George Forster to undertake a journey from Bengal to England and instructed him to gather information about the Sikhs. In his travelogue, Forster furnished an account of the Sikhs. Yet in another attempt, he employed Sayyid Gulam Hussain, a resident of Bareilly to write a history of India with special reference to the Sikhs. He too completed his work in 1784, entitled *Siyar-ul Mutakhrin*: H.R. Gupta, *Ibid,* pp. 343-44.

4. J.S. Grewal : 'The Present State of Sikh Studies', Miscellanous Articles, GNDU, Amritsar (1974), pp. 152-162; Darshan Singh, *Western Perspective on the Sikh Religion,* Sehgal Publishers, New Delhi, pp. 8-9; see also Darshan Singh (ed.) *Western Image of the Sikh Religion : A source Book,* National Book Organization, New Delhi (1999), pp. x-xii.
5. Alexander Burnes : *Travels into Bokhara containing the narrative of Voyage on the Indus from the sea to Lahore,* 3 vols., Oxford University Press, Karachi (1973) (first 1834), Vol.II, p. 286 (hereafter as *Travels*); Since, the system of taking regular census did not exist, therefore no exact figure of population can be given. European travellers and visitors at different times made their own estimates. In 1830s Steninbach enumerated the population of Punjab under Ranjit Singh as 12 lakhs. Another estimate given by a cavalry officer and Von Orlich of Ranjit Singh's Kingdom including Punjab, Jammu and Kashmir was at five millions. Henry Lawrence about the time of Ranjit Singh's death put the Punjab population at 15 lakh. We may venture to conjecture that the total population of the Punjab at the beginning of Ranjit Singh's rule should be taken at about 15 lakhs, and the time of his death at 30 lakhs.
6. *Ibid.,* III, pp. 110-11, 134.
7. *Ibid.,* I, pp. 3-4; III, p. 299.
8. *Ibid.,* I, pp. 45, 76; II, pp. 285-86; III, pp. 101, 140.
9. Victor Jacquoment : Letters from India, Describing a *Journey in the British Dominion of India, Tibet, Lahore and Cashmere During the years 1828, 1829, 1830 and 1831 undertaken by the order of the French Government,* Edward Churton, 2 Vol. London (1834), Vol. I, pp. 391-401. (hereafter *letters*)
10. Baron Charles Hugel : *Travels in Cashmere and the Punjab, containing a particular Account of the character and Government of the Sikhs* (tr. ed. T.B. Jarvis), Language Department Punjab, Patiala

(1970) (reprint-first 1845), p. 331; (hereafter as *Travels*).

11. Charles Masson : *Narrative of various Journeys in Baluchistan, Afghanistan and the Punjab, including a Residence in those countries from 1826 to 1838,* 3 Vols., Oxford Karachi (1974) (reprint-first 1842), Vol. I, pp. 433-34, (hereafter *Journeys*).
12. Masson : *Ibid.*, I, p. 434; *Burnes, Ibid.*, II, p. 285; III, p. 143.
13. Masson : *Op. cit.*
14. Victor Jacquoment and Solty koff, A. : *The Punjab : A Hundred years Ago* (ed. Garrett, H.L.O., Punjab Government Record office, Monograph No. 18, Lahore, 1935), Language Department Punjab, Patiala (1971), p. 67 (hereafter *Journal*).
15. Burnes: *Ibid.,* II, p. 288, III, pp. 138-39.
16. *Ibid.,* I, p. 10.
17. Jacquoment : *Journal*, p. 53.
18. Burnes : *Ibid.,*III, pp. 295-96.
19. G.T. Vigne : *Travels in Kashmir, Ladakh, Iskardo, the countries Adjoining the mountain course of the Indus and the Himalayas, North of the Punjab,* 2 Vols, Henny Colbum, London (1842) (hereafter *Travels*), I, pp.191-92; Masson, *Ibid.,* I, pp. 424, 450-51.
20. Jacquoment : *Journal,* pp. 81-82.
21. *Ibid.,* II, p. 153.
22. Vigne : *Op. cit.,* I, p. 135.
23. Jacquoment : *Op. cit.,* p. 121.
24. Masson : *Op. cit.,* I, pp. 436, 474.
25. Burnes : *Op. cit.,* I, pp. 13-14; III, pp. 101, 146; Jacquoment: *letters*, I, pp. 393-94, 396, 401; II, pp. 71-72, 163; *Journal* p. 34; Vigne, II, pp. 102-03; Hugel: *Op. cit.,* pp. 115, 191.
26. Jacquoment : *Journal*, pp. 25, 40; Masson: *Op. cit.,* I, pp. 433-34, 443; Hugel: *Op. cit.,* p. 380; Burnes: *Op. cit.,* I, p. 61; III, pp. 102, 136; Vigne, *Op. cit.,* II p. 140.
27. Burnes : *Ibid.,* I, pp. 13,14; Jacquoment : *Letters*, II, p. 16; *Journal*, pp. 26,28, 57-58; Vigne : *Op. cit.,* I, pp. 220, 236-37, 246; II, pp. 187-88; Hugel : *Op. cit.,* p. 207.
28. Burnes : *Ibid.,* I, p.14.
29. Jacquoment : *Journal*, p. 26.

30. Vigne : *Op. cit.,* I, pp. 174-75, 205; II, p. 189; William Moorcroft and Treback, G. : *Travels in the Himalayan Provinces and the Punjab, in Ladak and Kashmir, in Peshawar, Kabul and Kunduz and Bokhara from 1819 to 1825,* Language Department Punjab, Patiala (1970), (reprint-first printed 1837); p. 409 (hereafter *Travels*).

31. Jacquoment : *Journal*, pp. 26, 57-58.

32. Burnes : *Ibid.,* III, pp. 134, 166; Vigne : *Ibid.,* I, pp. 72, 81.

33. Jacquoment ; *Letters*, I, pp. 394-95; Hugel : *Ibid.,* p. 283.

34. Burnes : *Ibid.,* III, p. 166.

35. Moorcroft : *Op. cit.,* pp. 53, 108-09; Jacquoment : *Journal,* p. 9, Hugel : *Op. cit.,* p. 131; Burnes : *Ibid.,* I, pp. 27-28.

36. Vigne : *Ibid.,* II, p. 102.

37. Burnes : *Ibid.,* I, 62; III, pp. 82, 85, 146.

38. Masson : *Ibid.,* I, p. 435; Jacquoment : *letters,* II, pp. 91, 98; *Journal,* p. 73.

39. Masson : *Ibid.,* I, p. 436.

40. Vigne : *Ibid.,* I, pp. 83-84, 86; II, p. 151; Jacquoment : *Journal*, pp. 56, 207.

41. Hugel : *Ibid.,* pp. 283, 310-11, 338-340, Masson : *Ibid.,* I pp. 445-46; Jacquemont : *Letters,* I, p. 329; II, pp. 198, 182-83; Vigne : *Ibid.,* I, p. 43; II, p. 94; Burnes : *Ibid.,* pp. 26-27.

42. Masson : *Ibid.,* I, pp. 445-46; Jacquoment : *Letters,* I, p. 329.

43. Jacquoment : *Ibid.,* II, pp. 182-83, 198; Hugel : *Ibid.,* p. 283.

44. Hugel : *Ibid.,* p. 310; Jacquoment : *Ibid.,* I, p. 391; II, pp. 16, 55-56, 65-66; *Journal,* pp. 44-45.

45. Hugel : *Ibid.,* p. 146.

46. Hugel : *Ibid.,* pp. 145-46, 339.

47. Burnes : *Ibid.,* I, p. 44.

48. Hugel : *Ibid.,* pp. 121, 281; Burnes : *Ibid.,* I, p. 44; III, pp. 140-41.

## 13

# The Jats of the Punjab: A Demographic Study of the Colonial Period

*Manveer Kaur*

Jat is the dominant caste of most of the northern India. They are believed to be the descendants of Scythians whose kingdom's capital was Scythia, in the present Ukraine. However there are conflicting views about the race of the Jats. According to the British the Jats were lowly or Indo-Scythians and not Aryans. James Tod, Alexander Cunningham and H.M. Elliot maintained that they were of 'Indo-Scthian' stock. Tod classes the Jats as one of the great Rajput tribes. Cunningham identifies them with the 'Zanthii' of Strabo and the 'Jatii' of Pliny and Ptolemy and holds that they belong to a later wave of immigrants from the north-west of Scythian race and others relate them with the Aryans.[1] They entered Punjab from their home on the Oxus very shortly after the Meds or Mands (Indo-Scythian), who had settled in the region a century before Christ. The Jats had occupied Indus Valley as far down as Sindh. Different historical sources show the presence of Jats in Punjab and Sindh. Hiuen Tsang noted their presence in Sindh during the 7th century, he recognised them as pastoral people but did not named them as 'Jats'. In the *Chachmama,* (the celebrated account of the Arab conquest of Sindh) they were identified as Jats during the 8th century.[2] The Jats of Sindh had been a large primitive community. They were pastoral people with an egalitarian or semi-egalitarian social structure. They had firmly established in the Punjab during the beginning of the 11th century A.D., which has been proved from the various sources like; *Zainul*

*Akhbar, Tarikh-i-Baihaqi* and *Alberuni's India.* During the 16th century *Ain-i-Akbari* is the most important source for the presence of Jats in Punjab. The population of Jats showed a great expansion from the 11th to 16th centuries. Their economic position had also transformed from pastoralism to agriculture.[3]

According to Denzil Ibbetson the Jat is in every respect the most important of the Punjab peoples. Ethnologically, he is the peculiar and most prominent product of the plains of the five rivers. Politically, he ruled the Punjab till the Khalsa yielded to British Raj. Economically and administratively, he is the husbandman, the peasant, the revenue payer of the province. They spread all over the Punjab but especially numerous in the central Sikh districts and states, in the south eastern districts and in the south west parts. Beyond the Punjab, Jats were chiefly found in Sindh where they formed mass of the population, in Bikaner, Jaisalmer and Marwar where they equal in numbers all the Rajput races put together and along the upper valleys of the Ganges and Jamuna from Bareilly, Farukhabad and Gwalior upwards.[4] In 1881 there were 5.69 million Jats in India that increased to 8 million in 1931.[5]

The present paper studies the position of Jats in the Punjab during the colonial period from 1881 to 1931. It covers the province of Punjab consisted of British territory and the native states.[6] There were more than thirty princely states linked with Punjab. This paper intends to study the demographic picture of the Jats in the region mainly on the basis of Census information. The first section identifies the Jats in terms of number and their distribution in the different parts of the province and religious affiliations. It also highlights the changes in these aspects over this period. The second section intends to highlights the sex ratio, literacy rates and occupations among the Jats at that time. The third section presents an overview of the position of Jats in Punjab.

## I

Jats prevailed among the three main religious groups of Sikhs, Hindus and Muslims. There were a number of tribes among the Jats that were interrelated among these religious groups. The relationship of the Jats with the other groups was defined through their *gotra* or clan which is an exogamous kin-group. The Jats of the north and south west parts were looked upon as inferior race where they were nomadic tribes. Bhatti, Bhangu, Bhanhu, Bhutta, Chhina, Chhadhar, Hinjra, Joya, Langah, Punwar, Sipra, Sumra, Sial, Tahim, Tarar and Wattu inhabited southwest districts and princely state of Bahawalpur.[7] Aujla, Bajwa, Chatta, Deo, Dhotar, Ghuman, Goraya, Kahlon, Sarai, Sahi and Varaich were the Jat tribes found in almost all central districts of Amritsar, Gurdaspur, Sialkot, Lahore, Gujranwala, Gujarat and northwest districts of Rawalpindi, Jhelum and Shahpur. Chimma, Ghuman and Varaich also found in Kapurthala, Malerkotla and Phulkian states. Jats of the Sikh tracts were the typical Jats of the Punjab, including Aulakh, Bal, Bhullar, Brar, Buta, Bains, Chahil, Dhariwal, Dhillon, Dhindsa, Gills, Grewal, Her, Kang, Mann, Mahal, Odi, Pannun, Randhawa, Sandhu, Sidhu and Sohal. Though they spread over all districts but largely concentrated in central districts, Phulkian states, Kapurthala, Malerkotla, Nabha and Faridkot. The Ahlawat, Beniwal, Dalal, Deswal, Dhankar, Dagar, Gulia, Jakhar, Nain, Phogaat, Pawania, Rathi and Sangwan Jats inhabited the southeast districts of Delhi, Gurgaon, Karnal, Hisar and Rohtak.

The distribution of the Jats in the province had been changing during the period of study. The Jats constituted eighteen per cent of the total population of the province in 1868.[8] Among Hindus and Sikhs, Jats constituted about twenty six per cent and among the Muslim population, they were fourteen per cent. Hindu and Sikh Jats were concentrated in the central and southeast Punjab as these districts had most of the Hindu and Sikh population. About seventy four per cent of the Hindu and Sikh Jats inhabited Amritsar, Jalandhar, Ludhiana, Firozpur, Hoshiarpur, Hisar, Rohtak, Ambala and Delhi. In the northwest and southwest districts the number of Hindu and Sikh Jats was below one per cent. The Muslim Jats were concentrated in the north and southwest districts of the Punjab. About sixty per cent of the Muslim Jats lived in Shahpur, Dera Ismail Khan, Muzaffargarh, Gujranwala and Sialkot. The districts of Amritsar, Lahore, Rawalpindi and Jhelum contained about twenty one per cent of the population of Muslim Jats.

In 1881 there were 19 per cent Jats among the people of Punjab.[9] There were Jats among the followers of all major religions of the province. About 46 per cent of the Jats were Muslims, 33 per cent of them were Hindus and 21 per cent of all the Jats were Sikhs. The Jat population was spread over the whole province. Forty six per cent of them inhabited in the central districts, twenty nine per cent in the south east, nineteen per cent in the south western districts and only six per cent in the north west Punjab. Their religious composition followed the distribution pattern of their respective religion. The Jats formed around 65 per cent of the total Sikh population. Though they spread all over the province, yet most of the Sikh Jats inhabited the central Punjab, forming sixty five per cent. Around 17 per cent of the Hindus were Jats. The majority of Hindu Jats inhabited the southeast Punjab, where 62 per cent of them lived. Around 37 per cent of the Hindu Jats inhabited central Punjab. The Jats constituted around 16 per cent of the total Muslim population of the Punjab. The majority of Muslim Jats inhabited the north-west and south-western districts of the Punjab. The central Punjab also contained around 43 per cent of their population.[10]

In the next decennial year Jats were nineteen per cent. Twenty five per cent of them belonged to Sikhs, thirty per cent to Hindus and forty five to Muslims. As usual around forty six per cent of them inhabited central parts, twenty eight per cent in south-east, eighteen per cent in south-west and only eight per cent in north-west parts. In 1901 the Jats constituted almost fifty seven per cent of the Sikhs, about seventeen per cent of the Hindus and thirteen per cent of the Muslims. In 1911 one fifth of the population of the province were Jats.[11] In the British Punjab half of the Jats were Muslims, twenty eight per cent of them were Sikhs and twenty one per cent were Hindus. Their proportion had declined to forty one per cent in the central parts, about twenty five per cent in south-east and it had increased in south-west to twenty five per cent and nine per cent in north west parts. The Jats were prominent among the Sikhs among whom they formed almost fifty four per cent, nineteen per cent among the Muslims and thirteen per cent among the Hindus.

In 1921 they were one per cent more than in 1911 being twenty one per cent.[12] Forty seven per cent of the Jats were Muslims, thirty three per cent were Sikhs and only nineteen per cent were Hindus. Forty one per cent of them lived in central Punjab, about twenty four per cent in south-east, twenty seven per cent in south-west and little over eight per cent in the north-west parts of the province. Almost fifty six per cent of the Sikhs belonged to Jats, twenty per cent of the Muslims were Jats and about thirteen per cent of the Hindus were Jats. In 1931 the population of Punjab had about twenty one per cent Jats.[13] Forty two per cent of the Jats inhabited in central Punjab, twenty seven per cent in south-west, twenty two per cent in south-east and only nine per cent in north-west areas. In 1931 Jat population comprised of thirty five percent Sikhs, sixteen per cent Hindus and forty eight per cent Muslims. If we see their proportion among different religious groups, half of the Sikhs of Punjab were Jats, over one tenth of the Hindus and about one fifth of the Muslims were Jats.

The proportion of the Jats had also changed during this pcriod in the princely states of Punjab. They ranged between one fifth and one fourth of the total population in these states. In each of the Census of 1881, 1891 and 1901 Jats formed about twenty three per cent in the native states.[14] It fell to little over twenty one per cent in 1911, rose to twenty four per cent in 1921 and twenty fivc per cent in 1931. More than half of the Jats concentrated in Phulkian states especially in Patiala. About one fifth of them lived in Bahawalpur. The proportion of Jats in Patiala state reflected a decline from 45 per cent in 1911 to about 38 per cent in 1931. They increased from 21 per cent to 33 per cent in Bahawalpur. Their strength was almost same in Jind, Nabha, Faridkot and Kapurthala, forming four to ten per cent during this period. Their proportion was very low in Shimla hill states, Mandi, Suket, Chamba, Nahan, Pataudi, Kalsia, Loharu and Dujana. In 1881 they comprised of forty six per cent Sikhs, thirty seven per cent Hindus and seventeen per cent Muslims. In 1891 there were more Hindu Jats forming forty six per cent, thirty four per cent Sikhs and twenty per cent Muslims. In 1901 there were forty one per cent Sikhs, thirty seven per cent Hindus and twenty one per cent Muslims among the Jats. In 1911 more than half of the Jats belonged to Sikhs, twenty four per cent to Muslims and twenty two per cent to Hindus. In 1921 there were fifty one per cent Sikhs, twenty seven per cent Muslims and twenty one per cent Hindus among the Jats. In 1931 the Sikh Jats were forty nine per cent, Muslims were thirty three per cent and Hindus were eighteen per cent.

Jats of British Punjab had majority of Muslim Jats whereas Jats of native states had majority of Sikh Jats. Thus the population and distribution of Jats varied in the province. They represent a considerable growth of forty four per cent during 1881-1931. They had recorded an increase of almost fifty per cent in the British territory and of forty per cent in the princely states. However, the growth rate was not uniform over these decades. The proportion of increase was 6.5 per cent in 1891, 8.5 per cent in 1901, about 14 per cent in 1911, 10 per cent in 1921 and 11 per cent in 1931. The growth rate had increased in 1901 and 1911 while it had fallen in 1921 and 1931. There was also variation in the proportion of increase among the Jats of religious groups. The Sikh and Muslim Jats had increased considerably during fifty years, with ninety per cent each and Hindu Jats reflected a decline of thirty one per cent. The Hindu Jats represent a growth only in 1891 when they rose by sixteen per cent. They declined by forty per cent in the next two decades followed by minor increase in 1921 and again decline by five per cent in 1931. The Sikh Jats represented a continuous increase in each decade except a minor decline in 1891. They rose by twenty four per cent in 1901, by sixteen per cent in 1911, by thirteen per cent in 1921 and by seventeen per cent in 1931. The proportion of increase among Muslim Jats ranged between three to sixteen per cent from 1891 to 1931. However, the proportion of Sikh Jats had increased but their proportion had declined among the Sikh population of the province. The strength of Jats had fallen down from 65 per cent to 50 per cent in 1931 amongst the Sikhs of British Punjab. The proportion of Jats among the Hindus had also declined from 16 to 12 per cent. They increased among Muslim population from 16 to 20 per cent. The distribution in the region had also changed as the Jats had declined in the south eastern and central parts after 1901. They showed an increase of about seven per cent in the south western parts and of one per cent after 1901.

## II

It is significant to know about the literacy level and sex ratio among the Jats. The population of Jats remained illiterate during the colonial period as was the case of the whole province. In 1911 only two per cent of the Jats were literate that had increased to three per cent in 1921. About thirteen per cent of the literate Jats know English in 1931. The literacy rate among Jat male was 5.5 per cent and it was less than one per cent among the females. The married male numbered 365 per 1,000 males in 1911 that had increased to 371 in 1931. This number for females had decreased from 485 to 467 per 1,000 females. The number of widow male was 85 and of widow females were 137. Unmarried males were 547 and females were 419.

The Jats had lower sex ratio among the people of Punjab. The sex ratio was 799 females per 1,000 males in 1881, 805 in 1901, 764 in 1911, 781 in 1921 and 802 in 1931. The Sikh Jats had lowest sex ratio among the Jats of other religious groups. The Sikh Jats had recorded less than 760 females per 1,000 males in each decade. The Hindus had 785 to 813 females per 1,000 males. The Muslims had higher sex ratio than the Hindus and Sikhs. Their sex ratio ranged between 808 and 852 during this period. Most of the Jat clans belonged to all religions like Bal, Bhangu, Deo, Dhotar, Goraia, Mahil, Sahota, Sarai and Sumra had less than 800 females per 1,000 males.[15] There were a large number of Hindu and Sikh Jat clans having lower sex ratio namely Aulakh, Baidwan, Bajwa, Bhullar, Bhuttar, Chattha, Chima, Mangat, Dhariwal, Dhillon, Grewal, Her, Hinjra, Kahlon, Kang, Mann, Nain, Pannun, Pawania, Randhawa, Sahi, Sipra, Sohal, Varaich and Virk. The only Hindu Jat clans of Atwal, Bains, Bainiwal, Deswal, Chahal, Gill, Gulia, Sahrawat, Sarah and Sidhu had also lower sex ratio. The clans with more than 800 females per 1,000 males were the Jat Sikhs of Atwal, Dhindsa, Gill, Ghumman and Muslim clans of Bains, Bainiwal, Chahal, Sahi, Sidhu, Srah.

The Jats were involved in different kinds of occupations for their livelihood. The work participation rate of Jats had almost same from 1911 to 1931 being thirty seven per cent of the total Jats.[16] Hindu Jats had larger workers formed 42 per cent in 1911,

37 per cent in 1921 and 50 per cent in 1931. The Sikhs had 38 per cent in 1911, 36 per cent in 1921 and 37 per cent in 1931. Muslim Jats had 34 per cent in 1911, 32 per cent in 1921 and 33 per cent in 1931. The workers had declined in 1921 among all these Jats. In 1931 the workers had increased largely among Hindu Jats. Their connection with agriculture has become so close that the word 'Jat' can mean an agriculturist and they represent as typical peasant of Punjab.[17] Majority of Jat workers about eighty eight per cent engaged in agriculture. Thus only little over one tenth were non-agriculturists. A small proportion of them involved in industries, trade, transport, domestic and labour works. The number of Jats in industries and transport had declined. In 1911, 43,000 Jats involved in industrial vocations but in 1931 their number went down to 32,000. Similarly, in transport their number had declined from 29,000 in 1911 to 24,000 in 1931. In trade they had increased from 9,000 in 1911 to 13,700 in 1931. The number of Jats in administrative services was not varied so far as in 1911 they numbered 22,200 in 1911 and 22,900 in 1931. In 1931, 8,500 Jats served in army and 5,800 in police. The number of Sikhs was the largest in army; numbered 6,660. The lawyers, doctors and teachers had increased largely from 1,780 to 6,600. Their number as cashier, clerks and contractors was 800 in 1911 and 1,400 in 1931. It is noteworthy that the Jats were important not only because of their numerical strength but also the fact that the majority of the former *jagirdars* of the kingdom of Lahore and their descendants were Jats. They were looked upon as the natural leader of the community. The British administrators extended patronage to them especially after 1857-58, in terms of honorary positions, titles, employment as officers, in the civil administration and the army, nomination to local bodies and the legislative councils.[18]

## III

Jats were prominent among all castes in the society of Punjab. Jat gives importance to his tribal name or *gotra* more than religion. He tenaciously clings to his tribal name as a proud heritage. Jat is a Jat after all, whether he is a Hindu, Sikh or Muslim.[19] They found all over India especially in the northern India. In the north

India they concentrated in the province of Punjab. About one fifth of the people of British Punjab and little more than it in the native states were Jats during the period of study. Majority of the Jats concentrated in the central plains followed by the south east parts, north and south west parts. Jats of different religions followed the distribution pattern of their respective religion. Central Punjab contained Jats belonging to all major religions. These Jats were more superior both as politically and economically of all the Jats. The population of Muslim Jats in northwest and southwest Punjab and the population of Hindu Jats in the southeast Punjab were significant. Jats of the British Punjab had majority of Muslim Jats whereas Jats of native states had majority of Sikh Jats. Thus, the population and distribution of Jats varied in the province. Of the religious groups majority of the Sikhs belonged to Jat tribes. They were smaller in number amongst the Hindus and Muslims. They reflected a considerable growth during the colonial period. Jats formed the backbone of agriculture in the region. They were a dominant group among the agriculturists' castes of Punjab like Pathans, Bilochs, Rajputs and a number of other tribes. They also followed other occupations in industries, trade, transport, administrative and professional services. The literacy and the female sex ratio remained low among the Jats.

## References

1. Denzil lbbetson : *Report on the Census of Punjab,* Vol. I. Calcutta: Government Press (1883), p. 220. See also, Datta, Nonica : *Forming an Identity: A Social History of the Jats,* New Delhi: Oxford University Press, p. 7 (l999).
2. Irfan Habib : 'Jatts of Punjab And Sind' in Harbans Singh (ed.), *Essays in Honour of Dr. Ganda Singh,* Patiala : Punjabi University, p. 94 (1976).
3. *Ibid.,* pp. 95-6.
4. Denzil Ibbetson : *Report on the Census of Punjab,* Vol. I., pp. 221-22.
5. *A Compendium of the Castes and Tribes found in India,* Bombay: Education Society's Press.
6. For the present purpose British Punjab has been divided into four

broad areas–south-east and north-east; central; north-west and south-west. There were 32 districts in British Punjab from 1868 to 1891 and the number had decreased to 29 from 1901 to 1931 due to administrative changes. The southeast Punjab consisted of districts of Gurgaon, Karnal, Hisar, Rohtak, Sirsa, Ambala, Firozpur, Shimla and Kangra. The central districts consisted of Jalandhar, Hoshiarpur, Ludhiana, Amritsar, Gurdaspur, Sialkot, Gujranwala, Gujrat, Lahore and Sheikhupura. The northwest districts consisted of Bannu, Peshawar, Hazara and Kohat (till 1891), Rawalpindi, Jhelum, Shahpur, Attock and Mianwali. The southwest areas consisted of the districts of Lyallpur, Multan, Montgomery, Muzaffargarh, Dera Ghazi Khan, Dera Ismail Khan and Jhang.

7. *Census Punjab 1881,* Vol. I, Abstract No. 73 to 76, pp. 225-235.
8. *Census Punjab 1868,* General Statement No, III.
9. *Census Punjab 1881,* Table No, VII A.
10. Manveer Kaur : *Census As a Social Document: Punjabi Society in the Census of 1868 and 1881*, Unpublished M. Phil Thesis, Chandigarh, Punjab University, 2010, pp. 85-6.
11. *Census Punjab 1911*, Table XIII.
12. *Census Punjab 1921*, Table XIII.
13. *Census Punjab 1931*, Table XIII.
14. *Census Punjab 1881 to 1931.*
15. *Report on the Census of Punjab of 1911.*
16. *Census of 1911, 1921 and 1931*, Tables on Occupations of Selected Castes, Tribes and Races.
17. Irfan Habib : 'Jatts of Punjab And Sind' in Harbans Singh (ed.), *Essays in Honour of Dr Ganda Singh,* p. 97.
18. Joginder Singh : 'The Sikh Community: Demography and Occupational Change, 1881-1931' in Indu Banga : *Five Punjabi Centuries : Polity, Economy, Society, and Culture, c.1500-1900,* New Delhi: Manohar, p. 475 (2000).
19. K.R. Qanungo : *History of Jats : Contribution to the History of Northern India*, Delhi, Sunita Publication (1987), p. 1.

# 14

# Promotion of Unopposed Elections in Haryana Panchayats

*Dr. R.K. Kundu*
*Dr. S. L. Kundu*

Elections constitute an indispensable political activity and indicate the general will of the common masses as well as provide legitimacy to the government. They are the important mechanism for checking the use of governmental arbitrary power. Election is a process through which the political opinion of the people is shaped. Through elections a modern state creates amongst its citizens a sense of participation in public affairs, and in making the people aware of their rights. So, election is an essential for a vibrant democracy. Panchayats considered as mini republics. The success, growth and even survival of the sovereign, secular and socialist India depends upon the elected panchayats. These institutions of self-government are assigned powers and responsibilities for executing twin mission of economic development and social justice.

In pursuance of the 73rd Constitutional amendment, the Haryana Government enacted the Haryana Panchayati Raj Act, 1994. The Sarpanch and panchs are directly elected by gram sabha from amongst its voters by secret ballot. The Panchayati Raj Rules state that there shall be six panchs for a gram panchayat having population up to five hundred and for every additional five hundred populations or fraction thereof one extra seat shall be provided subject to a maximum of twenty seats. If a fraction forms part of the number of a seat or the office computed the number of seats or offices shall be increased to the next higher number in case the fraction consists of half or more of a seat or office and the fraction shall be ignored in case it consists of less than half of a seat or the office.[1]

Haryana Panchayati Raj (Election) Rules, 1994 section 37 depicts that if one candidate (whose nomination paper is found valid) remains after the date and time fixed for withdrawal of nomination paper then the duty of the Returning Officer (Panchayat) is to declare the candidate elected and inform the State Election Commissioner through District Election Officer (Panchayat).[2]

Unopposed election at the grassroot level is the most important aspect for democratic organizations and promotional schemes for encouraging this trend is the reflection of positivism in the present political scenario. Haryana Chief Minister Ch. Bhupinder Singh Hooda has emphasized on the promotion of unopposed elections in panchayats by providing special grant to these bodies. Under the provisions of above said grant, the village panchayats are classified population-wise into three categories The classified first, second and third categories are comprising upto 1,500 population villages, above 1,500 to 4,000 population and above 4,000 population villages respectively. In the first, second and third categories where the whole panchayat including sarpanch is elected unopposed the provisions of the grant are Rs. One lakh, two lakh and three lakh respectively. If only panchs are elected unopposed from first, second and third categories the provided amount is Rs. 75,000, 1.5 lakh and 2.5 lakh respectively. When only a sarpanch of a village is elected unopposed then the provisions of the grant are Rs. 50,000, one lakh and 1.5 lakh for respective category.[3] This is great step of Haryana Government regarding strengthening the democracy in the State as well as become a torch bearer for Indian democratic practices.

Originally this scheme of promotion of unopposed elections through providing incentives was launched in 1991 and closed in 2000 panchayat elections. At that time provision of incentives was Rs. 25,000/-, Rs. 15,000/- and Rs. 10,000/- for whole unopposed elected panchayat including sarpanch, only unopposed panchs and only unopposed sarpanch respectively.[4] This scheme has been restarted before 2010 panchayat elections as a visionary approach of the Chief Minister.

**Haryana Panchayati Raj Election, 2010 :**

In the last panchayati raj election, 2010, total 22931 (39.02 per cent) panchs were elected unopposed out of 58765 panchs. In this regard, Panchkula district secured first position with 65.36 per cent, Ambala and Fatehabad districts hold second and third positions respectively. The district Panipat is the backward district regarding unopposed elections with 25.85 per cent. If we consider the statistical data gender-wise and category-wise then we find that total 9724 (16.55 per cent) male and 6724 (11.44 per cent) female unopposed elected panchs belong to general category, 2004 (3.41 per cent) female and 1846 (3.14 per cent) male unopposed elected panchs belong to scheduled castes and 2492 (4.24 per cent) male and 141 (0.34 per cent) female backward class panchs are elected unopposed in this election. Only 175 (2.87 per cent) out of 6083 sarpanchs and 35 (1.26 per cent) out of 2772 members of panchayat samiti are elected unopposed. Overall 62 panchayats including sarpanchs and 90 panchayats excluding sarpanchs are elected unopposed in Haryana.

Total 8860 women panchs were elected unopposed in panchayat general elections, 2010. In this regard Bhiwani district holds first position with 725 women panchs followed by Jind (595) and Ambala (581). Faridabad district lags behind with 150 women panch in this hierarchy. There are total 228 women panchs belong to general category who are elected unopposed from other than their reserved seats and Rewari district secured first position with 52 women panchs in this regard followed by Sirsa (26), Bhiwani (26) and Sonipat (18) but Karnal and Kurukshetra districts on the backward line with only 2 women panch each. In case of scheduled castes, total 60 scheduled caste women panchs are elected unopposed from scheduled caste male reserved seats and Ambala district with 12 women panch is at the first place in this regard followed by Mahindergarh (06), Sonipat (06) and Karnal (05) but four districts (Faridabad, Jhajjar, Mewat and Rohtak) have no representation in this regard. It is analysed that the total strength of the unopposed women panch who were elected from other than their reserved seats is 288. In this context Rewari district has more representation with 56 women followed by Sirsa (28), Bhiwani (27), Sonipat (24) and the Mewat district has lowest representation with only 2 women panchayat members.[5]

**Main Observations :**

The main observations regarding unopposed elections of fourth general election, 2010 are :

- Out of total 140 gram panchayats where all panchs and sarpanchs have been elected unopposed, Kaithal district has 18 such panchayats followed by Kurukshetra (17) but Jhajjar and Rohtak districts don't have any such gram panchayat means no panchayat have been elected unopposed including sarpanchs in Jhajjar and Rohtak districts.
- There are total 176 gram panchayats, where all members have been elected unopposed means without sarpanchs. Ambala district is at the top with 25 such gram panchayats followed by Yamunanagar (18) and the district Panipat has no representation in this regard.
- Total 45 gram panchayats have elected unopposed sarpanchs means where only sarpanchs elected unopposed but not all members. In this context, Ambala district is at the top with 6 gram panchayats followed by Fatehabad and Kurukshetra with 5 sarpanchs and Panchkula, Panipat, Mahendergarh, Mewat and Sonepat districts have no such unopposed elected sarpanch.
- In Haryana 6 villages boycotted 2010 panchayat elections, Jind district is at the top with 2 villages i.e. Sangatpura of Jind block and Singhwal of Narwana block followed by Bhiwani district (Bapoda village of Bhiwani block), Kaithal district (Karora village of Rajound block), Panipat district (Khukhrana of Madlauda block) and Rewari district (Ramsingh Pura village of Bawal block) each have one village in this regard.
- All the seats (reserved and unreserved) have been won by women candidates in Lalheri village of Ganaur block in Sonepat district.

- Three backward class male panchs have been elected unopposed from SC reserved seats in Gurgaon district.
- Total 16 general category male panchayat members have been elected unopposed from women reserved seats in Rewari district.

**Haryana Panchayati Raj elections, 2005 :**

In Haryana Panchayati Raj election, 2005, total 36,645 (60.8 per cent) panchs were elected unopposed. The Panchkula district was at the first place with 75 per cent and Karnal district was in the last with 44.6 per cent regarding unopposed elected panchs. In case of sarpanchs, total 473 (7.7 per cent) seats were filled through unopposed elections. Total 302 (10.7 per cent) and 2 (0.5 per cent) members of panchayat samiti and zila parishad respectively were elected unopposed.[6]

**Second PRIs General Election, 2000**

The State Election Commission issued a notification for holding the second general election to PRIs in three phases and later modified it into two phases. The dates i.e., 22 and 29 March, 2000 were fixed but again changed to 12 and 16 March, 2000 due to annual examinations of Board of School Education Haryana. Total 85,90,880 voters casted their votes at 15,998 polling stations to elect 6,035 sarpanchs and 54,764 panchs out of which 701 (12 per cent) and 30,674 (56 per cent) were elected unopposed respectively.[7] Regarding panchayat samiti, total 2426 seats were fixed for members and 426 (18 per cent) candidates were elected unopposed. In case of zila parishad, out of 314 seats only 45 (14 per cent) candidates were elected unopposed. In gram panchayats, panchayat samitis & zila parishads the representation of women was 18037 (32.99 per cent) 842 (34.65 per cent) and 108 (34.39 per cent) respectively. For the posts of sarpanchs, chairpersons of panchayat samiti and zila parishads, the representation of women was significant i.e. 2009 (33.29 per cent), 52 (45.61per cent) and 7 (36.84 per cent) respectively.[8]

**Conclusion:**

After analysis of this data, it may be concluded that this trend of unopposed elections may lead to reduce the election violence, booth capturing, election criminalization, flow of liquor, money and vote sharing unhealthy trends at the time of elections and election expenditure etc. If we consider the only case of reduction or saving the election expenditure then the legal expenditure limits are Rs. 5,000, Rs. 20,000, Rs. 50,000 and Rs. One lakh for panch, sarpanch, member panchayat samiti and zila parishad respectively. We can calculate the expenditure incurred on the elections of panchayati raj bodies according to above said provisions and find the saved amount in crores.

Unopposed elections are the reflection of matured democratic trend in Haryana local governance process. So, such special grant decision which is taken by the Haryana Government not only saves the candidate's money but also preserves the social unity, promote bhaichara culture, avoid court disputes, develop the positive thinking in the village community and reduce the administrative work also. Some suggestions may be helpful for strengthening this trend. The provisions of the grant should be extended to the individual member of these institutions because of the less possibility to elect the whole panchayat unopposed. This support should be provided to panchayat samitis, zila parishads and urban local bodies also. There should be a separate ward fund for such types of grants. Last but not least it is the result of positive mind set of the Haryana Government headed by Ch. Bhupinder Singh Hooda. Due to this, Haryana may be a role model for India as well as for world also.

## References

1. Rule 3, Haryana Panchayati Raj Election Rules 1994, vide Haryana Government Notification No. GSR 56/HA 11/94/209/94 dated August 24, 1994.
2. Section 37, Haryana Panchayati Raj (Election) Rules, 1994, *Ibid.*
3. Dainik Jagran, April 16, 2010, p. 1.
4. *Ibid.*
5. Government of Haryana, Statistics of State Election Commission Haryana, Chandigarh: 2010 Panchayat Elections.
6. Government of Haryana, Report of State Election Commission

Haryana, Chandigarh: 2005, pp. 22-24.

7. Government of Haryana, Report of State Election Commission Haryana l994-2004, Chandigarh, pp. 102-103.

8. Government of Haryana, Report of 2nd State Finance Commission Haryana, Chandigarh, September, 2004, p. 58.

# 15

# Sir Chhotu Ram and Agrarian Questions in Punjab

*Dr. Nirmal Kumar*

As a leader of the Unionist Party in Legislative Assembly of Punjab 1926-31 and supporter of peasantry, Sir Chhotu Ram played a decisive role in trying to abolish peasant's obstacles like indebtedness, useries, exploitation by Mahajans, Sahukars as well as by British Indian governments.

By experience wc know historical forces tend to change the attitude of great men and sometimes strong thought and action with diplomacy to change the direction of the flow of historical currents. This trend is covered in G.B. Plekhnov's book entitled *Role of Individual in History*. He says, 'A personality is great because of specific qualities, the qualities that are lacking in ordinary people. Such a person holds progressive views and he tries to establish a just social order based on human welfare. His vast study and boldness for fighting the evils which had gone down in almost every society and to create the right way to achieve the emancipation from exploitation of individual by individual etc. are very important.

'He accomplishes these tasks through efforts and disciplined organization. He even trains workers and this becomes institutionalized. By moving among the people for creating political consciousness he speaks on the burning problem of the day. He is always ready to face all challenges thrown by the opponents, may be, state, capitalist, anti-social elements or misguided peoples.'[1]

Chhotu Ram was born on November 24, 1881 in a poor Jat family. His father, Chaudhary Sukhi Ram, owned a small piece of land and was a petty businessman. He completed primary education in his neighbouring village, Sampla in 1895. He passed his Matriculation Examination from Mission High School in 1892, graduated from St. Stephen's College, Delhi in 1905.

He was quite bold enough to lead any strike against the authorities. School authorities gave him title of 'General Roberts'.

He was drawn to the Indian National Congress in 1916. He was President of District Congress Committee, Rohtak in 1917-20. He was multifaceted personality. He had deep kind corner of heart for the downtrodden peasantry.

He had a view that progress and prosperity of India depended on progress of peasantry. This idea was very central to the nation builders. Chief point was the agrarian question. Landlord-tenants relations and to fight against British imperial interest in Punjab Assembly, were his chief works. The limited nature of government of India Act, 1919, could not do the justice. Therefore, it was realized that getting freedom was the first necessity to put the house in order.

His method was totally constitutional. This can be shown by his activities during Nonco-operation movements, 1920-22. He fully disagreed with the leadership over NCO. He rejected the ideas of non-payment of taxes and defiance of law. He was moderate in politics, and supported only constitutional methods for the achievement of Dominion Status.'[2] He was instrumental in passing such legislative measures as Debtor Protection Act, the Restoration of Mortgaged Lands Act, Punjab Agricultural Produce Marketing Bills. He had complete faith in Gandhian thought of rural India. India lives in villages. Reconstruction of village means upgradation of our country. Indian literature is full of peasant stories–their rich cultural heritage, hardship, confidence in life. Hindi literature is also not far behind in taking up such task.[3] His view, as other nationalist leaders thought, was that India lived in villages and development of peasantry would lead to the progress of the country.

But taking independent judgment in realm of various kinds of problems was not possible unless and until the country remained a colony to British empire. He was pro-peasant. He said, 'I have the mentality of a poor man. I have the mentality of an agriculturist and I prefer to have that mentality, the mentality of a worker and a peasant rather than the mentality of a capitalist.'[4]

Indian rural life attracted attention of our great leaders who belonged to rural life and who rose upto national leadership like Mahatma Gandhi. Dr. Rajendra Prasad[5] had vividly described the honesty, transparency and kind heartedness of a peasant in rural India in his Autobiography. Simplicity, modesty, honesty of villagers in 19th and early 20th century village India attracted much of the attention of Chhotu Ram, Dr. Rajendra Prasad vividly portraited it in his autobiography. This simplicity in village life of that time was great strength to the functioning of Indian nationalist movement.

Besides, Chhotu Ram's experience of village life was very vivid. He spoke against joint family. 'The old patrearchal system is still in full force. The will of the eldest male member is law, and such law is at times purely arbitrary while the system teaching the wholesome lessons of obedience, discipline, patience, tact, forebearance, sympathy, sacrifices, and secures economy and does away with the necessity of Poor laws. It is open to several serious objections. Every member has to throw his earnings into the joint-stock, and need not be taken into confidence in the disposition of the stock. The natural consequence is that the individual does not put forth his best efforts. Also, the advanced members of the family, cannot introduce reforms without disturbing the peace of the house. This is great hindrance in the way of social reform. The system also helps to increase the member of drones and loafers.'[6]

He further suggested in his speeches that individual responsibility and the privilege was to be recognized on a larger scale.

He also looked into various classes of a village like, landowners, *zamindars*,* *Banias*. He dwelt on heavily on *Bania*. He said,

---

* Cultivator is called *zamindar* in Haryana and Punjab.

'There is the much abused, much dreaded, and much despised *Bania*. Servility, selfishness, greediness are his characteristics. He is the incarnation of Shylock in our own times.'

Sir Chhotu Ram tried to inspire peasantry by progressive ideas of fearlessness, self sufficiency etc. Simultaneously, he got enacted the laws favourable to the peasantry in Punjab Legislative Assembly.

In Legislature, he played a decisive role against the mighty British Raj. Chhotu Ram's efforts were to rescue peasantry from exploitation. He looked up their cause in the legislature and succeeded in bringing about their freedom for economic slavery.[7]

It was Chhotu Ram's early conviction that one could hope to reach the summit of leadership of masses only through constitutional and democratic methods. A creed of bloody revolution was, in his view, heavily loaded in favour of fascist ideology that run counter to all accepted norms of human dignity, freedom and faith.[8] Why he was very much concern with peasantry? The section of society was backbone of the nation so, if then there is any trait that stands out must prominently in the entire personality of Chhotu Ram. It is his almost exclusive or absolute concern for the weal or woe of peasantry. Whether on the floor of the house or the public platform or in his write-up for the press, he never felt tired of talking about the various issues that confronted peasantry, and of finding some lasting remedial measures.[9] In this, his contribution is unique, and remains unbeaten even to this day. Every sentence of his speech or write-up reflected his deep sense of agony and anguish, and none could cow him down. Since the cause he espoused in the Punjab Legislature was unconventional, in the initial stage he could invite only the raised eye-brows of his colleagues. His arguments on the floor of the house were logical and consistent, and the urbanities could only marvel at his political ingenuity. The image of a poor, exploited, harassed and humiliated peasant always clung to his mind giving most of his critics the chance to have a dig at him that he had developed a mania.[10]

It was Chhotu Ram's considered view that the peasants were an intelligent lot and understood much as we do, but they needed some facilities which could put them on the right track.

By tracing the wide gap between rural and urban people and their capacity to influence the politics, he said, 'The tragedy was that the urban people on account of their prosperity and education (Punjab case) during the period of review were in a better position to wield so much political influence, and consequently, to bring to bear upon it so much political pressure that, as and whenever the government proceeds to do something for the welfare of the rural populace, they force the government to an extent that it diverts all funds for the benefit of these people, leaving the ruralities helplessly waiting for their turn. But Chhotu Ram concluded, 'All that we are doing and intend to do in the future to help the poor *zamindars* is from the purest of motives.'[11]

Chhotu Ram viewed that it was the foremost duty of every government, whatever its form, to promote and protect the interests of *zamindars* as a class. 'These *zamindars*–the hardy folk, as he calls them–were the only sections of our country's population which took hard knocks with smile. All other classes, in his view, raise an awful hue and cry at even the slight rise in taxes and prices of essential commodities. They display remarkable, unity in flouting government's directives, and create ugly situations by blocking roads, organizing demonstrations, and if deemed necessary, can indulge in violence. The agriculturists, on the contrary, are a class of docile type. It does not seem possible that the shearer will find a block of meeker sheep; but, let the shearer not take away skin with the wool. The *zamindar* is even ready to submit to any demand that is made upon him without murmur or grievance. He does not keep up a row. It is he who fills the government's exchequer even if he happens to be pennyless at the time. He may have to pay a high rate of interest, but he will never refuse payment of government dues, like the land revenue or abiana tax. Yet, Chhotu Ram argued, the poor *zamindar* does not generally bend himself in the good books of bureaucracy.'[12]

The British Raj run by strong bureaucracy stood for imperial interest at the cost of well being of the peasant class. Chhotu Ram understood the drawbacks of the peasantry. So it was one of his missions to awaken the *zamindar* to his legitimate grievances and to learn his rights as a respectable citizen of the country.

Simultaneously, he also confessed that the response to his efforts had not been encouraging. Nevertheless, he was optimistic that with the passage of time the peasant would shake his age old lethargy and understand in what direction his god lies. It is, indeed, remarkable that Chhotu Ram kept himself busy with all that could be of help in his mission. His public speeches, his speeches on the floor of the house and his writings in newspapers especially in the *Jat Gazette*, all combined to pull the *zamindars* out of their pessimism. He formed a group of rural legislators, and himself gave the lead. It bore the fruit. The grievances of the *zamindars* began to figure prominently in the speeches of these legislators and gradually the bureaucrats themselves began to realize that they had to be careful in their behaviour towards the *zamindars*. Chhotu Ram himself undertook tours of rural areas, heard their grievances and kept his fellow legislators well informed about them.

What often pained Chhotu Ram was the fact that the *zamindars* were not organized in any manner, had no press through which they could ventilate their grievances. Chhotu Ram often lamented, 'They are so circumstanced, and to be frank, so devoid of sense and feelings of self-respect that they have to bear with a show of cheerfulness any assent of insult offered to them. They may be disgraced publicly and they may even be given shoe-beating, but they cannot raise even their little finger in protest.'[13]

While showing his commitment to the cause of peasantry, Chhotu Ram burst out in emotion and remarked, 'I have always been advocating the cause of the *zamindars*, whether they be Hindus, Mohammedans, or Sikhs, and will continue to advocate the cause even if I am in a minority of one.'[14]

During his tenure of President, Public Legislative Assembly, he got enacted many enactments for the amelioration of the poor and the downtrodden which were hailed as 'pioneer measures in the modern economic history of India.' In respect of these enactments, Punjab was ahead of several other provinces. Apart from extending benefits to the agriculturists, he was among the first in India to move for a six-day week for employees of shops and business establishments, and fixed hours of duty for them.

It is indeed melancholy thought that most of the measures then condemned by the trading classes as retrograde have since been adopted by the welfare state of the Republic of India, and form the basis of the present-day-policies, including the core of the twenty point economic programme.

The economic advancement of downtrodden could be a solution of the communal problem. The communal problem, Chhotu Ram came to the conclusion, was basically an economic problem, and religion could not be the basis of political activity. If an economic programme for the amelioration of the poorer sections and the downtrodden could be drawn up and sold to the people, communalism would be obliterated from the provinces and the center. The fire of communalism would loose its fury and get ultimately extinguished for lack of fuel on which it feeds.[15]

Chhotu Ram disliked the statutory agriculturists' community of Haryana. He said "Members of this community had become tools in the hands of the moneylenders to take over lands of the Jat community. He disliked as a class only those of the community who joined hands with the moneylenders, mahajans, but not as individuals."[16]

Now, in order to evaluate the role of Chhotu Ram with regard to agrarian question, we pay attention towards his ideas in form of speeches/writings in Punjab legislature and outside. He openly presented his views there in clear terms, terrorized his opponents and educated the voiceless peasantry in a fitting way. Sometimes he pondered over the pathetic conditions not only due to the exploitative activities by government and government officials and *zamindars*, money lenders but also by their carelessness, ignorance, superstitions and uneducated attitudes and conservative outbooks.

By going through his approach in study and action of the agrarian problems, he always followed constitutional method in a peaceful way. So he may be called a mass leader of the Jat community.

Getting Indian independence was primary necessity for the betterment of Indian nation. History testifies the fact that peasantry progressed and nation prospered in France after French Revolution[17] of 1789 and the peasantry in Russia progressed after Russian revolution, 1917.[18]

Thus we see that Sir Chhotu Ram's thinking and activity on agrarian issue were significant during his life time's period. His thinking on the current issue is still relevant in our time.

## References


1. Kumar, Nirmal : *Rajendra Prasad and the Indian Freedom Struggle 1917-1947*, New Delhi, 1991, p. XI.
2. Sen, S.P. : *Dictionary of National Biography*, Institute of Historical Studies, No. 1, A-D, Calcutta, 1972 p. 310.
3. Sen, S.P. : *Ibid.*
4. Sen, S.P. : *Ibid.*, p. 310.
5. Kumar, Nirmal : *Op. cit.*
6. Gopal, Madan : *Sir Chhotu Ram: A Political Biography*, p. 26.
7. Singh, Balbir : *A Saga of Inspirational Leadership*, p. 101.
8. Singh, Balbir : *Op. cit.,* p. 101.
9. *Ibid.*, p. 102.
10. *Ibid.*, p. 102.
11. P.L.C. Vol.-XXVI, Feb 28, 1935 quoted from Singh, Balbir : *Saga of Inspirational Leadership*, p. 104.
12. *Ibid.*, p. 105.
13. PLC Vol. XXI 1939 quoted from Singh, Balbir : *Ibid.*, p. 107.
14. PLC Vol. XA-1927 quoted from Singh, Balbir, *Ibid.*, p. 34.
15. Madan Gopal : *Sir Chhotu Ram: A Political Biography*, Delhi, Preface, 1977, p. X.
16. *Ibid.,* Preface, p. XI.
17. Kropotkin : *The Great French Revolution 1909*, pp. 95-7 quoted from History of Modern Europe Since 1789.
18. Southgate, George W. : *A Text Book of Modern European History*, 1789-1960, London, 1964.

# 16

# Charan Singh's views on the Nagpur Resolution

*Dr. Etee Bahadur*

Chaudhary Charan Singh had been Prime Minister of India from 1979 July 1980, after the fall of the Janata Government and twice Chief Minister of Uttar Pradesh from 1967-68 and 1970. During his long political career in Uttar Pradesh, he served as Member Legislative Assembly, Uttar Pradesh, 1937-77, and was Minister in the Uttar Pradesh Government from 1951-67. He played major role in transforming the agricultural economy of North India in post-independence India. He belonged to a generation of politicians whose political experiences encompassed state and national politics. He was a political leader having rural roots in an agricultural district, with a sound base in his own Jat community. The Jats were the leading caste in Western Uttar Pradesh, Punjab and Haryana, the spokesman of the peasantry of agriculture over industry, and of an agricultural order based on a system of peasant proprietorship in which landlordism was abolished and the entire peasant held economically viable landlord ship. In his usual fortnightly Letters to the Chief Minister, Nehru wrote about the 64th annual session of the Indian National Congress held at Nagpur from 9 to 11 January 1959. There were two Resolutions on Planning and Agriculture apart from the Resolutions on Foreign Affairs and the condolence resolution which paid homage to Maulana Azad, Khan Sahib and others.[1] The Nagpur Congress adopted a Resolution in favour of the introduction of a joint co-operative farming. Charan Singh opposed the policy. Instead, he proposed policies that would strengthen the existing system of peasant proprietorship and would sustain 'rural democracy' rather than cooperative farming, which he thought could be maintained only by undemocratic means.

Questioning the need for a rapid, state-sponsored industrialization as advocated by Nehru, Charan Singh opposed to give priority to agriculture and to promote it by developing small farmer holdings, the only industrial investment. For him, agricultural cooperatives would annul the productivity gains resulting from the elimination of the *Zamindar*-like intermediaries because they would jeopardize the independence of the farmers. 'The thought that land has become his [the peasant's] and the children's in perpetuity lightens and cheers his labour and expands his horizon. The feeling that his is his own master, subject to no outside control, and has free, exclusive and untrammeled use of his land drives him to greater effort. Likewise any system of large-scale farming which his holding are pooled must affect the farmer, but in the reverse direction. No longer will he be his own master; he will become one of the many, his interest will be subordinated to the group interest.'[2]

Obviously, economic rationality was not the only reason for rejecting agricultural cooperation. Charan Singh admits that, 'ultimately it is not a question of economic efficiency or form of organization, but whether individualism or collectivism should prevail.' Indeed he argues, 'The peasant is an incorrigible individualist; for his avocation of Nature without the necessity of having to give orders to, or take order from anybody.'[3] On landless agricultural labour, Charan Singh's views are worth nothing too. Referring to peasants' and labourers' condition he notes that, 'if wages have at all to be paid, in view of the fact that a large supply of idle labours is almost always available the wages paid need only be subsistence wages.'[4] Indifferent to the condition of the landless labourers, Charan Singh was against too low a ceiling in the land reform program which could have benefited them because it weakens the peasant-proprietor pattern.[5] While Charan Singh is of course the representative of peasant-proprietors his whole strategy consists of forging a *kisan* identity in which all people working in the fields may be able to recognize themselves. He insisted on the dichotomy between the cities and the countryside in this very perspective. 'There has always been lack of equilibrium rather a sort of antagonism between cities and the countryside. This is particularly so in our land where the gulf of inequality between the capitalist class and the working class pales into significance before that which exists between the peasant farmer our villages and true middle-class town dwellers. India is really two worlds-rural and urban. The relationship between the countryside and the cities is therefore artal problem for us.'[6]

Charan Singh's *Kisan* politics was successful to a certain extent, since he was able to gradually involve a certain cultivating castes from different social ranks. This came to be known as AJGAR, an acronym where A stood for Ahir (or Yadav), J for Jat, G for Gujar, and R for Rajput. In fact his identification with the interest of the so called backward castes, Charan Singh always saw himself as a Jat which meant for him that he was not from an elite caste. He felt that the position of the backward classes in Uttar Pradesh was deplorable. 45% to 50% of Government services were dominated by Brahmins, *Banias* and Khatris. The late 1960's saw in North India, the shaping of a strategy by Charan Singh which aimed at empowering the peasant. On March 10, 1959 as Minister for revenue, irrigation and power addressing a public meeting at Nawabganj he said that without farm surplus, masses would not have sufficient purchasing power which was necessary for industrial growth. Larger agricultural production was also required for providing the industries, with the necessary raw material.[7] In Meerut on February 3, 1958 after concluding a four day tour of Meerut district he explained to the peasantry, the implications of the Nagpur Resolution on agrarian reform and declared that the consolidation of holdings scheme would continue in the state.[8] He said that certain news item which recently appeared in a section of the press suggesting that the scheme was likely to be withdrawn as a sequel to the Nagpur decision, were wrong and incorrect. He added that the scheme would be abandoned or not introduced in those villages where the landlords willing by desired to pool their lands and cultivate them on joint cooperative basic. Urging the peasants to form their own services, cooperatives for recurring credit, agricultural and manufacturing facilities, Charan Singh said that by doing so they would not only derive all the advantages of cooperation, but would exceed in eliminating to a great extent middlemen who reaped rich dividends at their cost. He always identified himself with the interests of the peasants. In 1939, before the executive committee of the Congress Parliamentary group in the Uttar Pradesh Assembly, where had been elected for the first time in 1937, he proposed a 50 per cent quota in public administration in favour of the sons of farmers. He framed his project in terms of a 'latent' urban India versus rural India 'conflict.' 'In our country the classes whose scions dominate the public services are either those which have been raised to unexampled prominence and importance' by the Britishers e.g. the money-lender, the big *zamindar* or the *taluqdar,* the *arhatia* or the trader, or those which have been, so to say, actually called into being by him—the *vakil* (advocate), the doctor, the contractor. These classes have, in subordinate cooperation with the foreigner, exploited the masses in all kinds of manner during these but two hundred years. The views and interests of these classes, on the whole are, therefore, manifestly opposed to those of the masses. The social philosophy of the member of the non- agricultural, urban classes is entirely different from that of a person belonging to the agricultural rural classes.'[9] Charan Singh dealt with the position of agriculture vis-a-vis industry in various countries and said that an essential pre-requisite for industrial growth was increased agricultural production. While he was not opposed to the starting of gigantic industries, he send, expansion of industry as a whole would require a strong agricultural base, as it had a vital effect on the industrial economy.[10]

Charan Singh opposed the entire resolution, with the exception of the provisions relating to the setting up of service cooperative and state farms on reclaimed lands. He said that he were not opposed to breaking up the bigger land holdings and their distribution among the landless, but this he wanted to be done without the government coming directly into the picture. He suggested that the government should formulate a tax programme for bigger holdings in such a way that they would be required to reduce them. If such a method was not adopted and government took the responsibility to distribute lands, there was bound to be dissatisfaction among the people, and opposition parties would exploit situation. Charan Singh disagreed with basic reasoning behind cooperation that pooling of lands would contribute towards increased production. Agricultural production was a biological production as different from mechanical production in industries. The way to increase agricultural production, in his opinion, was to pool the resources and not land. He supported the idea of service cooperatives because they would help to pool the resources. He said that cooperative farms would not succeed in India. They had not succeeded anywhere in the world even in Israel where the conditions were different. Even in China cooperative firms proved a temporary phase and ultimately gave place to collective farms and communes. He was of the opinion that they should consult the farmer and see if they were favourable to joint cooperative farming. Though technology and science had developed, Man's mind was as narrow as it was in the past. He said that if the government took over wholesale trade in food grains, the logical step would be to take over the retail trade too. If the retail trade left over with private traders, the state machinery would give licenses for retail trade which meant there would be scope for favouritism. He preferred warehousing cooperative to state trading.

In fact, the book *Joint Farming X-Rayed : the Problem and its Solution* was published in response to the Nagpur resolution of the Indian National Congress, which proclaimed as one of the principal goal of the Congress the establishment of large-scale cooperatives firms in India as a means of shifting Indian agricultural problems. Though the book takes off from the issues of large-scale cooperative farming and in an attack upon it, it is far more interesting as a positive statement and a proposal for an economic development strategy for India based upon agricultural rather than industrial growth and as a defense of the system of peasant proprietorship as the most suitable form of social organization to achieve both the economic goals of development of the political goals of Democracy. The book was published at the height of Nehru-era emphasis on economic development model based upon rapid industrialization with agriculture seen primarily as a resource base for industrialization, providing food for the cities and revenue for projects. Charan Singh's defense of peasant agriculture in India was based not only on an economic and ecological but also on ideological and political grounds. In an agricultural society, he insisted that democracy was dependent upon the existence of small farms. Large farms, whether capitalist or collectivist were inimical to democracy. Both types of big farms inevitably involve concentration of power and the direction of farm operations by a few offering to the peasantry the prospect of a countryside turned into huge barracks of "gigantic agricultural factories." Charan Singh's book *Joint Farming X-Rayed* and economic ideas are complex or scholarly, he did not present them for the edification of economist. In fact, he several times condensed them, represented them as the central section of the manifestoes of the political parties he led. As such, these manifestoes are by far the most sophisticated ever used in India.[11] Charan Singh's political life and economic ideas thus provide an entry point into a such broader set of issues both for India and for the political and economic development of the remaining agrarian societies of the world. His political career raises the issue of whether or not a genuine agrarian movement can be built into a political force in the twenty-first century. Then his economic ideas and his political programme raise the question of whether or not it is conceivable that a viable alternative strategy for economic development of agrarian societies can be pursed in the face of the economic pressure for industrialization. Clearly in the course of his political career Charan Singh played a central role in several of the most crucial turning points in the history of the politics of India's largest state of the country. He was involved at all levels of the Indian political system-as a spokesman for the middle peasantry. He was identified with rural peasant interests and values in political tradition in India. He was Nehru's principal rival for political power in the country after independence. He was the principal architect of the UP Zamindari Abolition Act, the most important piece of land reform enacted in the India state after independence and most carefully conceived of the acts of that type enacted by various Governments in India.

## References


1. *Letter to Chief Ministers,* Vol. V, 1957-1964. Delhi, Vikas, 1986, p. 203.
2. *Joint Farming X-Rayed-The Problem and Its Solution,* Charan Singh, Bombay, Bharatiya Vidya Bhavan, 1959.
3. *Ibid.,* p. 107.
4. *Ibid.,* p. 104.
5. *Ibid.,* p. 168.
6. *India's Poverty and its Solution,* Charan Singh, New York, Asia Publishing House, 1969, p. 212.
7. *The Pioneer,* 11 March 1959.
8. *The Hindustan Times,* 3 February 1959.
9. Charan Singh, *Land Reforms in UP and the Kulaks,* Delhi, Vikas, 1986, p. 203.
10. *Congress Bulletin,* 1959.
11. See *Bharatiya Kranti Dal: Aims and Principles,*signed by Charan Singh, Lucknow 1971 and Lok Dal Election Manifesto, 1979.

## References

1. *Letters to Chief Ministers*, Vol. 4, 1957–1964, Delhi, Viking, 1986, p. 361

2. *Joint Farming X-rayed: The Problem and Its Solution*, Charan Singh, Bombay: Bharatiya Vidya Bhavan, 1959

3. *Ibid.*, p. 107

4. *Ibid.*, p. 164

5. *Ibid.*, p. 166

6. *India's Poverty and its Solution*, Charan Singh, New York: Asia Publishing House, 1964, p. 212

7. *The Pioneer*, 11 March 1959

8. *The Hindustan Times*, 31 January 1959

9. Charan Singh, *Land Reforms in U.P. and the Kulaks*, Delhi: Vikas, 1986, p. 203

10. *Congress Bulletin*, 1959

11. See *BKD and Lok Dal: Policies and Principles*, signed by Charan Singh, Lucknow 1971 and Lok Dal Election Manifesto, 1977.

# 17

# जाट इतिहास से संबंधित फारसी आधार सामग्री और श्री नटनागर शोध संस्थान, सीतामऊ, जिला मन्दसौर (म.प्र.)

डा. मनोहरसिंह राणावत

जाट जाति देश की निधि है। वह देश का भरण पोषण भी करती है और रक्षा भी करती है। जिस कुशलता से वह खेत में हल चला सकती है, उसी कुशलता से युद्ध भूमि में यह तलवार चलाना भी जानती है। साहस, वीरता, दृढ़ता और परिश्रम में वह किसी से कम नहीं है।

17वीं शताब्दी के मध्य तक जाट जाति पूर्व में आगरा, मथुरा, कोइल (अलीगढ़) तथा पश्चिम में मेवात की पहाड़ियों या आमेर क्षेत्र की सीमाओं तक, उत्तर में दिल्ली से 50 मील दूर मेरठ, दक्षिण में चम्बल नदी का किनारा तथा उसके पार गोहद तक फैल गये। इन इलाकों में जाटों की संख्या सबसे अधिक थी।

श्री रघुवीर लायब्रेरी, श्री नटनागर शोध संस्थान, सीतामऊ (म.प्र.) में जाटों के इतिहास की प्राथमिक और समकालीन आधार सामग्री के फारसी, फ्रेंच, राजस्थानी, मराठी और अंग्रेजी में अनेक अप्रकाशित पाण्डुलिपियाँ और प्रकाशित ग्रंथ संग्रहीत है। उनमें प्रमुख निम्नानुसार हैं -

**प्रकाशित फारसी ग्रंथ :**

1. फतूहात-इ-आलमगीरी- ईश्वरदास नागर कृत (ब्रिटिश म्यूजियम, लंदन)
   अंग्रेजी अनुवाद सर यदुनाथ सरकार
   और डा. तसनीम अहमद कृत

2. मआसिर-इ-आलमगीरी - अंग्रेजी अनुवाद यदुनाथ सरकार कृत

3. तारीख-इ-आलमगीर - सानी (ब्रिटिश म्यूजियम, लंदन) अंग्रेजी अनुवाद सर यदुनाथ सरकार कृत

4. नजीबुद्दौला - अंग्रेजी अनुवाद सैय्यद नुरुद्दीन कृत; अंग्रेजी अनुवाद, अब्दुर्रशीद कृत, अलीगढ़

5. नजीबुद्दौला रुहेला चीफ - बिहारीलाल मुंशी कृत, अंग्रेजी अनुवाद सर यदुनाथ सरकार कृत (इस्लामिक कल्चर, जिल्द 10)

**अप्रकाशित फारसी ग्रंथ :**

1. अहवाल-इ-सलातीन-इ-मुताखेरीन-इ-हिन्द
2. अजाएब-उल-आफाक - फोटो कापी ब्रिटिश म्युजियम, लंदन
3. तजकीरात-उस-सलातीन-इ-चगताई - मुहम्मद हादी कामवर खाँ कृत
4. तारीख-इ-हिन्द - रुस्तम अली खाँ कृत
5. तारीख-इ-शाकीर खानी - शाकिर खाँ कृत
6. मीरात-इ-आफताबनुमा - अब्दुर्रहमान कृत
7. अखबारात-इ-दरबार-इ-मौला - औरंगजेब, बहादुरशाह, फर्रूखसियर और मोहम्मदशाह कालीन

**फ्रेंच :**

1. एन अकाउण्ट ऑफ जाट किंगडम - फादर वेण्डेल, यदुनाथ सरकार कृत, अंग्रेजी अनुवाद (अप्रकाशित)
2. मेमोयर्स ऑफ रैने मादे - यदुनाथ सरकार कृत, अंग्रेजी अनुवाद (बंगाल पास्ट एण्ड प्रजेण्ट, अप्रैल-जून, 1937, जि. 53, भाग 2, क्र.सं. 106)

**राजस्थानी :**

1. जोधपुर राज्य की ख्यात, भाग 3

**अंग्रेजी :**

1. केलेण्डर ऑफ पर्शियन कारेस्पाण्डेन्स, जिल्दें 1-2

2. पर्शियन रिकाई्स ऑफ मराठा हिस्ट्री - देहली अफयेर्स, जिल्द 1

3. स्टोरिया डी. मोगोर, मनुची कृत; अंग्रेजी अनुवाद विलियम इर्विन कृत, जिल्दें 1-4

**मराठी :**

1. चन्द्रचूड़ दफ्तर - द. वि. आपटे द्वारा संपादित, जिल्द 1 (पूना, 1919 ई.)

2. अठारहवीं शती के हिन्दी पत्र - डा. काशीनाथ केलकर द्वारा संपादित

3. हिंगणे दफ्तर- जी. एस. सरदेसाई द्वारा संपादित, जिल्द 2 (पूना, 1947 ई.)

4. होल्कर शहीच्या इतिहासाचीं साधने - वा. वा. ठाकुर द्वारा संपादित, जिल्द 1

5. सेलेक्शन्स फ्राम पेशवा दफ्तर - जी. एस. सरदेसाई द्वारा संपादित, भाग 21, 27, 29

6. सेलेक्शन्स फ्राम पेशवा दफ्तर (न्यू सिरीज) - पी. एम. जोशी द्वारा संपादित, भाग 1-3

7. मराठाच्या इतिहासांची साधने - वि. का. राजवाड़े द्वारा संपादित जिल्द 1

मैं यहाँ पर सर्वप्रथम श्री रघुबीर लायब्रेरी में संग्रहित अप्रकाशित फारसी पाण्डुलिपियों में वर्णित जाटों के विवरण की संक्षिप्त जानकारी दे रहा हूँ।

**अहवाल-इ-सलातीन-इ-मुताखेरीन-इ-हिन्द :** इस ग्रंथ का लेखन काल 1803 ई. है। इस ग्रंथ में औरंगजेब के शासनकाल के अन्तिम वर्ष से शाह आलम द्वितीय के शासनकाल तक का विवरण है। शाह आलम द्वितीय के शासन के 30 वर्षों की जानकारी क्रमबद्ध दी है।[1]

उपर्युक्त ग्रंथ में फर्रूखसियर द्वारा 1129 हि. में सवाई जयसिंह की चूड़ामन जाट के विद्रोह के दमन हेतु नियुक्ति और उसके सहायतार्थ कुतुबुल-मुल्क को भेजने का विवरण है। लगभग एक वर्ष तक सवाई जयसिंह और चूड़ामन के बीच छोटी-छोटी मुठभेड़ें हुई। अन्त में कुतुबुल-मुल्क की मध्यस्थता से बादशाही सेवा में पहुँचने का विवरण है।[2] इसके अतिरिक्त सूरजमल द्वारा पुरानी दिल्ली लूटने की जानकारी दी गयी है।[3]

**अजाएब-उल-आफाक** (ब्रिटिश म्यूजियम की फोटोस्टेट प्रति) : इस हस्तलिखित ग्रंथ में फर्रूखसियर और मुहम्मदशाह द्वारा राज्य के प्रमुख अधिकारियों को लिखे गये 200 पत्रों का संग्रह है। एक पत्र[4] राजा छबीलाराम को सम्बोधित कर लिखा है कि कुतुबुल-मुल्क, अजीतसिंह और चूड़ामन जाट में जो मेलजोल बढ़ा है उससे पुरानी समस्या को सुलझाने में मदद मिली है।

पृ. 55, 56, 57, 59, 60, 81, 82, 83, 122, 123 और 124 पर उल्लिखित पत्रों में राजा छबीलाराम द्वारा चूड़ामन जाट व उसकी सेना को दबाने के लिये किये गये प्रयासों की जानकारी मिलती है। ग्रंथ से जानकारी मिलती है कि न केवल छबीलाराम बल्कि कोई भी अन्य अधिकारी चूड़ामन के बढ़ते हुए प्रभाव को कम नहीं कर सकेगा। अतः बादशाह को सलाह दी गयी कि षड्यन्त्र द्वारा चूड़ामन की शक्ति को कम करने का प्रयास किया जाये। इस प्रकार इस ग्रंथ से चूड़ामन जाट की शक्ति और मुगल शासकों की स्थिति की महत्त्वपूर्ण और प्रामाणिक जानकारी मिलती है।

**तजकीरात-उस-सलातीन-इ-चगताई :** मुहम्मद हादी कामवर खां कृत इस ग्रंथ के दो भाग हैं। प्रथम भाग में चंगेज खां से बादशाह जहाँगीर (1627 ई.) तक का विवरण है और दूसरे भाग में शाहजहाँ से बादशाह मुहम्मदशाह के शासन काल के छठे वर्ष (1136 हि. से 1723-24 ई.) तक का विवरण है। लेखन काल 1122 हि. है।[5]

बहादुरशाह के शासन के द्वितीय वर्ष में लेखक अपने संरक्षक शाहजादा रफी-उस-शान के पुत्र मुहम्मद इब्राहिम की सेवा में मीर-इ-सामान के पद पर रहा। अतः बहादुरशाह और उससे आगे का विवरण उससे अधिक प्रामाणिक है।[6]

इस ग्रंथ में गोकुला जाट, राजाराम, चूड़ामन आदि जाटों ने मुगल बादशाहों के विरुद्ध आजादी का जो आन्दोलन छेड़ा उसकी विस्तृत जानकारी दी गयी है। लेखक के अनुसार औरंगजेब ने सैय्यद हसन अली खां को जाट विद्रोह को दबाने के लिये भेजा। उसे मथुरा की फौजदारी और 3500 जात व 2500 सवार का मनसब दिया। साथ ही अकबराबाद के फौजदार को उसकी सहायता करने का आदेश दिया।

हसन अली खाँ जाटों को दबाने में सफल रहा। गोकुला जाट अपने साथियों और परिवार सहित गिरफ्तार कर लिया गया, उसके पुत्र और पुत्री को मुसलमान बना दिया गया।[7]

राजाराम जाट ने अकबराबाद के आस-पास के क्षेत्रों में लूट मचा रखी थी। अतः उसे दबाने के लिये खानजहाँ बहादुर कोलकताश जफर जंग और उसके पुत्र को भेजा गया। लेखक के अनुसार, 'राजाराम ने अकबराबाद और शाहजहाँनाबाद के मध्य के क्षेत्र को लूट कर वीरान कर दिया है।[8] खानजहाँ बहादुर से हुई लड़ाई में राजाराम मारा गया। उसके दुर्गों को नेस्तनाबूद कर दिया गया और शाही सेना ने राजाराम के भाई जोरावर सिंह और अन्य संबंधियों को गिरफ्तार कर लिया।[9]

राजाराम के बाद मुगल विरोध की बागडोर चूड़ामन ने संभाली। तब चूड़ामन के दमन के लिये राजा छबीलाराम और सवाई जयसिंह को भेजा गया। उनके द्वारा की गयी

सैन्य कार्यवाही का संक्षिप्त में विवरण मिलता है तथा अन्त में चूड़ामन का शाही सेवा में जाना और बादशाह द्वारा खिलअत देने का उल्लेख है।[10]

**तारीख-इ-हिन्दी :** रुस्तम अली कृत (फोटोकापी, ब्रिटिश म्यूजियम, लंदन) इस ग्रंथ का लेखन 1741 ई. में भोपाल में किया गया। ग्रंथ में हिन्दू राजा से बादशाह मुहम्मदशाह तक का संक्षिप्त में विवरण अवश्य क्रमबद्ध और वर्षानुसार दिया गया है।[11]

उपर्युक्त ग्रंथ में जाट इतिहास की जानकारी बहुत संक्षिप्त में दी गयी है। उसमें लिखा है कि जब कुतुबुल मुल्क और बादशाही सेना में 8 घण्टे का घमासान युद्ध हुआ उस समय चूड़ामन जाट ने शाही सेना को लूट लिया। इसी कारण सेना को भागने तक की जगह नहीं मिली। तदन्तर लिखा है कि चूड़ामन के आतंक का दमन करने के लिये बादशाह ने अन्य सरदारों के साथ सवाई जयसिंह को भेजा। जयसिंह ने जाटों को दबाने के लिए आवश्यक कार्यवाही की और चूड़ामन की मृत्यु के बाद उसके भतीजे को वारिस बनवा दिया।[12]

इस ग्रंथ में यह भी जानकारी मिलती है कि जाटों ने कस्बा महावन में खूब लूटमार की और परगना फीरोजाबाद के फौजदार हकीम काजिम को मार डाला और लूट लिया तथा जाटों के सरदार ने 3000 सवारों को एकत्रित कर लिया और अपना-अपना छद्मनाम बन्तरशाह रखकर लूटमार शुरु कर दी।[13]

**फतुहात-ए-आलमगीरी :** ईश्वरदास नागर कृत इस ग्रंथ में औरंगजेब के काल के जाटों के संबंध में विस्तृत जानकारी दी गयी है जो निम्नानुसार है -

**गोकल जाट :**

**(पृ. 53 अ)** उन्हीं दिनों में गोकल जाट, जमींदार तलपट मुतअल्लका मथुरा ने एक बहुत बड़ा गिरोह जाटों में से और दूसरे देहातियों में से एकत्रित करके, झगड़ा-फिसाद, बगावत कर रखी थी एवं हसन अली खाँ, अब्दुन्नबी खाँ और दूसरे सरदारों को उस विरोधी नासमझ को दबाने के लिए शाही फरमान जारी हुआ। चुनाचे शाही आदेशानुसार जब ये लोग तलपट से इधर दस कोस की दूरी पर पहुँचे तब विरोधी अपनी जमइय्यत बीस हजार सवार योद्धाओं के साथ सामना करने हेतु आगे बढ़ा। सामना किया तत्पश्चात दोनों तरफ से सैनिकों की मोर्चेबन्दी की गई। लेकिन इससे पहले कि शाही सेना के जवान योद्धा सैनिक आगे बढ़ें, फिसादी विरोधी ने अपने घमण्ड में घोड़ों को मैदान में डाल दिया। ऐसी परिस्थिति में लड़ाकू जवान सैनिकों से मुठभेड़ हो गई। आमने-सामने युद्ध शुरु हो गया। यहाँ तक कि लड़ाई पूरे जोर-शोर से यानि घमासान युद्ध होने लगा। अन्त में शाही लश्कर के बहुत से काम के योद्धा लड़ाकू काम आ गये और बहुतेरे घायल

हो गये। ताहम मैदान को न छोड़ा और उधर उस विरोधी की तरफ से बहुत से मारे गये और बच गये। शाही सेना के सामने न ठहर सके ऐसी परिस्थिति में फिसादी बेमन हो गया, कुछ न सोच सका और हार को ही गनीमत समझकर भाग निकला और तलपट जाकर ठहरा। अन्त में शाही लश्कर ने पीछा किया और तलपट का घेरा डाल दिया। तीन रोज तक बराबर दोनों तरफ से लड़ाई **(पृ. 53 ब)** तीर और बन्दूकों से चलती रही। लेकिन चौथे रोज़ तजुर्बेकार सैनिक जवान योद्धा लड़ाकुओं ने चारों तरफ से धावा करते हुए तलपट में प्रवेश किया और हर तरफ से दीवाल में शिगाफ करके, अन्दर घुस गये। उधर विरोधी फिसादी भी जान से हाथ धोकर एक दिल होकर सब-के-सब शाही सेना के जवानों पर टूट पड़े और युद्ध के अन्दर बड़े जौहर दिखलाये। वहाँ भी करीब-करीब चार हजार तजुर्बेकार जवान योद्धा शाही लश्कर के काम आये और विरोधी झगड़ालू की तरफ से पाँच हजार आदमी मारे गये। और वह विरोधी सात हजार आदमियों के साथ शाही सेना के हाथों गिरफ्तार हो गया। और उक्त खान फिसादी विरोधी को और उसके साथियों को सबको पकड़कर शाही सेवा में लाये। हुकुम हुआ कि उस मरदूद (विरोधी) को सियासतगाह में ले जाकर उसके टुकड़े-टुकड़े कर दिये जाएं ताकि इस सजा से दूसरे फिसादी विरोधियों को भी डर हो और दूसरों को शाही सेना के कोतवाल के हवाले करदें ताकि वह उन्हें तोक और जन्जीरें डाल कर कैदी बना लें। इस विजय के बाद बादशाह ने मथुरा से कूच किया और तीन दिन के बाद बादशाह अकबराबाद में दाखिल हुआ।

**(पृ. 23 अ)** दारा अकबरावाद से निकलकर शम्भूगढ़ पहुँचा और वहाँ से एक कोस की दूरी पर मैदान में अपने सैनिकों को तोपखाने आदि को बाकायदा तरतीब से जमाकर युद्ध के लिये तैयार रहा।......उधर शाहजादा सिपर शिकोह ने चम्बल के घाट पर तोपें नसंब कर दीं ताकि घाट से कोई इधर पार नहीं कर सके................दोनों भाई ग्वालियर से रवाना हुए................चम्बल के इधर सात कोस की दूरी पर पड़ाव डाल दिया। घाट पर तो तोपें नसंब थी, इधर-उधर से चम्बल को पार करना कि जिसमें पानी बहुत गहरा था बहुत दुश्वार था। अब दोनों **(पृ. 23 ब)** भाई सोचने लगे, फिक्र में पड़ गये। लेकिन कुछ सौभाग्य से हाथीराज जाट परगना गोहद ताअल्लुका सरकार ग्वालियर का जमींदार जो ग्वालियर से ही मुलाजिमत कर सेना के साथ हो गया था, उसने अर्ज की कि यहाँ से पांच-छः कोस की दूरी पर घाट कन्नेरा है जहाँ से नदी को पार कर सकते हैं। और सारी की सारी सेना आराम से घाट उतर सकती है। इस आशा पर दोनों भाइयों ने हाथीराज को अगवा कर लिया और पीछे हो लिये। लेकिन रास्ता बहुत ही ऊबड़-खाबड़ था। नदी के दरारे थे। और सेना संध्या के समय रवाना हुई। और रात के आखिर हिस्से में घाट कनेरा पहुँची। रास्ते में करीब पाँच हजार आदमी भूखे

प्यासे मर गये। सबेरे सेना उस घाट से जिसमें पानी सीने के बराबर था पार हुई। नदी के उस पार पड़ाव डाला। तत्पश्चात दूसरे दिन भाई दारा शिकोह की तरफ और दारा शिकोह ने इनकी तरफ सेना को हरकत दी।

**(पृ. 131 ब)** राजा जाट का अकबराबाद के आसपास फिसाद फैलाना : राजा जाट फिसादी के हालात पहले के पृष्ठों में लिखे हैं कि कैसे फितना और फिसाद लूटमार मचा रखी है। बल्कि अब तो वह पहले से बहुत ज्यादा फिसाद करने पर तुल गया है और लोगों को नुकसान पहुँचा रहा है और इसकी लूटमार के कारण आमदोरफ्त, आने-जाने के रास्ते इतने बंद हो गये कि परिन्दों को अपने पर फड़फड़ाने की ही गुन्जाइश नहीं रही। इसके अलावा अकबराबाद के मुजाफ के परगनों को लूटमार कर वीरान कर दिया। और इसी तरह लूटमार करते हुए शाहजहाँबाद की तरफ बढ़ा। और उसने चाहा कि सिकन्दरा को लूटमार कर बरबाद कर दे। इस बीच वहाँ के फौजदार मीर अब्दुल फजल ने यह सूचना पाते ही अपने सैनिकों के साथ उस फिसादी, बदबख्त विरोधी का सामना करने हेतु अपनी जगह से पाँच कोस की दूरी पर जाकर उसका मुकाबला किया। जब दोनों तरफ से युद्ध की आग भड़की और हालांकि विरोधी बहुत ज्यादा और ये लोग गिनती के थे। लेकिन उक्त फौजदार ने बड़ी सावधानी वीरता से काम लिया तथा बहादुरी से सामना करता हुआ ही, विद्रोही लोगों को अपने सामने साफ करता रहा। जिसमें उसको भी घातक घाव लगे। उसके साथी सहायक बहुत से काम आ गये, जख्मी हुए और विरोधी दल में से भी बहुत मारे गये। और जख्मी **(पृ. 132 अ)** होकर भाग निकले। जब विरोधी फिसादी दल का सिकन्दरा को लौटने में कुछ बस न चल सका, न लूटमार कर सके तो वहाँ से असफल निराश होकर शिकारपुर जा धमके और उसको खूब लूटा। तमाम गहिमत का माल असबाब, सोना, चाँदी, नकद, जिन्स बहुत सा उठाकर रतनपुर की तरफ रवाना हुए। और जब इस फिसादी विरोधी की शिकस्त की (हार की) खबर शाही सेवा में अर्ज हुई तो उक्त मीर को इल्तिकातखाँ का खिताब...............और मनसब में दो सौ सवार का इजाफा देकर सम्मानित किया। इन्हीं फिसादी दिनों में महाबतखाँ को दारुस सल्तनत लाहौर की सूबेदारी मिली और वह तत्काल ही रवाना हो गया। जिस समय वह सिकन्दरा पहुँचा तो दरया जमन (यमुना) के किनारे अपना पड़ाव डाला तो वह फिसादी बदबख्त विरोधी, बहुत बड़ी जमइय्यत लेकर मुकाबला करने के इरादे से पहुँच गया। ऐसी परिस्थिति में उक्त खान ने, जो बहुत ही चतुर तथा अपनी सियासत में माना हुआ था, विरोधियों की तादात बहुत ज्यादा देखकर अपने सामने और सेना के चारों तरफ तोपखाना लगवा दिया। और डटकर सामना करने के लिए तैयार हो गया। लेकिन इस ख्याल से कि अशुभ विरोधी एक दो दिन की ढील में अपने फिसादी ख्याल से रुककर अपना रास्ता लें तो बहुत ही अच्छा है। वरना जो खुदा को मंजूर होगा हर हालत में

हो के रहेगा। लेकिन जब उस विरोधी को यह भनक पहुँची तो वह तो और ढीठ बनकर लड़ाई करने पर तुल गया। और बदबख्ती फिसाद की तरफ बड़ी शौखी से उतारु हो गया। अन्त में उक्त खान ने यह हालात देखी तो अपने साथी सवारों के साथ युद्ध के लिए सैनिक सिलसिले नियुक्त किये। और युद्ध छिड़ (**पृ. 132 ब.**) गया। लड़ाई बहुत जोर-शोर से हुई। उस विरोधी बदनसीब की तरफ से करीब चार सौ आदमी मारे गये। डेढ़ सौ आदमी उक्त खान की तरफ से काम आ गये और चालीस जख्मी हो गये। अन्त में जब उस विरोधी ने देखा कि सामना करते रहना बहुत कठिन है, तो युद्ध के मैदान से खिसक गया। तत्पश्चात् उक्त खान ने एक रोज और उसी जगह मुकाम किया। और दूसरे दिन अपनी मंजिल की तरफ रवाना हुआ।

इधर दिन प्रतिदिन उस फिसादी का फिसाद व लूटमार बढ़ती ही रही। और जब यह वारदातें शाही सेवा में अर्ज हुईं तो अकबराबाद की सूबेदारी अमीरुल उमरा को दी गई। और आदेशानुसार हुक्म मुहम्मद बका याने मुजफ्फरखाँ के नाम से पुकारा जाता था तथा जो खानजहाँ बहादुर का नायब था, जारी हुआ कि अमीरुल उमरा के वहाँ पहुँचने तक बराबर वहाँ की देख-रेख बन्दोबस्त सावधानी से करते रहो। इसी बीच अकबराबाद की घटनाओं से अर्ज हुई कि उस बदबख्त फिसादी ने सिकन्दरा में जो आगरे में ही है, वहाँ तक घुसकर हजरत अर्श आशियानी (अकबर) के रोजा को (कब्र को) लूट लिया और तमाम चीजें यहाँ तक कि फर्श बिछातें, बर्तन, कालीनें, जाजमें, सोने-चाँदी के बर्तन आदि सबके-सब लूट ले गया और वहाँ अकबर की कब्र और मजारात के आसपास थे सबको खोद डाला और मुहम्मद बका खानजहाँ का नायब जो अकबराबाद में था वह उस मरदूद फिसादी की रोकथाम हेतु सामने नहीं आया जिसके कारण बादशाह ने मुहम्मद बका के मनसब में से -

**(133 अ)** पाँच सदी और खानजहाँ के एक हजार सवार उसके पूरे मनसब में से कम किये और राजा रामसिंह को काबुल की तैनाती से इस अशुभ बदनसीब को सजा देने हेतु बुलवाया लेकिन उक्त राजा को मौत ने मोहलत न दी और उसकी वहीं पर मृत्यु हो गई। आखिर उसकी मृत्यु के बाद उसके लड़के बिशनसिंह को बादशाहाना मेहरबानियों से फरमाकर मनसब दो हजार जात, दो हजार सवार, हाथी, आलम (झण्डा), नक्कारा आंबेर का टीका और राजगी के खिताब से सम्मानित कर शहर मथुरा की फौजदारी की खिदमत और सनसनी की जमींदारी, जो कि उस गुमराह फिसादी का निवास स्थान है, उसको बरबाद करने तथा हलाक करने की शर्त पर नियुक्त किया....

**(पृ. 134 अ) राजा जाट की मृत्यु :** इन दिनों में जो शाही इकबाल से फतुहान (विजय) हुई उनमें एक राजा जाट के मार डालने की घटना है। जिसका सविस्तार बयान

यह है कि - शेखावाटी राजपूतों और चौहानों के बीच में परगना खतरिया आदि में जमींदारी हेतु आपसी झगड़ा पैदा हो गया और जिसने धीरे-धीरे बढ़ते-बढ़ते एक लड़ाई की शक्ल अख्तियार कर ली। दोनों तरफ से झुंड के झुंड एकत्रित हो गये। और कई मरतबा संघर्ष की नौबत **(पृ. 134 ब)** आई। ऐसी परिस्थिति में कभी तो शेखावत जीत जाते थे और कभी चौहान लेकिन कोई भी किसी पर पूर्णतया विजय नहीं पा सका था। इस पर चौहानों ने राजा जाट से सहायता लेने का निवेदन किया और उधर शेखावाटियों की पुकार पर सहपदारखाँ फौजदार मेवात का खालुजाद भाई शाहजी जो कि वहाँ मेवात में नायब था उन शेखावाटियों की मदद पर पहुँच गया।

मौज़ा बिचल.........के पास दोनों तरफ वालों की मुठभेड़ हो गई। राजपूत एक दूसरे से बड़ोती की ऊंच-नीच विचारधाराओं के इस संघर्ष में बहुत उलझ गये और घमासान युद्ध शुरु हो गया। जिसके कारण बहुत से लोग दोनों तरफ से मारे गये। इसी बीच राजा जाट स्वयं अपनी बहादुरी के नशे में अपने कुछ योद्धाओं के साथ जिनकी मौत सर पर चक्कर लगा रही थी लड़ाई में कूद पड़ा। इसी समय सपहदारखाँ का एक नौकर जो बरकन्दाजी निशाना लगाने में बहुत माहिर था उस विरोधी बदबख्त की खबर पाकर एक वृक्ष पर चढ़ गया और वहाँ से विद्रोही पर बन्दूक से ऐसा निशाना मारा कि उसके सीने से सीधा लगा और घोड़े की जीन से जमीन पर गिरा और तत्काल ही मृत्यु हो गई। तत्पश्चात हर तरफ से विजय-विजय की आवाज आने लगी और चौहानों के पांव उखड़ गये और युद्ध के मैदान से भाग निकले! पर शाहजी ने इस आसमानी विजय को अपने स्वयं के लिए शुभ समझकर उस विरोधी नाबकार के सर को उसके शरीर से काटकर अपने एक मुलाजिम के साथ **(पृ. 135 अ)** बादशाही सेवा में भिजवाया। जो अजमेर से बाईस दिन में शाही सेवा में पहुँचा। अर्जदाश्त बादशाह की सेवा में पेश की। और जब मौखिक भी अर्ज हुई कि इस ढंग से उसका सर लाये हैं तो आदेश दिया कि कोतवाली के चबूतरे पर उस बदनसीब अशुभ का सर लटका दिया जाय। उक्त खान को मनसब पाँच सदी जात से सम्मानित किया।

**(पृ. 135 ब.) राजा जाट के भतीजे चूड़ामन जाट का फिसाद फैलाना :**

राजा जाट के कत्ल करने की घटना, अकबराबाद के पास का बयान पहले गुजर चुका है अब इन दिनों में उस विरोधी फिसादी का भतीजा चूड़ामन जाट बदला लेने पर तुल गया। और इस इरादे से उसने अपने साथ बहुत से फिसादी झगड़ालू विरोधियों को कर लिया। और किला सनसनी और शिवगढ़............को मजबूत कर झगड़ा फिसाद लूटमार अपने भाई से भी अधिक शुरु कर दी। और तमाम परगने मुजाफ सूबा अकबराबाद और दारुल खिलाफत शाहजहाँबाद **(पृ. 136 अ)** को लूटना, वीरान

करना, बरबाद करना शुरु कर दिया। और उस अशुभ की लूटमार से यात्रियों के रास्ते भी बंद हो गये। जब यह खबर अकबराबाद की घटनाओं से और शाहजहाँबाद की वारदातों से शाही सेवा में पहुँची तो लगातार आदेश नाजिम मुसतकरूल खिलाफत दारूल खिलाफत और दूसरे उन जिलों के फौजदार आदि के नाम जारी हुए कि उस झगड़ालू, फिसादी विरोधी की तम्बीह की जाय, उसको दबाया जाय। अन्त में शाही आदेशानुसार शाही सेना को तरतीब दी और इन्हीं दिनों में राजा बिशनसिंह भी शाही हुक्म के अनुसार शीघ्र ही पहुँचकर लश्कर में शरीक हो गया। शाही सेना और राजा बिशनसिंह की सेना साथ-साथ इस विरोधी बदमाल को दबाने के लिए रवाना हुई। और चूँकि राजा को शुरु में ही.......बड़ा मनसब बख्श कर बादशाह ने सम्मानित किया था तो अपने नाम को रखने और शाही सेवा में मुजरा हो इस ख्याल से राजा ने अपने साथ दस हजार सैनिक और बीस हजार प्यादे नौक़र लिये और स्वयं शाही सेना की अगवा हरावल बना। और इस मकहूर विरोधी के निवास से पाँच कोस की दूरी पर सेना का पड़ाव डाला। अलगरज फिसादी अपनी बहादुरी के नशे में कभी दायें और कभी बाँयें, कभी इधर कभी उधर घुसकर लड़ाई करता रहा। लेकिन यह करते-करते उसका काम इस हद तक पहुँच गया कि तालाब से पानी भर कर ले जाना और रसद तक पहुंचना बहुत ही कठिन हो गया और रात को छापा मारने से लश्कर भी बहुत तंग आ गया। गल्ला और घास की इतनी कमी आ गई कि तीन चार रोज में ही गल्ला बहुत महँगा मिलने लगा। ऐसी परिस्थिति में आदमी भूख से निढाल **(पृ. 136 ब)** हो गये। और बहुत से चारपाये तो मर गये। और बहुत से ऐसे अशक्त हो गये कि जमीन से भी उठना दुश्वार हो गया। आखिर चार महीनों में किले के एक दरवाजे पर पहुँचकर सेना ने अपने पाँव जमाये। और तत्काल ही किले का घेरा डाल दिया। और ठोस और कड़क की आवाज वाली तोपों को मजबूत करने, नकब लगाने और रास्तों को साफ करने में सेना जुट गई। और किले के आस-पास के जंगलों को काटने में लग गये। और तब किले के दरवाजे में नकब लगाकर बारूद की थैलियाँ बिछादी और आग लगा दी गई। लेकिन विरोधी जाटों ने नकब लगाने की खबर पाकर नकब के मुँह को मिट्टी और पत्थरों से भर दिया था। लिहाजा जिस समय बारूद ने आग पकड़ी तो बारूद नकब के अगला हिस्सा उड़ाने के बजाय वापस ताकत से उल्टी लौटी जिसके कारण नकब का ऊपरी हिस्सा जो हवा में उड़ा तो बहुत से तोपखाने वाले, बन्दोबस्त वाले और दूसरे लश्करी जल गये हवा में उड़ गये और मर गये। तमाम शाही सैनिक फिर से नकब देने में लग गये। चुनाचे सुरंग खोदने वालों ने बड़ी तेजी से एक महीने में ही किले के नीचे नकब लगा दी और फिर से उस सुंरग को बारूद से भर दी और इसके बाद उक्त राजा और दूसरे बादशाही सैनिक सरदार अपनी-अपनी सेना सहित चारों तरफ से घेर कर डट गये। सुरंग

में आग लगाते ही बारूद की ताकत से कुछ तो किले की दीवार उड़ गई कुछ किले के भीतर और कुछ लश्कर की तरफ गिर गई। जिसके कारण वे विरोधी जाट अशुभ जो कि किले की दीवार पर सावधानी से बरकनदाज़ी निशाना लगाने को आतुर थे उनमें से बहुत **(पृ. 137 अ)** से जलकर खाक हो गये। और बहुत से किले की दीवार में दबकर मर गये। जब नकब की आग बुझी तो शाही सैनिक घुड़सवार किले की गिरी हुई दीवार से किले में घुस गये। उधर विरोधी जाटों ने भी डटकर सामना किया। और युद्ध करने में बड़ी सावधानी बरती जिसके कारण बराबर दो-तीन घड़ी तक घमासान युद्ध होता रहा। अन्त में शाही सेना की विजय हो गई और विरोधी हजारों निराशाओं के साथ इधर-उधर गुमनामी के जंगल में भाग निकले। फतह शाही सेना को नसीब हुई। फिसादी विरोधियों की तरफ से डेढ़ हजार आदमी मारे गये और जख्मी हुए और शाही सेना की तरफ से मामूरखाँ अपने दो सौ आदमियों के साथ इस युद्ध में मारा गया, और राजपूतों में से जो कि राजा के साथ थे और दूसरे सैनिक राजपूत करीब सात सौ आदमी इस युद्ध में काम आ गये और जख्मी हुए। तत्पश्चात राजा और शाही सैनिकों ने वहीं पड़ाव किया। इसी बीच में दूसरे दिन राजा को सूचना मिली कि फिसादी विरोधी शिवगढ़ के किले में जाकर ठहरा है और झगड़े के ख्याल से विरोधियों को एकत्रित करने में लग गया है। एवं राजा इस सूचना को पाते ही तत्काल अपने साथ बादशाही सेना को लेकर जा धमका। भाग्यवश उस समय किले का दरवाजा रसद के आने के लिये खुला हुआ था तो शाही सेना पहुँचते ही दरवाजे से किले में घुस गई और जिसने हाथ उठाया उसका वहीं खात्मा किया। और उस फिसादी विरोधी को **(पृ. 137 ब.)** उसके पाँच सौ सहायकों के साथ गिरफ्तार कर लिया और अपने डेरों की तरफ लौट आये। अंत में राजा ने अपने पड़ाव में पहुँच कर एक अर्जदाश्त की जिसमें बड़ी विजय और उस विरोधी मकहूर के उसके पाँच सौ साथियों के साथ गिरफ्तार करने के हालात लिखे थे, शाही सेवा में भिजवाये। जब शाही सेवा में अर्जी पेश हुई और सब हालात मालूम हुए तो बादशाह ने उक्त राजा को और दूसरे शाही सरदारों को उनके मुताबिक मनसब के आदेशानुसार हर एक को शाही इनायतों से सम्मानित किया...........और यह आदेश दिया कि गिरफ्तार लोगों की देख-रेख में बहुत ही सावधानी बरती जाय।

### आइज्जाखाँ या अगर खाँ के मारे जाने के हालात

**(पृ. 164 ब)** इन्हीं दिनों के दारुल खिलाफत अकबराबाद की घटनाओं के वाकेआत से अर्ज हुई कि आइज्जा खाँ को अकबराबाद के पास मार डाला है। जिसकी तफसील यह है कि उक्त खान तुरानी दारुलमुल्क काबुल में नियुक्त था। बहुत ही वीर खूबसूरत, दिखलौटा मनुष्य था और उससे कई बार वीरता के कार्य हुए। बहुत अर्से से वहीं उसी सरजमीन पर अपने कर्तव्य को निभाता रहा। लेकिन इस समय वहाँ की तैनाती

से अलग होकर शाही आदेशानुसार हुज़ूरेआला में रवाना हुआ था। और जब अकबराबाद से गुजरकर कस्बा धौलपुर के आस-पास पहुँचा और वहाँ से चूंकि सैनिक बेतरतीब इधर-उधर असावधानी से रास्ता तय कर रहे थे कि अचानक बदनसीब अशुभ जाटों ने एक बड़े गिरोह के साथ उस भीड़ (बेतरतीब सेना) पर धावा बोल दिया और कुछ घोड़े आदि सामान लूटकर ले गये। इस वक्त खान ने बगैर सोचे-समझे अपने गिने-चुने साथियों को साथ लेकर उनका पीछा किया और दो तीन कोस तक पीछा करता हुआ निकल गया। तिस पर विरोधी फिसादियों ने वापस पलट कर सामना किया और मारपीट लड़ाई शुरु हो गई। करीब दो सौ आदमी विरोधियों के मारे गये। और उक्त खान के करीब अस्सी आदमी इस लड़ाई में काम आ गये। अन्त में खान स्वयं बहादुरी के जौहर दिखाता हुआ मारा गया। जब यह घटना बादशाह की सेवा में अर्ज हुई तो आदेश दिया कि आशौर बेग खान आदि खान के साथियों को जिस जगह कि वे लोग पहुँचे हों वहीं से वापस काबुल की तरफ लौटा दिया जाए।

**अखबारात-ए-दरबार-ए-मुअल्ला (जयपुर रिकार्ड्स, भाग 7) :**

जाटों के विद्रोह को दबाकर उन्हें कत्लेआम करने का आदेश दिया गया है। इस कार्य के होने पर बादशाह का विश्वास बढ़ेगा तथा साथ ही पद और मनसब में वृद्धि की बात भी कही गयी है।[14] इसी तरह उपरोक्त कार्य को करने में विलम्ब होने का कारण जानना चाहा है, तथा तुरन्त आंबेर से कूच करके तुरन्त सनसनी पर अधिकार कर जाटों का कत्लेआम करना है। इस कार्य में डेढ़ महीने की देरी हुई इसका कारण भी जानना चाहा है।[15] केशव राय की अर्जी शाही दरबार में भेजी गयी जिसमें निष्ठा जतायी गयी है। अतः बादशाह ने इस पर ध्यान देकर आम्बेर राज्य का टीका महाराजा को दिया तथा 2000 जात और 4000 सवार, जिनमें से 2000 सवार बिना शर्त और 2000 सवार इस शर्त पर कि इस्लामाबाद की फौजदारी तथा जाटों का पूर्ण रूप से सफाया करना, और साथ ही बादशाह ने जाटों को पूर्ण रूप से दबाने के लिए अलग से मौखिक आदेश भी दिया।[16] आदेश मिलते ही एक बड़ी सेना एकत्रित करके जिसमें अनुभवी, साहसी और नये सैनिक भी हों जो सब मिलकर पूरे साहस और मजबूती से डटकर विद्रोही जाटों का सामना कर या तो उन्हें कत्ल कर दें या उन्हें गिरफ्तार कर लें।[17]

राजा जयसिंह द्वारा जाटों को दबाने का उल्लेख है। जिन चार महलों पर जाटों का अधिकार था राजा जयसिंह ने उन्हें वहाँ से बेदखल कर दिया है।[18] आगे कीरतसिंह के पुत्र कुशालसिंह आदि राजपूत जाटों के विद्रोह में सम्मिलित हो, इनका समर्थन करने का उल्लेख है। जाटों के समर्थकों को राजा जयसिंह द्वारा शाही सेना में मिलाना, उन्हें हरावल में स्थान देने का उल्लेख है। अतः शाही दरबार में यह माना जा रहा है कि वे

लोग जो जाटों के समर्थक हैं अपना काम पूर्ण ईमानदारी से नहीं कर रहे हैं। परन्तु ऐसा नहीं है। राजा जयसिंह ने ऐसा इसलिये किया कि कुछ जाट समर्थक तो जाटों के विरुद्ध लड़ाई में मारे जायेंगे और जो बचेंगे उन्हें राजा जयसिंह लड़ाई के बाद मरवा देंगे।[19]

परन्तु उपरोक्त षडयंत्र से भी जाटों को नहीं दबाया जा सका और वे लूट-पाट एवं अपना काम कर भाग निकले। उल्टा जब सनसनी का घेरा डाल रखा था तब ये विरोधी जाटों से जाकर मिल गये और शाही समस्या को और बढ़ा दिया।

बिहार की सूबेदारी का फरमान उम्मैद खां के नाम गुर्जदार लेकर जा रहा था जिसे जाट जो अकबराबाद में थे, अपने साथ लेकर अमीरुल-उमरा के पास आये। रात सनसनी में रखकर उसे पुनः शाही लश्कर में छोड़ आये।[20] अमीरुल उमरा ने राजा जयसिंह की तरफ शाही ध्यान आकर्षित किया और यह आदेश पाया कि विद्रोही जाटों को दबाने के लिये (शहजादा) जयसिंह ने सनसनी के किले एवं आस-पास के मौजों का घेरा डाल रखा है अतः उन्हें हर तरह की सुविधा उपलब्ध करायी जाये। रसद की तथा शस्त्रों की कमी न होने पाये। इस कार्य का उन्हें पर्याप्त प्रतिफल मिलेगा।[21]

**अखबारात-ए-दरबार-ए-मुअल्ला (8 जुलाई, 1723 ई. सोमवार) जयपुर रेकार्ड्स, सीतामऊ कलेक्शन, मुहम्मदशाह ग्रंथांक 1605 :**

अकबराबाद सूबा की घटनाओं की सूचना मोतकिद अली खाँ की सेवा में पहुँचायी इसमें एक घटना कपड़ों के थान रो भरी दो गंजिली गाड़ी नकीता या नाकता के पास जाट विद्रोहियों ने लूट ली। नायब निजामत सैय्यद मुजफ्फर अली खाँ ने तत्काल उनका पीछा किया। आपस में खुलकर मुठभेड़ हुई। इसमें बहुत से जख्मी हो गये। जाट विद्रोही ज्यादा देर तक नायब का सामना नहीं कर सके और भाग निकले।[22]

नायब मुहम्मद गोहर खाँ की अर्जी दि. 5 जिल्हिजा को अपनी सेना सहित परगना तरमाई पहुँचा। वहाँ सरकार अलवर के परगने के थानेदारों द्वारा लिखित सूचना से यह पता चला कि मीर अब्दुर्रहीमखाँ व मीर जाफर का भाई चूड़ामन जाट से मिल गये हैं, और शाही फौजदारी के परगनों के तमाम थानों को हटाकर स्वयं के थाने स्थापित कर लिये हैं। अतः इन्हें दबाने के लिय सवाई जयसिंह से सेना की मांग की गयी ताकि शीघ्र कार्यवाही की जा सके।[23]

चूड़ामन जाट भागकर बयाना जिले में घुसा है। कस्बा बसा कर और मौजा रूथमा आदि से शाही थाने हटाकर चूड़ामन ने अपने थाने स्थापित कर लिये हैं। बयाना और इब्राहीमाबाद के आस-पास लूटमार कर रहे हैं। ये इलाका शाही अधिकार में ही आता हैं, अतः एक शाही सेना का बन्दोबस्त करने की प्रार्थना की गयी है, ताकि जाट विद्रोहियों को दबाकर हर तरह से शांति कायम की जा सके।

## संदर्भ

1. *केटेलाग ऑफ पर्शियन मैनुस्क्रिप्ट्स एण्ड रेकार्ड्स इन द श्री रघुवीर लायब्रेरी*, सीतामऊ, अख्तर हुसैन निजामी कृत, पृ. 209-210।

2. अहवाल इ-सलातीन-इ-मुताखरीन-इ-हिन्द पृ. 59, 104, 105, 109।

3. *अहवाल*, पृ. 359।

4. *अजाएब-उल-आफाक*, पृ. 36।

5. निजामी, पृ. 179।

6. निजामी, पृ. 179।

7. *तजकीरात*, पृ. 116।

8. *तजकीरात*, पृ. 223, 231।

9. *तजकीरात*, पृ. 231।

10. *तजकीरात*, पृ. 315, 391, 399, 418, 425, 426।

11. निजामी, पृ. 181,-182।

12. *तारीख-इ-हिन्दी*, पृ. 488, 495।

13. *तारीख-इ-हिन्दी*, पृ. 543, 579।

14. *तारीख-इ-हिन्दी*, पृ. 85, 103।

15. *तारीख-इ-हिन्दी*, पृ. 107।

16. *तारीख-इ-हिन्दी*, पृ. 313, 314, 315।

17. *तारीख-इ-हिन्दी*, पृ. 317।

18. *तारीख-इ-हिन्दी*, पृ. 334, 335।

19. *तारीख-इ-हिन्दी*, पृ. 338, 339।

20. *तारीख-इ-हिन्दी*, पृ. 343, 344।

21. *तारीख-इ-हिन्दी*, पृ. 352, 353, 354।

22. *तारीख-इ-हिन्दी*, पृ. 17।

23. *तारीख-इ-हिन्दी*, पृ. 82।

18

# जाट इतिहास विषयक पुरालेखीय श्रृंखला- रामपुरिया रिकार्ड की कागदों की बहियाँ

डॉ. महेन्द्र खड़गावत

1

इतिहास निर्माण के दो मूलभूत आधार मनुष्य तथा भूमि हैं। इसलिए इतिहास में किसी भी देश के मनुष्यों के क्रिया कलाप, जो कि समय के प्रवाह के साथ प्रवाहित हो रहे है, एकत्रित किए जाते हैं। इतिहास का निर्माण काल की भित्ति पर होता है और उस के निर्धारण का आधार घटनाएें हैं। तात्पर्य यह है कि इतिहास में अतीत काल से सम्बन्धित मनुष्यों की सभी महत्वपूर्ण घटनाओं, प्रयत्नों तथा चरित्रों का विवरण है। इसमें समाज के विभिन्न समुदायों या वर्गों के सूक्ष्म भेदों तथा सम्बन्धों के रहस्यों का उद्घाटन भी है। भारतीय इतिहास की लिपिबद्ध सामग्री तथा विश्वस्तर विशुद्ध स्रोतभूत ऐतिहासिक सामग्री के अन्तर्गत इन अभिलेखों की गणना होती है। ये अभिलेख अतीत को प्रस्तुत करते हुए वर्तमान में प्रासंगिक तो हैं ही, शोध के विविध पक्षों को उद्घाटित करते हुए अनेक विध महत्त्वपूर्ण भी हैं।

राजस्थान राज्य अभिलेखागार, बीकानेर अभिलेखों की अपार एवं अमूल्य राष्ट्रीय धरोहर संरक्षित करने के कारण देश-विदेश में ख्यातिलब्ध हैं। विक्रम सं. 1700 से 2000 तक के अभिलेखों को संरक्षित करने वाले इस अभिलेखागार में मुगलकालीन फारसी अभिलेखों के साथ राजस्थान की भूतपूर्व रियासतों के अभिलेख संरक्षित हैं। यहां भाषा की दृष्टि से फारसी भाषा में बादशाह एवं शहजादों के फरमान, निशान, मन्शूर, अखबारात हैं, फारसी उर्दू एवं राजस्थानी भाषा-ढूंदाड़ी, मेवाड़ी मारवाड़ी और हाड़ौती में रियासतों के अभिलेख पट्‌टा, परवाना, ठक्का, बही, अर्जियां, खरीता, पानड़ी, तोजी, चौपनिया, पंचांग और अंग्रेजी भाषा में ब्रिटिश शासन की फाइलें हैं।

इस अभिलेखागार में उत्तर-पश्चिमी राजस्थान के थार मरुस्थलीय राज्य बीकानेर में एक खेतीहर समाज के रूप में वर्चस्व रखने वाले जाट समाज के इतिहास को संजोने वाली पुरालेखीय अभिलेख श्रृंखला के रूप में रामपुरिया रिकार्ड की बहियों का एक समृद्ध इतिहास उपलब्ध है। संख्या में 93 ये बहियां संवत् 1811 से प्रारम्भ होकर सं. 1857 तक की है। उन्हें स्थानीय भाषा मारवाड़ी में लिखा है तथा उनकी लिपि मोड़ी या कामदारी हैं, जो देवनागरी का एक रूप है। उन बहियों से जाट समाज से सम्बन्धित विभिन्न प्रारूपों पर उनकी उपस्थिति, विश्वास, रीति-रिवाज, आर्थिक, राजनैतिक स्वरूप, व्यवस्था, रीति-रिवाज और परम्पराओं का निरूपण किया जा सकता है।

राज्य अभिलेखागार की यह अभिलेखीय सामग्री जाट समाज की जन-जीवन विषयक सूचनायें देते हुए तत्कालीन सामाजिक एवं सांस्कृतिक जीवन के महत्वपूर्ण पक्षों - भूस्वामित्व, नगर-ग्राम, मुख्य धंधे, धार्मिक विश्वास, सामाजिक, आर्थिक तथा राजनैतिक तंत्र के रूप को प्रकट करती हैं। वैसे भी अभिलेख घटनाओं के निष्पक्ष वर्णन तथा ऐतिहासिक तथ्यों के वास्तविक मूल्यों से अवगत कराने के सर्वाधिक महत्वपूर्ण ऐतिहासिक साक्ष्य एवं आधार हैं।

समसामयिक बीकानेर राज्य में भी मुगलों की भांति कर निर्धारण भूमि की उत्पादकता पर आधारित था। गांव एक इकाई था और आबंटन के प्रयोजन का आधार जाति या उपजाति होता था। भूमि पर अधिकार का वर्गीकरण विभिन्न गांवों के मुखियाओं अथवा राजपूत कुलों के साथ उनके सम्बन्धों के आधार पर था। भूमिहीन किसानों तथा धार्मिक व्यक्तियों को भी आबंटन किया जाता था और जिनसे जाट काश्तकार प्रत्यक्ष रूप से प्रभावित होते थे। भू-कर निर्धारण में जाट जाति के चौधरी, डोलियार, काश्त और असामी वर्ग का प्रभुत्व था। 18वीं सदी में बीकानेर राज्य में भूमि चीरा एवं परगना में विभाजित थी। उस समय के कुछ प्रमुख चीरे- पूगल, जसरासर, सहीकोठी, गुसाईंसर, मगरा, खादर, खारीपती और शेखासर आदि थे। इन चीरों के निवासी काश्तकारों में जाटों का वर्चस्व था। एक चीरा औसत रूप से तीस से एक सौ एक और सोलह गांवों का होता है। चीरा और गांव राठौड़ों के आने से पूर्व में अस्तित्व में थे, जबकि दखली गांव प्रवासियों के द्वारा बसाये गये थे। इन गांवों को पाँच श्रेणियों-खालसा, पट्टा, शासन, गांव और हुजूरिया तथा भाई-परसंगी में विभाजन था। इन सभी गांवों के मूल काश्तकार प्रायः जाट जाति के थे।

खालसा गांवों में प्रशासनिक नियंत्रण था। राज्य के प्रशासनिक पदानुक्रम नियमित किये जाते थे। नियमों और परम्पराओं पर आधारित चौधरी पद के अतिरिक्त प्रशासनिक इकाई के रूप में 'हुजदार' पद भी था, जिसे हवलदार रूप में जाना जाता था। हवलदारों

का पारिश्रमिक राज्य द्वारा भुगतान किया जाता था। चौधरी राज्य के राजस्व एकत्रित कराने में सहायता करता था। जिन गांवों में जाट जाति का प्रामुख्य था वहां राज्य के द्वारा जाट समाज के प्रतिष्ठित व्यक्तियों को इन पदों पर नियुक्त किए जाने के सन्दर्भ समसामयिक कागदों की बहियों में देखने को मिलते हैं।

इसी प्रकार खालसा गांव के किसान साधारण तथा अस्थायी काश्तकारी अधिकार एवं अधिक करों के बोझ से पीड़ित थे। वस्तुतः शासक और किसानों के मध्य कोई सीधा सम्बन्ध नहीं था। राजस्व प्राप्ति में बिचौलिया वर्ग सहायता करता था।

रामपुरिया रिकार्ड की कागदों की बहियों से समसामयिक बीकानेर राज्य के काश्तकारों पर लगाये जाने वाले अनेक करों की भी जानकारी मिलती है जो तत्कालीन आर्थिक स्वरूप को प्रकट करती है। इन करों में 48 प्रकार के करों का उल्लेख प्राप्त हुआ है, जिनमें कुछ नाम इस प्रकार हैं - धुवान, देज, देसपथ, युक्त, अंगा, ठाकुरजी, गोसाईजी, मेलापड़ीखाती, देसपथ, मुर्ज, जाकिरा, कुंत्ता, सुखदा, एचएएल और पाद्दोक। ये वे कर थे, जिन्हें जाट काश्तकारों को प्रशासन को देना पड़ता था।

## 2

जैसा कि पूर्व में उल्लेख किया जा चुका है कि राजस्थान राज्य अभिलेखागार में रामपुरिया रिकार्ड बीकानेर की 94 बहियों में पूर्ववर्ती बीकानेर राज्य में प्रभुत्वशाली जाट समाज के सामाजिक, सांस्कृतिक ताने-बाने, रीति-रिवाज, परम्पराओं, सामाजिक विवादों, जाति पंचायतों आदि में विद्यमान महत्त्वपूर्ण सूचनाओं से युक्त दस्तावेज सन्दर्भ रूप में देखने को मिलते हैं। इनमें से कतिपय प्रमुख दस्तावेज मय मूल पाठ प्रस्तुत हैं -

बैसाख बदी 10 सम्वत् 1859 बही संख्या 12 पेज 129 में उल्लेख है कि डेलाणे का जाट खेमा अमरोणी 40 साल बाद गांव पुनवास मेडते के गाँव बसाने के लिए आया। इसको जमीन की बिजाई का लगान देना होगा : गांव नोरगंदेसर री रूखवाली री भाइद्द रो हुवालदार जोग तीथा गांव नोरंगदेसर रो चौधरी पेमों जीवणा रो बुढो छैः तिके ने रूखवाली भाछ रा रु. 2 लेज्यो बधती खेचल नां हुंसी साल तमाम अर सं. 1859 घोडा रेख मे मंतो मोडज्यो।[1]

बैसाख बदी 1 सं. 1859 बही नं. 12 पेज 122 गांव के चौधरियों को खालसा गाँव के लगान देने के सम्बन्ध में :

गांव डेलाणे ने चौधरी देवसी मेहा जोगतीथा डेलाणें रा जाट खेमे अमरोणी बरस 40 गांव पुनावास मेड़ते रे गांव सु आयो छैः सुं गांव में बससी इये बाप दादे रा खेत छैः

सुं इये नें सींव काडसी पैदा जो जीम से सुराओ देसी बिजाई गांव में नागौर रा गुवाड़ों बससी तोरी पीठ रहसी बैसाख बदी 1 सं. 1859 बही नं. 12 पेज 122।[2]

संवत 1898 मिति. दूज आसोज सुदी 110 पेलडी बही नं. 48 पृष्ठ 126 में सरदार शहर के हवलदार को रकम चुकाने के आदेश है :

गांव गिड़गचिये रा चौधरियां रे ईत सम सुता जोग तीथा थारो गांव तो खालसे छैः सुं थारे गांव री हासल बड़ी भाछ आगा भाछ रूखवाली री भाछ पानेइरी भाछ या गढ़ सुं रकम उतरे सुं सरब खालसे रे सरे श्रीसरदारशहर रै हुवालदार ने चुकाय देजो छः साहा हुक्मचन्द।[3]

बैसाख सुदी 9 सम्वत् 1899 बही नं. 49 पृष्ठ नं. 193 में गांव गणेशगढ़ के चौधरी मला, अर्जुन, चीमना, तुलछा, ताखड़ को दिया जाने का उल्लेख है :

गांव गुणेसगढ़ रै चौधरी मलो अरजन चीमनो तुलछो ताखर श्री दरबार मालूम कराई चौधर लारे रकनो हुवे सु सदामद जाटो रो हुवे छैः सुं मोहने दराई जे सुं हमें इये गांव रे चौधरियां रे रकनो लाग छैः सु अेलेसी।[4]

मिति आसाढ़ बदी 10 सं. 1896 बही नं. 46 पेज नं. 227-228 में दर्ज गांव खरसण्डी के चौधरी को आपसी 15 रु. के लेने-देने में भुगतान करने के आदेश का उल्लेख़ है :

गांव खरसंडी में चौधरी वीरा सोहू जोग तीथा गांव नगरासरी रे चौधरी रूधे सींवर श्री दरबार मालम कराई रु. 15 तेंमे मांगु छैः देवे नहीं रूपीया ब्याज सुधा परादेजे।[5]

संवत 1898 मिति दूजा असौज सुदी 13 में उल्लेख है कि गांव दादूरा के चौधरियों को आदेश दिया गया कि आपका गांव खालसा है अतः वर्ष की उपज में होने वाली आवक 'रिणी के कमठाने' तालके (मद) में लगाने के आदेश दिये गये।

गांव दादुरा चौधरिया रे सम सुता जोग तीथा थारो गांव खालसे छैः सु इये गांव री पैदा सं. 1899 साल सु रिणी लालके कमठाणें रे काम में जमा घात दीनी छैः सु कमठाणें तालके लागसी सुं हमे इये गांव री मुसदी हजुरी वीरामण वा दुजो कोई अरज न करसी माहरो बचन छैः दस्तखत साहा हुक्मचन्द।[6]

मिति बैसाख सुदी 5 सम्वत् 1896 बही नं. 46 पृष्ठ 189 में गांव अमरसर, घड़साना के चौधरी बुधर सारण को गांव खोखराने के चौधरी किसने गोदारे के मध्य और खरीद की बकाया रकम देने के सम्बन्ध में उल्लेख मिलता है :

गांव अमरसर घड़साना रे मैं चौधरी बुधर सारण जोग तीथा गांव खोखराणें रे चौ. किसने गोदारे श्री दरबार में मालूम कराई सं. 1890 साल ऊठ 1 रु. 34 में बेचीयो

थो ते में रु. 17 तो मने दिया बाकी रुपया दीया नहीं सुं हमें इये रा रूपीयारो सलुक कर दे जे सलुक न किया तो तलब हुसी दुजी तरह झगड़ो ऐडबी हुवे तो श्री दरबार अधजाब करजों।[7]

बैसाख सुदी 13 सम्वत् 1903 बही 53 पृष्ठ नं. 180 में राजपुरा तहसील नोहर के चौधरी खेतो नानू को गांव का जमींदार बनाने व गांव आबाद करने के सम्बन्ध में अन्य किसी द्वारा दखलंदाजी नहीं करने के आदेश हैं :

नोहर रा हवलदार जोग तीथा गांव राजपुरीये रा जमीदार चौधरी खेतो नानु सारण सदामद रा छैः सुं हुणे चौ. ताजीयो ईयां ने फोड़ा घाते छैः सुं जमीदारा सदामद रो इयां रो छैः इये गांव बसायो छैः सुं हमें इये गांव रो जमीदारा रो रकानो नोहर रे खालसे रे गांवा रे चौधरीयाँ रे सरे छुट मेल इये न छोडाय जाय जो इये री पीठ राखज्यो इये गांवा री जीम गैर ईलाके रे गांव जमाल रे बाणीयों मोती बावे छैः सूं मति बावण दिज्यों ओ गांव में गुवाड़ी लाय बसासी ताकी जीम बाहसी।[8]

सावण बदी 3 सम्वत् 1903 बही नं. 53 पृष्ठ नं. 205 में भादरा में जमीन के कागज बनाने व उसके नजराने के सम्बन्ध में उल्लेख है :

भादरा रे परगने रे गांव जीसागरी बड़ी रो चौधरी कस्बो बुधीयो सीरीराम चौधरी रो कागद सं. 1899 बैशाख वद 3 हुवो थो सुं हणे चौधरी मीसरी चौधरी आधी रो कागद कराय ले गयो थो तेरे नीजराणो रा रु. 50 दिया था तै ऊपर हणे श्री दरबार सुं चौधरी बुधीयो कस्वो ने चौधरी दीवी छैः तेरे सु गांव सापत री करसी तेरे नीजराणों रा रु. 150 ठाहारीया सुं भादरा रे साहै जमा हुसी है हस्ते मोहोतो माहेसंघ।[9]

सावरा सुदी 3 सम्वत् 1928 बही कागजो री बही नं. 74 के पृष्ठ नं. 59 में गांव दीनगढ़ परगने हनुमानगढ़ की चौधर कड़वासरे मारू धारणिये से लेकर 1000 बीघा सिक्खों को बसाने हेतु दी गई निम्नानुसार हासल भाग रकीगें आदि लिए जाने का उल्लेख है :

श्री हनुमानगढ़ रै प्रगने रे गांव दीनगढ़ री चौधर सदामद सुं कडवासरै मारू धारणीये सु खुरै छी सुं इये गांव लार जमी बीघा 20000 थी ते मांय सुं जमी बीघा 10000 काट गांव 1 सीखां ने बसावणा दे दीया जै सुं अे उदास हुव गया सुं जमी बीघा 10000 इये रे बास लारे रेहसी ते में मारू सुं बुने पुठा गांव दीनगढ़ में बसाया छैः सुं जमीं वीघा 10000 इये रे बास लारे रेहसी ते में मारू सुं बुरावतड़ खेत आय गया छैः सुं कांकड़ लगता जमी बीघा 10000 आसरे में आय जीसी तीके ईया ने पुठा दराय दी जासी अर बाकी खेत बेंतड फर सीखा सामल रय जासी तो अे आपरा बाहसी

हासल सीखा ने परगने रे सर मलबे सुधा दे देसी गांव आबाद करसी चौधरी री छुट वाधड़ तमा पा ढोल गुवाड़ी आगले कागाद मुजब लासी द पड़त मनफूल कमपनीयन ईस्टार ऑफ इण्डीया।[10]

सम्वत् 1933 बही कागदा री नम्बर 79 के पृष्ठ नम्बर 17-18 में गांव गणेशगढ़ के चौधरी माने ताखर और सारण मोटे वगैरा के जमीन बंटवारे का उल्लेख मिलता है:

श्री सूरतगढ़ रै परगने रे गांव गुणेशगढ़ रै चौ. मानै ताखर सादु मुमकै श्री दरबार मालुम कराई मोहारे गांव लारे जमी बीघा 150,000 आस रै माह रा. जाटो रे सीर री थी ते में जमी बीघा 35000 सारणा मोटे कान रे वास लारे पड़ी अर जमी बीघा 20000 दुरगे कासणीये रे बास लारे पड़ी ते में खेत महारों बेंतड़ आय गया तै बाबत हक्मां कोंन्सल सुं मोटे सामा लीख दीयो छैः सुं हुवालदार मोटे ने समझा कर मुनासब फैसला हुसी सुं कर देसी फैर म्हो इये बासा रा अजर न करसा बाकी जमी बीघा 95000 रही ते में आध मता राठा रा बास 4 पठ नुरेसुरा बमुमेका सादु मुमाराढढ़ी गेहण छैः सुं बासा रे अनमान मुजब बांट लेसी बाकी जीम आधी ताखर मले नरसे बैगर री ओलाद में रहसी बास नारा करसी तोरो नीजराण रा कागद नीयारा नीयारा कराय लेसी अर बास नारा बांध लासी हमे ऊपर मंडा मुजब जमीं सरब बासो ताल कै रहसी खत आप आपरी जमी में काठसी धन सारों बासा रो इयै गांव री रोही में खुसी आसी जठे चरसी दस्तखत मिमरान कोंसल मिति जेठ बदी 10 क. महक्का माल सुं।[11]

मिति आसाढ़ सुदी 8 सम्वत 1933 बही कागजों री नम्बर 79 के पृष्ठ नम्बर 26 पर दर्ज है। गांव सातु में जाटों की डोली में दी गई भूमि को सदाभद की तरह से जोतने देने हेतु भोगते को दिया आदेश है :

रा. नाहरसंघ सादुलसंघोत वणीरोत जोग तीथा गा. सातु मैं म्हैते सालम गीर रहे छैः तेने भोगता जाटा री डोली री जमीं बीघा 2000 दीयोड़ी छैः सु सदामद बाह छैः तै मुजब बाहण दे जो तेरो कागद सं. 1909 मिति आसोज बदी 5 रा दः प्रोहत चिमनराम री म्हैत प्रभातगीर रे नवे रा हुवा छैः तै ऊपर कागद दुजा सम्वत् 1919 मिति जेठ सुदी 3 रा दः मेहोत लीलाधर रा हुआ छैः सुं वीजनस हाजर छैः तै ऊपर नवो कर दियो।[12]

सम्वत् 1936 बही कागजो री बही नम्बर 82 के पृष्ठ नं. 31-32 पर गांव मलखेड़ के बैनीवाल तहसील भादरा के परगने में गांव डूंगरबास नया बसाने हेतु आदेश है :

भादरा रे परगने रे गांव मरखेड़े रे बेहणीवाल माजी श्री दरबार मालम कराई भादरा रै परगने मैं जीम बीघा 8000 मीने मीणाय दिजे तो गांव बसाय लेऊ

चौधर रो कागद माहरे नवे रा कराय यदीजे सुं हमें भादर रै परगने मैं गांव डुगरवास नवा बसासी तेरी चौधर वैणीवाल मोजी धोकल रे ने श्री दरबार सुं दीवी छैः तेरे नीजराणें रा रू. 201 ठाहारीया छैः सुं भादरा रे सारे जमा हुसी अर इये गांव लार जीम बीघा 8000 अखरे बीघा आठ हजार जोड़े खरथोण ऊपर गांव बसाती तै सुं लगती भादरा रे बासो री वा गांव भोजासर री मीणीय घताय दी जासी अर गांव में गुवाड़ी बसासी तेरी रकम परगने रे सेर भरसी आर चौधर पणे री छुट माजी री गुवाड़ी ने जीम बाहसी ते में अधखर छुटो जासी अर ढोल गुवाड़ छुट पचीतरो परगने रे सरे आलसी अर गांव बरस तीन में आबाद कर लेसी कैदास बरस तीन आबादी न करसी तो चौधर इये रे न रहसी अर हसाबी चाल चालसी गांव आबाद कर लेसी। तो चौधर इये सूं न उतरसी पीठ रेसी द. मिमरान सम्वत भादुबा बदी 3 छः महाराव हरी संघ।[13]

सम्वत 1934 बही नं. 45 पृष्ठ नम्बर 111-112 में गांव चंगाई के कस्बे आसे ओर गांव ढाणी के कालिया के बीच नाता के विवाद का निपटारा किया जाना व नजराना राजकोष में जमा किये जाने का उल्लेख है :

नीजराणेंरा 20 चंगोइ रे कस्वें आसे री बहूं आय कही के माहारो बेटो ठाकरीयो धीक गयो तेरी बहूं ने माहरे जेट पदमें रे बेट कालीये गांव ढाणी रे सीरावग मोहोके रे पले मने पुछीया बीना लगाय दीवी वा माहरे बेटे री बहू रे गहणो थो सु मोहोके म नदीयो नहीं तारो मोहोके कने सुं तो गहणों पाछो दरायो ने कालीये कने सुं रू. 40 आसै री बहू ने बैर रा दराया आपस में राजीपो करायो आगे कालीये रू. 90 बैर रा लीया था ते सुं कालीये कने सुं देराया तेरे नीजराणे रा आसे री बहूं सु लीया सु जमा मिति फागुण सुदी 5 ह. मोहोतो भीखाराम सावा बही राजगढ़।[14]

इसी प्रकार एक अभिलेख में सगाई विवाद का भी उल्लेख मिलता है। इसमें गांव बाबल परगना बिहाणी के जाट नेतराम और गांव चांद गोठड़ी के जाट मुखराम के बीच सगाई विवाद का निपटारा है :

नीजराणा रा सुं मिति चैत बदी 1 सम्वत् 1934 बही नम्बर 45 के पृष्ठ नम्बर 112 सावा बही राजगढ़ में 100 गांव बाबल प्रगने भीयाणी रे जाट नेतराम आपसी सगाई गांव, चान्द गोड़ी रे जाट मुखराम री बेटी सुं क़री थी अर आगे पहला सगाई गांव हुई प्ररगने दादरी रे सोवराण गोमद रे भाई सुं करी थी सुं गोमद आय टंटो कीयो तारा नेतराम मुखराम ने रु. 100) सगाई पेटे दिया था सुं पाछा तेय नेतराम मांगवा रुपीया रो राजीनामो मुखराम ने दीयो न मांग गांव हुई रे सोवराण गोमद रे रही तरे नीजराणे रा गांव हुई रे सोवण गोमद।[15]

मिति काती सुदी 5 सम्वत् 1944 बही कागदो री नम्बर 89 के पृष्ठ नम्बर 35, 36 में उल्लेख है कि चुरू परगने के गांव खासोली के चौधरी फरसे और इसी गांव के चौधरी डालू के बीच चौधर का बंटवारा हुआ :

चुरु रे परगने रे गोंव खासोली री चौधर चौधरी फरसे रूहल डालुदाय में रे छैः तेरी हणे तहकीकात कराय मीसल मुरतब हुई तो चौधर आधी फरसे रे अर चौधर आधी डालु रे साबत हुई पीण कागद मोहर छाप से ईयां रे हुवो नहीं ते सुं हमें श्री दरबार सुं गांव खासोली री चौधर आधी रो कागद चौधरी डालु किसने रे जाट दायमें ने कराय दीयो छैः तेरे नीजराणे रा रु. 35 अखरे रूपीया पैतीस चेरासाही ठहरीया छैः सुं चुरू रे साहे जमा हुसी अर चौधर पणें रो रकानो ढोल गुवाड़ नंदकार पांचोतरो वगैर परगने रे सरे आधो ओ लेसी अर गांव आबाद राखसी हसाबी चाल चालसी तो चौधर इये सुं न ऊतरसी पीठ रेहसी छैः मिमबरान कौंसल मिति काती सुदी 5 सम्वत् 1944 बही कागदो री नम्बर 89 के पृष्ठ नम्बर 35, 36।[16]

मिति प्रथम चैत सुदी 5 सम्वत् 1944 बही नं. 89 के पृष्ठ नम्बर 39-40 में भादरा परगने के गांव कूंजी के चौधरी नानू साहू के चौधर वंशानुगत नजराना लेकर जारी रखने का वर्णन है :

भादरा रे परगने रे गोंव कुंजी री चौधर आधी चौधरी नानु सोहू रे थी तेरा कागद मोहर छाप सं. 1983 मिति बैसाख बदी 11 हुवों थो अर नानु अेस धक गयो तेरी तहकीकात होकर मीसल मुरतब हुई तो नानु री पाती मैं नोनु रो बेटो जीवसुख साबत हुओ जे सुं हमें गांव कुंजी री चौधर आधी रो कागद चौ. जीव सुख नानु रे ने श्री दरबार सुँ कराय दीयो छैः तेरे नीजरारणे रा रू. 19 अखरे रूपीया उगणीस ठहरीया सुं भादरा रे सातै जमा हुसी अर चौधर पणें रो रकानो ढोल गुवाड़ पचोत्तरो आधो परगने रे सरे ओ लेसी अर गांव आबाद राखसी व हिसाबी चाल चालसी तो चौधर इये सं न उतरसी पीठ रेसी द. मिम्बरान कौंसल।[17]

मिति मगीसर बदी 7 सं. 1938 सावा बही नोहर बही नं. 43 के पृष्ठ नम्बर 88 में गांव भगवान रेऊ सिहाग की बहू को सिहाग हरजी के पल्ले लगाने पर रीठ लेने का हवाला है :

रीठ रे कांगदां रा 5 गांव भगवान रे रेऊ सीहाग री बहू वीधवा हुंती तेने सीहाग हरजी रे पले लगाई तेरे रीठ रे कागद रा लीया सु जमा।

सम्वत् 1938 सावा बही नोहर नं. 43 पृष्ठ नम्बर 88 में उल्लेख है कि : गांव सरदारपुरे के सेवे कड़वासरे के अपने काके के बेटे पेमे की बहू को नाते देने पर रीठ वसूल करने का कागद बनाया गया :

गांव सीरदार पुर रे सेवे कड़वासरे आपरे काके रे बेट पैम री बहूं वीधवा हुवती तेने पले लगाई तेरे रीठ रे कागद मिति पोहो बदी अमावश कर दीयो तेरा भराया सुं जमा ह. रूपो कासणीयों चौखा।[19]

मिति पौष सुदी 5 सं. 1938 बही पृष्ठ 43 के पृष्ठ नं. 89 पर गांव बरवाली के लक्ष्मण खीचड़ ने अपने भाई की बहू को पल्ले लगाने पर रीठ के कागद का उल्लेख किया है :

**गांव बरवाली रे लीछमण खीचड़ आपरे भाई री बहू ने पले लगाई तेरे रीठ 3 कागद रा लीया सुं जमा।[20]**

जाट समाज में गोद लेने की प्रथा का उल्लेख भी प्राप्त होता है। सम्वत् 1938 बही नं. 43 के पृष्ठ नं. 88 में गांव नवलखी के गोदारे पीथे द्वारा अपने भाई के लड़के को खोले (गोद) लेने का कागद मिलता है :

खोला कागद गांव नवलखी रे गोदारे पीथे रे औलाद नही से सुं आपसी खुस रजा सुं आप रे भाई कालु रे बेटे पोते ने आपरी राजी आसी तेने खोले राखसी तेरे कागद रा लीया सुं जमा।[21]

सम्वत् 1938 बही नं. 43 के पृष्ठ नम्बर 87-88 में गांव शोयराणी के टीकू साहू द्वारा अपने भतीजे लछु हणुते के बेटे को गोद लेने का कागद :

खोला कागद गांव शोयराणी रे टीकू सहु रे औलाद नही ते सु टीकु जीवते थके आपरे भतीजे लघु हणुते रे बेटे ने खोले लीयो छेः अर टीकु आपरा खने जीवत खरच कीयो छैः तारां इये ने खोले लेकर पाछे बधाई छी भाईपे री अर हणै टीकु धीक गयो तेरे मा. 1 हुवो तेरी खबर श्री दरबार में हुई तारा टीकु रो धन माल वगैर जबदी श्री दरबार सु कियो तारा गांव रा ठाकर खेतसंघ चौ. तखु सहू कुमों सीलु वा धाय भाई मुलचन्द रो आदमी लालु पुंवार आठे आयर जार कीवी के ओ खोलों आगे हुवोंड़ों छैः अर कागद श्री दरबार रो हुवोड़ो नहीं तांरो इये खोले री तकीकात करी सुं खोलो हुवोड़ों सही नीसरो ते सुं खोले रो कागद कर दीयो तेरा लीया सुं जमा।[22]

उस समय लगाये जाने वाले करों के विवरण भी इन बहियों में यत्र-तत्र मिलते हैं।

सम्वत् 1944 री के पृष्ठ नम्बर 36 पर गांव भादरा के गांव डूंगरसंघपुर की चौधर हिस्से चौथे की नोपे बिजाणिये को देने का उल्लेख मिलता है।

भादरा रे परगने रे गांव डुंगर संघपुरे री चौधर हिसे चौथे री चौधरी नापे बीजारणीये रे थी तेरा कागज मोहर छाप रो सम्वत् 1932 मिति कर्तिक सुदी 6 रो थो ते री नकल मीसल सांमल छै अर नोपो अस धक गयो अर नोपे रे खेले मनसो छैः तेरी तहकीकात

कराय मीसल मुरतब हुई तो नोपे रे खोले मनसो साबत हुवो ते सुं हमैं श्री दरबार सुं गांव डूंगरसंघ पुरै री चौधर हेसे चौथे री रो कागद चौधरी मनसे नोपे रे बीजारणिये ने कराय दीयो छैः तेरे नीजराणें रा रु. 8-00 अखरे रूपीया आठ ठहरीया छैः सु भादरा रै साहै जमा हुसी अर चौधर रो रकानो ढोल गुवाड़ पचोतरो हेसे चौथे रो परगने रे सरे ओ लेसी अर गांव आबाद राखसी हिसाबी चाल चालसी तो चौधर इये सुं न उत्तरसी पीठ रहेसी छैः मिम्बरान कौंसल मिति मीगसर बदी 7 सम्वत् 1944 बही नम्बर 89 कागजो री सम्वत् 1944 री के पृष्ठ नम्बर 36 पर दर्ज है।[23]

मिति पौष सुदी 11 दुजी सम्वत् 1944 बही कागजो री बही नम्बर 89 के पृष्ठ नम्बर 37-38 पर भादरा के बास डूंगरबास की चौधर आधी चौधरी चेने चतरे गोदारे को दी गई :

भादरा रे बास डूंगरवास री चौधर आधी चौधरी चेने चतरे रे गोदारे रे थी तेरी हणे तहकीकात कराय मिसल मुरतब हुई तो कागद इये रे मोहर छाप रो इये रे हुवाड़ो नहीं अर चौधर आधी इयो रे साबत हुई ते सुं हमें श्री दरबार सु बास डुंगरवास री चौधर आधी रो कागद चौधरी चेने चतरोणी गोदारे ने कराय दीयो छैः तेरे नीजराणे रा रु. 11 अखरे रूपीया ईगारे ठहरीया छैः सुं भादरा रे साहै जमा हुसी अर चौधर पणे रो रकानो ढोल गुवाड़ छुट पचोत रो आछो प्रगने रे सरे अरे लेसी अर बास आबाद राखसी हिसाबी चाल चालसी तो चौधर इये सुं न उत्तरसी पीठ रहेसी द. मिम्मबरान कौंसल।[24]

मिति आसोज बदी 11 सम्वत् 1944 बही कागदों री बही नम्बर 89 के पृष्ठ नम्बर 36 पर भादरा परगने के बास मोतीपुरे की चौधर चौधरी गेने देदाणी मील को दी गई।

भादरा रे परगने रे बास मोतीपुरे री चौधर चौधरी गेने देदाणी मील रे थी तेरी हणे तहकीकात कराय मीसल मुरतब हुई तो कागद मोहर छाप रो इये रे हुवोड़ो नहीं अर चौधर साल में इये रे साबत हुई ते सुं हमें श्री दरबार सु बास मोतीपुरे री चौधर रो कागद चौधरी गेने देदाणी ने कराय दीयो छैः तेरे नीजराणें रा रु. 21 अखरे रूपीया ईकीस ठहरीया छैः सु भादरा रै सहे जमा हुसी अर चौधर पणे रो रकनो ढोल गुवाड़ छूट पचोतरो रे प्रगने रे सरे ओ लेसी अर बास आबाद राखसी हिसाबी चाल चालसी तो चौधर इये सुं न उत्तरसी पीठ रहेसी द. मिम्बरान कौंसल।[25]

सारांशतः राजस्थान अभिलेखागार में जाट इतिहास विषयक अनेक अभिलेख संग्रहित हैं। इन अभिलेखों से अनेक तथ्यपरक उल्लेख प्राप्त होते हैं, जो इतिहास के साक्ष्य और शोध के आयाम हैं। इन बहियों में जाट समाज की सामाजिक, आर्थिक एवं सांस्कृतिक स्थितियों के साथ उनके योगदान का वर्णन प्राप्त होता है। विभिन्न रीतिरिवाजों से सम्बन्धित अभिलेख तत्कालीन समाज के स्वरूप का चित्रण करते हैं। निश्चय ही ये अभिलेख जाटों संबंधित नवीन प्रस्तुति में सहायक हैं।

## राजस्थान राज्य अभिलेखागार, बीकानेर
## बीकानेर में कागदों की बहियाँ की सूची

| क्रमांक | सम्वत् | क्रमांक | सम्वत् |
|---|---|---|---|
| 1 | 1811 | 40 | 1890 |
| 2 | 1820 | 41 | 1891 |
| 3 | 1827 | 42 | 1892 |
| 4 | 1831 | 43 | 1893 |
| 5 | 1838 | 44 | 1894 |
| 6 | 1839 | 45 | 1895 |
| 7 | 1840 | 46 | 1896 |
| 8 | 1846 | 47 | 1897 |
| 9 | 1851 | 48 | 1998 |
| 10 | 1854 | 49 | 1999 |
| 11 | 1857 | 50 | 1900 |
| 12 | 1859 | 51/1 | 1901 |
| 13 | 1861 | 51/2 | 1901 |
| 14 | 1863 | 52 | 1902 |
| 15 | 1866 | 53 | 1903 |
| 16 | 1867 | 54 | 1904 |
| 17 | 1867 | 55 | 1905 |
| 18 | 1868 | 56 | 1906 |
| 19/1 | 1870 | 57 | 1907 |
| 19/2 | 1870 | 58 | 1908 |
| 20 | 1871 | 59 | 1909 |
| 21 | 1872 | 60 | 1910 |
| 22 | 1873 | 61 | 1911–12 |
| 23 | 1874 | 62 | 1913 |
| 24 | 1875 | 63 | 1914 |
| 25 | 1876 | 64 | 1915 |
| 26 | 1877 | 65 | 1916–17 |
| 27 | 1878 | 66 | 1918–19 |
| 28 | 1879 | 67 | 1920 |
| 29 | 1880 | 68 | 1921–22 |
| 30 | 1881 | 69 | 1923 |
| 31 | 1882 | 70 | 1924 |
| 32 | 1883 | 71 | 1925 |
| 33/1 | 1884 | 72 | 1925–26 |
| 33/2 | 1884 | 73 | 1927 |
| 34 | 1885 | 74 | 1928 |
| 35/1 | 1886 | 75 | 1929 |
| 35/2 | 1886 | 76 | 1930 |
| 36 | 1886 | 77 | 1931 |
| 37 | 1888 | 78 | 1932 |
| 38 | 1889 | 79 | 1933 |
| 39 | 1890 | 80 | 1934 |

| क्रमांक | सम्वत् |
|---|---|
| 81 | 1935 |
| 82 | 1936 |
| 83 | 1937—38 |
| 84 | 1939 |
| 85 | 1940—41 |
| 86 | 1940—43 |
| 87 | 1942—43 |
| 88 | 1944 |
| 89 | 1945 |
| 90 | 1946 |
| 91 | 1947 |
| 92 | 1948—57 |

## संदर्भ

1. बैसाख बदी 10 सम्वत् 1859, बही नम्बर 12, पेज 129।
2. बैसाख वदी 1, सं. 1859, बही नं. 12 पेज 122
3. सं. 1898 मीति. दुजा आसोज सुद 10 पेलड़ी बही नं. 48 पाना 126
4. वैसाख सुद 9 सम्वत् 1899 बही नं. 49 पाना नं. 193
5. मिति आसाढ़ बद 10 सं. 1896 बही नं. 46 पेज नं. 227-228
6. सं. 1898 मी. दुजा आसौज सुद 13
7. मिति बैसाख सुद 5 सम्वत् 1896 बही नं. 46 पाना 189
8. बैसाख सुदी 13 सम्वत् 1903, बही 53, पाना नं. 180.
9. सावण बद 3 सम्वत् 1903, बही नं. 53 पाना नं. 205
10. सावरा सुद 3 सम्वत् 1928 बही कागजो रीबही नं. 74 के पाना नं. 59
11. सम्वत् 1933 बही कागदा री नम्बर 79 के पाना नम्बर 17-18
12. मिति आसाढ़ सुदी 8 सम्वत् 1933 बही कागजों री नम्बर 79 के पाना नम्बर 26
13. सम्वत् 1936 बही कागजो री बही नम्बर 82 के पाना नं. 31-32 पर दर्ज है।
14. सम्वत 1934 बही नं. 45 पाना नम्बर 111-112
15. मिति चैत बदी 1 सम्वत् 1934 बही नम्बर 45 के पाना नम्बर 112 सावा बही राजगढ़
16. मिति काती सुद 5 सम्वत् 1944 बही कागदो री नम्बर 89 के पाना नम्बर 35, 36
17. मिति प्रथम चैत सुद 5 सम्वत् 1944 बही नं. 89 के पाना नम्बर 39-40
18. मिति मीगसर बद 7 सं. 1938 सावा बही नोहर बही नं. 43 के पाना नम्बर 88

19. सम्वत् 1938 सावा बही नोहर नं. 43 पाना नम्बर 88 पर
20. मिति चैत बदी 11 सम्वत् 1938 सावा बही नोहर सं. 1938 बही नम्बर 43 के पाना नं. 89
21. मिति चैत बदी अमावस्या सम्वत् 1938 सावा बही नोहर सम्वत् 1938 बही नं. 43 के पाना नं. 89
22. मिति पोटो सुद 5 सम्वत् 1938 सावा बही नोहर सम्वत् 1938 बही नं. 43 के पाना नम्बर 87-88 पर।
23. मिति मंगसर बद 7 सम्वत् 1944 बही नम्बर 89 कागजों री सम्वत् 1944 री के पाना नम्बर 36 पर दर्ज है।
24. मिति पोहो सुद 11 दुजी सम्वत् 1944 बही कागजो री बही नम्बर 89 के पाना नम्बर 37-38 पर।
25. मिति आसोज बद 11 सम्वत् 1944 बही कागदों री बहीनम्बर 89 के पाना नम्बर 36 पर।

## 19

# जाट आन्दोलन का प्रणेता सरदार गोकुला जाट

**डॉ. मलिका बोहरा**

राजपूताने में जाटों का राजनैतिक उत्कर्ष दिल्ली के सम्राट औरंगजेब के शासनकाल में सन् 1660-69 में आरंभ हुआ, जब मथुरा के जाटों ने उसकी धर्मान्धिता के विरुद्ध विद्रोह का झंडा गाड़ दिया। तब उत्तरप्रदेश के सादाबाद, हाथरस या महामाया नगर) के पास स्थित स्थान तिलपत के जमींदार गोकुला जाट के नेतृत्व में जाटों ने साहसपूर्ण कार्य करके एक फौजदार अब्दुल नबी खां को मार डाला। इसका कारण राजस्व संग्रहण कार्य तथा फौजदारों द्वारा बलपूर्वक कर की वसूली कृषक जाटों से करनी थी।[1] ऐसे प्रतिकारात्मक आन्दोलन की शुरुआत यू तो मुगल सम्राट शाहजहां के समय (1628-58 ई.) में हो चुकी थी, जब मथुरा, (जिसका नाम मुआसिल-ए-आलमगीरी में इस्लामाबाद बताया है) महावन तथा कामां पहाड़ी का फौजदार मुर्शीद कुली खान था, जो काश्तकारों के अभियानों का उपयोग अपनी कामपिपासा की संतुष्टि हेतु करता था। *मुआसिर-उल-उमरा* में बताया गया है कि मथुरा में जब कृष्ण जन्माष्टमी के अवसर पर विशाल मेला आयोजित होता था, उस दौरान वहां का गवर्नर मुर्शीद खां हिन्दुओं जैसा लिबास धारणकर, धोती पहनकर व माथे पर टीका लगाकर भीड़ में घुस जाता था तथा सुन्दर रमणी को पकड़कर उसे नाव में बिठाकर यमुना पार कर आगरा के शाही महल के अपने कक्ष में ले जाता था, लेकिन बदनामी के डर के मारे गायब युवती के परिजन कोई खैर-खबर नहीं करते थे।[2] आखिरकार वह सन् 1638 में संभल के अन्तर्गत जटवाड़ा (जाटों की एक बस्ती) में आक्रमण के दौरान गोली लगने से मारा गया था।

शाही आदेशानुसार उस समय मिर्जा राजा जयसिंह सन् 1637 में हिण्डोन में, सन् 1647 में महावन में तथा 1650 ई. में कांमा की पहाड़ी तथा खोह में विद्रोही किसान जाटों का दमन करने हेतु गये थे।[3] शाहजहां के शासनकाल के अंतिम वर्षों में

उत्तराधिकार युद्ध के समय व्याप्त अराजकता तथा अव्यवस्थाओं का लाभ उठाकर मथुरा, आगरा तथा अलीगढ़ के किसानों ने लुटेरों का सा व्यवहार किया था। ठेनुवा जाटों ने अपने मुखिया नंदराम के नेतृत्व में राजस्व देना बंद कर दिया। यद्यपि उत्तराधिकार युद्ध समाप्त होते ही सन् 1660 में बादशाह औरंगजेब के समक्ष उन्होंने आत्म समर्पण कर दिया[4] मगर जाटों की विद्रोहात्मक गतिविधियां जारी रही। जून 1662 ई. में अलीगढ़ में इतनी अशांति फैल गई कि उनके दमन हेतु सम्राट को सेना भेजनी पड़ी।[5]

औरंगजेब की कट्टर धार्मिक नीति से ब्रजमण्डल में एक नवीन आन्दोलन की चिनगारी भड़क उठी थी, जिसका नेतृत्व सिनसिनवार गोत्री जाट सरदार गोकुला कर रहा था।[6] मुंशी देवी प्रसाद ने *औरंगजेबनामा* ग्रंथ की पाद टिप्पणी में लिखा है कि गोकुला नाम भरतपुर महाराजाओं की वंशावली में आया है, परन्तु जागाओं की पोथी से पता चलता है कि जाट सरदार ओला ही आगे जाकर 'गोकुला' के नाम से विख्यात हुआ। उसका जन्म सिनसिनी गांव के महिपाल जाट के यहां हुआ था। महिपाल के चार पुत्र थे-सिंधुराज, ओला, झमन तथा समन, जिसमें ओला (गोकुला) दूसरे नम्बर का पुत्र था।[7] जाति नियमों के अनुसार पैतृक जमींदारी व सम्पदा का हकदार बड़ा पुत्र सिन्धुराज तथा उसका पुत्र पृथ्वीराज था। तत्कालीन साहित्यों से पता चलता है कि सन् 1650-51 में महिपाल व उसके पुत्र सिन्धुराज ने मिर्जा राजा जयसिंह का सामना किया था। मुठभेड़ में सिंधुराज मारा गया। इसी वजह से उत्तराधिकार में उसे सिनसिनी गांव की जागीर मिली थी।[8] ओला का आरंभिक जीवन गोकुल महावन में शुरु हुआ था।[9] भोजसिंह सिनसिनवार के पुत्र गंगदेवा की संततियों ने इसका साथ दिया था। गोकुला स्वभाव से क्रान्तिकारी था, इसलिए अपनी क्रांतिकारी भावनाओं को सबल बनाने के लिए उसने शुरूआत में राहजनी व लूटमार को पेशे के रूप में अपनाया था, मगर बाद में इसे छोड़कर दिल्ली के पास तिलपत गांव की जमींदारी प्राप्त करली थी, इसलिए जमींदार के रूप में युवावस्था में उसने अच्छी साख बना ली थी। यहां रहकर उसने जाट किसानों को संगठित किया और उनकी टोलियों का सरदार बन गया। उसने तथा उसके ताऊ उदयसिंह सिंधी ने किसान जाट युवकों के हाथों में लाठी, फरसा, बाण की जगह बन्दूकें थमाकर उन्हें सिपाही बना लिया था। इस प्रकार उसने 20 हजार जाट नवयुवकों का संगठन बना लिया। गोकुला धर्मनिष्ठ, देशप्रेमी, साहसी, स्वाभिमानी, निर्भीक, स्वाधीनताप्रेमी, पराक्रमी, सामाजिक एकता को महत्व देने वाला, मुगल साम्राज्य में अपनी सशक्त क्रांति की जड़ों को जमाने वाला पहला जाट सरदार रहा है।

दूसरी तरफ औरंगजेब की धार्मिक असहिष्णुता की नीति से ब्रजमण्डल के हिन्दुओं का जीवन दुश्वार हो गया था। यहां के जमींदार, किसान, मजदूर सभी के दिलों में बादशाह के विरुद्ध आक्रोश उत्पन्न हो गया था। ऐसे में फौजदारी का प्रबन्ध संभालने

के लिए बादशाह ने सितम्बर सन् 1668 में अब्दुलनबी खां को 2 हजार जात व 2 हजार सवार का मनसब देकर मथुरा भेजा, जो औरंगजेब के समान ही धर्मान्ध था। वहीं पर उसने प्रशासनिक दृष्टि से यमुना नदी के पार गोकुल के दक्षिण में अपने नाम से एक छावनी स्थापित करली तथा अपने सैनिक दस्ते को किसानों से लगान वसूल करने का आदेश दिया, लेकिन जाट किसानों के विरोध के कारण अब्दुल नबी को विद्रोह का सामना करना पड़ा। इसका कारण अपने सरदार गोकुला जाट का लगान न अदा करने का आदेश था, जिसकी कमान गोकुला ने स्वयं संभाली थी। उसे मथुरा, सिनसिनवार, सिंघोली व चावली के जाटों का समर्थन मिला था। जब अप्रैल 1669 ई. में फौजदार अब्दुलनबी खां आन्दोलनकारियों के प्रमुख गढ़ सुरहा (सहोर, मथुरा के खंदोली थाने का एक गांव, जिसे *मुआसिर-उल-उमरा*[10] में महावन परगने का एक मौजा बताया है) गांव की तरफ बढ़ा तथा उसे आक्रमण कर बरबाद कर दिया। आमने-सामने की लड़ाई में गोकुला जाट के संगठन के क्रांतिकारियों ने उसे गोली से उड़ा दिया। उसकी मृत्यु से मुगल सेना में खलबली मच गई। जैसे-तैसे मुगल सैनिक अपनी युद्ध सामग्री को वहीं छोड़कर भागने में सफल हुए, जिस पर जाटों ने कब्जा कर लिया। इससे उत्साहित होकर गोकुला के जाट दस्तों ने सादाबाद कस्बे को भी लूटकर जला दिया। इस प्रकार आगरा के अनेक स्थानों पर अव्यवस्था का माहौल पैदा हो गया। आगरा, मथुरा, सादाबाद, महावन आदि परगने जाट आन्दोलन के केन्द्र बन गये। जाटों का समर्थन यहां के अन्य हिन्दुओं ने भी किया।[11]

अब्दुलनबी की हत्या के बाद 23 मई 1669 में सम्राट ने सैफशिकन खां को मथुरा का फौजदार बनाकर भेजा। साथ ही आगरा के सेनापति राद्दन्दाज खां को तोपखान के साथ मथुरा रवाना किया। साथ ही उसकी सहायता हेतु सम्राट ने राजपूत सरदार वीरमदेव सिसौदिया, हमीद खां, समीर खां, सैयद मुरतया व उसका पिता साइया खां, नजीब खां, कमालुद्दीन, नुरूद्दीन मेवाती, शाहजहां मुहम्मद, अकबर खां बक्शी, इस्कन्दियार आदि को भी भेजा[12] लेकिन उन्हें आन्दोलनकारियों को दबाने में सफलता नहीं मिली। गोकुला के आतंक ने भंयकर रूप धारण कर लिया। सैफशिकन खां ने समस्त लूट का माल वापस करने तथा लूटमार व आगजनी की घटना बंद करने हेतु एक शांति प्रस्ताव भी उसके पास भेजा, लेकिन उसने उसे ठुकरा दिया।[13]

गोकुला जाट की उपरोक्त गतिविधियों से क्रुद्ध होकर अन्त में औरंगजेब 28 नवम्बर 1669 को स्वयं विशाल सेना लेकर मथुरा की तरफ रवाना हुआ। यमुना नदी के किनारे सैनिक छावनी बनाई। उसने अपनी अग्रिम सैनिक टुकड़ियों को आगरा की तरफ रवाना कर दिया तथा स्वयं मथुरा छावनी में रुककर गोकुला के विरुद्ध सेना का संचालन किया।[14]

दिसम्बर 1669 ई. में औरंगजेब ने अली वर्दी खां के द्वितीय पुत्र हसनअली खां[15] को सादाबाद तथा मुरसान की जाट गढ़ियों की तरफ रवाना किया। हसन अली खां ने शाही सेना के साथ जाटों की रेवाड़ा, चन्दरख तथा सरखरू नामक तीन गढ़ियों पर अचानक आक्रमण कर सफलता प्राप्त की। इस हेतु उसे बहुत बड़ी कीमत चुकानी पड़ी। इस युद्ध में जाटों ने वीरता का प्रदर्शन कर हसन खां को लोहे के चने चबाने पर मजबूर कर दिया। मुगल सेना के दस्तों को भारी क्षति उठानी पड़ी थी, फिर भी मुगलों ने कई नागरिकों को बंदी बनाया तथा उनके मवेशियों पर अधिकार कर लिया, लेकिन यहां औरंगजेब ने मानवता का परिचय दिया। उसने यहां खड़ी फसलों की रक्षा करने, लूटमार तथा अत्याचार को रोकने तथा बच्चों को गिरफ्तार न करने की आज्ञा देकर फौजदार सैफशिकन खां को 200 सवारों के साथ रवाना किया तथा हसन अली खां की सफलता पर प्रसन्न होकर उसे 3 हजार जात व 2 हजार सवार का मनसबदार बनाया। उसे तलवार तथा घोड़ा भी भेंट किया। उसने आलमगीर शाही के पुत्र अमानुल्लाह खां को मथुरा बुलाकर 300 सवार की तरक्की देकर हसनअली खां की कमान में सैन्यसंचालन का दायित्व सौंपा। इसी तरह से मुरादाबाद के फौजदार नामदार खां तथा आगरा के फौजदार होशियार खां को भी हसनअली खां की सेना में शामिल होने की आज्ञा दी। *मुआसिर-उल-उमरा* तथा *औरंगजेबनामा* के अनुसार हसनअली खां के नेतृत्व में एक विशाल सेना का गठन हुआ, जिसने मथुरा तथा सादाबाद परगने को पूरी तरह से घेर लिया। इसे देखते हुए जाटों ने सादाबाद परगने को खाली कर दिया तथा तिलपत नामक स्थल पर युद्ध की घोषणा कर दी। गोकुला ने यहां के जंगलों की आड़ में मुगल सेना की नाक में दम कर दिया, लेकिन आखिरकार मुगलों की शाही सेना ने गांव को घेर कर धावा बोल दिया। मुगल सेना ने तिलपत की गढ़ी पर अधिकार कर लिया। इस युद्ध में 4000 मुगल सैनिक मारे गये, हजारों घायल हुए। साथ ही 5 हजार से अधिक जाट सैनिक मारे गये। गोकुला जाट तथा उसका ताऊ उदयसिंह सिंधी परिवार सहित बंदी बना लिये गये। साथ ही 7 हजार से अधिक जाट किसान बंदी बना लिये गये। जाटों की कई युद्ध सामग्रियां मुगलों के हाथ आई जो कई गाड़ियों में भरकर शाही शिविर की ओर ले जाई गई।[16]

1 जनवरी 1670[17] शनिवार के दिन औरंगजेब ने मथुरा से अपना शाही सैन्य शिविर उठा लिया तथा आगरा के महलों में आ गया। दूसरी तरफ हसनअली खां ने शेख कयाम खां के निरीक्षण में गोकुला जाट व उसके ताऊ को मय परिवार तथा अन्य युद्धबंदियों को भी तिलपत से आगरा रवाना किया, जहां गोकुला को आलमगीर औरंगजेब के दरबार में उपस्थित किया गया। धर्मान्ध औरंगजेब ने समस्त युद्धबंदियों को इस्लाम धर्म स्वीकार करने का आदेश दिया जिसका कतिपय जाट किसानों ने विरोध किया, लेकिन अंततः

सम्राट के क्रोध तथा क्रूरता के आगे विवश होकर उन्होंने अपने प्राण बचाये। औरंगजेब ने दोनों क्रांतिकारी नेताओं को नृशंस कत्ल करने का आदेश दिया।

जनवरी 1670 के पहले सप्ताह में गोकुला तथा उदयसिंह को आगरा की कोतवाली के सामने एक चबूतरे पर जंजीरों से बांधकर जल्लादों के सामने लाया गया। जल्लादों ने नृशंसता पूर्वक उनकी हत्याकर उनके अंगों को एक-एक करके काट डाला तथा आगरा की सड़कों पर फेंका गया। इस वीभत्स दृश्य को आगरा की जनता ने देखा, मगर वे हृदय में करूणा तथा आंखों में आँसू लिये इस दृश्य को देखते रहे। इस प्रकार से जाट नेता गोकुला व उसके ताऊ उदयसिंह का अंत हुआ, लेकिन उनका बलिदान व्यर्थ नहीं गया। जाटों के हृदय में अब भी स्वतंत्रता की ज्वाला प्रज्जवलित हो रही थी, इसलिए उक्त नृशंस हत्याकाण्ड के 15 दिन बाद सिनसिनी (भरतपुर से 16 मील दूर उत्तर-पश्चिम में स्थित) में वहां के जमीदार भज्जासिंह के पुत्र राजाराम ने एक योग्य नेता के रूप में उभरकर इस आन्दोलन को जारी रखा।

औरंगजेब ने गोकुला के पुत्र व पुत्री के पालन पोषण की जिम्मेदारी जवाहर खां नाजिर को सौंपी तथा उन्हें मुसलमान बनाया। लड़की का विवाह उसने मुगल उच्चाधिकारी गुलाम शाह अली से करवाया तथा लड़के को कुरान-ए-हाफिज़ (कुराअने पाक की तिलावत करने वाला) बनाया। *मुहासिर-उल-उमरा* तथा *औरंगजेबनामा* के अनुसार गोकुला का पुत्र स्पष्ट तथा शुद्ध रूप से कुरआने शरीफ का उच्चारण करता था। स्वयं सम्राट भी उसके इस उच्चारण का कायल था। वह उसके बिना किसी ओर से कुरआने शरीफ की तिलावत करवाना पसंद नहीं करता था। इसलिए सम्राट ने उसे 'फाजिल' की उपाधि दी थी।[18]

## संदर्भ

1. जदुनाथ सरकार : *हिस्ट्री ऑफ औरंगजेब,* जिल्द 3, पृ. 291; फारूकी : *औरंगजेब एण्ड हिज़ टाइम्स,* पृ. 125

2. मोहम्मद साकी मुस्तइद खां द्वारा *मुआसिर-उल-उमरा* फारसी में लिखा ग्रंथ है। *मुआसिर-एल-उमरा* (हिन्दी), जिल्द-4, पृ. 486; डॉ. पी. सी. चान्दावत : *महाराजा सूरजमल और उनका युग,* पृ. 20

3. (1) *ए डेस्क्रिप्टिव लिस्ट ऑफ फरमान मंसूर एण्ड निशान फरमान,* सं. 34 (4 जून 1637) व 58 (1 जुलाई 1650 ई.)
   (2) उपेन्द्रनाथ शर्मा : *जाटों का नवीन इतिहास,* पृ. 90

4. वी. एस. भार्गव ने *मुआसिर-उल-उमरा* ग्रंथ का हवाला देते हुए अलीगढ़ का गवर्नर

नंदराम को बताया है, जो मृत्युपर्यन्त तक वहीं रहा जिसे औरंगजेब ने नियुक्त किया था। इससे पूर्व सम्राट ने नए फौजदार को नियुक्त करने का सोचा था, मगर बाद में जाटों को संगठित तथा विकसित देखकर उसने उस विचार को त्याग दिया। नंदराम को फौजदार के पद पर नियुक्ति देकर तोछीगढ़ परगने का प्रबन्धक बनाया।

5. जदुनाथ सरकार : *औरंगजेब*, जिल्द 3, पृ. 20-21
6. *मुआसिर-उल-उमरा*, पृ. 436
7. उपेन्द्र शर्मा : *जाटों का नवीन इतिहास*, पृ. 89 (1977)
8. *वाकिया-ए-राजपूताना*, भाग-2 (उर्दू) पृ. 42 ज्वाला सहाय मुंसिफ संस्करण (1878)
9. (1) *औरंगजेब नामा*, भाग 2 के पृ. 20 पर उसे सादाबाद परगने के उपद्रवग्रस्त गांवों का रईस बताया है, जबकि *मुआसिर-उल-उमरा* ने पनाह गांव का रईस लिखा है।
   (2) उपेन्द्रनाथ शर्मा : *जाटों का नवीन इतिहास*, पृ. 89
10. *मुआसिर-उल-उमरा*, 1 को तथा 4 को
11. (1) *मुआसिर-उल-उमरा*, पृ. 436,
    (2) *औरंगजेबनामा* भाग 2, पृ. 14
    (3) जदुनाथ सरकार : *औरंगजेब*, भाग 3, पृ. 332
    (4) कानूनगो : *जाट*, पृ. 38
12. *मुआसिर-उल-उमरा*, पृ. 131
13. (1) जदुनाथ सरकार : *औरंगजेब*, भाग 3, पृ. 334
    (2) कालिका रंजन कानूनगो : *जाटों का इतिहास*, पृ. 22
14. *मुआसिर आलमगीरी*, पृ. 57
15. (1) इर्विन : द *मुगल*, भाग 1, पृ. 321
    (2) *मुआसिर-उल-उमरा*, भाग 5, पृ. 423
16. *(1)* *मुआसिर-उल-उमरा*, पृ. 58
    (2) *औरंगजेबनामा*, भाग 2, पृ. 21
    (3) महाराज कुमार : *बृज*, भाग 1, पृ. 161
17. उपेन्द्रनाथ शर्मा, पृ. 96
18. *मुगलकालीन ब्रज प्रदेश 1586-1718 ई.*, भाग 1, पृ. 162

# 20

# 17वीं सदी में मुगलों के विरुद्ध जाट कृषकों का आन्दोलन और मालवा पर प्रभाव

डॉ. एस. एल. वरे

17वीं शताब्दी भारतीय इतिहास की उथल-पुथल एवं अराजकतापूर्ण सदी मानी जाती है। प्रसिद्ध मालव इतिहासकार महाराज कुमार डॉ. रघुवीरसिंह भी इस शताब्दी को युगान्तरकारी घटना मानते हैं।[1] क्योंकि इस सदी के अन्तिम दशकों में मुगल सम्राट औरंगजेब (1658-1707) की कट्टर धर्मान्धता से देश में चहुँओर मुगल सल्तनत के विरुद्ध बगावत, उत्पात, उपद्रव एवं विद्रोही आन्दोलन बढ़ते जा रहे थे। जिनका असर भी देश के कोने-कोने में दृष्टिगोचर होने लगा था। इन उपद्रवों एवं आन्दोलनों में उत्तरी भारत के जाट कृषकों का आन्दोलन भी प्रमुख था। जिनका प्रभाव देश के मध्य भाग के मालवा प्रान्त पर भी पड़े बिना नहीं रहा। यद्यपि आरम्भ में जाट कृषक शांतिपूर्ण खेतीबाड़ी कर अपना जीवनयापन करते थे परन्तु दिल्ली के मुस्लिम शासकों, विशेषकर औरंगजेब, की हिन्दू विरोधी नीति के कारण यह लोग अपने परम्परागत व्यवसाय कृषि एवं पशुपालन से हटकर उत्पात पर उतर आये थे।[2]

मालवा मध्यकालीन भारतीय इतिहास का एक महत्वपूर्ण केन्द्र बिन्दु वर्षों तक रहा है। यहाँ की समशीतोष्ण जलवायु, उपजाऊ मिट्टी, शुद्ध आबोहवा आदि से इतिहास के विद्व न साहित्यकार, लेखक एवं पाठक इसके किसी भी पक्ष से अपरिचित नहीं है। कबीर की इस जगप्रसिद्ध कहावत ने तो इसमें और चार चाँद लगा दिये कि 'मालव धरती गहन गंभीर, डग-डग रोटी पग-पग नीर'[3] तो शायरों ने यह कहकर कि - ''शामे अवध सुबह बनारस और शबे मालवा'' ने इसकी प्रसिद्धि को सातवें आसमान पर बैठा दिया।

अतः इस समृद्ध, सम्पन्न, धन-धान्य से परिपूर्ण हृदय प्रांत मालवा पर 16वीं सदी के इस जाट कृषक आन्दोलन व उपद्रव का जो औरंगजेब के शासन के दौरान लगभग

तीन दशक तक चलता रहा, बहुत प्रभाव पड़ा। यहाँ के उत्तर से दक्षिण (दक्कन) जाने वाले शाही राजमार्गों पर जाट कृषकों का अधिकार हो गया था जिससे उत्तर से दक्कन एवं दक्कन से उत्तर जाने वाले सभी राजमार्ग अवरुद्ध हो गये थे। वहीं प्रान्त में राजनैतिक असमंजस की स्थिति पैदा हो गई थी जिसके कारण प्रान्त का उत्पादन एवं प्रान्त का राजस्व निरन्तर घटता गया तथा शाही राजकोष में घाटा होता गया। उत्तर भारत से दक्षिण की ओर जाने वाले व्यापारियों के काफिले, बंजारों की बालोद, शाही खजाने, सैनिक साजो-सामान, और अमीरों के कुटुम्ब और उनके शिविर आदि लूटे जाने लगे। जो शाही रास्ता (शाही मार्ग) दिल्ली से आगरा, धौलपुर तथा मालवा से होकर दक्षिण में जाटों के मुल्क से होकर गुजरता था वह अब पूर्णतः असुरक्षित हो गया था।[4]

अब जाट अन्नदाता किसान, उत्तर भारत के आगरा, ब्रजप्रदेश और उसके आसपास के क्षेत्रों में लूटपाट कर औरंगजेब की धर्मान्धिता को कड़ी चुनौती दे रहे थे तभी उनसे प्रभावित होकर मालवा क्षेत्र के किसान भी यहाँ से गुजरने वाले शाही काफिलों तथा उनकी हुकूमत के खिलाफ गड़बड़ियाँ पैदा करने लगे थे। उत्तरी भारत के जाट कृषक तो शुरु में शाही माल-असबाब आदि को लूटा करते थे पर मालवा के विद्रोही इन्हें मध्य में लूटते थे। इससे यह बात स्पष्ट होती है कि उत्तरी भारत में शाही नियंत्रण पूरी तरह शिथिल हो चुका था। इसका लाभ उठाकर मालवा में छोटी-छोटी लड़ाई व झड़पें मुगल सूबेदारों के विरुद्ध जनता भी करने लग गई थी। इन जाट किसानों की झड़पों में पहाड़सिंह व अन्य राजपूत शासक भी मालवा के इस विद्रोह में 'बहती गंगा में हाथ धोना' वाली कहावत के अनुसार शामिल हो गये थे। यह विद्रोह कालान्तर में मालवा के साथ ग्वालियर और उसके आसपास पूरे बुन्देलखण्ड तक फैल गया। आगे चलकर मराठे आक्रमणकारी भी शामिल हो गये। यानि कि लोग आते गये और कारवाँ जुड़ता गया। सन् 1704 अर्थात् औरंगजेब की मृत्यु के तीन वर्ष पूर्व उत्तर-दक्षिण मार्ग इस तरह अवरुद्ध हुआ कि 355 शाही एवं गैर शाही पत्रों के थैले और फलों से भरे हुए टोकरे बहुत दिन बाद में मिले थे।[5]

उत्तर भारत की जाट कृषक आवाम का इतना असर हुआ कि मालवा की आवाम का यह विद्रोह दिन दूना और रात चौगुना बढ़ता गया जिससे भयभीत होकर मालवा का सूबेदार अबुनसरखाँ उज्जैन के दुर्ग कालियादह के महल में आकर छुप गया तथा माण्डू का फौजदार भागकर धार चला गया। मालवा की यह दशा देखकर औरंगजेब चिंतित हुआ तथा उसने यहाँ एक साहसी, वीर एवं विश्वसनीय सूबेदार की आवश्यकता महसूस करते हुए शहजादा बिदारबख्श को मालवा का सूबेदार (अगस्त 1703 से मई 1705) नियुक्त कर दिया और जयसिंह को उसका नायब नियुक्त किया। बिदारबख्श यहाँ कुल 19 माह रहा।

औरंगजेब के अन्तिम दिनों में तो उत्तर भारत से दक्षिण सहित देश के लगभग सभी राज्यों की राजनीतिक स्थिति विशृंखलित हो चुकी थी। अकेले मालवा में राजपूत, मराठे, बुन्देले, अफगान सभी लूटपाट पर उतारू हो गये थे।

जिस समय उत्तर भारत में चूड़ामन जाट के नेतृत्व में मुगलों के विरुद्ध जाटों का विद्रोह जोर पकड़ता जा रहा था, मुगल सम्राट ने मालवा से सवाई जयसिंह को चूड़ामन जाट एवं उनके सभी कृषक जाटों को दबाने हेतु भेजा था। जयसिंह के साथ बुद्धसिंह, नरवर के राजा गजसिंह और कोटा के राव भीमसिंह को भी भेजा था। जाट आन्दोलन को दबाने हेतु मालवा से जयसिंह की इतने समय तक अनुपस्थिति और शासन कार्य की उपेक्षा करने का लाभ मराठों ने उठाया, क्योंकि मालवा का सूबेदार जयसिंह उत्तर भारत में जाटों के विद्रोह को दबाने में दो वर्ष तक लगा रहा। यह सोचकर कि अब मालवा का मुखिया कोई नहीं था; मालवा में अब वे बेरोकटोक आक्रमण और लूटपाट करने लग गये थे।

इस तरह औरंगजेब के अनेक दुष्टतापूर्ण, घृणित, अधार्मिक व अत्याचारपूर्ण कार्यों से उसके समूचे साम्राज्य में गैर मुस्लिम आवाम का उपद्रव व असंतोष शुरु होकर उसके अंतिम दिनों में जंगल में आग की तरह फैल गया था। जिनमें जाट जमींदार, उनके परिवार के सदस्य, उत्तर भारत के जाट कृषक, जाट श्रमिक, अन्य खेतिहर, हिन्दू मजदूर यानि कि राजा से रंक तक सभी शामिल हुए और अपने धर्म, दर्शन, संस्कृति एवं मानवता की रक्षार्थ संगठित होकर अपनी आहुति देते नजर आये, जिसका असर पंजाब, राजपूताना, गोंडवाना एवं मालवा क्षेत्र में भी हुआ। यहाँ के हिन्दू जमींदारों, कृषकों एवं श्रमिकों ने समय-समय पर विद्रोह आरम्भ कर दिये। यहाँ तक कि इन विद्रोहियों में मालवा के शाही इलाकों में खूब लूटपाट मचाकर कई गांवों एवं कस्बों को उजाड़ दिया था। बुरहानपुर से सिरोंज तक और अकबरपुर के मार्ग से उज्जैन तक के इलाके लूटपाट से ऐसे नष्ट कर दिये गये थे कि लम्बी दूरी तक कहीं बस्ती तक नहीं दिखाई पड़ती थी।[5]

17वीं सदी के इन बड़े पैमाने के विद्रोह के अतिरिक्त औरंगजेब के शासन के अन्तिम वर्षों में उसके साम्राज्य में अन्य कई छोटे बड़े विद्रोह भी हुए थे। इनमें उसके स्वयं के रिश्तेदार अप्रत्यक्ष रूप से लगे थे।

## संदर्भ

1. डॉ. रघुवीरसिंह : *मालवा में युगान्तर,* मध्यभारत, हिन्दी साहित्य समिति इन्दौर (1938) पृ. 1-51; गर्ग, दामोदरलाल : *जाट शासकों का इतिहास,* साहित्यागार, जयपुर (2009), पृ. 41-50

2. श्रीवास्तव, आशीर्वादीलाल : *भारत का इतिहास,* लक्ष्मीनारायण अग्रवाल, आगरा (1967), पृ. 637-38; नागर, ईश्वरदास : *एक शार्ट हिस्ट्री आव औरंगजेब;* सरकार, जदुनाथ : *औरंगजेब,* भाग 5, हिन्दी ग्रंथ अकादमी रत्नाकर प्रा.लि. बम्बई (1970), पृ. 359-362
3. वरे, एस. एस. : *मालवांचल का इतिहास,* म. प्र. हिन्दी ग्रन्थ अकादमी, भोपाल, (2008) पृ. 8-10। ईश्वरीप्रसाद : *मध्यभारत का इतिहास,* इण्डियन प्रेस प्रा. लि. इलाहाबाद (1969 व 1984), पृ. 485; शर्मा, मथुरालाल : *मुगल साम्राज्य का पतन,* कैलाश पुस्तक सदन, भोपाल, (1977) पृ. 125-128; शर्मा, एल. पी. : *मध्यकालीन भारत,* लक्ष्मीनारायण अग्रवाल, आगरा (1975), पृ. 138।
4. रघुवीरसिंह : *मुगलकालीन ब्रजप्रदेश भारत,* पृ. 256; देशराज : *जाट इतिहास,* पृ. 559-60; इलियट एवं डाउसन : *भारत का इतिहास, भाग 5,* दिल्ली (1981), पृ. 361
5. शर्मा, एस. आर. : *भारत में मुस्लिम शासन का इतिहास,* लक्ष्मीनारायण अग्रवाल, आगरा (1937), पृ. 521; शर्मा, मथुरालाल : *मुगल साम्राज्य का पतन,* कैलाश पुस्तक सदन, भोपाल (1977), पृ. 125
6. लुणिया, बी. एन. : *औरंगजेब आलमगीर,* कमल प्रकाशन, इन्दौर (1981), पृ. 193-200; लुणिया, बी. एन. : *मराठा प्रभुत्व,* भाग 2, लक्ष्मीनारायण अग्रवाल, आगरा (1982); इर्विन, डब्ल्यू : *लेटर मुगल्स,* भाग 1 (51-52) (सम्पादित जदुनाथ सरकार); रघुवीरसिंह : *मालवा में युगान्तर मध्यभारत,* हिन्दी साहित्य समिति, इन्दौर, 1938 एवं सरदेसाई, गोविन्द सखाराम : *मराठों का नवीन इतिहास,* भाग 3, नई दिल्ली (1960), पृ. 335

---

नोट- स्वयं औरंगजेब का जन्म 24 अक्टूबर 1618 में मालवा एवं गुजरात की सीमा पर स्थित दाहोद में हुआ था। सरकार : *मुगल साम्राज्य का पतन*

# 21

# महारानी किशोरी : राजनीतिक कौशल एवं उपलब्धियाँ

**डॉ. राकेश कुमार शर्मा**

भरतपुर के जाट राज्य का गौरव अक्षुण्ण बनाये रखने में यशस्वी महाराजा सूरजमल की महिमामयी अर्धांगिनी किशोरी का ठोस योगदान है। संकटपूर्ण परिस्थितियों में राजनीतिक कौशल का परिचय देकर अनेकों बार महारानी किशोरी ने भरतपुर राज्य का संरक्षण किया और उसके अस्तित्व पर आँच न आने दी। जाटों के समान ही मुगलों और मराठों में उसका सम्मान था। मुगल सेनापति नजफ खाँ और मराठों के मूर्धन्य सेनापति महादजी सिंधिया महारानी किशोरी को मातृतुल्य समझते थे।

महारानी किशोरी ने राजनीति के क्षेत्र में ही अपनी कुशाग्रता और बुद्धिमता का परिचय नहीं दिया, साहित्य और कला के क्षेत्र में भी अग्रणी थी। उसने साहित्यिक प्रतिभाओं को समय-समय कर प्रोत्साहन दिया। कविवर जय सिंह, रामानन्द, सुधाकर, शिवराम आदि ने उसके आश्रय में रहकर साहित्य-सृजन का कार्य किया। इसी काल में रामानंद कवि ने *लीला रतन चूड़ामणि* नामक ग्रन्थ की रचना की।[1] दूरदर्शिता, आतिथ्य, संवाद-निपुणता, आत्मसम्मान एवं धर्मपरायणता की प्रतिमूर्ति महारानी किशोरी का चरित्र निश्चय ही जीवन को गरिमापूर्ण बनाने के लिए प्रेरणास्रोत है। किशोरी की शिक्षा-दीक्षा के विषय में इतिहास में कोई जानकारी उपलब्ध नहीं है। परन्तु लोककथाओं में सूरजमल से उसके विवाह के प्रसंग से यह स्पष्ट होता है कि वह अत्यन्त सुस्कारित, आत्म सम्मान से भरपूर किन्तु लकीर की फकीर नहीं थी। हाथी पर विराजमान राजकुमार सूरजमल के लिए होडल के बाजार में रास्ता खाली कराने के लिए सैनिकों के प्रयास को बालिका किशोरी ने मार्ग में खड़े होकर चुनौती देते हुए कहा कि रास्ता तो काफी खाली पड़ा है और अगर आदमियों से इतनी नफरत है तो राजकुमार अपनी सवारी बाजार के बजाए जंगल से निकाल लेते। एक ग्रामबाला के इस प्रकार के साहस ने राजकुमार सूरजमल का

हृदय जीत लिया। उसके पिता काशीराम की सामान्य स्थिति को दृष्टिगत रख सूरजमल ने विवाह हेतु फेंटा और कटारी भिजवा दी परन्तु किशोरी ने इसे अपना अपमान समझा। उसके पिता ने बेटी के मन की बात रखते हुए राजकुमार से कहला दिया कि राजकुमार स्वयं पधारें तथा ब्याह कर ले जाएं। राजकुमार सूरजमल ने किशोरी का मान रखा तथा स्वयं होडल पधारकर उन्होंने किशोरी से विवाह किया।[2] आत्मसम्मान की रक्षा के लिए बचपन से ही किशोरी को प्रचलित परम्पराओं तथा कन्याओं की अन्यान्य वर्जनाओं को तोड़ने की पहल करने में कोई हिचक न थी।

नेत्ररोग की भयंकरता से पीड़ित बदन सिंह के राजकार्यों से निवृत्त होने के कारण नवम्बर 1745 ई. में युवराज सूरजमल शासन संचालन के पूरे अधिकारों के साथ जाट राज्य का वास्तविक शासक बन गया था। किशोरी केवल अपने अप्रतिम लावण्य के कारण ही सूरजमल के हृदय की अधिष्ठात्री नहीं बनी थी, अपितु अपने साहस एवं नीति नैपुण्य से भी उसने अपने पति के राज्य के परिवर्धन-परिरक्षण में एक महत्वपूर्ण भूमिका निभाई।[3]

उस काल के निरन्तर बदलते शक्ति-सन्तुलनों और राजनीतिक उथल-पुथल से भरतपुर एक बहुत ही नाजुक केन्द्र बन गया था। मुगलों, मराठों, राजपूतों और रुहेला अफगानों को भरतपुर का उत्थान फूटी आँखों न सुहाता था। इन शक्तियों के मध्य सूरजमल ने अपनी स्थिति को काफी दृढ़ कर लिया था।

मुगल सम्राट के विरुद्ध हुए गृहयुद्ध में सूरजमल ने सफदरजंग का साथ दिया था। यद्यपि सम्राट ने उसको विधिपूर्वक क्षमा कर दिया था परन्तु वह दिल्ली दरबार तथा गाजीउद्दीन द्वितीय की घृणा का पात्र था। गाजीउद्दीन ने इस समय सूरजमल को दण्ड देने का निश्चय कर लिया। मराठों को हाल ही में आगरा तथा अजमेर के सूबे प्राप्त हुए थे, तथा उनका विचार वहां पर अपना वास्तविक नियंत्रण स्थापित करने का था। आगरा का सूबा सूरजमल के लिए विशेष लाभकारी था क्योंकि वह उसके भरतपुर तथा मथुरा के प्रदेशों के निकट था। अजमेर का सूबा मारवाड़ के राजा को समान रूप से प्रिय था तथा उसने जयप्पा सिन्धिया के लोभ को भी जागृत कर दिया था। मल्हारराव होल्कर ने अपने पुत्र खाण्डेराव को अपने विश्वस्त गंगाधर तात्या के साथ दिल्ली भेजा ताकि वह गाजीउद्दीन से मिलकर अभियान की योजना की रचना करें।

सूरजमल अपनी चतुर पत्नी रानी किशोरी उर्फ हंसिया से प्रत्येक संकट के अवसर पर सदैव परामर्श करता था।[4] रानी की राजकाज में रुचि थी और वह अपने आँख-कान खोलकर रखती थी और संकट के समय सुविचारित परामर्श देकर कोई न कोई मार्ग निकाल देती थी। कुम्हेर के घेरे के अवसर पर सन् 1754 में ऐसी ही विकट स्थिति

उत्पन्न हो गई। यह ही वह स्थान था जहाँ सूरजमल ने 80,000 सैनिकों की सम्मिलित मुगल-मराठा सेना का 20 जनवरी 1754 से 18 मई 1754 तक डटकर सामना किया।[5] भीषण संघर्ष में एक गोली से 17 मार्च को मल्हारराव होल्कर के प्रिय एवं इकलौते पुत्र खाण्डेराव होल्कर का देहांत हो गया जिसके कारण उसके पिता को वृद्धावस्था में भारी दुःख हुआ।[6] इस घोर वेदना में मल्हारराव होल्कर ने जाटों के विरुद्ध भीषण प्रतिशोध की प्रतिज्ञा की और किसी समझौते को स्वीकार न किया और आक्रमणों का दबाव इतना बढ़ा दिया कि सूरजमल हतप्रभ हो गया। उसकी सहायता को कोई नहीं आया। यहाँ तक कि सफदरजंग भी नहीं, जिसे मुसीबत में मदद देने में उसने कोई कसर न छोड़ी थी। जीवन में पहली और अन्तिम बार सूरजमल को निराशा और उदासी ने आ घेरा। पराजय और विनाश को अब देर तक टाला नहीं जा सकता था। जब ऐसा लगने लगा था कि सब कुछ नष्ट होकर ही रहेगा तब रानी किशोरी उर्फ हंसिया ने अपने पति के भग्न होते उत्साह को फिर जगाया और कहा कि मुझ पर भरोसा रखो। अपने मन से निराशा को बिल्कुल निकाल दो।[7] रानी किशोरी को मराठा शिविर की फूट और गुटबन्दियों का पूरा ज्ञान था। मल्हारराव होल्कर और जियाजीराव सिन्धिया एक दूसरे से जलते थे। रानी को इस विषय में पूरी जानकारी थी और वह यह भी जानती थी कि सिन्धिया उदारचित्त और निष्कपट स्वभाव का व्यक्ति है। एक रात रानी किशोरी उर्फ हंसिया ने रूपराम के पुत्र तेजराम कटारिया को सूरजमल का एक पत्र देकर उसके पास भेजा। उसने सहायता मांगने और मित्रता स्थापित करने के लिए सूरजमल की पगड़ी भी जियाजीराव सिन्धिया के पास भेजी। उन दिनों मैत्री स्थापना के लिए पगड़ियों के विनिमय की प्रथा प्रचलित थी। ग्वालियर के सरदार ने तुरंत उत्साह एवं उदारता के साथ उत्तर दिया। उसने बदले में एक पगड़ी, उसके साथ एक बिल्व पत्र भी भेजा जो उसकी सत्यनिष्ठा का सबसे पक्का प्रमाण था। इस प्रकार किशोरी ने उसे उपहारों तथा मैत्रीपूर्ण प्रार्थनाओं द्वारा अपने पक्ष में कर लिया।[8] सिन्धिया और सिनसिनवार के मध्य हुए इस सम्पर्क का समाचार शीघ्र ही प्रकट हो गया और इसका यह अभीष्ट परिणाम हुआ कि मल्हारराव होल्कर के हौसले टूट गये।[9] जियाजीराव अपने प्रभाव का उपयोग करके रघुनाथराव से घेरा उठवा देने के लिए सहमत हो गया। जियाजीराव (जयप्पा) ने आग्रह किया कि जाटों से समझौता कर लेना ठीक है और इस निरर्थक युद्ध को समाप्त कर देना ही उत्तम होगा। उधर जाट राजा मराठों को 30 लाख रुपये वार्षिक किश्तों में देने को सहमत हो गया। शान्ति स्थापित हो गई। सरदेसाई लिखते हैं कि यह रघुनाथराव की असफलता थी। चूंकि युद्ध से पूर्व राजा सूरजमल शान्ति बनाये रखने के एवज में 40 लाख रुपये देने को तत्पर था जबकि रघुनाथराव एक करोड़ की मांग कर रहा था। कुम्हेर के इस प्रकरण की समीक्षा करते हुए फादर वैंदेल कहते हैं, 'सूरजमल की धाक इस घेरे के दिनों में और भी बढ़ गयी थी

और सारे हिन्दुस्तान पर छा गयी थी। अब उसे यह यश और प्राप्त हो गया कि उन दो सरदारों से जो अपनी-अपनी सेनाओं में उसके समकक्ष थे, सौदेबाजी करने में और उनसे अपनी मनचाही शर्तें मनवाने में सफल हुआ।[10] कुम्हेर के घेरे में मराठों और मुगलों से सूरजमल के सकुशल और अक्षत बच जाने में रानी किशोरी उर्फ हंसिया के साहस एवं बुद्धिचातुर्य की जितनी सराहना की जाये, कम है।

14 जून 1761 में मराठों और अहमदशाह अब्दाली का पानीपत में भयानक युद्ध हुआ जिसमें मराठे पराजित हो गये। इस युद्ध में बचे हुए लगभग एक लाख मराठे शस्त्रहीन, वस्त्रहीन और भूखे, कोई चारा न पाकर महाराजा सूरजमल के राज्य क्षेत्र की ओर जान बचाकर दौड़े। यद्यपि युद्ध से पूर्व महाराज सूरजमल ने मराठा सेनापति सदाशिवराव भाऊ का उसकी हठधर्मिता के कारण साथ छोड़ दिया था परन्तु इस अवसर पर उसने तथा उसकी महारानी किशोरी ने प्रेम और उत्साह से उन्हें सांत्वना दी, उनका सत्कार और आतिथ्य किया। हारे मराठे सैनिक अनुचरों को मुफ्त खाना-पीना दिया तथा घायलों की सेवा शुश्रुषा की। ग्रांट डफ ने मराठे शरणार्थियों के साथ किये गये व्यवहार के विषय में लिखा है, 'जो भी भगोड़े उसके राज्य में आये, उनके साथ सूरजमल ने अत्यन्त दयालुता का बरताव किया और मराठे उस अवसर पर किये गये जाटों के व्यवहार को आज भी कृतज्ञता तथा आदर के साथ याद करते हैं।' नाना फड़नवीस ने एक पत्र में लिखा था- 'सूरजमल के व्यवहार से पेशवा के चित्त को बड़ी सांत्वना मिली।'[12] यह सब महारानी किशोरी का प्रभाव था कि उसने इस संकट के समय अनुकरणीय मानवीय दृष्टिकोण का परिचय दिया। भाऊ की पत्नी पार्वतीबाई डीग पहुंचकर कई दिन तक रोती बिलखती रही। महारानी किशोरी ने उसे धैर्य बंधाया, सांत्वना दी और दक्षिण तक अपने सैनिकों की सुरक्षा में भेजा। अन्य शरणार्थियों को भी सुरक्षित ग्वालियर तक पहुँचाया। यह सहायता ऐसे समय की जा रही थी कि जब मराठों को सहायता का अर्थ था अब्दाली को रुष्ट करना।[13] इस संकट के समय किसी राजपूत शासक ने मराठा शरणार्थियों की तरफ मौखिक सहानुभूति तक के लिए दृष्टिपात नहीं किया।

महारानी किशोरी ने महाराष्ट्रीय ब्राह्मणों को पांच-पांच रुपया तथा वस्त्रादि भेंट देकर पुण्य अर्जित किया। मराठों की आवभगत में दस लाख रुपया व्यय हुआ।[14] सर जान मार्शल माल्कोल्म जाटों द्वारा की गई इस सहृदयता के लिए, जिसकी प्रेरणास्रोत महारानी किशोरी थी, लिखते हैं, 'मराठों का जाटों के प्रति आज भी अत्यधिक सम्मान है जिन्होंने पानीपत की भयानक पराजय के उपरान्त उनके पूर्वजों को शरण, सहायता और सुरक्षा दी। उन्हें वस्त्र और भोजन ही नहीं दक्षिण में अपने घरों के पहुंचने तक सुविधा एवं सुरक्षा प्रदान की। इसी के परिणामस्वरूप मराठा जाति में कोई ही बिरला होगा जो जाटों के प्रति कृतज्ञता अनुभव न करता हो।'[15] इतिहास में ऐसे उदाहरण प्रायः नगण्य ही हैं

जहां मन-मुटाव के उपरान्त भी किसी महारानी ने इतनी सदाशयता, उदारता और विशाल हृदयता का परिचय दिया है।

25 दिसम्बर 1763 को नजीब रुहेले से युद्ध में रहस्यमय परिस्थितियों में सूरजमल के देहावसान पर के. आर. कानूनगो लिखते हैं, 'जाट की आँख और ज्योति, गत पन्द्रह वर्षों से हिन्दुस्तान का सबसे दुर्धष राजा अपने काम को अधूरा छोड़कर जीवन के रंगमंच से लुप्त हो गया।[16] अपराजित, नेताविहीन भग्न हृदय जाट सेना रणभूमि से लौट गई। राजकुमार तथा विधवा महारानियां शोक-विह्वल हो गई और मार्ग पूरी तरह अंधकारमय हो गया। महारानी किशोरी के भाई बलराम ने तुरन्त महाराजा के ज्येष्ठ पुत्र जवाहर सिंह के बजाय कनिष्ठ पुत्र नाहर सिंह को, जिसे महाराजा सूरजमल भी चाहते थे, राजा घोषित करके डीग में गद्दी पर बैठा दिया। यह अत्यन्त संकट की घड़ी थी क्योंकि इस समय के किसी भी गलत निर्णय के दूरगामी परिणाम होते। उत्तराधिकार के इस निर्णय के समर्थन में खाप के वृद्ध नेताओं की परिषद ने भी नाहर सिंह को ही उत्तराधिकारी मान लिया। परन्तु महारानी किशोरी ने सारी परिस्थितियों का विश्लेषण करते हुए बड़े मार्मिक ढंग से अपील की कि उसकी एकमात्र इच्छा यह है कि महाराज की हत्या का बदला लेने में समर्थ उत्तराधिकारियों में से ही राजा बनाया जाये। यद्यपि महारानी किशोरी निःसन्तान थी परन्तु सामरिक कुशलता और साहस को देखते हुए उसने अपने दत्तक पुत्र जवाहर सिंह के पक्ष में अपना समर्थन दिया। स्वयं जवाहर सिंह ने इस संकट की घड़ी में अपने भीष्म संकल्प को दोहराया। दरबारी स्वयं समझते थे कि इस कार्य को जवाहर सिंह के अतिरिक्त कोई अन्य नहीं कर सकता। फलतः सभी ने जवाहर सिंह को अपना राजा स्वीकार कर लिया और बलराम का षड्यंत्र विफल हो गया। सिंहासनासीन होते समय जब पगड़ी बांधी जाती है उस समय भी महारानी किशोरी ने जो नीतिपूर्ण वचन कहे उन्हें आज तक भी लोक गीतों में गाया जाता है। लोक गायकों के शब्दों में महारानी किशोरी ने बड़े ही मार्मिक शब्दों में जवाहर सिंह से कहा था—

बांधियों तो बांधिये प्रताप की पगड़ी
दिल्ली में धक्के ना खाती फिरै तेरे बाप की पगड़ी।

अपने पिता की हत्या के प्रतिशोध के लिए तुरन्त ही जवाहर सिंह ने आक्रमण का निश्चय किया। परन्तु नजीबुद्दौला से युद्ध करने के लिए धन और सैनिक शक्ति दोनों की आवश्यकता थी। अतः उसने अपनी माता महारानी किशोरी से आर्थिक सहायता के लिए निवेदन किया, तब उसे राजमाता किशोरी से पर्याप्त धन प्राप्त हो गया।[17] इस स्थिति में अनिच्छुक होते हुए भी जाट सामन्तों को जवाहर सिंह का साथ देने के लिए सहमत होना पड़ा।[18] राजमाता किशोरी से पर्याप्त धन-सम्पत्ति प्राप्त करके जवाहर सिंह

ने मल्हाराव होल्कर से सम्पर्क किया और 22 लाख रुपये से 20,000 मराठा अश्व सेना का सहयोग प्राप्त कर लिया एवं 15,000 सिक्खों की सेना भी आमंत्रित की। मध्य दोआब की चौकियों पर कब्जा कर नवम्बर 1764 में नजीबुद्दौला पर आक्रमण कर दिया। यह दिल्ली अभियान नवम्बर 1764 से फरवरी 1765 तक चला।[19] इस युद्ध से वांछित परिणाम तो नहीं निकल सके परन्तु तत्कालीन राजनीतिक शक्तियों की सेनाओं का गौरवपूर्ण सेनापतित्व करते हुए जवाहर सिंह ने इस दिल्ली अभियान को राष्ट्रीय महत्ता प्रदान कर दी और दिल्ली आक्रमण में लूट की आधी सामग्री भरतपुर में आई। इस क्षेत्र में 'दिल्लीवाड़े की लूट' नामक कहावत आज भी सुनी जाती है। जवाहर सिंह के इस अभियान की प्रेरणास्रोत महारानी किशोरी थी। लोक गीतों में आज भी ये पंक्तियां सुनने को मिलती हैं :

किंयो सिंहगढ़ फतह सिवा ने सुनते ही माता के बैन।
मेरे सिवा करें सर दिल्ली तब आवेगो मो को चैन।।

महारानी किशोरी धर्मपरायण महिला थी। धार्मिक स्नान की महिमा के अन्तर्गत पुष्कर मेले का वर्णन, पुराणों में भी मिलता है। ऐसी मान्यता है कि जब तक पुष्कर के कुण्ड में स्नान न कर लिया जाये, चारों धामों की यात्रा सम्पूर्ण नहीं मानी जाती। पुष्कर में ब्रह्मा की बड़ी प्राचीन मूर्ति है। इस स्थान पर तीर्थ यात्री स्नान कर अपने को पुण्य लाभ के भागी समझते हैं। उस समय राजपूत जाटों को हीन भावना से देखते थे तथा उन्हें पुष्कर स्नान के पात्र ही नहीं मानते थे। जवाहर सिंह राजपूतों को हेय दृष्टि से देखता था, विशेषतया जयपुर के राजपूतों को जिन्होंने मुगलों को अपनी बेटियां दी थी। अपनी माता की पुष्कर स्नान की इच्छा जानकर किशोरी के साथ जवाहर सिंह गाजे-बाजे के साथ पुष्कर पहुंचा, महारानी किशोरी ने स्नान-ध्यान किया तथा अतुल राशि दान-पुण्य में ब्राह्मणों तथा अन्य सुपात्रों को वितरित की। परन्तु वापिस लौटते समय 14 दिसम्बर 1767 को राजपूतों ने जवाहर सिंह पर धावा बोल दिया। जवाहर सिंह अपने कौशल तथा अपने सेना सहायक समरू और रैन मादे की वीरता से सुरक्षित बच निकला।[20] सन् 1768 ई में अगस्त मास में महाराज जवाहर सिंह की हत्या कर दी गई।[21]

महाराजा जवाहर सिंह की हत्या से भरतपुर राज्य पर संकट के बादल छा गये। जवाहर सिंह का उत्तराधिकारी रतन सिंह पूर्णतया अयोग्य था और केवल नौ मास ही शासन कर पाया। उसका पुत्र केशरी सिंह अल्प वयस्क था और शासन की बागडोर नवल सिंह को दी गई परन्तु उसका भाई रणजीत सिंह उसके विरुद्ध था। इस पारिवारिक कलह से लाभ उठाकर नजफखां ने नवल सिंह को बरसाना के युद्ध में परास्त कर सन् 1774 में डीग भी जाटों से छीन लिया।[22] और, जाटों की शक्ति को छिन्न-भिन्न कर

दिया। भरतपुर परगने के अतिरिक्त जाटों के सारे क्षेत्र को अपने अधिकार में ले लिया। धौलपुर क्षेत्र पर भी उसी का अधिकार हो गया।[23] इन विषम और भयानक परिस्थितियों में महारानी किशोरी ने चरम आत्मविश्वास, उत्कट दूरदर्शिता और अपूर्व साहस का परिचय दिया। वह स्वयं नजफ खां के खेमे में गई और अपनी कुशलता, वाक्पटुता और धैर्य से नजफ खां को प्रभावित करने में सफल हो गई। नजफ खां ने महारानी किशोरी से मातृतुल्य व्यवहार किया और उसकी अपील पर भरतपुर राज्य के दस परगने वापिस लौटा दिये।[24] नजफखां के उत्तराधिकारी मिर्जा शफी खां ने इन पर अपना अधिकार जताया। महारानी किशोरी ने तुरंत चौथ वसूली की प्रथा चालू की तथा राजकोष में धन संग्रह किया। इस प्रकार चरमराई अर्थव्यवस्था को महारानी ने दुरुस्त कर सेना का खर्चा निकाला और मिर्जा शफी खां की योजनाओं को निष्फल कर दिया। उधर मिर्जा शफी की डीग में हत्या हो गई और रणजीत सिंह ने परगनों पर पूर्ण नियंत्रण कर लिया।[25]

अभी रणजीत सिंह अपनी स्थिति पूरी तरह दृढ़ भी नहीं पर पाया था कि सन् 1784 में मराठा सरदार महादजी सिन्धिया ने भरतपुर और धौलपुर क्षेत्र पर अपना अधिकार कर लिया। जाटों की स्थिति पुनः संकटग्रस्त हो गई। इस विषम स्थिति में भी भरतपुर राज्य की संरक्षिका के रूप में महारानी किशोरी ने अटूट धैर्य और अपूर्व कुशलता का परिचय दिया। महारानी किशोरी ने तुरंत महाराज सिंधिया से भेंट करने का प्रस्ताव रखा। पानीपत के तृतीय युद्ध के उपरान्त महारानी किशोरी ने परास्त मराठों की आवभगत में कोई कसर न छोड़ी थी। महादजी सिंधिया ने महारानी किशोरी के प्रस्ताव का मान रखा और उनसे मिले। महारानी किशोरी से महादजी सिंधिया अत्यन्त प्रभावित हुए और उन्होंने भरतपुर नरेश रणजीत सिंह को 11 परगने वापिस लौटा दिये। महारानी किशोरी के निर्देशानुसार रणजीत सिंह ने भी महादजी के प्रति अत्यन्त अच्छा व्यवहार रखा और सदैव समर्थन में रहा। इससे प्रभावित होकर महादजी सिंधिया ने डीग क्षेत्र भी रणजीत सिंह को वापिस लौटा दिया।[26] आगे चलकर रणजीत सिंह के सक्रिय और विश्वसनीय सहयोग के कारण उसे 1795 में तीन परगने और प्राप्त हो गये।[27] इस प्रकार महारानी किशोरी ने अपनी सूझबूझ से भरतपुर राज्य की रक्षा की। यदि रानी नहीं होती तो रंजीत सिंह के हटते ही सिन्धिया के हाथों भरतपुर का अस्तित्व हमेशा-हमेशा के लिए समाप्त हो जाता।[28]

महारानी किशोरी के व्यक्तित्व और उसकी उपलब्धियों का आकलन यदि प्रसिद्ध विद्वान कोजुब्सका द्वारा उल्लिखित करिश्माई नेतृत्व के सात तत्वों के आधार पर किया जाये तो उसकी गणना विश्व की शिरोमणि महिलाओं में की जा सकती है। चरम आत्मविश्वास, गरिमामय लक्ष्य से युक्त विचक्षणता, सम्प्रेषण क्षमता, आग्रहपूर्ण दृढ़ता एवं धुन, विशिष्ट शैली, दूरदर्शिता तथा चुम्बकीय रहस्यपूर्ण व्यक्तित्व के मानकों पर महारानी किशोरी खरी उतरती है। उसका व्यक्तित्व चुम्बकीय था। कुम्हेर पर मराठा

अभियान के समय जब महाराज सूरजमल और उनका विश्वसनीय परामर्शदाता रूपराम कटारिया हतप्रभ थे तो महारानी किशोरी ने. चरम आत्मविश्वास प्रदर्शित करते हुए समस्या का समाधान कर डाला। उसकी सम्प्रेषण क्षमता अदभुत थी। नजफ खां और महादजी सिन्धिया जैसे महान सेनानायकों से वार्तालाप करने में उसे थोड़ी भी हिचक नहीं हुई और अपनी विशिष्ट शैली तथा गरिमामय लक्ष्य से युक्त विचक्षणता के आधार पर आग्रहपूर्ण दृढ़ता का परिचय दिया तथा खोये हुए राज्य को प्राप्त करने में आश्चर्यजनक राजनीतिक कौशल का परिचय दिया। ऐतिहासिक दृष्टि से यदि सुप्रसिद्ध महिलाओं से उसकी तुलना की जाय तो भी महारानी किशोरी का व्यक्तित्व सर्वोपरि उभर कर आता है। रजिया सुल्तान अत्यन्त योग्य होते हुए भी अमीर उमरावों के कोपभाजन का शिकार बन गई। नूरजहां की चमक जहांगीर के मरने के बाद तिराहित हो गई, बेगम समरू ने यद्यपि अपनी जागीर पर 58 वर्ष तक अपने कौशल से आधिपत्य बनाये रखा परन्तु वह अपने दत्तक पुत्र को उत्तराधिकार दिलाने में असफल रही। राजनीतिक कौशल एवं उपलब्धियों को दृष्टिगत रखते हुए, महारानी किशोरी का स्थान भारतीय इतिहास में सर्वोपरि कहना तर्कसंगत होगा।

## संदर्भ

1. डॉ. उषा भार्गव : *राजस्थान के नारी रत्न*, प्रकाशन विभाग, सूचना एवं प्रसारण मंत्रालय, भारत सरकार, नई दिल्ली (1992), पृ. 16
2. उपर्युक्त, पृष्ठ 13
3. सुखबीर सिंह दलाल : *जाट वीरांगनाएँ* (1995), पृ. 70
4. जी. एस. सरदेसाई : *मराठों का नवीन इतिहास*, शिवलाल अग्रवाल एण्ड कम्पनी (1961), पृ. 486
5. उपर्युक्त, पृ. 486
6. फाल्के सीरीज, ग्वालियर बी. 204
7. के. आर. कानूनगो : *हिस्ट्री ऑफ द जाट्स*, ओरिजिनल्स, दिल्ली (2003), पृ. 54
8. उपर्युक्त, पृ. 54
9. कुँ. नटवर सिंह : *महाराजा सूरजमल*, राधाकृष्ण प्रकाशन, नई दिल्ली (1985), पृ. 76
10. उपर्युक्त, पृ. 77-78
11. ग्रांट डफ : *ए हिस्ट्री ऑफ द मराठाज*, पृ. 30
12. कुँ. नटवर सिंह : पूर्वोक्त, पृ. 118

13. के. आर. कानूनगो : पूर्वोक्त, पृ. 82
14. उपर्युक्त, पृ. 118
15. *मैमायर्स ऑफ सैन्ट्रल इण्डिया* (1880), पृ. 129
16. के. आर. कानूनगो : पूर्वोक्त, पृ. 90
17. मनोहर सिंह राणावत : *भरतपुर महाराज जवाहर सिंह जाट*, हिन्दी साहित्य मन्दिर, जोधपुर, पृ. 40
18. उपर्युक्त, पृ. 40; यदुनाथ सरकार : *फाल आफ द मुगल एम्पायर* 2, पृ. 335
19. *राजस्थान डिस्ट्रिक्ट गंजेटियर*, भरतपुर पृ. 67
20. मनोहर सिंह : पूर्वोक्त, पृ. 83
21. उपर्युक्त, पृ. 90
22. के. के. सहगल : *राजस्थान डिस्ट्रिक्ट गजेटियर - भरतपुर* (1971), पृ. 69
23. उपर्युक्त, पृ. 69
24. उपर्युक्त, पृ. 69
25. उपर्युक्त, पृ. 69
26. उपर्युक्त, पृ. 69
27. उपर्युक्त, पृ. 69
28. डॉ. उषा भार्गव : पूर्वोक्त, पृ. 15

22

# भरतपुर के जाट राजाओं का दुर्ग स्थापत्य और पर्यटन

**डॉ. प्रणव देव**

राजस्थान का दुर्ग स्थापत्य जिन उत्कृष्ट उपादनों से महिमा मण्डित होकर देशी-विदेशी पर्यटकों, शोधकों एवं इतिहासवेत्ताओं के आकर्षण का केन्द्र बना है उसमें भरतपुर के राजाओं का अनूठा दुर्ग स्थापत्य, अद्‌भुत शिल्प सौन्दर्य और भव्य राजप्रासादों का कलात्मक वैभव उल्लेखनीय है। इन राजाओं के दुर्ग स्थापत्य को देखकर कहीं-कहीं दुर्गों के शास्त्रीय विधान[1] तो कहीं संस्कृति के अनूठे अनमोल खजाने का स्मरण हो आता है। तभी तो भरतपुर के दुर्ग के बारे में यह उक्ति लोक में प्रसिद्ध है—

दुर्ग भरतपुर उडगजिमि, हिमगिरि की चट्‌टआन।
सूरजमल के तेज को, अब लौं करत बखान।।

प्रस्तुत शोध पत्र में भरतपुर के जाट राजाओं के दुर्ग स्थापत्य के परिचय एवं संक्षिप्त सांगोपांग वर्णन के साथ-साथ उनकी विविध विशदताओं की चर्चा की गई है। यद्यपि, राजस्थान सहित भारतीय इतिहास में दुर्ग निर्माण की प्राचीन परम्परा रही है। युद्ध परम्परा तथा यहां की भौगोलिक स्थिति के कारण दुर्गों का सर्वाधिक महत्व रहा है। प्राचीन साहित्य में दुर्गों के स्थापत्य के विविध विधानों को निर्धारित किया गया है। भरतपुर के जाट राजाओं ने दुर्ग स्थापत्य में जहाँ एक ओर शास्त्रीय विधान से अपने दुर्ग स्थापत्य को सम्वर्धित किया, वहीं दूसरी ओर समसामायिक आवश्यकताओं का भी ध्यान रखा।

राजस्थान के सिंह द्वार भरतपुर में स्थापित दुर्ग 'लोहागढ़' जाट राजाओं की कीर्ति को न सिर्फ दिगदिगन्त में फैला रहा है अपितु उनकी पर्यटन, पर्यावरण एवं सैन्य सुरक्षा की समझ का जीवन्त प्रमाण है। लोहागढ़ नामक इस अजेय दुर्ग के साथ जाट राजाओं की वीरता और पराक्रम के रोमांचक आख्यान जुड़े हुए है। इस किले का निर्माण 19 फरवरी 1733 ई. में महाराजा (तब कुंवर) सूरजमल द्वारा प्रारम्भ किया

गया था।[2] किले का सम्पूर्ण निर्माण कार्य लगभग 8 वर्ष मे पूरा हुआ। किले के निर्माण से राज्य की राजनैतिक गतिविधियां अब डीग के स्थान पर भरतपुर से संचालित होने लगीं। शास्त्रीय दृष्टि से भरतपुर का यह 'लोहागढ़' भूमिदुर्ग की श्रेणी में आता है।[3] इस दुर्ग के बनने से पूर्व इस स्थल पर बाणगंगा, रूपारेल एवं गम्भीरी नदियों के पानी का संगम होता था। इसकी जल से भरी हुई विस्तृत खाई (परिखा) तथा बाहरी मिट्टी की विशाल प्राचीर इसके स्थापत्य का अनुपम अंग है। जिसमें जाट राजाओं की उत्कृष्ट सैन्य समझ के दर्शन होते हैं। तोपों की गोलाबारी भी किले को इस व्यवस्था के कारण कोई नुकसान नहीं पहुंचा पाती थी। भरतपुर दुर्ग के निर्माण के सम्बन्ध में कुंवर नटवर सिंह ने लिखा है- 'एक बार निर्माण कार्य शुरु हो जाने के बाद साठ वर्ष तक रुका नहीं। मुख्य किलेबन्दियां आठ वर्षों में पूरी हो गयीं। .................. इनमें दो खाइयां भी थी। एक तो शहर की बाहर वाली चारदीवारी के पास थी और दूसरी कम चौड़ी पर ज्यादा गहरी, किले को घेरे हुए थी। बाढ़ के पानी को रोकने और अकाल के समय सहायता पहुंचाने के लिए दो बांध और दो जलाशय बनाये गये थे। परिवर्तन, रूपान्तरण सिंह (1853-1893 ई.) के राज्यकाल तक चलता रहा। इस किले को पूरा बनकर तैयार हो जाने पर यह हिन्दुस्तान का सबसे अजेय किला माना जाता था। विमान के आविष्कार से पूर्व इसे जीतना प्रायः असम्भव था।[4] आयताकार आकृति वाले इस दुर्ग का विस्तार 6.4 वर्ग कि.मी. क्षेत्र में हैं। दो विशाल गोलाकार मिट्टी की दीवारें एक-दूसरे को घेरकर खड़ी की गई हैं। बीच में एक अत्यांधिक चौड़ी 150-200 फीट और 20-50 फीट गहरी खाई (परिखा) जल से पूर्ण होकर दुर्ग को अभय रखती हैं। इस खाई में पानी कोहनी बांध से आता है। उत्तर-दक्षिण शहरपनाह सहित कच्चे किले की लम्बाई डेढ़ मील सौ फुट है। जबकि पूर्व-पश्चिम तक इसकी दूरी डेढ़ मील से 400 कीट कम है। इस किले के बाहरी भाग को चार भागों में विभक्त किया गया है जो गोपालगढ़, रामगढ़, किशनगढ़ तथा फतहगढ़ के नाम से प्रसिद्ध हुए। दुर्ग की दो विशाल प्राचीरें है। जिनमें भीतरी ईंट-पत्थरों से पक्की बनी है तथा बाहरी प्राचीर मिट्टी की है जो युद्ध के समय तोपों के गोलों को निष्क्रिय कर किले के भीतरी भाग में स्थित महलों आदि को सुरक्षित रखती थी। ऐसा प्रतीत होता है कि महाराजा सूरजमल ने मानसार में वर्णित मानकों के अनुसार भरतपुर दुर्ग का निर्माण करवाया।[5] भरतपुर दुर्ग के सुदृढ़ परकोटे में आठ विशाल बुर्जे, 40 अर्धचन्द्राकार बुर्जे तथा दो विशाल दरवाजे हैं इनमें से उत्तरी द्वार अष्टधातु दरवाजा तथा दक्षिणी द्वार लोहिया दरवाजा कहलाता है।[6] उत्तरी द्वार के अष्टधातु दरवाजे को सन 1764 ई. में महाराजा जवाहर सिंह द्वारा दिल्ली विजय के स्मारक के रूप में स्थापित किया गया था।[7] भरतपुर के शासकों के गद्दी पर बैठने का संस्कार इसी बुर्ज में किया जाता था। इसे पवित्र और मांगलिक माना जाता है।[8] दुर्ग की

अन्य बुर्जों में सिनसिनी बुर्ज, भैंसावाली बुर्ज उल्लेखनीय है। दुर्ग में बारह अन्य दरवाजे थे जिनमें अब कई ध्वस्त हो गए हैं। इनके नाम मथुरापोल, चांदपोल, गोवर्द्धनपोल, जधीनापोल, सूरजपोल और दिल्ली दरवाजा हैं। किले में पर्यटन की दृष्टि से कई इमारतें उल्लेखनीय है। जिनमें किशोरी महल, महलखास, कोठीखास, दादी मां का महल, वजीर की कोठी, दरबार खास, सिपहखाना, बिहारी व मोहन जी के मन्दिर मुख्य हैं। महलखास व दरबार खास में भरतपुर का संग्रहालय बना हुआ है, जिसमें शिलालेख, मूर्तियां, जाट राजाओं के अस्त्र-शस्त्र एवं अन्य पुरामहत्व की सामग्री प्रदर्शित है। यह सामग्री पर्यटकों एवं शोधकों को सहज ही अपनी ओर आकर्षित कर लेती है। किले का मुख्यद्वार सुदृढ़ एवं भव्य है। इसके पार्श्व भाग पर दोनों ओर 60 से 80 फीट ऊँची विशाल बुर्जे खड़ी है। पार्श्व की बुर्जों के मध्य दो अर्ध चन्द्राकार बुर्जे बनी है। प्राचीरों के शीर्श मार्ग तथा बुर्जों के बीच तोपों और गोलियों की मार के स्थल बने हुए हैं। इसके साथ ही किले के बाहरी ओर थोड़ी दूर शहर में गंगा मन्दिर, तथा लक्ष्मण मन्दिर बने हैं, जो राजस्थान के पार्यटनिक वैभव में एक अनूठा अध्याय जोड़ते हैं।

7 फरवरी 1805 को जब अंग्रेजों ने इस दुर्ग को घेर कर क्रमशः 9 जनवरी, 21 जनवरी, 21 फरवरी 1805 को आक्रमण कर अपने 3200 सैनिक खोये व 65 तोपे खराब कर लीं, तो ब्रिटिश अफसरों को असफलता का आस्वादन कराने का श्रेय इस दुर्ग की स्थापत्य तकनीकी को भी देना होगा। इस असफलता पर अंग्रेजों के टूटे मनोबल का आभास सर चार्ल्स मेटकाफ द्वारा गवर्नर जनरल को लिखे पत्र की इन पंक्तियों से मिलता है- ''ब्रिटिश फौजों की सैनिक प्रतिष्ठा का अधिकांश हिस्सा भरतपुर के दुर्भाग्यपूर्ण घेरे में दब गया है।''[9]

अगले बीस वर्ष तक अंग्रेज इस दुर्ग पर आक्रमण का साहस न कर सके तथापि यह दुर्ग सैन्य सफलता का अनुपम उदाहरण बना रहा। अंग्रेज अपनी हार की टीस को भूले नहीं थे, अतः उन्होंने सन् 1825 ई. में भरतपुर के जाट राजाओं के आपसी गृहकलेश का फायदा उठाकर पुनः हमला किया। ब्रिटिश सेनापति कोम्बर मेयर ने 20 हजार सैनिकों एवं विशाल तोपखाने को लेकर भरतपुर को पुनः घेर लिया। आन्तरिक संघर्ष के कारण इस बार 18 जनवरी 1826 ई. को जाट शासक पराजित हुआ, किले पर अंग्रेजों का अधिकार हो गया, किन्तु मेजर स्ट्राटन जैसे अंग्रेज अधिकारियों ने भी इस अजेय दुर्ग के स्थापत्य की प्रशंसा की।[10] भले ही भरतपुर पर अंग्रेजों का कब्जा हो गया है परन्तु जन मानस आज भी ''गोरा हट जा रे राज भरतपुर को'' जैसे लोक गीतों के माध्यम से इस दुर्ग के संस्थापकों को राष्ट्रीय चेतना के प्रतीक मानकर याद करता है।

महाराजा सूरजमल से पूर्व महाराजा बदन सिंह ने डीग, कुम्हेर और बैर के किलों का निर्माण कराके डीग को अपनी राजधानी बनाया था। उन्होंने डीग के किले का निर्माण सन् 1725 ई. में किया था।[11] डीग के किले के चारों ओर 20 फीट गहरी खाई का निर्माण भी करवाया। महाराजा बदनसिंह के भाई रूपसिंह द्वारा निर्मित रूप सागर के सामानान्तर बारह बुर्जें भी बनाई गई। किले की प्राचीर अत्याधिक ऊँची बनाई गई थी। इनमें प्रसिद्ध बुर्ज का नाम लक्खा बुर्ज है जिस पर विशालकाय तोपें अपने प्राचीन शौर्य की स्मृति आज भी ताजा कर देती है। ध्रुव टीला नामक बुर्ज, लक्खा बुर्ज से भी अधिक ऊँचा है। दुर्ग के मध्य में महाराजा सूरजमल का महल है जिसमें वे प्रारम्भिक समय में रहते थे। इस महल के पीछे उनके भाई सुल्तान सिंह की समाधि बनी हुई है। उसके निकट एक अन्य कब्र है जिसे देहली के वजीर मिर्जा सफी की समाधि बताया जाता है जो 3 सितम्बर 1783 ई. को मारा गया था। उसके पास ही बड़ी खासें है जिनमें सैन्य सामान रखा जाता था। दुर्ग के उत्तर-पश्चिम में शाह बुर्ज है। डीग कस्बे के 10 द्वार बनाए गए थे। भूड़ा, पान्होरी, शाहपुरा, बंधा, कामा, देहली, जसौंधी, गोवर्धन और रामचेला दरवाजे प्रसिद्ध है। नगर कोट के बाहर चारों ओर बड़ी-बड़ी बुर्जें बनी हुई हैं। इस किले के पास ही जाट शासकों ने डीग के जल महलों का निर्माण भी करवाया था। डीग का सम्पूर्ण स्थापत्य भरतपुर के जाट राजाओं के स्थापत्य का मूलाधार माना जा सकता है जो शिल्प एवं सौन्दर्य में बेजोड़ है।

महाराजा बदन सिंह ने सन् 1725 ई. में परगना भुसावर, बयाना तथा कस्बा उज्जैन के मध्य भाग में बैर नामक परगना गठित किया था।[12] जिसे उन्होंने अपने पुत्र प्रतापसिंह को पांच लाख रुपयों के साथ जागीर के रूप में दिया था। राजा प्रताप सिंह ने एक प्राचीन टीले को घेर कर बैरगढ़ का निर्माण प्रारम्भ किया। यह बैर का दुर्ग लगभग 70 फीट की ऊँचाई पर है जिसके चारों और प्रताप नहर बनी हुई है। इस किले में 8 बुर्जे बनाई गई थीं। यहां बुर्जों पर दो तोपें भी रखी हुई हैं। किले के अन्दर जनाना महल, जल का कुँआ, राजा की एक कचहरी एवं दरवाजे के पास घुड़साल बनी हुई है। इसके अन्दर कांच का महल और एक बारादरी भी है। यहां दो कुण्ड हैं। दुर्ग के पास ही महाराजा बदन सिंह ने नौलक्खा बाग भी बनवाया था।

डीग और भरतपुर के बीच में कुम्हेर का दुर्ग स्थित है जहां कुछ समय के लिए भरतपुर राज्य का राजकोष भी संरक्षित रहा था। भरतपुर के राजाओं की सैन्य व्यूह रचना को कुम्हेर, भरतपुर, डीग एवं बैर के दुर्गों के माध्यम से समझा जा सकता है। कुम्हेर दुर्ग की प्रंशसा थीफेन्थडर, फादर वैंदल, सूडान आदि अंग्रेज अधिकारियों के प्रतिवेदनों में मिलती है।[13] समासतः कुम्हेर का किला जहां एक ओर जाट शासकों की सैन्य दृष्टि का अनुपम उदाहरण है वहीं दूसरी और पर्यटकों के आकर्षण का एक अनूठा

केन्द्र हो सकता है। इसके अलावा बल्लभगढ़ का किला, कामा का कामसेन महल भी भरतपुर के जाट राजाओं के अनूठे शिल्प निर्माण के प्रतीक हैं जिनका पार्यटनिक विकास राजस्थान के पर्यटन में एक नया अध्याय जोड़ सकता है। उपर्युक्त दुर्गों के अतिरिक्त जाट राजाओं के संरक्षण में थून की गढ़ी, सोगर गढ़ी, सिनसिनी की गढ़ी, नीमराना की गढ़ी, सोनकगढी आदि का निर्माण हुआ जो निःसन्देह राजस्थान के स्थापत्य एवं शिल्प में अनोखी श्रीवृद्धि करता है।

आज आवश्यकता इस बात की है कि भरतपुर के जाट राजाओं के दुर्ग स्थापत्य को संरक्षित कर पर्यटन की दृष्टि से विकसित किया जाए जिससे इन राजाओं के शिल्प एवं प्रकृति प्रेम के अनोखे आयाम से विश्व परिचित हो सके।

## संदर्भ

1. *शुक्रनीति* : चतुर्थ अध्याय, षष्ट प्रकरण, पृ. 324-326, सं. ब्रह्मशंकर मिश्र; कौटिल्यकृत *अर्थशास्त्र;* विष्णु धर्मसूत्र; *मानसोल्लास* (2/5); *मनुस्मृति* अध्याय 7, श्लोक सं. 70-76 *विष्णु धर्मोत्तर पुराण* (2/26/20-88); *नीतिवाक्यामृत* (*दुर्गसमुद्दैश,* पृ. 199); *याज्ञवक्य स्मृति* (1/231); *नरपतिजयचर्या* (पृ. 175-176) आदि में दुर्ग प्रकारादि की चर्चा की गई है।
2. ऐसी मान्यता है कि इस दुर्ग का संस्थापन एवं निर्माण रुस्तम नामक एक जाट द्वारा करवाया गया था। सूरजमल ने इस दुर्ग को खेमकरन से लिया था फिर उसे नये सिरे से बनवाया। उसने शहर के चारों और मिट्टी की प्राचीर बनवाई। सन् 1733 ई. से यह उसकी राजधानी के रूप में रही। इससे पूर्व रुस्तम से खेमकरन को जो गढ़ी प्राप्त हुई उसे चौबुर्जा कहा जाता था। (*राजस्थान डिस्ट्रिक्ट गजेटियर भरतपुर,* पृ. 477-479)
3. *सुजस* : दुर्ग विशेषांक, अप्रैल-मई 1998 ई., वर्ष 7, अंक-3 के पृ. 24-25 पर के. एल. मीणा का लेख, 'गोराहट जा रे राज भरतपुर को', सूचना एवं प्रकाशन विभाग, राजस्थान सरकार।
4. कुंवर नटवर सिंह : *महाराजा सूरजमल,* पृ. 46, राधाकृष्ण प्रकाशन, दिल्ली, सन् 1985 ई.।
5. दीनानाथ दुबे : *भारत के दुर्ग,* पृ. 95, प्रकाशन विभाग भारत सरकार।
6. जनश्रुति है कि यह अष्टधातु दरवाजे पहले चित्तौड़ दुर्ग में लगे थे जिन्हें अलाउद्दीन खिलजी अपने मेवाड़ अभियान के समय दिल्ली ले गया था। (राघवेन्द्र सिंह मनोहर : *राजस्थान के प्रमुख दुर्ग,* पृ. 69, राजस्थान हिन्दी ग्रन्थ अकादमी, जयपुर, 1997, प्रथम संस्करण)

7. *राजस्थान डिस्ट्रिक्ट गजेटियर भरतपुर,* पृ. 479
8. रतनलाल मिश्र : *राजस्थान के दुर्ग,* पृ. 159, साहित्यागार जयपुर, 2008
9. राघवेन्द्र सिंह मनोहर द्वारा पूर्वोक्त पृ. 71 पर उद्धृत।
10. This place drives a considerable degree of its strength from the great quantity of water, which enables it to command its ditch being filled with this, presents and obstacle very difficult to be overcome. A large expense of water on the north-west side of Bharatpur disappeared suddenly on the arrival of my Army, and I afterwards discovered that the whole of this had been admitted into the ditch by which the fort and town were surrounded. Dinesh Chandra Sharma and Reeta Pareek: *Military system of the Jats of the Bharatpur State (1732 A-D to 1947 A-D)* p. 136] Competition Plus Sansthan, Ajmer, 2005 पर उद्धृत।
11. के. एल. मीणा ने इसे सुजस दुर्ग विशेषांक में सन् 1730 में निर्मित होना बताया है।
12. आचार्य सोमनाथ तथा कविवर सूदन के अनुसार इसका नाम बैरीगढ़ था जिसे आजकल बैर कहते हैं। दूसरे लेखक ओ-डायर का मत है कि इस भू-भाग में बेर के पेड़ बहुत होने के कारण यह बैर के नाम से प्रसिद्ध हुआ (रतन लाल मिश्र, *पूर्वोक्त,* पृ. 188 से उद्धृत)
13. फादर एफ. एक्स. वैंदेल द्वारा *वैंदेल्स मेमायर्स ऑन द ओरिजन, ग्रोथ एण्ड प्रेजेन्ट स्टेट ऑफ जाट पावर इन हिन्दुस्तान* (1768), में कुम्हेर का उल्लेख है। वैंदेल के जाट सत्ता सम्बन्धी वृत्तलेख का विश्लेषण डॉ. वीरसिंह ने किया। डॉ. पेमाराम सम्पादित *सम आस्पेक्ट्स ऑफ राजस्थान हिस्ट्री एण्ड कल्चर,* क्लासिक पब्लिकेशन, जयपुर, 2002, पृ. 16-29।

# 23

# पश्चिमी राजस्थान में जाट समाज की जाति-पंचायतें एवं सामाजिक विवादों का निस्तारण (1700-1800 ई.)

**प्रो. शिव कुमार भनोत**

अठारहवीं शताब्दी कालीन पश्चिमी राजस्थान के बीकानेर एवं जोधपुर राज्यों में जाति-पंचायतें सामाजिक स्तर पर एक प्रभावशाली और अति सक्रिय न्यायिक संस्थाएं रही हैं।[1] अपनी गहन सामाजिक सम्पृक्ति के कारण यह पंचायतें कई अर्थों में अपने क्षेत्र की गांव पंचायतों[2] तथा व्यावसायिक पंचायतों[3] की तुलना में कहीं अधिक प्रभावी और गतिशील दृष्टिगत होती हैं।[4] हमारे अध्ययन काल और क्षेत्र में विविध जातियों की पृथक-पृथक जाति पंचायतों के अस्तित्वमान होने के प्रमाण मिलते हैं[5] जिनमें से जाट समाज की जाति पंचायतें अपने सामाजिक सरोकार और विविध सामाजिक विवादों के निस्तारण की दृष्टि से विशेष रूप से उल्लेखनीय है। जाट समाज में प्रचलित सामाजिक नियमों, परम्पराओं, रीति-रिवाजों एवं मान्यताओं-मर्यादाओं को सुरक्षा प्रदान करने तथा जाति सदस्यों के मध्य उत्पन्न होने वाले विविध प्रकार के सामाजिक विवादों के निपटारे की दृष्टि से इन जाति पंचायतों को एक स्वायत्तशाली, सामाजिक न्यायिक संस्था के रूप में देखा जा सकता है।[6] राजस्थान राज्य अभिलेखागार, बीकानेर में ऐसी विपुल स्रोत सामग्री समुपलब्ध है जो अठारहवीं शताब्दीकालीन पश्चिमी राजस्थान के जाट समाज में विद्यमान रही जाति पंचायतों के स्वरूप, गठन, कार्यपद्धति, कार्यक्षेत्र एवं इनके समक्ष प्रस्तुत होने वाले सामाजिक विवादों के प्रकार तथा उनके निस्तारण में रही इनकी भूमिका पर बहुत मूल्यवान जानकारियाँ प्रदान करती है।[7] इस स्रोत-सामग्री को आधार बना कर कतिपय इतिहासकारों ने कई उल्लेखनीय कार्य प्रकाशित किये हैं जिनमें प्रो. दिलबाग सिंह[8], प्रो. जी.एस.एल. देवड़ा[9], प्रो. एस.पी. गुप्ता[10], प्रो. बी.एल. भादाणी[11], प्रो. के. एल. शर्मा[12], प्रो. पेमाराम[13], प्रो, शिव कुमार भनोत[14], डॉ. शशि अरोड़ा[15], डॉ. गिरिजा

शंकर[16] आदि के नाम विशेष रूप से उद्धृत किये जाने योग्य हैं। पूनम जोइया[17] तथा जिब्राइल[18] आदि शोधार्थियों ने भी इस पुरालेखीय स्रोत-सामग्री को आधार बना कर तद्विषयक शोध-लेख लिखे हैं। परन्तु, फिर भी हमारे अध्ययन क्षेत्र में मुख्य रूप से खेतीहर वर्ग का प्रतिनिधित्व करने वाले जाट समाज की इन जाति पंचायतों द्वारा अपने सामाजिक स्तर के विवादों को निस्तारित करने में रही इनकी भूमिका पर अभी बहुत कुछ शोध करना और उसे प्रकाश में लाया जाना शेष है। प्रस्तुत शोध-पत्र इसी दिशा में अग्रसर होने का एक विनम्र प्रयास है।

## 1

उल्लेखनीय है कि हमारे अध्ययन क्षेत्र में जाट समाज की जाति पंचायतें खापों के स्तर पर गठित हुई दिखाई नहीं देती हैं[19] वरन् गांव अथवा गांवों के समूह-स्तर पर गठित दिखाई देती हैं जिसे इनके एक वैशिष्ट्य के रूप में देखा जा सकता है। जाति पंच कौन होते थे एवं उनके चयन या नियुक्ति का आधार क्या था इस बिन्दु पर उपलब्ध स्रोत-सामग्री खुल कर प्रकाश नहीं डालती है। जो संदर्भ या उल्लेख देखने को मिलते हैं उनके आधार पर जाति पंचों के रूप में चयनित या नियुक्त होने वाले व्यक्तियों को मुख्य रूप से पांच श्रेणियों में वर्गीकृत कर देखा जा सकता है। प्रथम श्रेणी में हम जाट समाज के उन सदस्यों को जाति पंच के रूप में नियुक्त पाते हैं जो गांव में 'चौधरी',[20] 'जमींदार'[21] या 'सहाणा'[22] के रूप में नियुक्त एक स्थानीय अधिकारी के रूप में अपनी एक विशेष हैसियत रखते थे।[23] उल्लेखनीय है कि चूंकि इस संभाग में चौधरी का पद वंशानुगत माना जा चुका है अतएव ऐसे जाति पंच जो गांव में चौधरी भी हुआ करते थे, निःसंदेह वंशानुगत आधार पर जाति-पंच के रूप में स्वतः ही नियुक्ति पा जाते थे।[24] दूसरी श्रेणी में हम जाट समाज के उस प्रभावशाली आसामी[25] को जाति पंचायत का सदस्य बना देखते हैं जिसके पास वंशानुगत आधार पर अपेक्षाकृत अधिक जमीन हुआ करती थी और बड़ा आसामी होने के कारण उस व्यक्ति को अपने स्वजातीय सदस्यों के मध्य अधिक मान-सम्मान प्राप्त होता था।[26] तृतीय श्रेणी में हम उस क्षेत्र विशेष के जाट समाज के पुराने वासी या आबाद परिवार के सम्मानित सदस्य को जाति पंच के रूप में नियुक्त पाते हैं[27] तो चौथी श्रेणी में हम ऐसे व्यक्ति को अपनी जाति पंचायत का सदस्य नियुक्त पाते हैं जो अपनी विशिष्ट पारिवारिक स्थिति के कारण अपने स्वजातीय परिवारों के मध्य विशेष आदर का पात्र हो।[28] पाँचवी स्थिति में हम जाट समाज के 'जमादार'[29] नामक सम्मानजनक पद पर नियुक्त व्यक्ति को भी अपनी जाति-पंचायत में सदस्य के रूप में नियुक्त पाते हैं जो राज्य तथा अपने जातीय सदस्यों के मध्य एक महत्वपूर्ण सम्पर्क-सूत्र की भूमिका भी निभाया करता था।[30]

## 2

समसामयिक मूल स्रोत-सामग्री का अध्ययन करने पर यह ज्ञात होता है कि मुख्य रूप से चार परिस्थितियों में जाति-पंचायत की बैठक बुलाई जाती थी या सम्बन्धित निपटारे के लिये जाति पंच नियुक्त होते थे। प्रथम, जब कभी किसी जातीय सदस्य या सदस्यों द्वारा अपने किसी सामाजिक विवाद के निपटारे या सामाजिक समस्या के समाधान के लिये अपनी जाति पंचायत से तद्विषयक प्रार्थना की जाती थी।[31] द्वितीय, किसी सामाजिक रीति-रिवाज, परम्परा या जातीय मर्यादा की जाति के किसी सदस्य या सदस्यों द्वारा अवमाननना या उल्लंघन करने की स्थिति में जाति पंचों द्वारा स्वतः ही सक्रिय होकर पंचायत की बैठक बुलाई जाती थी;[32] तृतीय, जाति पंचायत के किसी निर्णय से असंतुष्ट होने की स्थिति में राज्य के समक्ष जाति पंचायत के निर्णय के विरुद्ध अपील होने की स्थिति में राज्य द्वारा जाति-पंचों की नियुक्ति की जाती थी[33] एवं चतुर्थ, किसी सामाजिक विवाद को निपटारे हेतु राज्य के समक्ष प्रस्तुत किये जाने की दशा में राज्य द्वारा सम्बन्धित जाति पंचायतों को नियुक्त किया जाता था अथवा सम्बन्धित जाति पंचायत को इस कार्य के लिये नियुक्त किया जाता था कि वह इस मामले से सम्बन्धित सही-सही ब्यौरा जांच-पड़ताल कर राज्य को प्रदान करे।[34] जाति पंचायतों की बैठक बुलाये जाने की उक्त चारों परिस्थितियों का विश्लेषण करने पर एक महत्वपूर्ण निष्कर्ष यह निकलता है कि राज्य को भी जाति-पंचों को नियुक्त करने विषयक अधिकार प्राप्त था एवं आवश्यकता पड़ने पर राज्य ऐसा करता भी था।[35]

जाति पंचायत की बैठक बुलाते समय विवाद का स्वरूप तथा प्रभावित पक्षों से सम्बन्धित स्थान महत्वपूर्ण भूमिका निभाते थे। जैसे, सामान्यतः एक ही गांव के जाट समाज के सदस्यों के पारस्परिक सामाजिक विवादों का निपटारा करने के लिये उसी गांव के जाति पंचों की पंचायत बैठती थी।[36] यद्यपि, विशिष्ट परिस्थितियों में दूसरे गांव के जाति पंच भी नियुक्त किये जा सकते थे।[37] इसी प्रकार दो भिन्न गांवों के समान जाति के सदस्यों के पारस्परिक सामाजिक विवादों का निपटारा करने के लिये तीसरे गांव के समान जाति के पंच नियुक्त किये जाने सम्बन्धी प्रमाण भी मिलते हैं।[38] एक गांव में जाट जाति के थोड़े से परिवार होने की स्थिति में वे अपने सामाजिक विवादों के निपटारों के लिये अपने निकटस्थ गांव की जाति पंचायत से जुड़ते हुए भी दिखाई देते थे।[39]

जाति पंचायत की बैठक किसी निश्चित स्थान विशेष पर ही आयोजित किये जाने की बाध्यता नहीं थी। प्राप्त पुरालेखीय सामग्री में वर्णित संदर्भों से यह पता चलता है कि तत्सम्बन्धी बैठक सामान्यतः किसी जातीय सदस्य के मकान, जाति के मंदिर, नोहरे, चौपाल, कुएं की मेड़ या किसी पेड़ के नीचे आयोजित हुआ करती थी।[40] प्रारम्भ में पंच

वादी द्वारा प्रतिवादी पर लगाये गये आरोप को सुनते थे। वादी, प्रतिवादी एवं साक्षियों से सत्य वृतान्त कराने के लिये उन्हें शपथ या कसम खिलाई जाती थी।[41] आवश्यकता पड़ने पर पंच लिखित प्रमाणों की जांच भी करते थे।[42] जाति पंचों के निर्णय से संतुष्ट नहीं होने पर वादी उस निर्णय के विरुद्ध राज्य से अपील कर सकता था।[43] दस्तावेजों के अवलोकन से एक ध्यान देने योग्य बात यह मुखरित होकर सामने आती है कि राज्य द्वारा सामान्यतः जाट समाज के सामाजिक विवादों के मामलों में दखल नहीं दिया जाता था। राज्य के समक्ष प्रस्तुत होने वाले ऐसे विवादों को राज्य द्वारा जाट समाज की ही अन्य पंचायत को सौंपे जाने के उदाहरण मिलते हैं।[44] ऐसा करते समय राज्य द्वारा सम्बन्धित पंचों को ईश्वर को साक्षी मान कर निर्णय देने के स्पष्ट निर्देश दिये जाते थे और उन्हें दूध, पूत, खेती आदि की विविध कसमें भी खिलाई जाती थी।[45]

**3**

हमारे अध्ययन क्षेत्र एवं काल में जाट समाज की जाति पंचायतों के समक्ष प्रस्तुत होने वाले सामाजिक विवाद मुख्य रूप से सगाई, विवाह, विवाहित जीवन, पति की मृत्यु के उपरान्त विधवा स्त्री की दशा, पुनर्विवाह जैसे नाता, पले लगाई, घर में घालना आदि, खोला (गोद लेना), नारी के क्रय-विक्रय, पैतृक सम्पत्ति, खेत-जमीन के बंटवारे आदि से सम्बन्धित हुआ करते थे।[46] इनके कार्यक्षेत्र में जातीय व सामाजिक नियमों-परम्पराओं को संरक्षण एवं सुरक्षा प्रदान करने का कार्य भी सम्मिलित था।[47] सगाई सम्बन्धी विवाद मुख्यतः सगाई की बात तय कर मुकर जाने; परस्पर विरोधी दोषारोपण करने कि सगाई दूसरे पक्ष द्वारा देनी की थी परन्तु अब मुकर रहा है तथा सगाई तयशुदा स्थान से अन्यत्र कर देने जैसे प्रकरणों से सम्बन्धित हुआ करते थे। जिनके जाति पंचों के समक्ष निपटारे के लिये पहुंचने के अनेकानेक उल्लेख देखने को मिलते हैं।[48] सगाई के उपरांत लड़के या लड़की में से किसी एक की मृत्यु को जाने पर या किसी एक में शारीरिक दोष उत्पन्न हो जाने की स्थिति में सगाई तोड़ने या छोड़ने की अनुमति प्राप्त करने आदि मामले भी सम्बन्धित जाति पंचों के द्वारा ही सुलझाये जाते थे।[49] सगाई के उपरांत अकाल या सूखे की मार के कारण लड़के के अन्यत्र चले जाने, निर्धारित रीत के रुपये नहीं चुकाने तथा पारस्परिक झगड़ा हो जाने के चलते सगाई अन्यत्र करने के मामले भी ये जाति पंचायतें ही निपटाती थी।[50] सगाई सम्बन्ध विच्छेद हो जाने पर पूर्व में दी गई धनराशि की मांग को लेकर उत्पन्न विवाद[51] तथा 'वेर की रकम' या 'वेर के कागद' को लेकर उत्पन्न विवाद भी जाति-पंचों की मध्यस्थता से ही निपटाये जाते थे। सगाई सम्बन्धों में विधिवत सम्बन्ध विच्छेद को लौकिक भाषा के शब्द 'वेर' में समाहित किया जा सकता था। वेर एक प्रकार का आर्थिक दण्ड था, जिसमें दोषी पक्ष दूसरे पक्ष को एक रकम चुकाता था।

दण्ड की राशि दोषी पक्ष की आर्थिक स्थिति तथा मामले की गम्भीरता को देखते हुए तय की जाती थी जिसके निर्धारण में जाति पंचों को अहम भूमिका रहा करती थी।[52]

इन जाति पंचायतों के समक्ष पहुंचने वाले विवाह से सम्बन्धित सामाजिक विवाद भी अनेक प्रकार के हुआ करते थे। इनमें कन्या पक्ष के द्वारा बारम्बार आग्रह करने के बावजूद वर पक्ष के द्वारा जानबूझ कर विवाह में अनावश्यक विलम्ब करने, तयशुदा स्थान पर विवाह न करके विवाह अन्यत्र कर देने तथा न्याय अर्थात् जाति के नियम-परम्पराओं का उल्लंघन कर किसी नीची जाति की महिला को घर में रख लेने या समाज की गरिमा को ठेस पहुंचाने आदि से सम्बन्धित विवाद स्थूलतः हमारी जानकारी में आते हैं।[53] उदाहरणार्थ - वि. सं. 1811 में बीकानेर राज्य के गांव किलाणसर के चौधरी हरदास भोजोणी की पुत्री का विवाह उसी राज्य के गांव लोहरे के चौधरी सुरजे के पुत्र के साथ होना निश्चित हुआ था परन्तु, विवाह के समय चौध ारी सुरजे के पुत्र के स्थान पर दूसरे चौधरी के विवाह करने पहुंचने का मामला जातीय गरिमा व प्रतिष्ठा को ठेस पहुंचाने वाले कृत्य के रूप में देखा गया एवं सम्बन्धित जाति-पंचायत के विचार का विषय बना।[54]

विवाहित जीवन के दौरान भी कभी-कभी ऐसी समस्याएं उत्पन्न हो जाती थीं, जो गम्भीर सामाजिक विवाद का रूप लेकर निबटारे के लिये जाति पंचायत के समक्ष पहुंचती थी। ये विवाद मुख्य रूप से पति द्वारा अपनी विवाहिता को ठीक से न रखने, उसके साथ उचित व्यवहार नहीं करने, एक पत्नी के होते दूसरी को घर में लाने या दूसरा विवाह कर लेने पर प्रथम पत्नी को उसके अधिकार व हक से वंचित करने, विवाहित स्त्री के दुराचारिणी या निःसंतान होने पर पुरुष द्वारा अन्यत्र विवाह कर लेने, इत्यादि से उत्पन्न झगड़ों से सम्बन्धित होते थे, जो सम्बन्धित जाति पंचायत के विचार के विषय बनते हुए दिखाई देते थे।[55] जैसे वि. सं. 1828 में जोधपुर राज्य के गांव हरियाडाणा के जाट कुसला द्वारा अपनी पहली पत्नी के होते हुए दूसरी स्त्री से नाता कर घर में प्रथम पत्नी द्वारा राज्य से न्याय मांगे जाने पर राज्य द्वारा यह मामला निपटाने हेतु सम्बन्धित जाति-पंचायत को सौंप दिया गया ओर यह उसके कार्यक्षेत्र का विषय बनता हुआ दिखाई दिया।[56]

इस सम्भाग में पति की मृत्यु के उपरांत विधवा स्त्री के पुनर्विवाह सम्बन्धी उल्लेख प्रचुर मात्रा में मिलते हैं। नारकीय वैधव्य जीवन का परित्याग कर पुनर्विवाह से नये जीवन की शुरुआत करने की व्यवस्था पश्चिमी राजस्थान के जाट समाज ने प्रदान की है।[57] लौकिक भाषा में इन पुनर्विवाह को 'नाता', 'घर में घालना', 'पल्ले लगाई', 'गांठ बंधाई', 'चूड़ी पहराई' आदि नामों से अभिलेखों में दर्शाया गया है।[58] नाता-प्रथा के

नियमों और परम्पराओं की अनुपालना कराना और तत्सम्बन्धी विवादों का निपटारा करना पश्चिमी राजस्थान के जाट समाज की जाति पंचायतों का एक महत्वपूर्ण कार्यक्षेत्र था तथा उनके द्वारा किये गये फैसलों को राज्य सरकार का संरक्षण भी प्राप्त था।[59] इस संभाग के जाट समाज में प्रचलित परम्परानुसार प्रथम विवाह तो बेटी के बाप पर निर्भर करता था परन्तु, पुनर्विवाह अर्थात् 'नाता' करना नारी की स्वयं की इच्छा पर निर्भर करता था। वह 'नाता' चाहे तो कर सकती थी अन्यथा पीहर या ससुराल में, जहां पर भी वह रहना चाहती, रह कर अपना शेष जीवन व्यतीत कर सकती थी। जाट समाज में नाता देने का अधिकारी नारी का पूर्व ससुराल पक्ष था, जिसकी बिना सहमति के नारी के मां-बाप, भाई-बन्धु उसे नाते नहीं दे सकते थे।[60]

हमारे अध्ययनकाल में पश्चिमी राजस्थान के जाट समाज में 'नाता-प्रथा' से सम्बन्धित कतिपय नियम और परम्पराएं प्रचलित थी[61], जिनका उल्लंघन होने पर वह विषय जाति पंचायत के कार्यक्षेत्र का विषय बनता दिखाई देता था। 'नाता' करने वाले दोनों पक्षों का शादीशुदा होना आवश्यक था। यदि कोई कुंवारा पुरुष नाता करना चाहता था तो पहले उसका कुंवारापन उतारना जरूरी था।[62] नाता करते समय चार गोत्र - मां-बाप, दादी-नानी के गोत्रों को टाला जाता था।[63] विधवा से नाता करने का पहला अधिकार देवर का माना जाता था। स्त्री अपने जेठ अथवा जेठूते से नाता नहीं कर सकती थी। ऐसा कर लेने पर 'घर जब्त' या 'न्याय बाहर' करने का प्रावधान था।[64] पति के जीवित रहते स्त्री नाता नहीं कर सकती थी तथा ऐसी स्त्री ही नाता कर सकती थी जिसका फैसला जाति-पंचायत या दरबार ने कर दिया हो।[65] धरम छोड़ी हुई औरत से नाता किया जा सकता था।[66] जाति पंचायतें दोनों पक्षों को घर बसाने के लिये बाध्य करती थीं और फिर भी वे नहीं मानते तो 'गुनहगारी' लगा कर फैसला कर 'नाता' करने की छूट प्रदान कर दी जाती थी।[67] नाता-प्रथा में 'बैर' की रकम वसूल कर स्त्री को नाते जाने की छूट दे दी जाती थी। पंचायत 'बैर' की रकम का निर्धारण दोनों पक्षों की आर्थिक स्थिति को देख कर करती थीं।[68] यह रकम ले लेने के पश्चात् मृत पति के परिवार वालों की तरफ से सम्बन्ध विच्छेद का परिचायक बैर का कागद दिया जाता था।[69] नारी स्वयं अपना बैर चुका कर भी नाता कर सकती थी।[70] बैर की रकम में से जाति पंचायत अपना हिस्सा रख लेती थी।[71] नाता ले जाने वाला पक्ष देने वाले पक्ष से आपसी सहमति का परिचायक एक कागज बनवाता था, जिसे फारगती का कागज कहते थे। इसमें बैर की रकम का हवाला, बाल-बच्चे, धन-दौलत या अन्य सम्पत्ति आदि का जिक्र होता था। जाति पंच इसे तस्दीक करते थे और यह कागज विवाद की स्थिति में साक्ष्य के रूप में स्वीकारा जाता था।[72] राज्य सरकार द्वारा 'नाते' के लिये 'रीठ' नामक कर वसूला जाता था परन्तु सगे भाई की विधवा को

घर में डालने पर 'रीठ' नहीं लगता था।[73] नाता जाने वाली स्त्री अपने पूर्व ससुराल के उत्तराधिकारी एवं दायित्वों से पूरी तरह वंचित हो जाती थी।[74] पश्चिमी राजस्थान के जाट समाज में प्रचलित यह परम्परा पुनर्विवाह का एक सम्मानजनक प्रकार था क्योंकि जाति पंचायत और राज्य दोनों में इन्हें मान्यता प्राप्त थी और उनकी दृष्टि में ये निन्दनीय नहीं थे।[75] पश्चिमी राजस्थान के समसामयिक जाट समाज में पुनर्विवाह का एक और स्वरूप देखने में आता है जो राज्य और समाज दोनों की दृष्टि में अच्छा नहीं माना जाता था। इसे घर में घालना कहा जाता था। किसी विवाहिता को उसके पति के होते हुए किसी अन्य व्यक्ति द्वारा अपने घर में रख लेना[76] तथा पूर्व पत्नी के होते हुए भी दूसरी स्त्री को घर में डाल लेना[77] इस श्रेणी में आता था। ऐसे सभी मामले सामाजिक विवाद का रूप धारण कर तद्विषयक निपटारे के लिये जाति पंचायतों के समक्ष प्रस्तुत होते दिखाई देते थे। प्राप्त पुरालेखीय संदर्भों का अवलोकन करने पर यह विदित होता है कि ऐसे मामलों में जाट समाज की सम्बन्धित जाति पंचायतों की हरसंभव चेष्टा यही रहा करती थी कि समाज की सामाजिक निरन्तरता और स्थिरता बनाये रखने के लिये इस प्रकार अनाधिकृत रूप में रखी गई स्त्री को उसके मूल पति के घर वापस पहुंचा दिया जाये।[78]

हमारे अध्ययनकाल में पश्चिमी राजस्थान में लड़कियों व स्त्रियों का क्रय-विक्रय एक अप्रत्याशित घटना नहीं थी और तत्कालीन जाट समाज भी इससे प्रभावित हुए बिना नहीं रह सका। साधारणतया ऐसी स्थिति अकाल व सूखे के समय उत्पन्न होती थी जबकि या तो वे अकाल से मुक्ति पाने के उपाय में पुरुषों द्वारा बेच दी जाती थीं अथवा पुरुषों के अन्यत्र चले जाने पर असहाय अवस्था में मजबूरन स्वयं बिक जाती थीं। ऐसे मामलों में सम्बन्धित जाति पंचायतों के द्वारा मध्यस्थता व लिखा-पढ़ी भी की जाती थी।[79] अवैध तरीकों से किये गये विक्रय सम्बन्धी विविध प्रकार के विवाद सम्बन्धित जाति-पंचायत के द्वारा ही सुलझाये जाते थे।[80] इन सभी विवादों के अतिरिक्त जाति-पंचायत अपने जातीय सदस्यों के मध्य उत्पन्न पैतृक सम्पत्ति के बंटवारे सम्बन्धी विवाद, किसी जातीय सदस्य की पत्नी के दुराचारिणी होने से उत्पन्न विवाद आदि को भी सुलझाती थी, साथ ही जातीय सदस्यों के क्रिया-कलापों पर यह दृष्टि भी रखती थी कि उनके किसी कार्य से जातीय सम्मान व गरिमा को ठेस नहीं पहुंचे।[81]

आत्महत्या, अधूरा गर्भ गिराने, बलात्कार, व्यभिचार आदि फौजदारी मामले यद्यपि राज्य के कार्यक्षेत्र में आते थे परन्तु जाट समाज की सम्बन्धित जाति पंचायतें भी अपने जातीय सम्मान को बनाये रखने के लिये जातीय स्तर पर भी ऐसे अपराधियों के अपराधों पर विचार करती थीं तथा ऐसे मामलों में सम्बन्धित जाति-पंचायतों द्वारा दिया गया दण्ड राज्य द्वारा प्रदत्त दण्ड से अतिरिक्त होता था।[82]

**4**

जाट समाज की जाति पंचायतों द्वारा विविध प्रकार के सामाजिक विवादों को निपटाने के लिये जो निर्णय समय-समय पर विविध मामलों के संदर्भ में दिये गये, उनमें से कतिपय निर्णय उदाहरणस्वरूप द्रष्टव्य हैं - वर पक्ष के द्वारा सगाई तोड़े जाने की स्थिति में जाति-पंचायत कन्या पक्ष को उचित हरजाना मय रीत की रकम के दिलाती थी। बीकानेर राज्य के गांव रामसर के जाट द्वारा सगाई तोड़ने पर उसे कन्या पक्ष से मय रीत के 50 रुपये लौटाने पड़े थे।[83] कभी-कभी जाति-पंचायत सगाई तोड़ने वाले पक्ष से यह आग्रह भी करती हुई दिखाई देती थी कि वे लड़की के लिये नया वर तलाश करें। इस तरह के आदेश बीकानेर राज्य के गांव गजरूपदेसर के ढुढोणी चेतन को तथा जोधपुर राज्य के परबतसर गांव के जाट भेजे को दिये गये थे।[84]

इस प्रकार हम देखते हैं कि हमारे अध्ययनकाल में इस संभाग में जाट समाज की जाति पंचायतों का अपना व्यापक कार्यक्षेत्र था तथा जातीय व सामाजिक विवादों के निपटारे एवं सम्बन्धित समस्याओं के समाधान में उनकी महत्वपूर्ण भूमिका थी। राज्य भी इन जाति पंचायतों, इनकी भूमिका तथा इनके निर्णयों को समुचित महत्व व संरक्षण प्रदान करता था और इन्हें पर्याप्त स्वायत्ततता व संरक्षण प्रदान करने की नीति पर चलता था। जाट समाज की जाति-पंचायतों ने क्षमा याचना, त्रुटि सुधार, अर्थदण्ड, जाति-भोज, जाति बहिष्कार जैसे दण्डों के माध्यम से जातीय सदस्यों में अपने प्रचलित सामाजिक नियम परम्पराओं की अनुपालना के प्रति जागरूकता व सतर्कता उत्पन्न की और अपनी सामाजिक परम्पराओं को संरक्षित किया। राज्य द्वारा यथासंभव इन जाति-पंचायतों के क्षेत्राधिकार में दखल नहीं दिया जाता था फिर भी हम पाते हैं कि सर्वोच्च सत्ता की हैसियत का उपयोग करते हुए राज्य किसी-किसी मामले में इन जाति पंचायतों के निर्णयों को उलटता हुआ और एक निश्चित आर्थिक कर लेकर प्राणी को संरक्षण प्रदान करता हुआ भी दृष्टिगोचर होता है। इससे इन जाति पंचायतों पर राज्य की सर्वोच्चता का होना प्रमाणित होता है। तथापि, समसामयिक पुरालेखीय स्रोत-सामग्री के विश्लेषण के आधार पर यह कहना अतिशयोक्तिपूर्ण नहीं होगा कि अठारहवीं शताब्दी कालीन पश्चिमी राजस्थान में जाट समाज की जाति-पंचायतों ने जाति एवं समाज से जुड़े विविध प्रकार के सामाजिक विवादों व समस्याओं को स्थानीय स्तर पर सुलझाने व सामाजिक नियमों-परम्पराओं एवं मर्यादाओं के समुचित संरक्षण प्रदान करने का कार्य निष्पादित कर राज्य को अप्रत्यक्ष रूप से बहुत सहायता प्रदान की।

## संदर्भ

1. डॉ. शिव कुमार भनोत : *राजस्थान में पंचायत व्यवस्था,* पृ. 74-105, जयपुर (2000)
2. *वही,* पृ. 106-139
3. जी. एस. एल. देवड़ा : *ए रीथिंकिंग ऑन दि पोलिटिक्स ऑफ कमर्शियल सोसायटी ऑफ दी कोलोनियल इण्डिया,* ओकेजनल पेपर, एन.एम.एम.एल., तीन मूर्ति हाउस, नई दिल्ली (1987); शिव कुमार भनोतः *पश्चिमी राजपूताना में व्यावसायिक पंचायतें,* शोध पत्र, प्रकाशित, राजस्थान हिस्ट्री कांग्रेस प्रोसीडिंग्स ऑफ सिरोही सेशन, पृ. 97-102, जोधपुर (1984)
4. शिव कुमार भनोत : *ऑर्गेनाईजेशन एण्ड रोल ऑफ कास्ट पंचायत्स इन वैस्टर्न राजपूताना,* शोध लेख, प्रकाशित, *सम आस्पैक्ट्स ऑफ सोशो-इकोनोमिक हिस्ट्री ऑफ राजस्थान* (सं. जी.एस.एल. देवड़ा), पृ. 226-246, जोधपुर (1980)
5. उदाहरणार्थ - मोचियों री पंचायत दर्जियों री पंचायत; बामणां री पंचायत; तेलियों री पंचायत; अग्रवालों री पंचायत; सुनारों री पंचायत; जाटां री पंचागत आदि।
6. *सनद परवाना बही (मारवाड़)* वि.सं. 1823 नं. 5, पृ. 28, राजस्थान राज्य अभिलेखागार, बीकानेर; वहीं, वि. सं. 1828, नं. 10, पृ. 261; *कागदों की बही* (बीकानेर), वि. सं. 1839, नं. 6, पृ. 20, 43, रा.रा.अ.बी.
7. शिव कुमार भनोत : *पश्चिमी राजस्थान (बीकानेर, जोधपुर) में पंचायत प्रणाली के पुरालेखीय स्रोत* (1700-1800 ए.डी.), शोध लेख, प्रकाशित, *सम आस्पैक्ट्स ऑफ सोशो-इकोनोमिक हिस्ट्री ऑफ राजस्थान एण्ड मालवा* (सं. डॉ. नारायण सिंह भाटी), पृ. 155-165, जोधपुर (1989)
8. प्रो. दिलबाग सिंह : *आस्पैक्ट्स ऑफ जाट अपराइजिंग,* शोध लेख, प्रकाशित, *दी जाट्स दियर रोल एण्ड कन्ट्रीब्यूशन टू दि सोशो-इकोनोमिक लाइफ एण्ड पोलिटी ऑफ नार्थ वैस्ट इण्डिया,* वोल्यूम-1 (सं. डॉ. वीर सिंह), पृ. 78-86, दिल्ली (2004); वही- *माइग्रेशन एण्ड मूवमेन्ट : दी रोल ऑफ जाट्स इन रूरल सेटलमेन्ट्स इन राजस्थान ड्यूरिंग दि मिडीवल पीरियड,* शोध लेख, *दी जाट्स,* वोल्यूम-2 (सं. डॉ. वीरसिंह), पृ. 213-220, दिल्ली (2006)
9. प्रो. जी.एस.एल. देवड़ा : *राजस्थान की प्रशासनिक व्यवस्था (1574-1818 ई.), पृ. 3-4, बीकानेर (1981);* वही : *फोरमेशन एण्ड सेटलमेन्ट ऑफ जाट सोसाइटीज इन दी नोर्थ वेस्ट रीजन्स ऑफ दि इण्डियन सबकोन्टिनेन्ट ड्यूरिंग दी अर्ली मिडीवल पीरियड,* की-नोट एड्रैस, *दी जाट्स,* वोल्यूम-3 (सं. डॉ. वीर सिंह), पृ. 11-32, दिल्ली (2007)
10. प्रो. एस.पी.गुप्ता : *एग्रेरियन कंडीशन्स इन दि टेरीटरीज ऑफ जाट्स,* शोध लेख प्रकाशित, *दी जाट्स,* वोल्यूम-1 (सं. डॉ. वीरसिंह), पृ. 87-100, दिल्ली (2004)

11. प्रो. बी.एल. भादाणी : *दी रोल ऑफ जाट्स इन दी इकोनोमिक डवलपमेन्ट ऑफ मारवाड़, शोध लेख, प्रकाशित, दी जाट्स,* वाल्यूम-1 (सं. डॉ. वीर सिंह), पृ. 65-77, दिल्ली (2004); वही : *ए नोट ऑन दी जाट जमींदार्स इन दि डेजर्ट स्टेट ऑफ बीकानेर,* शोध लेख, प्रकाशित, *दी जाट्स,* वोल्यूम-2 (सं. डॉ. वीरसिंह), 61-68, दिल्ली (2007)

12. प्रो. के.एल. शर्मा : *ए सोशो कल्चरल प्रोफाइल ऑफ जाट्स इन नोर्थ वेस्ट इण्डिया,* शोध लेख, प्रकाशित, *दी जाट्स,* वोल्यूम-1 (सं. डॉ. वीरसिंह), पृ. 11-20 दिल्ली (2004); वही : *इमर्जेन्स ऑफ जाट्स,* शोध लेख, प्रकाशित, *दी जाट्स,* वोल्यूम-2 (सं. डॉ. वीरसिंह), पृ. 1-8, दिल्ली (2006)

13. प्रो. पेमाराम : *मारवाड़ में किसान जागृति के कर्णधार जाट,* शोध लेख, प्रकाशित, *दी जाट्स,* वोल्यूम-1 (सं. डॉ. वीरसिंह), पृ. 247-265, दिल्ली (2004); वही : *मध्यकालीन राजस्थान में जाट गणराज्य एवं उनका पतन,* शोध लेख, प्रकाशित, *दी जाट्स,* वोल्यूम-3 (सं. डॉ. वीरसिंह), पृ. 201-214, दिल्ली (2007)

14. प्रो. शिव कुमार भनोत : *ऑर्गेनाइजेशन एण्ड रोल ऑफ कास्ट पंचायत इन वेस्टर्न राजपूताना, शोध लेख, प्रकाशित, सम आस्पैक्टस ऑफ सोशियो इकोनोमिक हिस्ट्री ऑफ राजस्थान* (सं. जी.एस.एल. देवड़ा), पृ. 226-246, जोधपुर (1980); वही : *पश्चिमी राजपूताना में व्यावसायिक पंचायतें,* शोध लेख, प्रकाशित, *राजस्थान हिस्ट्री कांग्रेस प्रोसीडिंग्स ऑफ सिरोही सेशन,* पृ. 97-102, जोधपुर (1984); वही : *पश्चिमी राजस्थान में पंचायत प्रणाली के पुरालेखीय स्रोत (1700-1800 ई.),* शोध लेख, प्रकाशित, *सम आस्पैक्ट्स ऑफ सोशो इकोनोमिक हिस्ट्री ऑफ राजस्थान एण्ड मालवा* (सं. डॉ. नारायण सिंह भाटी), पृ. 155-165, जोधपुर (1989); वही : *राजस्थान में पंचायत व्यवस्था, जयपुर (2000)* वही : पश्चिमी राजस्थान में ग्रामीण जनजीवन में सौहाद्र एवं समन्वय स्थापना में पंचायतों की भूमिका (1700-1800 ई.), शोध लेख, प्रकाशित, *राजस्थान हिस्ट्री कांग्रेस प्रोसीडिंग्स,* वोल्यूम-25, सुजानगढ़ सेशन, पृ. 144-52, जोधपुर (2008); वही : पश्चिमी राजस्थान के ग्राम्य जीवन में पंचायतें और पर्यावरण (1750-1800 ई.), शोध लेख, प्रकाशित, *वैचारिकी रिसर्च जर्नल,* जुलाई-सितम्बर, 2009, भाग : 25, अंक 2, पृ. 62-66, कोलकाता (2009); वही : *पश्चिमी राजस्थान में पंचायत-राज्य सम्बन्ध* (1750-1800 ई.), शोध लेख, प्रकाशित, *राजस्थान हिस्ट्री कांग्रेस प्रोसीडिंग्स,* वोल्यूम-25, जोधपुर सेशन, पृ. 463-470, जोधपुर (2009)

15. डॉ. शशि अरोड़ा : पश्चिमी व उत्तर पश्चिमी राजस्थान की पंचायतों के सम्मुख नारी की स्थिति, शोध लेख, प्रकाशित, *राजस्थान हिस्ट्री कांग्रेस प्रोसीडिंग्स ऑफ उदयपुर सेशन,* पृ. 36-40, जोधपुर (1978)

16. डॉ. गिरिजाशंकर : *राजस्थान राज्य अभिलेखागार, बीकानेर में जाट जाति के*

*महत्वपूर्ण स्रोत,* शोध लेख, प्रकाशित, *दी जाट्स,* वोल्यूम-1 (सं. डॉ. वीरसिंह), पृ. 193-96, दिल्ली (2004); वही : *जनचेतना के अग्रदूत बीकानेर के जाट (19वीं-20वीं सदी),* शोध लेख, प्रकाशित, *दी जाट्स,* वोल्यूम-2 (सं. डॉ. वीरसिंह), पृ. 243-248, दिल्ली (2006)

17. पूनमचंद जोइया : *पश्चिमी राजस्थान में जाट समाज में नाता प्रथा,* शोध लेख, प्रकाशित, *दी जाट्स,* वोल्यूम-1 (सं. डॉ. वीर सिंह), पृ. 182-192, दिल्ली (2004); वही : *जाट संदर्भिका सनद परवाना बही,* जोधपुर (1763-1939), शोध लेख, प्रकाशित, *दी जाट्स,* वोल्यूम-1 (सं. डॉ. वीर सिंह), पृ. 197-206, दिल्ली (2004)

18. जिब्राइल : *पोजीशन ऑफ जॉट्स इन चूरू रीजन,* शोध लेख, प्रकाशित, *दी जाट्स,* वोल्यूम-2 (सं. डॉ. वीरसिंह), पृ. 221-226, दिल्ली (2006)

19. पूर्ववर्ती बीकानेर राज्य में जाटों की कई खापें अस्तित्वमान थीं जिनमें निम्नांकित सात प्रमुख रूप से उल्लेखनीय थीं- शेखसर के गोदारा, सुई के सिहाग; धाणसिया के सोहुना; सिधमुख के कसवां; रायसलाणा के बेणीवाल; भाड़ग के सारण तथा लुद्दी के पुनिया। इनके अतिरिक्त भादू, भूकर, जाखड़, कलहेर, नैण इत्यादि कतिपय छोटी शाखाएं भी थीं। *दयालदास री ख्यात* में इनके लिये ''सात पट्टी, सत्तावन मंझरा'' उल्लेख आया है, जिसका अर्थ है कि इनके सात बड़े और सत्तावन छोटे राज्य थे।

20. गांव का मुखिया।

21. भूमिपति, जिसे वंशानुगत भूमि सम्बन्धी अधिकार प्राप्त थे।

22. भूमि के मापन, कर निर्धारण व वसूली के कार्य में सहयोग करने वाला स्थानीय अधिकारी।

23. प्रो. शिवकुमार भनोत : *राजस्थान में पंचायत व्यवस्था,* जयपुर (2000) पृ. 76

24. दीवानी पत्र - मोहता संग्रह, रा.रा.अ.बी.

25. *सनद परवाना बही* (मारवाड़) वि.स. 1821. नं. 1, पृ. 22; *कागदों की बही* (बीकानेर), वि.सं. 1828 नं. 10, पृ. 261, रा.रा.अ.बी.

26. *कागदों की बही* (बीकानेर), वि. सं. 1827, नं. 3, पृ. 44, 45, 47; *सनद परवाना बही* (मारवाड़), वि.सं. 1830, नं. 13, पृ. 74, रा.रा.अ.बी.

27. *बही पानवाला ठिकाणा री,* वि.सं. 1800, नं. 40/5, रा.रा.अ.बी.

28. *गांवां रे हलगत री बही,* वि.सं. 1739, नं. 133, रा.रा.अ.बी.

29. जाति विशेष का नेता/मुखिया, जो अन्य व अपनी जाति के मध्य एक प्रतिनिधि होता था।

30. *खाता बही रीणी,* वि.सं. 1834-35, नं. 5, पृ. 33-34, रामपुरिया रिकाड्र्स, बीकानेर, रा.रा.अ.बी.

31. *सनद परवाना बही* (मारवाड़) वि.सं. 1822, नं. 3, पृ. 90; *कागदों की बही* (बीकानेर), वि.सं. 1859, नं. 12, पृ. 140, 155, रा.रा.अ.बी.

32. *सनद परवाना बही* (मारवाड़) वि.सं. 1822, नं. 3, पृ. 90; *कागदों की बही* (बीकानेर), वि.सं. 1857, नं. 11, पृ. 22, रा.रा.अ.बी.

33. *सनद परवाना बही* (मारवाड़) वि. सं. 1822, नं. 3, पृ. 30, 90; कागदों की बही (बीकानेर), वि.सं. 1839, नं. 6, पृ. 19, 35, रा.रा.अ.बी.

34. *सनद परवाना बही* (मारवाड़) वि.सं. 1823, नं. 5, पृ. 52; *कागदों की बही* (बीकानेर), वि.सं. 1840 नं. 7, पृ. 27, रा.रा.अ.बी.

35. *सनद परवाना बही* (मारवाड़) वि.सं. 1822, नं. 3, पृ. 93-94; *कागदों की बही* (बीकानेर), वि.सं. 1857, नं. 11, पृ. 284, रा.रा.अ.बी.

36. *सनद परवाना बही* (मारवाड़) वि. सं. 1823, नं. 5, पृ. 52; *कागदों की बही* (बीकानेर), वि.सं. 1857, नं. 11, पृ. 196, रा.रा.अ.बी.

37. *सनद परवाना बही* (मारवाड़) वि.सं. 1822, नं. 3, पृ. 25; *कागदों की बही* (बीकानेर), वि.सं. 1840, नं. 7, पृ. 18, रा.रा.अ.बी.

38. ऐसे एक लेख का मूल पाठ द्रष्टव्य है - 1 मी. जेठ सुद 13 1 तथा गांव जूंझणदा नै जनांणा रा जाटां रे सगाई रो असरचो है सुं असरचो है सुं पाखती रा गांवां रा जाट पंचां ऊपर थाप ने हुआ जबी समझाय देजो श्री हजूर से हुकम है दुहोड़ीदार भवानीदास - *सनद परवाना बही* (मारवाड), वि.सं. 1822, नं. 3, पृ. 24, रा.रा.अ.बी.

39. *बही पेशकसी रे लेखे री* (बीकानेर), वि.सं. 1833, नं. 38, पृ. 1; सनद परवाना बही (मारवाड़) वि.सं. 1822, नं. 3, पृ. 56, रा.रा.अ.बी.

40. बीकानेर की रामपुरिया रिकार्ड की कागदों की बहियों में तथा जोधपुर की सनद परवाना बहियों में तद्‌विषयक उल्लेख देखने को मिलते हैं।

41. *सनद परवाना बही* (मारवाड़), वि. सं. 1822, नं. 3, पृ. 22; *कागदों की बही* (बीकानेर) वि. सं. 1859, नं. 6, पृ. 36-37, रा.रा.अ.बी.

42. *सनद परवाना बही* (मारवाड़), वि. सं. 1830, नं. 13, पृ. 74; *कागदों की बही* (बीकानेर), वि.सं. 1839, नं. 6, पृ. 37, रा.रा.अ.बी.

43. *सनद परवाना बही* (मारवाड़), वि. सं. 1824, नं. 6, पृ. 30; *कागदों की बही* (बीकानेर), वि.सं. 1839, नं. 6, पृ. 1, 9, 35, रा.रा.अ.बी.

44. *सनद परवाना बही* (मारवाड़), वि. सं. 1822, नं. 11, पृ. 261; *कागदों की बही* (बीकानेर), वि.सं. 1839, नं. 6, पृ. 19, 35, रा.रा.अ.बी.

45. *सनद परवाना बही* (मारवाड़), वि. सं. 1822, नं. 6, पृ. 22; *कागदों की बही* (बीकानेर), वि.सं. 1859, नं. 12, पृ. 36, 37, रा.रा.अ.बी.

उदाहरणार्थ- गो. बुधणाऊ रा चौधरी कुसला राम जोग्य तीथा भींवसर रे चौ. हरदासीये रे भाई री सगाई गो. जाजुसर रे वीको रे सगे गुड़े री बेटी ने ले जाय दुजे ने प्रणाय दीवी सुं थे पंच जाणेऊ छो सुं वरा प्रमेसरी नीवेड़ देजो हरकुर कही रीमत राखजो थोने थोरे दूध पूत री सीतस छै थारौ कहो उथ्यासी तेतु रु. 11 गुनेहगारी रा लागसी आसाढ़ सुद 1 थोरे कने दुनो आसी सुं नीवेड़ देजो। - *कागदों की बही* (बीकानेर), वि.सं. 1859, नं. 12, पृ. 202, रा.रा.अ.बी.

46. *सनद परवाना बही* (मारवाड़), वि.सं. 1823, नं. 5, पृ. 236, 257; *बही पेशकसी रे लेखे री* (बीकानेर), वि.सं. 1833, नं. 38, पृ. 58, 60; *कागदों की बही* (बीकानेर), वि.सं. 1839, नं. 6, पृ. 36, 37, रा.रा.अ.बी.

47. *सनद परवाना बही* (मारवाड़), वि.सं. 1823, नं. 5, पृ. 26, 252, 257; *कागदों की बही* (बीकानेर), वि.सं. 1854, नं. 10, पृ. 105, रा.रा.अ.बी.

48. *बही पेशकसी रे लेखे री* (बीकानेर), वि.सं. 1833 सू, पृ. 58, 70; *कागदों की बही* (बीकानेर), वि.सं. 1840, नं. 7, पृ. 18, 27, रा.रा.अ.बी.

49. पैर से लंगड़ा हो जाना, अंधा हो जाना, पीठ में कूबड़ निकल जाना आदि। *बही पेशकसी रे लेखे री* (बीकानेर), वि.सं. 1833, नं. 38, पृ. 36, 60; *कागदों की बही* (बीकानेर), वि.सं. 1857, नं. 11, पृ. 196, रा.रा.अ.बी.

50. *सनद परवाना बही* (मारवाड़), वि. सं. 1824, नं. 6, पृ. 3; *कागदों की बही* (बीकानेर), वि.सं. 1811, नं. 11, रीठ के कागज, रा.रा.अ.बी.

51. *सनद परवाना बही* (मारवाड़) वि.सं. 1823, नं. 5, पृ. 28; *कागदों की बही* (बीकानेर), वि.सं. 1840, नं. 7, पृ. 18; वही, वि.सं. 1859, नं. 12, पृ. 222, रा.रा.अ.बी.

52. *सनद परवाना बही* (मारवाड़) वि.सं. 1825, नं. 8, पृ. 149; कागदों की बही (बीकानेर), वि.सं. 1838, नं. 5, सनद के कागज; वही, वि.सं. 1840, नं. 7, पृ. 48, रा.रा.अ.बी.

53. *सनद परवाना बही* (मारवाड़) वि.सं. 1823, नं. 5, पृ. 14; *कागदों की बही* (बीकानेर), वि.सं. 1854, नं. 10, पृ. 105; रा.रा.अ.बी.

54. *सनद परवाना बही* (मारवाड़), वि.सं. 1811, नं. 1, *सनद के कागद*, रा.रा.अ.बी.

55. *सनद परवाना बही* (मारवाड़) वि.सं. 1823, नं. 5, पृ. 106; *कागदों की बही* (बीकानेर), वि.सं. 1857, नं. 11, पृ. 301; रा.रा.अ.बी.

56. *सनद परवाना बही* (मारवाड़), वि.सं. 1828, नं. 11, पृ. 10, रा.रा.अ.बी.

57. *मरदुमशुमारी रिपोर्ट राज मारवाड़,* सन् 1891 ई., अप्रकाशित, रा.रा.अ.बी.

58. *सनद परवाना बही* (मारवाड़) वि.सं. 1824, नं. 6, पृ. 14; *कागदों की बही* (बीकानेर), वि.सं. 1840, नं. 6, रा.रा.अ.बी.

59. *कागदों की बही* (बीकानेर), वि.सं. 1854, नं. 10, पृ. 205; *सनद परवाना बही* (मारवाड़) वि.सं. 1822, नं. 1, पृ. 303, रा.रा.अ.बी.

60. *मरदुमशुमारी रिपोर्ट राज मारवाड़,* सन् 1891, पृ. 42, रा.रा.अ.बी.

61. पूनमचंद जोइया : पश्चिमी राजस्थान के जाट समाज में नाता प्रथा (सन् 1700 से 1800 ई.), शोध लेख, प्रकाशित, *दी जाट्स,* वोल्यूम-1, पृ. 183-187, दिल्ली, 2004

62. *कागदों की बही* (बीकानेर), वि.सं. 1861, पृ. 1-2, रा.रा.अ.बी.

63. *मरदुमशुमारी रिपोर्ट राज मारवाड़,* सन् 1891 ई., पृ. 52, रा.रा.अ.बी.

64. वही

65. *कागदों की बही* (बीकानेर), वि.सं. 1826, नं. 3, पृ. 41, रा.रा.अ.बी.

66. *वही,* वि.सं. 1857, नं. 11, पृ. 35, रा.रा.अ.बी.

67. *सनद परवाना बही* (मारवाड़), वि.सं. 1832, नं. 15, पृ. 151, रा.रा.अ.बी.

68. *कागदों की बही* (बीकानेर), वि.सं. 1820, नं. 2, पृ. 40, रा.रा.अ.बी.

69. *कागदों की बही* (बीकानेर), वि.सं. 1839, नं. 6, पृ. 12 एवं बही नं. 7, वि.सं. 1840, पृ. 23, रा.रा.अ.बी.

70. *सनद परवाना बही* (मारवाड़), वि.सं. 1832, नं. 15 पृ. 7, रा.रा.अ.बी.

71. *मरदुमशुमारी, रिपोर्ट राज मारवाड़,* 1891, पृ. 92; *कागदों की बही* (बीकानेर), वि.सं. 1940, पृ. 18, रा.रा.अ.बी.

72. *मरदुमशुमारी रिपोर्ट राज मारवाड़,* सन् 1891, पृ. 44, रा.रा.अ.बी.

73. *कागदों की बही* (बीकानेर), वि.सं. 1859, नं. 12, पृ. 69, 70, रा.रा.अ.बी.

74. *कागदों की बही* (बीकानेर), वि.सं. 1845, नं. 38, पृ. 12; *कागदों की बही* (बीकानेर), वि.सं. 1840, नं. 4, पृ. 10, रा.रा.अ.बी.

75. पश्चिमी राजस्थान में नाता प्रथा के तीन रूप देखने को मिलते थे। द्रष्टव्य- पूनमचंद जोइया का लेख, पूर्वोक्त, पृ. 186-189

76. *सनद परवाना बही* (मारवाड़), वि.सं. 1832, नं. 15, 201; *बही पेशकसी रे लेखे री,* वि.सं. 1833, नं. 38, पृ. 125; *कागदों की बही* (बीकानेर), वि.सं. 1840, नं. 7, पृ. 11, रा.रा.अ.बी.

77. *सनद परवाना बही* (मारवाड़), वि.सं. 1823, नं. 5, पृ. 87; *कागदों की बही* (बीकानेर),

वि.सं. 1838, नं. 5 के सनद के कागद, रा.रा.अ.बी.

78. *सनद परवाना बही* (मारवाड), वि.सं. 1823, नं. 6, पृ. 21-22; *कागदों की बही* (बीकानेर), वि.सं. 1839, नं. 6, रीठ के कागद, रा.रा.अ.बी.

79. *सनद परवाना बही* (मारवाड़), वि.सं. 1822, नं. 3, पृ. 130; *कागदों की बही* (बीकानेर), वि.सं. 1827, नं. 3, आसोम बद 7 का कागद, रा.रा.अ.बी.

80. *बही पेशकसी रे लेखे री* (बीकानेर), वि.सं. 1833, नं. 38, पृ. 16, 24, 32, रा.रा. अ.बी.

81. *सनद परवाना बही* (मारवाड़), वि.सं. 1822, नं. 2, पृ. 68; वही, वि.सं. 1823, नं. पृ. 119, 132, 133, 135; *कागदों की बही* (बीकानेर), वि.सं. 1854, नं. 10, पृ. 128, रा.रा.अ.बी.

82. *सनद परवाना बही* (मारवाड़), वि.सं. 1823, नं. 5, पृ. 71, 164; *कागदों की बही* (बीकानेर), वि.सं. 1854, नं. 10, पृ. 131; वही, वि.सं. 1859, नं. 12, पृ. 203, रा.रा.अ.बी.

83. *कागदों की बही* (बीकानेर), वि.सं. 1854, नं. 10, माघ वदि 10 कागद, रा.रा.अ.बी.

84. *सनद परवाना बही* (मारवाड़), वि.सं. 1823, नं. 4, पृ. 260; *कागदों की बही* (बीकानेर), वि.सं. 1853, नं. 9 आसाढ़ वद 14 का कागद, रा.रा.अ.बी.

# 24

# उत्तर-पश्चिमी भारत में जाटों की सामाजिक, आर्थिक और राजनैतिक भागीदारी - विशिष्ट संदर्भ बीकानेर एवं जोधपुर संभाग

**ब्रह्माराम चौधरी, जसवंत सिंह खीचड़,**
**श्रीमती कल्पना चौधरी एवं डॉ. आरती चौधरी**

जाट जाति पशुपालन एवं कृषि में संलग्न रही है। कालीबंगा में गाय, भैंस, भेड़, बकरी, ऊंट, खच्चर, श्वान और घोड़ा पाला जाता था और गेहूँ, जौ, काला तिल, सरसों, खजूर, चना, बाजरी की खेती होती थी। कालीबंगा (2400-1500 ई. पू.) पूर्णरूपेण नगरीय संस्कृति थी जो बीकानेर से 200 कि.मी. सरस्वती नदी के किनारे बसी हुई थी।[1] चावल की खेती 4530 ई. पू. प्रारंभ हुई। यह कार्बन-14 की अर्द्धआयु जो 5568 वर्षों की आधी हो जाती है, द्वारा पाया गया। अर्थव्यवस्था गौ-पशु आधारित थी। मरुस्थल में आज भी 2 लाख वर्ग कि.मी. में थारपारकर, कांकरेज, राठी, शाहीवाल, रेड-सिंधी, धन्नी नस्ल दूधदात्री गाय तथा शक्ति के आधार पर हरियाणवी, नागौर नस्ल के अनुवांशिकीय गुणों का चयन जाटों ने किया जो उनके सामाजिक रिवाज से पता चलता है। जाट 12वें दिन पर टोगड़े की शादी सात फेरा देकर टोगड़ी के साथ कर, सांड बनाते हैं जो पूरे गांव को लाभ पहुंचाता है। सांड के खैंग पर गोलाकार शून्य का दाग लगाते हैं। जाटों की याददाश्त तेज होती हैं। भारत ने ही शून्य और दशमलव ईजाद किया है। आर्यभट्ट ने 522 ई. में शून्य का प्रयोग अपनी पुस्तक में किया।[2] सिंधु घाटी सभ्यता (3400-300 ई.पू.) के बाद उत्तरी-पश्चिमी भारत में कृषि एवं पशुपालन में विकास जाट जाति ने किया। गजनी के अन्तिम आक्रमण (1030 ई.) के बाद जाटों ने राजस्थान में प्रवेश किया। इसके बाद बाबर ने 20 जनवरी 1505 को हिन्दुस्तान पर हमला किया। सिंध के किनारे-किनारे नीचे को 3 कूच माल मिल रहा था। निरी गायें ही

गायें थी। बाबर[3] लिखता है जाट अभी भी गण थे। जात नहीं बने थे। गूजर भी जाटों की तरह अभी गण ही थे.... लूटमार करना और डाके डालना ही उनका पेशा हो गया था।

सच यह था कि बाबर हमलावर लुटेरा था। मरुस्थल में बीकानेर की स्थापना से पूर्व 7 जाट गोत्रों के 1664 गांवों में 7 जनपद थे–[4]

| | जाट गोत्र | गांवों की संख्या | मुख्य गांव | मुखिया का नाम |
|---|---|---|---|---|
| 1. | गोदारा | 360 | लादड़ी, शेखसर | पांडू जी |
| 2. | सारण | 360 | भांडंग | पूलो जी |
| 3. | कसवां | 360 | सिद्धमुख | कोरपाल जी |
| 4. | बेनीवाल | - | रेसालान | रैसाल जी |
| 5. | पूनिया | 360 | वारांलूड़ी | काना जी |
| 6. | सिहाग | 140 | सूई | चौखो जी |
| 7. | सोडूआन (सोहुआ) | 84 | घांसी | अमरा जी |

यहां नेरा जी जाट की भूमि पर गढ़ बना तो बीका+नेर=बीकानेर नाम से 1488 में अक्षय तृतीया के दिन बसाया गया।[5] यहां जाट ही 24 राजाओं के तिलक करते आये थे। 1488 से 1947 तक परस्पर सामाजिक सौहार्द्र रहा; यद्यपि जाटों पर 24 टैक्स लगाये गये और आर्थिक शोषण किया और शिक्षा से वंचित रखा। स्वामी केशवानन्द जी ने सेवा सदन शिक्षा केन्द्र 1932 में संगरिया विद्यापीठ से प्रारंभ किया। जागीरी 60 प्रतिशत और खालसा 40 प्रतिशत भूमि थी। बीकानेर के राज्य में जागीरदार और लाग-बाग किसानों से लेते थे। जैसे- (1) पारन घास लाग, (2) बकरा लाग : बेचने पर रकम देना, (3) कानूनगो लाग : प्रशासनिक खर्च, (4) डेरा खर्च : घर खर्च पूरा करने हेतु (5) विदा : जागीरी से बाहर जाने पर, (6) कस : यात्रा कर, (7) तलबः बुलाये जाने पर नजराना देना, (8) लवाजमा : रख-रखाव के लिए खर्च, (9) फारखतीः बंटवारा करने पर, (10) ओथी रोजगार : नौकरों के खर्च के लिये, (11) दरोगा खर्च: नौकर खर्च, (12) लिखना : लिखने वाले के नाम लाग, (13) प्रतिष्ठा भाछ : घर प्रवेश लाग। जाटों को पक्का मकान बनाना, 'सिंह' पर नाम रखना, बराबर खाट पर सामने बैठना, ऊंट पर चढ़कर गांव से निकलना, गढ़ या ठाकुर के घर के आगे से जूती पहनकर निकलना बिल्कुल मना था। यह सामाजिक तिरस्कार था कि जाटों को 'गधा' कहा जाता था। (14) पाग लाग - उत्तराधिकारी पर लाग। जाटों को ये लागें जागीरदार को देनी

होती थी ऊपर सापर थीं। सरकार की लागें कानूनन थी यथा[6]- (1) धुंआ लागः प्रत्येक चूल्हे-घर से ली जाती थी, (2) देश परठ : सैनिक खर्च लाग, (3) करोर भूंकराः घास लाग, (4) रूखवाली लाग : सुरक्षा खर्च, (5) तलीबाब : चराई लागः पशु चारागाहों पर, (6) पंचोराई : सीगोठी लाग- हर सींगवाले जानवर पर, (7) भांडा बाछ : बर्तन लाग (9) नाई बाछ : नाई खर्च लाग, (10) घोड़ा बाछ : घोड़ा खर्च लाग।[7] इस प्रकार की 24 लागें बीकानेर राज्य में और 41 लागें जाट किसानों पर जोधपुर राज्य में लगती थी। जोधा को जोधपुर जीतने में जाटणी ने राय दी थी कि राजधानी पर हमला न कर पहले गांव जीतें।[8] जोधा का पुत्र बीका 30 सितम्बर, 1465 ई. में जोधपुर से चलकर 180 घोड़े और 500 पैदल सवार लेकर आया। पांडू जी गोदारा और पूला जी सारण की अनबन पत्नी मलकी के कारण उग्र हो गई। बीका ने सिकनी के नरसिंह जाटू के सहयोग से हमला किया परन्तु पांडू जी के पुत्र नकोदर ने जोधा के कांधल का साथ लेकर नरसिंह का उसकी ससुराल में वध कर दिया। यदि पांडू जी गोदारा राव बीका जी से मेल कर उन्हें सहयोग न देते तो संभव है, दूसरे जाट भी उसकी अधीनता स्वीकार न करते।[9] लोदी गृहयुद्ध में फंसा था। राणा सांगा बाबर से हाथ मिलाने को तैयार था (बाबरनामा, पृ. 324)। पश्तो कवि कुशाल खाँ खटक ने राजाओं की स्थिति बताते हुए बाबर को दिल्ली का सुलतान बनने का निमंत्रण भेजा। (बाबरनामा, पृ. 328)

आपस की लड़ाई ने भारत को परतंत्र बनाया। समाज का शोषण हुआ। उत्तरी भारत में महाराज रणजीत सिंह ने विजय पाई, सदैव के लिये हमले रोके और 1799 में लाहौर के महाराजा 19 वर्ष की आयु में राजा बने। अपनी स्वाधीनता बनाये रखी 1839 तक यद्यपि भारत के सभी राजाओं ने अंग्रेजों की अधीनता स्वीकारी थी[10]। कोहिनूर हीरा जो शाहशुजा को सरंक्षण दे कर प्राप्त किया था, अंग्रेजों ने उनके उत्तराधिकारी दिलीप सिंह से लेकर महारानी विक्टोरिया को 3 जुलाई, 1850 को 108.93 कैरेट का हीरा दिया।

सामाजिक उत्थान के लिये शिक्षा जरूरी है। बीकानेर में पहला हाई स्कूल 8 जून 1885 में खुला जिसमें कुल 526 छात्र थे। इनमें जाट एक भी नहीं था। बीकानेर राज्य के गजट में पहली बार 1927 में शिक्षा के प्रतिशत का ब्योरा जातिवार मिलता है जिसमें जाट 0.6 प्रतिशत एवं विश्नोई 1.1 प्रतिशत साक्षर थे।[11] बीकानेर राज्य की जनगणना रिपोर्ट 1911 के अनुसार जैन 6.5 प्रतिशत, हिन्दू 2.5 प्रतिशत, मुसलमान 1.2 प्रतिशत साक्षर थे। किसान की शिक्षा का उल्लेख नहीं है।

'मद्रम शुमारी राज मारवाड़ 1891' के अनुसार-"मारवाड़ में जाट खेती करते हैं और बड़े दर्जे में नहीं समझे जाते। संख्या में जाट सन 1881 में 1,89,828 थे। सन् 1891 में 3,15,443 हो गये जिसमें संख्या में 1,71,881 मर्द एवं 1,43,562 औरतें थीं।

ज्यादा बस्ती जाटों की परगने नागौर में थी। यहां से जाट थली में गये हैं। कुल मारवाड़ के जाटों में गांव ईदाणा, खियाला, परगना नागौर, डांगावास, कालू, परगना मेड़ता और झंवर, धवा परगने, जोधपुर, लोहावट के जाटा (फलौदी) सरपंच है। इन गांवों के जाटों का हुक्म कुल जाट मानते हैं। इनके पास बादशाही फरमान है और बादशाही राज में अपने-अपने परगनों का हासिल उगाह कर भरा करते थे।"

झंवर के जाट इंसाफ करने में मशहूर रहे हैं। श्री बखतसिंह महाराजा अक्सर मुश्किल और पेचसर मुकदमे फैसले के वास्ते झंवर के जाटों के पास भेजते थे। जाट कानूनगो बाणा खाप के, गांव भदाणा के निवासी थे। जाट गुड़ को बड़ी अमोलक चीज समझते हैं। सगाई में सिर्फ एक रुपया और गुड़ की डली देते हैं। जाट अच्छी तरह से मेहनत कर उत्पादन करते है। जाट जहां ठाट का ओखाण इसी सबब से चला है। नागौरी बैल जाटों के पाले हुए होते हैं। जाटों में मसखरापन, उनकी उत्पाती प्रवृत्ति भी बहुत खूब है। "नट बुद्ध आवे पर जट बुद्ध नहीं आवे" का ओखाण प्रसिद्ध है। जाट बहादुर और मजबूत, सूरत-शक्ल और बोलचाल मरदाना, दबते भी कम और जंगल में शेर ही होते हैं। जाट जागीरदारों और हाकिम के वास्ते तेरहवां ग्रह कहलाते थे, क्योंकि वे जिसके पीछे पड़ जाते थे चैन नहीं लेने देते।[12] भाटी राजपूतों की जाति का उद्भव यदु जाट जाति से हुआ।[13] अभय राव के दो बेटे में से अभेराव लाखी ने जंगल अधिकार में कर लिया और शासक बना और छोटा खेती कर सारण जाट कहलाने लगा (टॉड, 1829, पृ. 179)। 'The most extensive agricultural races spread all over India called Jats or Jits, have a tradition that they are descended from Yadu race (Tod)' लेकिन तिहरी गुलामी से प्रताड़ित यह झूंझा आंचल हमेशा कुचला जाता रहा, पशुपालन और मामूली कृषि उपज के बलबूते शासकों को झेलता रहा, जागीरदार का एक मात्र उद्देश्य धन उगाहना और मौज मस्ती करना था। ठिकानेदार लाग-बाग से साधारण जन को लूटने लगे।[14] शेखावाटी में किसानों पर सात लाग-बाग और मारवाड़ जोधपुर में 41 लागें ले कर जाट-किसानों का शोषण किया जाता था।[15] जाट जाति पर लाग लगाने सम्बन्धी पत्र जोधपुर प्रजामण्डल की फाइल में 1941 में मिलता है।

| *क्र. लाग* | *तादाद धन एवं धान* |
|---|---|
| 1. फेर | मोठ फली समेत ऊपड़ा हुआ एक ऊंट का बोरा |
| 2. कोरड़ | बिना कूटा गुणा एक सलीता (बोरा) और माद 20-25 सेर |
| 3. चरी का हल | एक दिन हल से काम कराये या एक रुपया देना |

| | |
|---|---|
| 4. लास हल | एक दिन हल से ठिकाना अपना काम कराये या एक रुपया रोकड़ा दे। |
| 5. खर-खर | निनाण कराने के लिये चार आदमी या एक रुपया रोकड़ा |
| 6. लास-घास | घास काटने के लिए एक आदमी और अधिक |
| 7. लास पाला | पाला काटने के लिये |
| 8. लास लावणी | मोठ गंवार पाड़ने के लिये एक आदमी और ज्यादा भी या चार आने फी. आदमी |
| 9. भिंटोरा | एक गाड़ी कांटों का रेट के अनुसार चार आना और छः आना भी हर एक से। |
| 10. भरोटी | चार आना |
| 11. भैंस | मुँह देख (चार और आठ आना भी) कंवरानी का शादी पर मुंह देखने की लाग प्रति भैंस |
| 12. पान चराई | प्रत्येक भेड़ बकरी पर चार-चार आना |
| 13. मांचा | ठिकाणे में मेहमान आने पर मांचा ले आना |
| 14. गूदड़ा | कपड़े मांचे के साथ |
| 15. थेपड़ी | हर तीन-चार दिन बाद थेपड़ी लाना |
| 16. दूध लाग | ठिकाणे में मेहमान आने पर जबरन दूध लाना और श्राद्धों के दिनों में 16 दिन तक बराबर दूध लाना। |
| 17. ऊंट | बेगार में ले जाना |
| 18. माया | बेची हुई वस्तु या पशु पर पैसा-रुपया |
| 19. सीटा | आठ आना या 360 सीटा |
| 20. भांभी सीटा | जीमन नापने के लिये जाने पर करीब 20 सेर बाजरी या सीटा लाना। |
| 21. साढ़ी नारियल | चंवरी सवा दो रुपया (घोड़ी, डोली, चंवरी कुल दो रुपया छः आना) |
| 22. ढोल | पांच रुपया |

| | |
|---|---|
| 23. कांसा | शादी और मोसर पर चावल लापसी पर 6 रुपया, सीरा गुड़ का 20 रुपया, सीरा गुड़ का चीरा 25 रुपया, लड्डू 30 रुपया और बाकी मनचाहा वसूल करे। |
| 24. लावणा | सीरा, चावल या लापसी की दो कढ़ाई आठ आना |
| 25. नौता | ब्याह कंवर साहब प्रति 100 बीघा 5 रुपया<br>ब्याह बाईजी लाल प्रति 100 बीघा 5 रुपया<br>मोसर माजी या ठाकुर प्रति 100 बीघा 5 रुपया<br>यह रकम मनचाही भी वसूल की जा सकती है। |
| 26. खूद | जौ अथवा गेहूँ ही हासल से अलग प्रति कुआँ नौ क्यारी या ढाई सेर अनाज |
| 27. तमाखू | प्रति कुआँ हासल अलग ढाई सेर तमाखू |
| 28. सब्जी | प्रति कुएँ पर से जब तक कुएँ पर हो, हर दूसरे दिन कच्ची छः सेर सब्जी |
| 29. पी | माफ ठाकुर सा की |
| 30. आंगा | प्रति पुरुष तागड़ी बंद एक रुपया |
| 31. धुवा | आठ आना प्रति चूल्हा |
| 32. झूंपी | सवा रुपया |
| 33. मूहरी | प्रत्येक ऊंट को बेचने पर एक रुपया |
| 34. होली नजराना | एक रुपया |
| 35. दिवाली नजराना | एक रुपया |
| 36. डोरी बटाई (सुगन भेंट) | साठी डोरी नापने के लिये डोरी बांटने के मौकों पर एक रुपया |
| 37. लादा लाग | एक रुपया प्रति माह |
| 38. बैगार कुम्हार | बर्तन देना |
| 39. पानी लाग | पानी भरना |
| 40. बैगार भांभी | हर काम को निःशुल्क करना |
| 41. भारा लाग | एक भारा रोज हरी घास का चार माह तक |

इस प्रकार राजशाही, ठाकुरशाही और औपनिवेशी परतंत्रता में उत्तरी-पश्चिमी भारत का किसान कुचला जाता रहा। दूधवा खारा के हनुमान सिंह किसानों के हितैषी बने तो हनुमान जाट के खिलाफ कार्यवाही शीर्षक का वर्णन गोपनीय फाइल 1946/15 में मिलता है। 'किसानों को लगान व हबूब देने के विरुद्ध खुल्लमखुल्ला भड़का रहा था। कृषि सम्बन्धी आन्दोलन में सुई जितनी समस्या को मूसल बनाने में लगा हुआ रहा, सरकार ने नजरबंद कर देने का निर्णय लिया है।'[16] गांधी, नेहरू और पटेल की जन-जागृति की आवाज भारतीय किसानों ने सुनी और आजादी के संग्राम में कूद पड़े। इतिहास कितना अजीब और मिथ्यावादी होता है। जब माउंटबैटन गांधी के बारे में कहते हैं, "वह तहस-नहस कर सकते थे, कुछ बना नहीं सकते थे।"[17] "ब्रिटिश राज्य के अधीन भारत खुश है..... 99 प्रतिशत लोग हमारे साथ..... 1 प्रतिशत जो हमारे खिलाफ हैं, वे पढ़े-लिखे नेता लोग हैं।" तीहरे शोषण की इस पराकाष्ठा से समाज जागा जिसका नेतृत्व चौ. कुंभाराम जी आर्य, चौ. बलदेवराम जी मिर्धा, चौ. हरलाल सिंह, चौ. नाथूराम जी मिर्धा ने किया। शिक्षा के लिये किसान छात्रावास बनाये। सन् 1931 में श्री पोकर राम जी बेंदा ने रानीबाजार में श्री पोकरराम पूर्णराम धर्मशाला बनवाई जो अब किसान छात्रावास और धर्मशाला दोनों हैं।[18] राजस्थान में सन् 1931 की जनगणना के अनुसार कुल जनसंख्या एक करोड़ में जाट 10.72 लाख थे। कुल अन्य पिछड़ी जातियाँ 27 थीं जो 45.53 लाख थी (अब 82 अ. जातियां हैं जिनका 21 प्रतिशत आरक्षण है) अनुसूचित जातियां 16.54 लाख थी (अब 58 हैं और 16 प्रतिशत आरक्षण है)। ये सभी 75 लाख शोषण का शिकार हुई। राजपूत 6.50 लाख, वैश्य 5.68 लाख, अन्य सिंधी कायस्थ 0.67 लाख तथा मुसलमान 3.06 लाख थे। सामन्त मात्र 9 लाख थे। माउंटबैटन के साथ 99 प्रतिशत नहीं मात्र 9 प्रतिशत ही थे।

आजादी के बाद जमीन के मालिकाना हक प्राप्त होने के बाद अब नहरों और कुंओं से सिंचाई कर किसान मूंगफली, सरसों, गेहूँ, चना, ईसबगोल, सौंफ की खेती आधुनिक तकनीक अपना कर आर्थिक दृष्टि से सबल हुए हैं और पंचायती राज आने से 50 प्रतिशत नारी का आरक्षण होने से समाज में नारी शिक्षा की प्रेरणा जागी है। जमीन के टुकड़े होने से नये रोजगार की तलाश में अन्य राज्य एवं मध्यपूर्व में जाने लगे हैं। आने वाला समय उज्ज्वल होगा, ये आशाएं जगने लगी हैं। जिला प्रमुख, प्रधान एवं सरपंच, पंच बन कर ग्राम स्तर पर प्रशासनिक पकड़ एवं जिम्मेदारी निभाने लगे हैं। यद्यपि राज्य की सर्वोच्च सत्ता का पद पाना अभी शेष है।

मनरेगा से ग्रामीण आंचल में रोजगार मिलने लगा है। लेकिन खेती मजदूरी बढ़ने से मंहगी होने लगी हैं। विकल्प एक ही है कि मनरेगा के श्रमिक खेतों में मदद करें।

## संदर्भ


1. ब्रह्माराम चौधरी : *वसुंधरा,* अर्चनालोक प्रकाशन, बीकानेर (2008), पृ. 32
2. जयंत विष्णु नारलीकर : *भारत की विज्ञान यात्रा,* प्रभात प्रकाशन, दिल्ली (2008)
3. युगजीत नवलपुरी (अनु.) : *बाबर नामा,* साहित्य अकादमी, नई दिल्ली (2004), पृ. 200
4. करणी सिंह : *द रिलेशन्स ऑफ द हाऊस ऑफ बीकानेर विथ द सेन्ट्रल पावर्स,* मुंशीराम मनोहरलाल पब्लि. प्रा. लि., नई दिल्ली (1974)
5. जैम्स टॉड : *एनल्स एण्ड एन्टीक्वीटीज ऑफ राजस्थान,* रोलेज एण्ड केगान लि., लंदन
6. चेतना मुदगल : *बीकानेर में जन आन्दोलन,* रचना प्रकाशन, जयपुर (1999), पृ. 185
7. होम डिपार्टमेन्ट, बीकानेर, (1946) नं. 71, पृ. 1021
8. रघुवीर सिंह और मनोहर सिंह : *जोधपुर राज्य की ख्यात, नैणसी की ख्यात,* पंचशील प्रकाशन, जयपुर (1988)
9. चंद्रदान चारण : बीकानेर राज्य की स्थापना में जाट समाज का सहयोग, किसान छात्रावास स्मारिका, बीकानेर (1994), पृ. 12-13
10. ब्रह्माराम चौधरी : *"वसुंधरा",* बीकानेर, अर्चनालोक प्रकाशन, 2008, पृ. 76, 77, 78
11. कल्पना चौधरी : जाट समाज में शिक्षा, समाज में शिक्षा एवं शिक्षा प्रेरक, किसान छात्रावास स्मारिका, बीकानेर (1994), पृ. 57
12. मद्रम शुमारी, राज मारवाड़, जोधपुर, 1891, पृ. 47, 50, भाग 3, खण्ड प्रथम
13. कर्नल टॉड : *"एनल्स एण्ड एण्टीक्वीटीज ऑफ राजस्थान",* भाग एक (1829), व भाग दो (1832), जैसलमेर का एनल, पृ. 169-231, 259, 294
14. राजेन्द्र कसवां : *किसान योद्धा चौधरी घासी राम,* कमल प्रकाशन, झूंझुनू (2009), पृ. 8-9
15. जोधपुर प्रजामण्डल, फाईल संख्या 17-75, दिनांक 15.03.1941
16. दाऊलाल आचार्य : *भारत के स्वतंत्रता संग्राम में बीकानेर का योगदान,* चेतना प्रकाशन, बीकानेर, 7 अ 30, द, पवनीपुरी (1997), पृ. 321-22.
17. लैरी कालिन्स एवं दौमिनिक लौपियर : *माउंटबैटन और भारत का विभाजन,* अनु प्रकाशन, जयपुर (2005), पृ. 31, 35
18. कल्पना चौधरी : किसान छात्रावास स्मारिका, बीकानेर, 1994, पृ. 59

# 25

# हरदा जिले में जाटों की सामाजिक, आर्थिक एवं राजनैतिक स्थिति

**डॉ. धर्मेन्द्र पारे**

मध्यप्रदेश में हरदा जिला अपेक्षाकृत नया है। यह जिला पहले होशंगाबाद जिले की एक तहसील हुआ करता था। हरदा की जिले के रूप में स्थापना 6 जुलाई 1998 को हुई। उत्तर भारत से दक्षिण में जाने के लिए नर्मदा को पार करने के लिए हरदा हंडिया का नर्मदा तट सर्वाधिक उपयुक्त था। कारण दक्षिण के विशाल सतपुड़ा पर्वत की अंतिम इकाई मकड़ाई यहाँ समाप्त हो जाती है और उसके आगे मैदानी भाग प्रारंभ हो जाता है। हरदा जिले में हंडिया नामक जगह पौराणिक युग से लेकर मुगल-मराठा-ब्रिटिश युग तक महत्वपूर्ण स्थल रहा है। हंडिया नगर के ध्वंसावशेष इसके साक्षी हैं। हरदा जिले में प्राचीन आबादी कोरकू और गोंड जनजाति की है। मुगल काल या उसके कुछ पूर्व राजपूत, गुर्जर, ब्राह्मण, तिलोरिया, गोंड, कुर्मी तथा कुछ अनुसूचित जातियों के लोग गुजरात की तरफ से आकर यहाँ बसे थे। इन जातियों के साथ कृषि सभ्यता में काम करने वाली शिल्पकार और पारंपरिक पेशों को करने वाली जातियों के भी साथ आने का अनुमान है। गुजरात से यहाँ आकर बसने के कोई दस्तावेजी प्रमाण तो उपलब्ध नहीं है किन्तु पारिवारिक श्रुतियों, वंशावलियों और लोकगीतों से इस बात की कई जगह पुष्टि होती है।

कालांतर में राजस्थान के मारवाड़ कहे जाने वाले क्षेत्र से भी कई जातियों का यहाँ आगमन हुआ। इन जातियों को आमतौर पर मारवाड़ी जाति के रूप में ही जाना जाता है, यथा आदिगौड़ ब्राह्मण, जाट, विश्नोई, खाती, माली, अग्रवाल-बनिया आदि। मारवाड़ से आने वाली जातियों का इस क्षेत्र में आगमन अपेक्षाकृत बहुत हाल की घटना है। बमुश्किल डेढ़ दो सौ वर्ष पूर्व की। मारवाड़ से आनेवाली इन जातियों के अधिकांश

परिवारों का अपने पैतृक गांवों और कुटुम्ब परिवार से संपर्क आज भी बना हुआ है। बीच के दौर में कई परिवारों के संपर्क अपने पैतृक गाँव से टूट गये थे। जड़ों को तलाशने में आवागमन और दूरसंचार के नवीन साधनों ने बहुत मदद की है। लोगों ने अपने पैतृक गांवों को पुनः खोज लिया है। मारवाड़ से आकर यहाँ बसी हुई जातियों को अपने पैतृक परिवार से जोड़कर रखने का काम राव भाट और रामदेवरा तीर्थ की यात्रा ने भी किया है।

जाट इस क्षेत्र में कब और कैसे आये इस विषय में सर्वेक्षण करने पर स्पष्ट हुआ कि अधिकांश जाट पाँच से लेकर आठ पीढ़ी पहले राजस्थान के *नागौर* जिले की मेड़ता तहसील और जोधपुर जिले के गाँवों में अकाल पड़ने से यहाँ आये थे। कतिपय लोगों का यह भी कहना था कि व्यवसाय के सिलसिले में वे मालवा होते हुए यहाँ आ बसे हैं। आज भी राजस्थान के इन जिलों के गांवों से यहाँ के जाट समुदाय का रिश्ता बना हुआ है। जाटों के हरदा अंचल में आगमन के विषय में कतिपय अन्य मान्यताएँ भी मिलती हैं, मसलन - जाट लोग रोजगार के सिलसिले में इधर आये थे। एक अन्य मान्यता के अनुसार मराठा साम्राज्य अपने अंतिम चरण में था, तब मराठा सरदार अपने साथ बेहद श्रमशील जाट और विश्नोई लोगों को भी साथ ले आये थे। हरदा क्षेत्र में जाट और विश्नोई जातियाँ ज्यादातर उन्हीं गाँवों में निवास करती हैं जहाँ कभी मराठा लोगों की जागीर और मालगुजारी कायम थी। जहाँ आज जाट बसे हैं कहा जाता है कि तत्कालीन समय में वह लगभग उजाड़ और वीरान हुआ करता था। जगह-जगह बरू नामक घास उगी थी। उस समय की सत्ता ने जाट लोगों से कहा कि जंगलों को साफ कर खेती करो। यह श्रुति आज भी कई जाट परिवारों में सुनने को मिलती है। अपने कठोर परिश्रम से जाटों ने खेती को बहुत उन्नत बनाया। इसी जमीन पर वे पुश्तों से खेती करते चले आ रहे हैं। मराठों के पतन के अंतिम दौर में पिंडारगर्दी का दौर प्रारंभ होता है। पिंडारियों में कई जातियों के लोग शामिल थे। पिंडारियों में चीतू पिंडारी का नाम सर्वाधिक दुर्दांत लोगों में शामिल है।

'चीतू जन्म से जाट था, जब वह बालक था तभी एक अकाल के दौरान किसी अश्वारोही पिंडारी सरदार ने उसे खरीद लिया था .... वह अपनी योग्यता के कारण दौलतराव सिंधिया को प्रभावित कर सका.... दौलतराव सिंधिया ने उसे 1804 में एक जागीर दी और नवाब की उपाधि प्रदान की ..... चीतू नर्मदा के किनारे सतवास, हंडिया के निकट रहता था।'[1]

चीतू के इस उद्धरण से स्पष्ट होता है कि जाटों का इस क्षेत्र में आगमन और निवास कैसे और किन परिस्थितियों में हुआ है। कतिपय लोगों के द्वारा एक अन्य उदाहरण से

यह भी बनाया जाता है कि जाट इस क्षेत्र में कई सौ वर्षो ... रह रहे हैं किन्तु इतिहास से इस मत की कतई पुष्टि नहीं हो पाती। बताया गया है ... के हरदा जिले में प्रसिद्ध ऐतिहासिक स्थल जोगा पर जाट जाति का आधिपत्य था। जाट इतिहास पुस्तक में डॉ. रवीन्द्र भारती लिखते हैं, 'आल्हा ऊदल के समकालीन चंदेल या परमार राजाओं की सेना में भोगा और जोगा नामक दो वीर जाट हुआ करते थे.... इनके वंशज मुगलों और मराठों के जमाने में भी जोगा को राजधानी बनाकर लगभग 600 वर्षों तक राज्य करते रहे। जोगा के द्वारा ही इस जिले का निर्माण करवाया गया था। ... किले के चारों ओर बुर्जों और किनारों की दीवारों से 30-40 मील तक दूर-दूर का सौंदर्य देखा जा सकता है। नेमावर हंडिया का नवनिर्मित पुल पूर्वी झेरोखे से साफ-साफ दिखता है...।'[2] ऐसा लगता है लेखक ने किसी सुनी सुनाई बात के आधार पर वर्णन कर दिया है। जोगा के किले से नेमावर हंडिया का नवनिर्मित किला संभवतः अच्छी खासी दूरबीन से भी नहीं दिख सकता। इसकी दूरी लगभग 26 किलोमीटर है। इसके अलावा उक्त मत की इतिहास से पुष्टि संभव नहीं जान पड़ती। जिस 'जोगा नागक किले' का जिक्र किया गया है उसे मालवा के द्वितीय सुल्तान होशंगशाह गोरी ने बनवाया था।[3] होशंगशाह गोरी मालवा की गद्दी पर ई. सन् 1406 में बैठा था।[4] यह तथ्य इस बात से भी त्रुटिपूर्ण जान पड़ता है कि समकालीन दस्तावेजों और ग्रंथों से इसकी कहीं पुष्टि नहीं होती। 'आइने अकबरी' आदि में भी इसका जिक्र नहीं आता। फिर परमारों के बाद जिन 600 वर्षों तक जोगा और भोगा के वंशजों में राज्य करने की बात है वह भी सिद्ध नहीं हो पाती है क्योंकि भोज द्वितीय के पश्चात 1305 ई. में महलक देव जब मालवा का राजा था उस समय अलाउद्दीन खिलजी ने देश पर आक्रमण किया था। मांडू के किले में महलक देव को मार डाला गया था।[5] सन् 1306 में 600 वर्ष जोड़ने पर सन् 1906 तक सीमा आ जाती है। इस गणित से तो श्री रवीन्द्र भारती का कथन बहुत अतार्किक हो जाता है। जोगा में किसी समय पुलिस थाना भी था जो सन् 1879 में हंडिया में स्थानान्तरित कर दिया गया। परमारों के बाद इस क्षेत्र पर खिलजियों, तुगलकों, हुमायूं, शेरशाह और बाद में अकबर से लेकर औरंगजेब तथा मराठों और अंग्रेजों तक का आधिपत्य रहा। किन्तु किसी काल के समकालीन दस्तावेजों में इस बात का उल्लेख नहीं मिलता कि किसी जाट अधिपति का यहाँ शासन रहा है। इस किले पर पूर्व में बैड़ी के कोरकू ठाकुरों का आधिपत्य रहा, इस बात का जिक्र अवश्य मिलता है।[6] बहरहाल जाट जाति इस क्षेत्र में लगभग 150 से 200 वर्षों से निवास कर रही है, यह ज्यादा तर्कसंगत और वैज्ञानिक प्रतीत होता है। जाट जाति मध्यप्रदेश के हरदा क्षेत्र में सर्वाधिक संख्या में निवास करती है। मध्यप्रदेश 1956 के पूर्व सेन्ट्रल प्रोविन्स के नाम से जाना जाता था, तब वर्तमान हरदा जिला होशंगाबाद जिले की एक तहसील हुआ करता था। सेन्ट्रल प्रोविन्स में सन

1911 में जाट जाति की [illegible] 10000 थी जिसमें से होशंगाबाद में 5000 लोग निवास करते थे। 1867 में प्रकाशित सेटलमेंट रिपोर्ट में बताया गया है कि जाट लोग केवल चार पीढ़ी पूर्व ही इस क्षेत्र में भरतपुर से मारवाड़ होते हुए यहाँ आये हैं।[7] आज भी जाट हरदा जिले की हरदा और टिमरनी तहसील के अलावा होशंगाबाद जिले की सिवनी तहसील में निवास करते हैं। यह पूरा क्षेत्र नर्मदा का तटवर्ती इलाका है।

जाट जाति में आज भी विवाह की सामान्य आयु 18 से 22 वर्ष है। पूर्व के वर्षों में तो बाल-विवाह प्रथा थी। एक पीढ़ी लगभग 20 से 25 वर्षों में परिवार में जुड़ जाती थी। इस हिसाब से भी जाट जाति का इस क्षेत्र में आगमन लगभग 200 वर्ष पूर्व ठहरता है।

जाट जाति ने अपने रीति रिवाज और परंपरा को अन्य जातियों की तुलना में बहुत हद तक बचाये रखा है। इस जाति की सबसे बड़ी विशेषता तो यही लगती है कि परंपरा और विरासत के प्रति इनके मन में अगाध जगह है। 200 वर्षों से इस क्षेत्र में साथ साथ निवास कर रही इस जाति के विषय में कम लोग ही जानते होंगे कि जाटों के गाँवों में भले ही मंदिर कम हों, भले ही कर्मकांड अनुष्ठान कम होते हों किन्तु हर जाट घर में प्रतिदिन अपने पुरखों की पूजा-अर्चना और भोग दीप लगाया जाता है। जाट जाति के घर में एक बार हिन्दू देवी देवताओं की तांबे पीतल पत्थर की प्रतिमा भले ही न मिलें पर घरों में 'पितर स्थान' अवश्य ही होता है। जाट जाति के घरों में अपने लोकनायकों और लोकदेवों रामदेवजी, तेजाजी और 'पितर' की पूजा अवश्य होती है। अमावस्या और पूर्णिमा के दिन 'पितर' की पूजा आवश्यक रूप से की जाती है। चंद्र पक्ष में भी 'पितरों' की पूजा अवश्य की जाती है। जाटों में भादों, बैसाख आदि को बड़ा माह माना जाता है। इन बड़े माहों में पुरखों की रात जगाने का कार्य होता है। जाट जाति में यह विश्वास किया जाता है कि पितरों की आत्मा का हमेशा संतुष्ट रहना आवश्यक है। यदि वे नाराज हो गये तो अनिष्ट हो सकता है। जाट जाति में कुछ लोगों के शरीर में कुछ देवता की पवन भी आती है। यह व्यक्ति परिवार में आई व्याधि के विषय में बताते हैं। कुछ लोग 'पितर' को गले में ताबीज की तरह भी धारण करते हैं।

जाट जाति में प्रचलित कुछ कुप्रथाओं को लेकर अब युवाओं में विरोध हो रहा है। फिजूलखर्ची व दिखावे के प्रतिरोध के चलते ही इस क्षेत्र में बड़े पैमाने पर सामूहिक विवाह होना बहुत पहले ही प्रारंभ हो गया था। यह तब की बात है जब अन्य जातियाँ सामूहिक विवाह के प्रति संकोची भी या जानकारी भी नहीं रखती थी। इस क्षेत्र में संभवतः अन्य किसी जाति में इससे पूर्व सामूहिक विवाह प्रारंभ नहीं हुए थे। जाट जाति में अब तक प्रचलित बत्तीसी प्रथा का भी विरोध हो रहा है। बत्तीसी प्रथा (भात न्योतना) वह है

जिसमें बहन जब निमंत्रण देने अपने मायके जाती है तो उसके साथ उसके सारे रिश्तेदार भी आते हैं। एक अन्य प्रथा जिसे 'समटावनी देना' कहा जाता है का भी विरोध हो रहा है। इस प्रथा में लड़की पक्ष द्वारा लड़के पक्ष में दूर-दूर तक के रिश्तेदार परिजनों को वस्त्र भेंट किये जाते हैं। किसी दिवंगत के शरीर पर भी वस्त्र चढ़ाने का व्यापक रिवाज इस क्षेत्र में है। ये वस्त्र चढ़ावा भी बंद करने की आवाज अब उठाई जा रही है। शवयात्रा के पश्चात होने वाले भोज का भी विरोध किया जा सकता है।

जाटों के प्रमुख गोत्रों में इस क्षेत्र में सिरोही, सारन, टोडा, डूडी, देहड़, चोयल, खैरवा, जलवानिया, बडियार, जेवल्या, बेड़ा, मातवा, बगडवा, भारी, खोकर, ओडग, हुंडा, लेगा, गुलिया, मेरिया, जाखड़, चमेल, बराड़ आदि पाये जाते हैं। परंपरा में बिंधी इस जाति की एक और सहकार भावना की सराहना की जानी चाहिए कि जो परिवार गरीब है उनका शादी विवाह या अन्त्येष्टि आदि जाति के लोग मिलकर सम्पन्न करते हैं।

इस क्षेत्र के जाटों की दूसरी बड़ी विशेषता मातृ भाषा के प्रति सम्मान और लगाव की भावना को माना जाना चाहिए। भले ही बच्चे कितनी ही अंग्रेजी शिक्षा प्राप्त कर लें वे आपस में और घरों में आवश्यक रूप से अपनी मातृभाषा मारवाड़ी में ही बात करते हैं। डॉक्टर, इंजीनियर, प्रोफेसर, अधिवक्ता अपनी मारवाड़ी भाषा में ही सामान्य व्यवहार करते हैं। परिधान के मामले में अब अवश्य बदलाव आ रहा है किन्तु अन्य जातियों की तुलना में यह परिवर्तन बहुत धीमा है। पच्चीस तीस वर्ष की महिलाएँ अवश्य साड़ी सलवार जैसा परिधान पहनने लगी हैं किन्तु आज भी प्रौढ़ और वृद्ध महिलाओं का परिधान पारंपरिक राजस्थानी ही है। यही स्थिति कमोबेश पुरुषों के मामले में है।

जाट जाति के धार्मिक और सामाजिक रीति रिवाज राजस्थान में प्रचलित रीति रिवाजों की तरह ही हैं। इसे विडम्बना ही कहा जाना चाहिए कि राजस्थान की इस जाति को सही परिप्रेक्ष्य में समझा ही नहीं गया। जब तथाकथित ऊंची कही जाने वाली जातियों में विधवा विवाह की कल्पना भी नहीं की गई थी, जाट जाति में तब से ही विधवा विवाह प्रचलित है। गोत्र के विषय में इस क्षेत्र में भी सगोत्रीय ही नहीं माँ और नानी के गोत्रों में भी विवाह वर्जित है। यहाँ खाप जैसी पंचायत प्रथा नहीं है, न ही कोई जाति पटेल होता है। इस अंचल में जाट जाति में तलाक बहुत कम होता है। विधवा का 'नातरा' कर दिया जाता है। परिवार प्रायः संयुक्त होते हैं जिसमें निर्णय का अधिकार बड़े व्यक्ति को होता है। खान-पान में घर-परिवार और विवाह आदि अनुष्ठान में शाकाहारी भोजन ही मान्य है। महिलाएँ मांसाहार बिल्कुल नहीं करती, किन्तु कहीं कहीं पुरुष वर्ग में मांस-मदिरा का सेवन घर के बाहर चोरी-छिपे प्रचलित है।

महिलाओं में हमेल, बोरबंद, काठली, बालडी, झुमरा, बावटया, उग्न्या, कड़ी, ठुस्सी नामक आभूषण बहुत प्रचलित हैं। जाट जाति में कार्तिक स्नान लगभग सभी महिलाएँ करती हैं। इस पर्व पर पूरे माह ब्रह्म मुहूर्त में पवित्र नदियों में स्नान किया जाता है। यदि नदी में संभव न हो तो कुँआ या बावड़ी के पानी से भी यह अनुष्ठान सम्पन्न होता है। अतिम पाँच दिन उपवास किया जाता है जिसे 'पंच पीपरी' कहा जाता है। इन पाँच दिनों में दोनों समय अन्न ग्रहण नहीं किया जाता है।

यहाँ की कुछ प्रथाएँ बड़ी विशिष्ट रही हैं, पर अब ये प्रथाएँ लुप्तप्राय हैं। एक प्रथा का नाम 'पेढ़ा चढ़ाना' कहलाता है। पेढ़ा 'पेढ़ी' अर्थात सीढ़ी को कहा जाता है। कुछ लोग पेढ़े का पर्याय चक्र को भी बताते हैं। इस प्रथा के अंतर्गत धनी-मानी व्यक्ति यह अनुष्ठान वैवाहिक अवसरों पर करता है। इसमें लकड़ी के एक खंबे के ऊपर बैलगाड़ी के चक्के के समान एक गोल चक्र को लकड़ियों के ऊपर रखा जाता है। इस पेढ़े का शृंगार भी किया जाता है। इस लकड़ी में और लकड़ियाँ जोड़ी जाती है और उसके ऊपर चक्र को सरकाया जाता है। जितनी लकड़ियाँ जोड़ी जाती हैं, उतने पेढ़े गिने जाते हैं और उतने ही दिनों तक गांव के चारों ओर के रास्ते बंद कर दिये जाते हैं। केवल आने का एक रास्ता खुला रहता है। गांव के ही नहीं आसपास के दस-बीस गाँवों के लोगों को इस अनुष्ठान के चलते पूरे दिन मिष्ठानयुक्त भोजन करवाया जाता है। हरदा क्षेत्र में यह अनुष्ठान अब तक सोनतलाई, गोयत, भमोरी, अबगाँव, रन्हाई, बिछौला, भुन्नास के पटेल परिवारों ने सम्पन्न किया है। जाट जाति के लोगों का ही कहना है कि इसके पीछे अपनी श्रेष्ठता सिद्ध करने की भावना ज्यादा होती थी। इसके चलते कई परिवार लाखों रुपये पानी में बहाते रहे हैं, और कई परिवार आर्थिक दुरावस्था में भी चले गये। बहरहाल कई सालों से अब यह प्रथा देखने में नहीं आ रही है।

हमारे संदर्भित जिले में जाट जाति हरदा और टिमरनी तहसील के पचास साठ गाँवों में निवास करती है। इन गाँवों में जाट जाति की खेती बहुत उन्नत मानी जाती है। लगभग 95 प्रतिशत जाटों के पास खेती है। मजूदरी जैसे कामों पर निर्भरता बहुत कम मात्रा में है। तत्कालीन होशंगाबाद जिला जिसकी हरदा एक तहसील हुआ करता था, की 1867 की सेटलमेंट रिपोर्ट में बताया गया है कि जाट 47 मौजों में किसानी करते थे और उनका कुल राजस्व 17,125 रुपये था। इस अवधि में सर्वाधिक राजस्व ब्राह्मणों के द्वारा 1,44,256 रुपये, राजपूतों के द्वारा 66,159 रुपये तथा गूजरों से 18,680 रुपये और कुर्मियों से 46,460 रुपये राजस्व प्राप्त होता था।[8] ये सभी जातियाँ खेती स्वामी थी। तुलनात्मक रूप से जाट सबसे कम संख्या में थे, जबकि ब्राह्मण 42,044 और कुर्मी 17,385 थे। अफसोस कि इस सेटलमेंट रिपोर्ट में जाटों के राजस्व का तो जिक्र है किन्तु उनकी संख्या का कतई नहीं। आगे जाकर 1911 की जनगणना में इस जिले में

जाट जाति की संख्या 5,058[9] बताई गई है। इन आकड़ों का विश्लेषण करने से मोटे तौर पर लगता है कि जाट खेती स्वामी के रूप में ब्राह्मणों के बाद आते हैं किन्तु अन्य तुलनात्मक जातियों यथा राजपूत, गुर्जर, कुर्मी की तुलना में काफी आगे हैं। फिलहाल के वर्षों में जाट जाति के युवाओं ने डम्पर, जेसीबी मशीन, हार्वेस्टर, खनिज परिवहन तथा उत्खनन के क्षेत्रों सहित अन्य व्यापार व्यवसाय में भी शुरूआत की है। हरदा जिले में जाट जिन गाँवों में निवास करते हैं वे गाँव तवा नहर से सिंचित हैं, साथ ही भूमि भी अत्यंत उपजाऊ है। इस सबका परिणाम यह है कि जाट यहाँ पर्याप्त खुशहाल स्थिति में है। राजनीति के क्षेत्र में भी जाट जिन गाँवों मे निवास करते हैं वहाँ उनका पर्याप्त प्रभुत्व कायम रहता है। 1993 से आज तक हरदा क्षेत्र से विधायक कमल पटेल, जो बीच में प्रदेश में मंत्री भी रहे जाट जाति के ही हैं। इससे पूर्व होशंगाबाद जिले की जनपद पंचायत एवं मंडी में रामदीन पटेल अध्यक्ष रहे हैं। आशय यह है कि कम संख्या के बावजूद जाट जाति हरदा क्षेत्र में राजनैतिक रूप से काफी प्रभावशाली है।[9]

स्वतंत्रता संग्राम के दिनों में इस क्षेत्र में अभूतपूर्व चेतना रही। हरदा क्षेत्र से 1857 के पश्चात केवल एक शहीद का नाम आता है वह है श्री मामराज जाट। खेद का विषय है कि इनके विषय में हरदा क्षेत्र में ही ज्यादा जानकारी उपलब्ध नहीं है। श्री मामराज जाट हरदा क्षेत्र में पंजाब हरियाणा की तरफ से आये थे। उनका जन्म 1915 में हुआ था।[10] उनके विषग में बताया जाता है कि वे कम्युनिस्ट विचारधारा के थे। वे हरदा में 1930-31 के आंदोलनों में बहुत सक्रिय थे। विदेशी वस्त्रों की होली जलाना, वानर सेना के साथ सारे शहर में नारे लगाते घूमना तथा "नहीं रखनी, नहीं रखनी, यह जालिम सरकार नहीं रखनी", इनका प्रसिद्ध नारा था। 1942 में आंदोलन में बम्बई में ये पुलिस की गोली से शहीद हो गये।[11]

जाट जाति के युवा स्वयं स्वीकारते हैं कि उनके स्वभाव में एक किस्म की वक्रता विद्यमान होती है। इसके पीछे वे कारण बताते हैं कि श्रम और जीवन की बीहड़ परिस्थितियाँ ने ऐसा मनोभाव उत्पन्न कर दिया है। दूसरा कारण वे गिनाते हैं कि स्वाभिमान की भावना और किसी का दबाव न सहन करने की मानसिकता ने भी उन्हें यह स्वभाव प्रदान किया है। बहरहाल हरदा क्षेत्र के जाटों की प्रगतिशीलता, श्रमशीलता, परंपरा के प्रति अगाध लगाव की प्रशंसा की जाना चाहिए।

## संदर्भ

1. Horace Hayman Wilson: *The History of British India,* Vol. II, London, p. 132

2. महेन्द्रकुमार शास्त्री (संपादक), *जाट इतिहास,* मधुर प्रकाशन, दिल्ली, पृ. 572
3. G. L. Corbett : *Gazetteer of India, Dist. Hoshangabad,* 1908 (Reprint-1997) Gazetteers Unit, Govt. of M.P., Bhopal, p. 319
4. ए.एम. सिन्हा एवं एस.डी. गुरु : *मध्यप्रदेश जिला गजेटियर-होशंगाबाद,* गजेटियर संचालनालय संस्कृति विभाग, भोपाल, प्रथम संस्करण (1994), पृ. 38
5. पूर्वोक्त, पृ. 38
6. G. L. Corbett : *Op. cit.,* p. 319
7. Charles Alfred Elliott : *Report of the Land Revenue Settlement of the Dist. of Hoshangabad,* Allahabad (1867), p. 62
8. Charles Alfred Elliot: *Op. cit.,* p. 66
9. G. L. Corbett: *Op. cit.,* p. 319
10. Hiralal Gupta : *Freedom Fighters of Madhya Pradesh and Chattisgarh,* Vol. I, Om Pub., N. Delhi (2002), p. 213
11. महेशदत्त मिश्र एवं अन्य (संपादक) : *हरदा और स्वतंत्रता संग्राम,* प्रकाशक-चंद्रगोपाल जनकदुलारी मिश्र परमार्थ ट्रस्ट, हरदा (2010), पृ. 113

---

नोट - इस आलेख को तैयार करने में श्री हरिशंकर सारन ग्राम अतरसमा, श्री प्रहलाद पटेल, ग्राम छोटी हरदा, डॉ, महेन्द्र सिरोही ग्राम-भैरोपुर, श्री पन्नालाल डूडी, ग्राम बिछौला, श्री रामा पटेल, ग्राम राताललाई, श्री रेवाराम पटेल, ग्राम छोटी हरदा ने सर्वेक्षण में सहयोग प्रदान किया है।

## 26

# उत्तर-पश्चिमी भारत में शिक्षा प्रसार, समाज सुधार एवं जनजागृति में स्वामी केशवानन्द जी का योगदान विशेष सन्दर्भ : बीकानेर संभाग

जसंवत सिंह खीचड़

भारत के उत्तर-पश्चिमी भाग का अधिकांश क्षेत्र सूखा, रेतीला, बंजर एवं दुर्गम है जहाँ पर जीवन यापन अत्यंत कठिन था। लोग कृषि एवं पशुपालन से जीवन यापन करते थे। वर्षा के अभाव में कृषि उत्पादन भी नगण्य था, पानी का सर्वथा अभाव था। राहगीर द्वारा पीने के लिए पानी मांगने पर पानी के स्थान पर घी देने की कहावतें प्रचलित हैं। इस क्षेत्र को मरुस्थल कहा जाता है जिसका अर्थ है 'मौत का स्थान'।[1] विषमताओं तथा अभावों के विरुद्ध संघर्ष ने इस क्षेत्र के लोगों को हर विपरीत परिस्थिति का सामना करने में सक्षम एवं संघर्षशील बना दिया। इस दुर्गम क्षेत्र में अधिकांशतः जाट जाति के किसान रहते थे, जो जीवन संघर्ष के प्रतिरूप थे।[2] इस सम्बन्ध में एक फारसी कहावत प्रचलित है, "हर बला के अज आसमाने आयद, वो पुरश्त कि खानए किसान कुजा अश्त", अर्थात् स्वर्ग (आसमान) से जो भी मुसीबत जमीन पर आती है वह सबसे पहले यही पूछती है कि किसान का घर कहाँ है?[3] तात्पर्य यह है कि किसान (विशेषकर जाट जाति) ने सदैव मुसीबतों का सामना कर स्वाभिमान एवं परिश्रम से जीवन जिया है। कालांतर में पंजाब एवं राजस्थान के श्रीगंगानगर-हनुमानगढ़ क्षेत्र में गंग नहर एवं तत्पश्चात् राजस्थान नहर परियोजना (वर्तमान में इंदिरा गांधी नहर परियोजना) से सिंचाई सुविधा प्राप्त होने पर कठिन परिश्रमी किसानों ने कृषि उत्पादन में उल्लेखनीय वृद्धि की जिससे न केवल इस क्षेत्र में समृद्धि व विकास हुआ बल्कि सम्पूर्ण भारतीय अर्थव्यवस्था पर इसका सकारात्मक प्रभाव पड़ा। उत्तर पश्चिमी भारत के इस भू-भाग का जो परिदृश्य आज हमारे समक्ष है उसके निर्माण में स्वामी केशवानन्द जी का अहम् योगदान है।[4] बीसवीं

सदी के प्रारम्भ में बीकानेर संभाग (श्रीगंगानगर, हनुमानगढ़, बीकानेर एवं चूरू जिलों का क्षेत्र) में शिक्षा का सर्वथा अभाव था। शिक्षा के अभाव में अनेक सामाजिक कुरीतियाँ यथा मृत्युभोज, छुआ-छूत, बालविवाह, पर्दाप्रथा, दहेजप्रथा, अंधविश्वास आदि व्याप्त थीं।[5] यद्यपि 19वी सदी में प्रथम स्वतंत्रता आंदोलन हो चुका था तथा विश्व भर में अनेक उल्लेखनीय व दीर्घ प्रभावी सामाजिक-राजनैतिक घटनाएँ घटित हुई किन्तु भारत का यह भू-भाग अशिक्षा के अंधेरे के कारण 20वीं सदी के प्रारम्भ तक सुषुप्त था।

सन् 1883 ई. में इसी दुर्गम भू-भाग से लगते शेखावाटी क्षेत्र (सीकर जिले) के मंगलूणा गांव में एक सामान्य किसान (ढाका गोत्र के जाट) परिवार में श्री स्वामी जी का शिशु बीरमा के रूप में जन्म हुआ।[6] 4 वर्ष की आयु में ही बालक बीरमा के सिर से पिता श्री ठाकर सी का साया उठ गया। पहले से ही विपत्तियों का सामना कर रही बीरमा की माँ श्रीमती सारा के लिए तत्कालीन सामाजिक परिवेश में जीवनयापन एवं बालक की परवरिश करना कितना कठिन था इसका सहज ही अन्दाजा लगाया जा सकता है। किन्तु सारां एक साहसी एवं निर्भीक महिला थी जिसने अभावों, कष्टों एवं ईश्वर प्रदत्त दुर्भाग्य का दृढ़ता से मुकाबला करते हुए बालक बीरमा का लालन-पालन किया तथापि उन्हें बार-बार विस्थापित अवश्य होना पड़ा। श्री स्वामी जी के साहस, निर्भयता एवं धैर्यशीलता की प्रेरणा स्रोत वीरांगना सारां ही थी। सन् 1899 का भयावह छप्पना (सम्वत 1956 में) अकाल राजस्थान के भू-भाग के लिए अत्यंत दुर्भाग्यपूर्ण था, जिसमें भूख एवं महामारी के कारण हजारों लोग मर गये एवं अनेक लोग पंजाब की ओर कूच कर गये, गाँव के गाँव खाली हो गये। वीरांगना सारां भी इस विपदा को सहन नहीं कर सकी और सन् 1899 में केलणिया गाँव (तहसील नोहर, जिला-हनुमानगढ़) में उनकी मृत्यु हो गई।[7]

बाल्यकाल से जीवन संघर्ष को करीब से देखते आ रहे तरुण बीरमा को जीवन की दुर्गम डगर पर अब अकेले ही अपनी मंजिल तलाशनी थी। छप्पना अकाल में प्राण बचाने के लिए लोग इधर-उधर पलायन कर रहे थे। बालक बीरमा भी चल पड़ा अनजाने व अनदेखे रास्ते पर और नोहर, सिरसा, भटिण्डा, अबोहर होता हुआ पंजाब के झूमियांवाली तथा वहाँ से आर्य समाज फिरोजपुर द्वारा संचालित अनाथालाय में पहुँच गया। प्रखर बुद्धि बीरमा ने 17 वर्ष की उम्र में हिन्दी-संस्कृत का प्रारम्भिक ज्ञान फिरोजपुर अनाथालय में ही प्राप्त किया। बालक बीरमा की संस्कृत पढ़ने की उत्कृष्ट इच्छा थी, जिसके वशीभूत सन् 1904 में 150 कि.मी. पैदल यात्रा कर फाजिल्का पहुँचे जहाँ दैवयोग से उदासी पंथ के डेरे के संत खुशालदास से इनकी भेंट हुई। बीरमा ने महंत जी को संस्कृत पढ़ने का प्रयोजन बताया, किन्तु जब महंत खुशालदास को पता चला कि बीरमा जाट जाति से है तो उन्होंने कहा कि तुम तो संस्कृत नहीं पढ़ सकते।[8] इसे

सामाजिक विडम्बना ही कहा जा सकता है कि उस जमाने में जाटों को संस्कृत पढ़ने का अधिकार नहीं था। अपने लक्ष्य के प्रति प्रतिबद्ध बीरमा ने जब महंत जी से इसका उपाय पूछा तो उन्होंने कहा कि यदि तुम साधु बन जाओ तो संस्कृत पढ़ सकते हो क्योंकि तब तुम्हारी कोई जाति नहीं होगी और तुम जातिबंधन से मुक्त हो जाओगे। इतना सुनते ही बीरमा को तो जैसे अपनी मंजिल की राह मिल गई और तुरन्त साधुत्व धारण कर महंत खुशालदास के शिष्य बन गये। संस्कृत अध्ययन हेतु बीरमा जी 600 कि.मी. पैदल यात्रा कर आगरा पहुँचे, वहाँ से इलाहाबाद होते हुए बनारस गये किन्तु वहाँ उचित व्यवस्था न पाने पर वापस इलाहाबाद लौट आये। सन् 1905 में प्रयाग के प्रसिद्ध कुम्भ मेले में अवधूत अखाड़े के महंत हीरानन्द ने बीरमा जी के शुद्ध हिन्दी उच्चारण से प्रभावित हो उन्हें केशवानन्द नाम दिया।[9] सन् 1905 से 1908 तक केशवानन्द ने हरिद्वार व अमृतसर में संस्कृत का अध्ययन किया तथा अपनी ज्ञान-पिपासा शांत करने हेतु सिंध, बलूचिस्तान व पंजाब की यात्रा करते हुए अंतिम पड़ाव के रूप में नोहर (जिला-हनुमानगढ़) पहुँच कर वेदान्त का अध्ययन किया। शिक्षा यात्रा पूर्ण कर 1908 में वापस फाजिल्का पहुँचे तथा महंत खुशालदास के उत्तराधिकारी के रूप में अपने डेरे के महंत बने। अब उनके साथी व अन्य लोग उन्हें स्वामी जी कहने लगे। इस प्रकार सीकर जिले के मंगलूणा गाँव में जन्मा बालक बीरमा से स्वामी केशवानन्द हो गया और कालांतर में उत्तर-पश्चिमी भारत में स्वामी जी के नाम से लोकप्रिय हुआ।

**कर्मयात्रा :**

सन् 1908 में स्वामी जी भारत के इस सुदूर एवं दुर्गम क्षेत्र में शिक्षा का प्रकाश फैलाने एवं सामाजिक जागृति पैदा करने के लिए अपनी कर्मयात्रा पर निकल पड़े जिस पर जीवनपर्यन्त चलते रहे। स्वामी जी में भ्रमणशीलता व सीखने की प्रवृत्ति बचपन से थी तथा युवावस्था में पहुंचते-पहुंचते स्वामी जी को यह व्यावहारिक ज्ञान प्राप्त हो गया था कि शिक्षा ही एकमात्र अमोघ अस्त्र है जिसके द्वारा इस पिछड़े क्षेत्र के सोये हुए मानस को सामाजिक बुराइयों के प्रति सचेत एवं सामान्य नागरिक अधिकारों के प्रति सजग किया जा सकता है। इसी प्रयोजन से सन 1909 में स्वामी जी ने लाहौर यात्रा की। सन 1911 में साधु आश्रम फाजिल्का में 'वेदान्त पुष्प वाटिका' नाम के पुस्तकालय की स्थापना की तथा 1912 में संस्कृत पाठशाला प्रारम्भ की। सन 1913 से 1915 तक सम्पूर्ण उत्तर भारत में लाहौर, अमृतसर, दिल्ली, आगरा, श्रीनगर आदि शहरों में भ्रमण कर पुस्तकालयों, वाचनालयों, संग्रहालयों, शिक्षा केन्द्रों, विश्वविद्यालयों में शिक्षा साधनों का अध्ययन किया। स्वामी जी सन 1916 ई. में गुरुगद्दी स्वेच्छा से त्याग कर स्वाध्याय व हिन्दी भाषा के प्रचार में लग गये। इसी दौरान सन् 1917 में पंजाब के दानेवाला गांव में प्रवास के दौरान 'गीता रहस्य' एवं 'भारत भारती' का अध्ययन

किया जो उनके प्रमुख प्रेरणास्रोत बने।[10] सन् 1920 में उन्होंने अबोहर में 'नागरी प्रचारिणी सभा' की स्थापना की। गांधी जी से प्रभावित होकर स्वामी जी 1921 में असहयोग आन्दोलन में भाग लेने के कारण दो वर्ष तक फिरोजपुर जेल में रहे। जेल से रिहा होने के पश्चात् 24 जनवरी 1924 को स्वामी जी ने साहित्य सदन, अबोहर की स्थापना की। इसी कड़ी में स्वामी जी के प्रयासों से श्रीगंगानगर में सार्वजनिक पुस्तकालय, एलनाबाद (हरियाणा) में साहित्य सदन व मुक्तसर में हिन्दी प्रचार मण्डल की स्थापना हुई। इसी दौरान स्वामी जी स्वतंत्रता आंदोलन में भी सक्रिय भूमिका निभाते रहे तथा डॉ. राजेन्द्र प्रसाद, मोती लाल नेहरु, सुरेन्द्र नाथ बनर्जी, चितरंजन दास, गांधी जी जैसे बड़े नेताओं के सम्पर्क में आये। सविनय अवज्ञा आन्दोलन में सन् 1930 में फिर एक साल स्वामी जी जेल में रहे। 1931 में जेल से रिहा होने पर स्वामी जी ने अबोहर फाजिल्का क्षेत्र में जागृति के लिए चलता-फिरता पुस्तकालय प्रारम्भ किया। सन् 1932 में जाट स्कूल, संगरिया की प्रबन्ध समिति ने उन्हें विशेष रूप से आमंत्रित कर स्कूल संचालन में आ रही कठिनाइयों से अवगत कराते हुए उनसे स्कूल संचालन का अनुरोध किया। पहले से अनेक संस्थाओं व सामाजिक कार्यों का भार होते हुए भी शिक्षा प्रसार के प्रति समर्पित संत से सन 1933 में तत्कालीन जाट स्कूल, संगरिया के संचालन का विधिवत कार्यभार ग्रहण कर लिया और जीवन के शेष 40 वर्षों की तपस्या से पूर्ण अभावों के बावजूद इस छोटे से स्कूलरूपी पौधे को वट वृक्ष के रूप में विकसित कर दिया।

इसी दौरान 24-26 सितम्बर, 1933 को साहित्य सदन, अबोहर में पंजाब प्रांतीय हिन्दी साहित्य सम्मेलन का वार्षिक अधिवेशन सफलतापूर्वक सम्पन्न कराया। सन 1933 में ही अबोहर से प्रसिद्ध हिन्दी मासिक पत्रिका 'दीपक' का प्रकाशन प्रारम्भ कराया जो इस क्षेत्र में सामाजिक-राजनीतिक जागृति का बड़ा आधार बन गई थी। हिन्दी भाषा के प्रचार-प्रसार के क्षेत्र में उल्लेखनीय कार्य करने के कारण स्वामी जी की ख्याति राष्ट्रीय स्तर पर फैल गई। यह इस घटना से साबित होता है कि जब निजाम हैदराबाद में सन 1941 में हैदराबाद में होने वाले 'अखिल भारतीय हिन्दी साहित्य सम्मेलन' का आयोजन अपनी रियासत में नहीं करने देने का फरमान जारी कर दिया तो यह सम्मेलन कराने की जिम्मेदारी स्वामी जी पर डाली गई। स्वामी जी ने इसे चुनौती के रूप में स्वीकार कर अबोहर जैसे छोटे कस्बे में 27-30 सितम्बर को 'अखिल भारतीय हिन्दी साहित्य सम्मेलन' का सफलतापूर्वक आयोजन किया।[11] एक वर्ष पश्चात ही 13-14 सितम्बर, 1942 में स्वामी जी ने जाट स्कूल, संगरिया का रजत जयंती समारोह आयोजित किया जिसमें रहबरे आजम सर छोटू राम तथा के. एम. पनिक्कर मुख्य अतिथि थे। जाट स्कूल, संगरिया में सन 1943 में स्वामी जी ने साहित्य सम्मेलन, प्रयोग की सभी परीक्षाओं का केन्द्र बनवाया तथा इसी वर्ष इसे हाईस्कूल में क्रमोन्नत कराया। हिन्दी जगत में स्वामी

जी द्वारा की गई सेवाओं के कारण साहित्य सम्मेलन प्रयाग ने उन्हें 'साहित्य वाचस्पति' की उपाधि से भी सम्मानित किया।[12]

स्वामी जी ने तत्कालीन बीकानेर राज्य के ग्रामीण अंचल में शिक्षा द्वारा चेतना और साहस का दिया जलाकर निरक्षर को साक्षर किया। साथ ही गांवों में व्याप्त सामाजिक कुरीतियों तथा ओसर-मौसर (मृत्युभोज), पर्दा प्रथा, बाल विवाह, शादी-विवाह में कांकड़ जिमाना (गांव की सीमा से लगने वाले सब गांवों को खाना खिलाना) आदि के विरुद्ध जन-जागृति की मुहिम चलाई। स्वामी जी ने 1944 में 'मरुभूमि सेवा कार्य योजना' प्रारम्भ की जिसके अन्तर्गत इस मरुधरा के सैंकड़ों गांवों में 1959 तक 287 पाठशालाएं स्थापित की।[13] स्वामी जी जाति व्यवस्था की संकीर्ण भावना के खिलाफ थे इसलिए 1948 में जाट स्कूल, संगरिया में जाति सूचक शब्द (जाट) हटाकर स्कूल का नामकरण 'ग्रामोत्थान विद्यापीठ' कर दिया। स्वामी जी ने सन 1949 में संगरिया में महिला शिक्षा प्रारम्भ की तथा 1955 में स्कूल को उच्चतर माध्यमिक में क्रमोन्नत कराने के साथ ही कृषि संकाय भी प्रारम्भ कराया। ग्रामोत्थान विद्यापीठ में सन 1963 में कृषि महाविद्यालय तथा सन 1965 में शिक्षक प्रशिक्षण महाविद्यालय प्रारम्भ हुए। 13 सितम्बर, 1972 को स्वामी जी देहावसान से पूर्व ही वे इसे वास्तविक अर्थों में ''विद्यापीठ'' का स्वरूप दे चुके थे।

उत्तर पश्चिमी भारत के इस निर्धनतम एवं पिछड़े क्षेत्र में शिक्षा का अलख जगाने वाले इस महायज्ञ में महान संत स्वामी केशवानन्द जी के साथ-साथ श्री बहादुर सिंह जी भोबिया, स्वामी गोपाल दास जी,[14] हरीशचन्द्र जी नैण, दौलतराम जी सारण, ठाकुर गोपाल सिंह जी (जिन्होंने अपनी 14 बीघा 3 बिरध जमीन जाट स्कूल को प्रदान की), कुम्भाराम जी, हंसराज जी, चौ. हनुमान सिंह जी दूधवा खारा, बलदेव राम जी मिर्धा, गुल्लाराम जी बैंदा, चौ. गंगाराम जी मिस्त्री, चौधरी रामदीन जी बाड़मेर, मूलचन्द जी नागौर, चौ. घासी राम जी झुंझनू, चौ. रूपाराम जी, चौ. जीवन राम जी, श्री नित्यानंद जी आदि का नाम भी स्मरणीय है।

इस भू-भाग में स्वामी केशवानन्द जी द्वारा जलाई गई शिक्षा की लौ का ही परिणाम एवं स्वामी जी का आशीर्वाद है कि पश्चिमी राजस्थान में स्थित बीकानेर शहर में आज तीन राजकीय विश्वविद्यालय स्थापित है, जहाँ उच्च शिक्षा के विभिन्न क्षेत्रों में शिक्षा प्रसार एवं अनुसंधान कार्य को बखूबी अंजाम दिया जा रहा है। बीकानेर स्थित कृषि विश्वविद्यालय का नामकरण स्वामी केशवानन्द जी के नाम से 'स्वामी केशवानन्द राजस्थान कृषि विश्वविद्यालय, बीकानेर' किया गया है जो स्वामी जी जैसे संत के प्रति श्रद्धा एवं सम्मान का प्रतीक है। हाल ही में कृषि विश्वविद्यालय परिसर में राजस्थान के

मुख्यमंत्री श्री अशोक गहलोत द्वारा स्वामी जी की प्रतिमा का अनावरण किया गया है जो कृषि शिक्षा एवं अनुसंधान से सम्बन्धित छात्रों एवं शिक्षकों के लिए प्रेरणास्रोत है।

## संदर्भ


1. कर्नल टॉड : *एनल्स एण्ड एन्टिक्विटीज ऑफ राजस्थान* पार्ट - I, 1829 एवं पार्ट - II, 1832; *जैसलमेर का एनल*, पृ. 169-231, 259, 294
2. डॉ. करणी सिंह : *दि रिलेशन्स ऑफ दि हाउस ऑफ बीकानेर विद दि सेन्ट्रल पॉवर्स*, नई दिल्ली, मुंशीराम मनोहरलाल पब्लिशिंग प्राईवेट लिमिटेड, 54, रानी झांसी रोड (1974)
3. डॉ. तमन्ना सिंह मोटसरा : *स्वामी केशवानन्द - एक युग पुरुष की अमर कथा*, पृ. 7 (2010)
4. गोविन्द शर्मा : 2008 स्मारिका चौधरी बहादुर सिंह समाज जागृति परमार्थ ट्रस्ट, ग्रामोत्थान विद्यापीठ, संगरिया, पृ. 21
5. गोविन्द शर्मा : *स्वामी केशवानन्द जी का साहित्यिक योगदान*, उपरोक्त, पृ. 24-31
6. उपरोक्तानुसार।
7. रामनारायण ज्याणी : उपरोक्त, पृ. 34-35
8. ज्ञानप्रकाश पिलानिया : *कर्मयोगी शिक्षा संत स्वामी केशवानन्द जी*
9. उपरोक्तानुसार।
10. उपरोक्तानुसार।
11. गोविन्द शर्मा : उपरोक्त, पृ. 24-31
12. ज्ञानप्रकाश पिलानिया : *कर्मयोगी शिक्षा संत स्वामी केशवानन्द जी*
13. उपरोक्तानुसार।
14. गोविन्द अग्रवाल : *स्वामी गोपालदास जी का व्यक्तित्व एवं कृतित्व*, पृ. 46

27

# बाड़मेर में जागीरदारी प्रथा के विरुद्ध जाटों का आंदोलन (1925-1960)

**जोगाराम सारण**

पश्चिमी राजस्थान में स्थित वर्तमान बाड़मेर जिले कों राजशाही में मालाणी परगना कहा जाता था, जो मारवाड़ (जोधपुर) राज्य का अंग था। रेगिस्तानी क्षेत्र में स्थित मालाणी में व्याप्त अराजकता की समस्या को हल करने के लिये कैप्टन जैक्सन, कर्नल टॉड (पालिटिकल एजेण्ट, मारवाड़), जोधपुर दरबार, मारवाड़ के हाकिम, मालाजी के जागीरदारों तथा जाटों के बीच तय किया गया कि मालाणी के जागीरदार जाट काश्तकारों से केवल बाजरा फसल का चौदहवां (1/14) हिस्सा हासिल (कर) लेंगे। अन्य किसी फसल पर लाग बाग नहीं ली जायेगी।[1] समय के साथ जागीरदारों का ऐशोआराम पर होने वाला व्यय बढ़ने लगा तो जाट काश्तकारों पर लगान बढ़ा दिया। बाजरे के अलावा ग्वार, मोठ, मूंग पर कर लगा दिया। इसके अलावा तो जाट की प्रत्येक चीज पर लाग थी। प्रत्येक घर पर धूंवा भाछ (गृहकर), गांव में नया घर बसने पर देसप्रठ लाग, जाट द्वारा अपनी बच्ची की शादी पर चंवरी कर, मृत्यु भोज पर कांसा लाग, जानवर बांधने पर खूंटा लाग, औरत के मरने पर दूसरी औरत लाने पर नाता लाग, घर के दरवाजे पर कियाड़ी लाग, बकरी व भेड़ पर पान चराई लाग, बैलों के जोड़ों पर हल लाग, कमठा लाग, परवाना लाग, चूड़ा लाग, माहेरा लाग, जागीरदार की मृत्यु पर खाण्ड बार, लानी लाग, राली लाग, माचा लाग, थेपड़ी लाग, बैड़ी लाग आदि कई-कई प्रकार के लाग जाटों पर आरोपित थे।[2] जागीरदार मौके-बेमौके जाटों से भेंट लेता रहता था। किसान को कुंवर के जन्म से लेकर जागीरदार की मृत्यु तक प्रत्येक कार्य में कर देना पड़ता था।[3] होली, दीपावली पर उसे जागीरदार को भेंट देनी पड़ती थी। इन तमाम कुकृत्यों के बाद भी जागीरदारों के दिल में रहम नहीं था। जाटों को बेगार की चक्की में पिसना

पड़ता था। जाट को अपना आवश्यक ही नहीं अनिवार्य कार्य छोड़कर भी जागीरदार के काम के लिये जाना पड़ता था। जागीरदार के घर वालों के लिये खाने-पीने, घास, लकड़ी लाने, गढ़ को लीपने-पोतने का कार्य किसानों को ही करना पड़ता था। बेगार न देने या आनाकानी करने या असमर्थता प्रकट करने पर सरेआम बेइज्जत करना, गढ़ में बुलाकर बंद कर देना, गोडा लकड़ी देना, मुर्गा बनाकर धूप में खड़ा कर देना आदि आम बातें थी।[4]

इन सबके अलावा साहूकार अपने तरीके से ही अनपढ़ जाटों का शोषण करते थे। कुल मिलाकर जाटों की स्थिति अत्यंत ही शोचनीय हो चुकी थी। जाट मोटा अनाज, मोठ की दाल और बाजरे की रोटी खाकर और मोटा कपड़ा, एक पैर में जूती, कंधे पर अंगरखी और घुटनों तक फटी धोती पहनकर दिन निकालता था।[5]

मालाणी का सम्बन्ध देश के अन्य भागों से भी न के बराबर था। ग्राम्यांचल में ढाणियों में रहने के कारण वह देश-दुनिया से कटा हुआ था। खेती व मवेशियों में सर खपाने वाले जाट के लिये जागीरदार ही सब कुछ था।

सन् 1900 में जोधपुर सादीपल्ली रेलवेलाइन ने मालाणी के किसानों की भाग्य रेखा बदल दी।[6] रेल पटरी बिछाने के लिये अंग्रेजों को मजदूरों की आवश्यकता थी। सौभाग्य से मालाणी के जाट हृष्ट-पुष्ट शरीर तथा मजबूत कद-काठी के थे। इसलिए जाटों को मजदूरों के रूप में रेललाइन पर रख लिया। यहीं से मालाणी के जाटों के भाग्य का सितारा चमकना प्रारम्भ हो गया। अंग्रेज अफसरों के सम्पर्क में आने पर इन जाट मजदूरों को उनकी वेशभूषा, भाषा, रहन-सहन को देखकर शिक्षा के महत्व का ज्ञान होने लगा।

इसी बीच मालाणी में एक ऐसे शख्स का प्रादुर्भाव हुआ जो यहां के किसानों के लिये भगवान बनकर उभरा। रामदान चौधरी रेलवे में भर्ती तो एक मजदूर के रूप में हुए थे लेकिन अपनी अक्ल-होशियारी व योग्यता से रेल पथ निरीक्षक (P.W.I.) के पद तक पहुंच गये। इनके सहयोग से और भी जाट रेलवे में भर्ती होने लगे। चौधरी रामदान ने सन् 1925 में पुष्कर के अखिल भारतीय जाट महासभा के सम्मेलन में भाग लिया।[7] इस सम्मेलन में रामदान सरीखे कार्यकर्ता के मन में यह बात समा गई कि पिछड़ेपन का मूल कारण अशिक्षा है। इसलिये मालाणी में भी शिक्षण संस्थाएँ खोलने तथा जाटों को अपने बच्चों को पढ़ाने को प्रेरित करने का निर्णय लिया।

1926 ई. को जोधपुर में जाट बोर्डिंग हाउस खोला गया तो रामदानजी के सहयोग से 6-7 छात्रों को वहां भेज दिया गया। रामदानजी ने मालाणी के मुखियाओं को इस हेतु प्रेरित किया कि वे बच्चों को शिक्षित करें। आप विवाह-शादी के अवसर पर जहां भी जाते जाटों को शिक्षा के बारे में प्रेरित करते तथा बाड़मेर में जाट बोर्डिंग की स्थापना की बात करते।

30 जून 1934 ई. को 'जाट बोर्डिंग हाउस, बाड़मेर' की स्थापना की गयी।[8] अब बाड़मेर के जाटों के बच्चे भी पढ़ने लगे। उधर रेलवे में काम करने वाले जाट शख्स भी थोड़ा बहुत पढ़ना-लिखना सीख गये तो उन्हें समझ में आ गया कि जागीरदार लोग किस प्रकार उनके साथ अन्याय कर रहे हैं, किस प्रकार उनका अनैतिक शोषण कर रहे हैं।

पढ़ाई के साथ-साथ किसान नेताओं यथा जोधपुर के बलदेवराम मिर्धा, बाबू गुल्लाराम, बागौर से मूलचन्द सियाग, फूसाराम जी तथा बाड़मेर से चौधरी रामदान का उद्देश्य एक ऐसे किसान संगठन की स्थापना था, जो किसान में शिक्षा के साथ समाज सुधार, शोषण से मुक्ति, किसानों के अधिकारों की रक्षा तथा दैवीय विपदा के समय किसानों की मदद कर सके। लम्बे विचार-विमर्श के पश्चात् 22 अगस्त सन 1938 को तेजादशमी के दिन परबतसर के प्रसिद्ध पशु मेले में 'मारवाड़ जाट कृषक सुधारक सभा' का गठन किया गया।[9]

मालाणी के परगने में इस सभा का कार्य संचालन रामदानजी के निर्देशन में उनके पुत्र चौधरी केसरीमल देखते थे। जाट कृषक सुधारक सभा ने कृषकों से लिये जाने वाली नाजायज लागबाग व बैठ-बेगार के सम्बन्ध में तथा संवत् 1996 में भयंकर अकाल में किसानों की सहायता का प्रशंसनीय कार्य किया।

इन दिनों जागीरदारों का आतंक एवं अन्याय अपने चरम बिन्दु पर था। वे किसानों को बुरी तरह परेशान करते थे। लटाई से पहले किसान सिट्टा भी नहीं तोड़ सकता था एवं उस फसल में से एक दाना भी काम में नहीं ले सकता था। वे नाजायज तौर पर कूंता कर देते थे। जो किसान एतराज करते थे उनको पिटवाना, उनके घरों में चोरी-डकैती करवाना आम बात हो गई थी।[10] जाट कृषक सुधारक सभा इस प्रकार की घटनाओं की जानकारी सरकार तक पहुंचाने तथा किसानों के दावों-मुकदमों में सलाह देने का कार्य करती थी।

कई बार कूंतों के मामले में कानूनी लड़ाई लड़नी पड़ती थी। मालाणी के खड़ीन व बूठ गांवों के किसानों को वकील कर कोर्ट में मामला दायर करना पड़ा। सन् 1941 में इस सभा का उद्देश्य वृहद कर इसका नाम श्री बलदेवराम मिर्धा की सलाह पर 'मारवाड़ किसान सभा' रख दिया गया। मारवाड़ किसान सभा द्वारा जो भी ज्ञापन-पर्चे जारी किये जाते, बाड़मेर में केसरीमलजी गांव-गांव, ढाणी-ढाणी घूमकर उन पर हस्ताक्षर, अंगूठे करवाकर, डाक द्वारा जोधपुर सरकार तक भेज देते थे। बाड़मेर में कूंता, हासिल व लाग बाग की जानकारी मारवाड़ किसान सभा के केन्द्रीय कार्यालय को समय-समय पर दी जाती थी।

जैसे-जैसे किसान जागृत होने लगे, छटपटाये हुए जागीरदारों ने किसानों पर दावे करने शुरू कर दिये। इस प्रकार के मुकदमों की सुनवाई व जांच 'हाकिम' या जोधपुर सरकार के मिनिस्टर किया करते थे। मारवाड़ किसान सभा के कार्यकर्ता इन दावों-मुकदमों में किसानों को परामर्श, सलाह, मार्गदर्शन एवं वकील आदि की सेवा उपलब्ध करवाने का कार्य करते थे।[11]

दोनों तरफ से दावों-मुकदमों की झड़ी लग गई। जागीरदार अपनी मनमानी पर उतर आये। 24 फरवरी 1942 ई. को गांव शिवकर, परगना बाड़मेर में लाटे के विवाद के कारण किसानों के ऊंट, बकरी, भेड़ आदि जानवरों को पकड़कर बाड़मेर फाटक में बंद करवा दिया तथा विरोध करने पर जाट अचला जाखड़ की ढाणी को वहां के जागीरदार ने आग लगा दी। जब पास के किसानों ने ढाणी को जलते देखा और उसे बुझाने को दौड़े तो जागीरदारों के समूह ने एकाएक हमला बोल दिया, जिससे 9-10 आदमी बुरी तरह घायल हो गये। उनमें से चार को जोधपुर तथा बाकी को बाड़मेर के अस्पताल के भर्ती कराया गया।

25-26 अप्रैल 1943 को मारवाड़ किसान सभा ने अपना द्वितीय अधिवेशन सर चौधरी छोटूराम, राजस्व मंत्री पंजाब की अध्यक्षता में जोधपुर में आयोजित किया।[12] इस सम्मेलन में चौधरी रामदान के नेतृत्व में बाड़मेर से कई क़िसानों ने भाग लिया। इस सम्मेलन में मंच पर जोधपुर दरबार उम्मेदसिंह के साथ दो जाटों, सर छोटूराम व बलदेवराम मिर्धा, डी.आई.जी. को बैठे देखकर जाट पुलकित हो उठे। इस अधिवेशन में करीब 40 प्रस्ताव पारित किये गये।

इस अवसर पर महाराणा उम्मेदसिंह के समक्ष मांग रखी गई कि भागरी क्षेत्रों में भूमि बंदोबस्त किया जाये। इस पर दरबार ने कहा कि उनके पास भूमि पैमाईश का जानकार स्टाफ नहीं है। तब सर छोटूराम ने अमीन-कानूनगो को भेजने का वादा किया। इस पर महाराणा ने भूमि बंदोबस्त की घोषणा की। छोटूरामजी ने वापस पंजाब जाते ही वादे के मुताबिक खान अली मोहम्मद नामक एक जानकार अधिकारी को जोधपुर प्रशिक्षण देने के लिये भेज दिया। बाड़मेर में खेमाराम बांगड़वा तथा गुमनाराम गोदारा कोलू को अमीन पद पर नियुक्ति दिलाई।[13]

जोधपुर के इस सम्मेलन में पधारे चौधरी रामदान सहित अन्य महानुभावों ने वापस बाड़मेर आकर यह प्रचारित किया कि जब मारवाड़ के मालिक के बराबर मंच पर जाट बैठ सकता है तो गांवों में जागीरदारों के बराबर जाट खाट पर क्यों नहीं बैठ सकता है?

किसान सभा ने बाड़मेर में जगह-जगह बैठकें आयोजित कर लोगों को समझाने व जागृत करने का कार्य किया। इस कड़ी में मारवाड़ किसान सभा ने अपना दो दिवसीय

अधिवेशन 9 व 10 जनवरी 1944 ई. को जाट बोर्डिंग हाउस, बाड़मेर में बलदेवराम मिर्धा की अध्यक्षता में किया जिसमें मालाणी परगने के करीब 1000 चौधरी एकत्रित हुए। इसमें किसानों को सलाह दी गई कि वे अपने बच्चों को ज्यादा से ज्यादा पढ़ाएं, मौसर व अमल गालने की प्रथा को समाप्त करें, ज्यादा से ज्यादा फौज में भर्ती हों तथा बोर्डिंग हाउस के सुचारू संचालन के लिये प्रति घर से चार आना चंदा दें।[14] इस सम्मेलन को चौधरी बलदेवराम मिर्धा के अलावा गोवर्द्धनसिंह चौधरी, मूलचंद सियाग, सूबेदार पन्नाराम तथा चौधरी रामदान ने सम्बोधित किया। इस सम्मेलन को सफल बनाने एवं प्रचार-प्रसार करने में चौधरी देवराजजी व आईदानजी भादू शिवकर ने महत्वपूर्ण भूमिका निभाई।

सन् 1946 में मारवाड़ किसान सभा का पुनर्गठन किया गया जिसमें बाड़मेर से रामदान चौधरी, अमराराम सारण सवाऊ के अतिरिक्त अब्दुल हादी को कार्यकारिणी सदस्य के रूप में शामिल किया गया। बाड़मेर इकाई का अध्यक्ष चौधरी रामदान तथा हुकमसिंह कच्छवाह को मंत्री बनाया गया। ज्यों-ज्यों जाट जागृत होने लगे यहां के जागीरदार जुल्म बढ़ाने लगे। मारपीट, अंग-भंग करना, चोरियां करवाना, खेतों से बेदखल करवाना, ढाणियों को जलाना, झूठे फौजदारी मुकदमे बनाना, अनाज लूट लेना, पशुओं को फाटक में बंद कर देना, कणवारियों से जासूसी करवाना आम बात हो गई। इन ज्यादतियों से जाट घबराये नहीं अपितु दुगने जोश से मुकाबला करने लगे। इसी बीच ग्राम तारातरा के जागीरदारों ने जाटों से जबरदस्ती लगान वसूल किया जिसका जाटों ने विरोध किया। इसकी सूचना बाड़मेर व जोधपुर किसान नेताओं को मिलने पर इन करतूतों का विरोध करने तथा जाटों में जोश का संचार करने के लिये तारातरा में बलदेवराम मिर्धा के सान्निध्य में बैठक रखी गई। जागीरदारों के भारी विरोध के कारण बैठक तारातरा के स्थान पर भोमाणियों की ढाणी में रखी गई। बाबा धर्मपुरी व विरधाराम सियाग ने दो माह बाद तारातरा में बददेवराम मिर्धा की बैठक रखवाई। इसके बाद जागीरदारों द्वारा जबरन वसूली गई लाग वापस किसानों को देने के लिये बाध्य होना पड़ा। इस घटना से वे स्वयं को अपमानित समझने लगे। जागीरदार हेमसिंह राठौड़ के नेतृत्व में डाकू ऊमपुरी के दल द्वारा धूड़ाराम जाट की 'कराई' जलाकर लगभग 10 टन बाजरा राख कर दिया।[15]

जाटों ने विरोध दर्ज कराना शुरू किया तो पीढ़ियों से ऐशो-आराम की जिन्दगी जीने वाले जागीरदारों के आराम में खलल पड़ने लगा। इससे बौखलाकर उन्होंने जाटों-किसानों पर हमले तेज कर दिये। मालाणी (बाड़मेर) में लगभग 24 जाट जागीरी जुल्मों का विरोध करते हुए शहीद हो गये- 1. देदाराम गोरसिया करना, 2. अन्नाराम मूंढ, चिड़िया, 3. जगराम खोथ अकदड़ा व उनके परिवार के तीन अन्य सदस्य,

4. नाथाराम गोदारा, बींजराड़ की तीन वर्षीया दोहिती, 5. देराजराम कड़वासरा, सेलाऊ, 6. रूपाराम कड़वासरा, सेलाऊ, 7. ऊदाराम जाखड़, 8. हरचंद सियोल, जैसार, 9. गोमाराम सारण, कानोड़, 10. विमाराम सियाग, सवाऊ, 11. नरसिंगाराम गूजर, पोशाल, 12. भोमाराम डूडी, चोखला, 13. ठाकराराम सियाग, गंगासरा, 14. कलाराम डूडी, चोखला, 15. पेमाराम पालीवाल, मेहलू, 16. खींयाराम सारण, गोलिया, 17. भीखाराम डऊकिया, लोहारवा, 18. डूंगरराम डऊकिया, कुण्डावा, 19. कलाराम सारण, सांवलोर, 20. रूगाराम सारण, सांवलोर, 21. आदूराम बाना, देरासर।[16]

बाड़मेर परगने के ईसरोल गांव की एक जाटनी को बंदूक की नोक के ठूंसों से जागीरी राक्षसों ने मार डाला। इसी परगने के शिवकर, लखवारा और दूधू गांव पर हमला किया गया जिसमें लखवारा का एक जाट और शिवकर का एक माली मारा गया।[17] इसके अलावा कई जाटों के अंग भंग कर दिये गये आंखें फोड़ दी गई। रेगिस्तान के 'लाईफ लाईन' ऊंटों की चोरियां करना आम बात हो गई। ऊंटों के अलावा घी, सोने-चांदी के गहने व ऊनी वस्त्रों की चोरी कर देते थे। कभी-कभी तो डकैत लाग जागीरदारी की शह पर महिलाओं का अपहरण तक कर लेते थे। शिवकर गांव की झीमों नामक महिला को वहां के जागीरदारों ने अपहरण कर सिंघ में बेच दिया। तत्कालीन एस.पी. भागीरथराम विश्नोई के प्रयासों से उसे बरामद कर वापस परिजनों को सौंपा। मीठड़ा गांव की गवरी नामक महिला को जैसलमेर से 8 वर्ष पश्चात् 1958 में मुक्त करवाया।[18]

उस समय जागीरदारों के विरुद्ध जुबान खोलना आफत को अमंत्रित करना था। किन्तु हिम्मतवान लोगों ने दिलेरी से मुकाबला किया। जाट परिश्रमी, बलवान, साहसी व हिम्मतवान तो थे किन्तु हमलावरों एवं डकैतों की गोली एवं तलवार का मुकाबला करने के लिये लाठी ही थी जो बंदूक व तलवार का मुकाबला करने में सक्षम नहीं थी। तब मारवाड़ किसान सभा की बाड़मेर शाखा ने 'धारिये' बनवाकर दिये। साथ ही सीमावर्ती गांवों बींजराड़, जैसार, रतासर, शोभाला, नेतराड़ क्षेत्र के 13 जाटों को बंदूकों के लाईसेंस दिलवाये। ऊंटों की चोरी रोकने के लिये अलग-अलग गांवों के लिये अंग्रेजी वर्णमाला के अक्षरों के लोहे के दाग बनाये।

इन अत्याचारों के खिलाफ मारवाड़ किसान सभा की बाड़मेर इकाई के अध्यक्ष रामदान चौधरी तथा कर्मठ कार्यकर्ता केसरीमल चौधरी, बन्नाराम जाखड़, अमराराम सारण के अलावा वृद्धिचन्द जैन, अब्दुल हादी, हुकमसिंह कच्छवाह आदि गांव-गांव जाकर जागीरी जुल्मों के खिलाफ लोगों में जागृति उत्पन्न करते, समझाईश करते। जोधपुर से बलदेवराम मिर्धा, पूरमचन्द विश्नोई, नाथूराम मिर्धा, परसराम मदेरणा,

मूलचन्द सियाग आदि नेताओं को आमंत्रित किया जाता था। ये नेता जाटों व किसानों की बैठक लेते। उन्हें जागीरदारों के अत्याचारों का विरोध तथा बच्चों को अधिक से अधिक पढ़ाने का आह्वान करते। ऐसी ही एक मीटिंग डाबड़ गांव में जागीरदारों के अत्याचारों के खिलाफ हुई। यह मीटिंग दो दिन चली। इसमें जोधपुर से बलदेवराम मिर्धा, बाड़मेर से रामदान चौधरी, गंगाराम चौधरी, अमराराम सारण सवाऊ, लूंभाराम सारण पाटियाल, पनाराम माचरा होडू, वीरमाराम ढाका सड़ा, जोधाराम सारण रावतसर, ताजाराम बेनीवाल आडेल, धनाराम सरणू, गंगाराम कलबी ऊंदड़ी सहित कई लोग आए। लोग दूर-दूर के गांवों से पैदल या ऊंटों पर चढ़कर आये। मीटिंग में पढ़ाई, बोर्डिंग के चंदे तथा लाग-बाग, बेगार के विरुद्ध चर्चा हुई। नाथूराम मिर्धा, बलदेवराम मिर्धा, रामदानजी ने तारातरा, धारासर, मांगता, खानजी का तला आदि कई स्थानों पर बैठकें लेकर जाटों की हौसला अफजाई की तथा जालंग-बोरा, जट की बेड़ी, पाला, हासिल, बेगार, पागीपा का विरोध किया। इन लोगों ने समझाया कि हम सब एक रहेंगे तो हासिल, लाग, चीरा, ताली, कुंता सब बंद हो जायेंगे, अपना राज होगा, अपनी जमीन होगी, जमीन की खातेदारी अपने नाम दर्ज होगी, अपने ही हाकिम होंगे और अपने ही हुकम।

जसोल जागीरी के क्षेत्र के गांवों परेऊ, रतेऊ, सवाऊ, सणतरा, चीबी, कूंपलिया, गिड़ा, सोहड़ा, कालेवा, पाटियाला, खोखसर, पोशाल, पनावड़ा आदि गावों में बाजरी की हासिल के अलावा हरे ग्वार का एक बोरा लिया जाता था जिसे 'बोरा बाग' कहा जाता था। 1948 ई. में मारवाड़ टिनेन्सी एक्ट लागू होने के पश्चात् कानूगी रूग से लाग-बाग, बेगार बंद हो गये। मारवाड़ किसान सभा के कार्यकर्ताओं अमराराम सारण सवाऊ, हरचन्द गोदारा कूंपलिया, लूंभाराम सारण, राणाराम गोदारा पाटियाल, गंगाराम लेघा परेऊ, ऊदाराम जाखड़, मोटाराम जाखड़, शिवदान जाखड़, मेहाराम कूकणा, ऊदाराम घाट, डूंगराराम डेलू सोहड़ा, जेठाराम गोदारा पनावड़ा, आदाराम गोदारा कूंपलिया, चिमाराम डऊकिया चीबी, जगमाल लेघा होलानी, अरजनराम सारण पोशाल, प्रभुराम डऊकिया गिड़ा[19] आदि ने चौधरी रामदान के नेतृत्व में इस ऐतिहासिक फैसले को आमजन तक पहुंचाने के उद्देश्य से बैठकें प्रारम्भ की तथा लोगों से बोरा लाग नहीं देने का आह्वान किया। कानून की समझाईश से जाटों ने बोरा लाग देना बंद कर दिया। जागीरदारों ने जबरदस्ती की परन्तु वे कामयाब नहीं हो पा रहे थे। जागीरदारों ने सन् 1949 तत्कालीन मुख्यमंत्री हीरालाल शास्त्री से झूठी शिकायत की कि जाट उनके ठिकानों की लाग अदा नहीं कर रहे हैं। लगान वसूली में उनकी सहायता के लिये प्रशासनिक व पुलिस बल से मदद दिलवाई जाये। तत्कालीन मुख्यमंत्री ने मारवाड़ टिनेन्सी एक्ट 1948 के प्रावधानों की अवहेलना करते हुए बाड़मेर कलेक्टर के नाम आदेश जारी किया कि जसोल ठिकाने के जागीरदारों

को लगान वसूली में आवश्यक सरकारी सहायता उपलब्ध करवाई जाये। वास्तव में जागीरदार लगान के बहाने बोरा लाग वसूलना चाहते थे ताकि उन्हें आय भी होती रहे व जाट किसान भी दबे रहें। राज्य सरकार से आदेश प्राप्त होते ही बाड़मेर जिला कलेक्टर जयनाथ कुंजरू स्वयं राजस्व व पुलिस अधिकारियों व कर्मचारियों को लेकर जागीरदारों के अमले सहित सणतरा गांव पहुंचे। गांव के सभी मुखियाओं को बुलाकर कलेक्टर साहब ने बोरा लाग देने हेतु दबाव डाला।[20] इस हालत में गांव में माहौल गरमा गया। पड़ोसी गांव गिड़ा के मुखिया उदाराम जाखड़ को समाचार मिलने पर उन्होंने बाड़मेर रामदानजी के पास समाचार पहुंचाया। ऊदाराम गिड़ा से करीबन एक सौ आदमियों को लेकर लाठियों, धारियों व कुल्हाड़ियों के साथ सणतरा पहुंचे। अमराराम सारण सवाऊ को समाचार मिलने पर वे भी सणतरा पहुंच गये। सणतरा पहुंचने पर उन दोनों की आंखें खुल गई। पहले तो उन्होंने समझ रखा था कि जागीरदार जबरन वसूली का प्रयास कर रहे हैं लेकिन वास्तव में कलेक्टर मय पुलिस अमले के साथ जागीरदारों का साथ देकर जाटों पर बोरा लाग देने का दबाव दे रहे थे। पुलिस ने जाटों के अस्त्र-शस्त्र छीनकर जागीरदारों को दे रखे थे।

अमराराम ने कलेक्टर से निवेदन किया कि यह आदेश गलती से हो गया है। नाथूराम मिर्धा व बलदेवराम मिर्धा से बात कर ठीक करवा देंगे। कलेक्टर साहब ने अमराराम को धमकाकर वहां से चले जाने को कहा। अमराराम वहां से सीधे जोधपुर बलदेवराम मिर्धा के पास गये। मिर्धाजी ने उनके साथ पूनमचन्द विश्नोई वकील को भेजा तथा एस.डी.ओ. सम्पतराज के नाम पत्र लिखकर दिया कि यह गैरकानूनी वसूली बंद कराओ।[21]

सणतरा में बहुत ही कम लोगों ने हासिल जमा करवाया। वहां से सरकारी अमला व जागीरदार शेर की मांद 'सवाऊ' में आ गये। दूसरे दिन अमराराम उस अमले के पास जागीरदारों की कोटड़ी पहुंचे। पुलिस उपअधीक्षक भैरूसिंह ने अमराराम को झुककर मुजरा करने को कहा। किन्तु अमराराम ने मुजरा नहीं किया। वहां उपस्थित किसानों को अमराराम ने छुड़वा दिया। सवाऊ में एक भी जाट से लगान या बोरा लाग नहीं भरवा सके।[22]

जसोल क्षेत्र के गांवों में किसान सभा के बाड़मेर अध्यक्ष चौधरी रामदान व केन्द्रीय कार्यकारिणी सदस्य अमराराम सारण के नेतृत्व में गांव-गांव, ढाणी-ढाणी बैठकें आयोजित की। इसी कड़ी में परेऊ गांव में किसान केसरी बलदेवराम मिर्धा की अध्यक्षता में बैठक की। इस बैठक में लगभग 50 गांवों के जाटों ने भाग लिया। इसमें परसराम मदेरणा (बाद में मंत्री व विधानसभाध्यक्ष बने) सहित मुखियाओं ने बोरा लाग नहीं देने,

संगठित रहने, अन्याय का साहस के साथ मुकाबला करने तथा शिक्षा हेतु बच्चों को बाड़मेर जाट बोर्डिंग हाउस भेजने तथा छात्रावास हेतु सहायता देने की बातें कही।

सन 1949 में हीरालाल शास्त्री सरकार ने एक काला कानून बनाया कि यदि किसान किसी भी कारण से लगान देने से मनाही करते हैं तो तहसीलदार, जागीरदार तथा गांव चौधरी मिलकर फसल का कूंता कर दें तथा घोषणा कर दें कि इतनी रकम अमुक काश्तकार पर बाकी है। इस तरह बकाया अदालत की डिक्री मानी जायेगी तथा यह रकम पुलिस व मजिस्ट्रेट की सहायता से वसूल की जायेगी। बाड़मेर के जसोल, गुड़ा, नगर, चौहटन आदि जागीरदारों ने किसानों द्वारा लगान न देने की जिलाधीश से शिकायतें की। किसानों द्वारा मना करने पर झगड़े, मारपीट भी होने लगी। परेऊ गांव में तहसीलदार व पुलिस बल के साथ जाटों का झगड़ा हो गया जिसमें तहसीलदार व पुलिस थानेदार को चोटें लगी और उसी दिन यह कार्यवाही रुक गई।[23] तारातरा में विराधाराम सियाग ने, महाबार में सरदारराम गोदारा ने, रावतसर में जोधाराम सारण ने, बायतु में नंदराम बेनीवाल व मूलाराम धतरवाल ने, चांदेसरा में चोलाराम पाबड़ा ने, खड़ीन में देवराज P.W.I. ने जाट जागृति का उल्लेखनीय कार्य किया।[24]

यहां के स्थानीय जागीरदार जाट किसानों को दबाने व आतंकित करने के लिये जैसलमेर एवं पाकिस्तान से डकैत दलों को आमंत्रित करते थे। डकैत दल ऊँटों व घोड़ों पर सवार होकर शस्त्रास्त्रों से लैस होकर जाटों की ढाणियों पर हमला बोल देते थे। हमला उसी ढाणी पर किया जाता था जो कि जाट जागृति का हिमायती होता था तथा जागीरदारों के आदेशों का अक्षरशः पालन नहीं करता था। देदाराम गोरसिया निवासी करना को जागीरदारों के गुण्डों ने मारकर उसकी लाश लूणी नदी में फेंक दी। नाथूराम निवासी बींजराड़ के घर पर हमला बोलकर जेवर, घी के घड़े, कीमती सामान व तीन ऊंटनियां ले गये। सन 1950 में तेगसिंह निवासी चिड़िया ने बंदूक से अनाराम मूंढ कर हमला कर मार दिया। 5 जुलाई 1950 को सेलाऊ में कड़वासरों की ढाणी पर हमला कर देराजराम को तथा अगले दिन 6 जुलाई 1950 को रूपाराम कड़वासरा को मारकर ढाणी लूटकर डाकू पाकिस्तान भाग गये। इसी साल चिमाराम सियाग निवासी सवाऊ डकैतों के हाथों मारे गये। इसी तरह कानोड़ निवासी गोमाराम सारण डकैतों का विरोध करते हुए वीरगति को प्राप्त हुए।[25] संवत् 2009 वैशाख सुदी दशमी को गोलिया गांव लूटा। मेहलू की सरहद में डकैत दल का जाटों ने मुकाबला किया। इस मुकाबले में दो जाट सींयाराम सारण व पेमाराम पालीवाल तथा एक डकैत मारा गया। 22 अप्रैल 1951 को बाड़मेर की लखानियां डकैती, 13 जून 1952 को भेडाणा की डकैती, संवत् 2009 को अरणियाली को लूट, संवत् 2019 की कार्तिक वदी 11 को लोहारवा गांव की डकैती इसी शृंखला में शुमार थी।

ऊमपुरी डकैत दल द्वारा तारातरा गांव को लूटा गया। पाबूराम कड़वासरा व ऊदाराम डूडी के ऊंट व भीयोणी गोदारों की ऊंटनियां ले गये। इसी समय नेनू पत्नी टीकमाराम गोदारा, धापू पत्नी हरुराम सियाग ने इस गिरोह का मुकाबला किया।[26] सवाऊ गांव के सुनार महाजनों को लूटने वाले डकैत दल का अमराराम सारण ने मुकाबला किया। तीनों डकैतों को पकड़कर पुलिस के हवाले कर दिया। इनमें एक कानासर का इनायत मुसलमान, दूसरा सांकड़ा का पोकरणा तथा तीसरा दरोगा था।

गिड़ा थाने के होनहार थानेदार गोपालसिंह जाखड़ ने खानूड़ा राईका व सागरमल महाजन के डकैत दल से हीरा की ढाणी गांव की सरहद में मुकाबला किया। इस मुठभेड़ में सागरमल अपने कई साथियों सहित मारा गया तथा शेष गिरफ्तार कर लिये गये।[27] ऊमपुरी के दुर्दान्त डकैत दल का खरथाराम जाखड़ भणियाणा की सहायता से डिप्टी रामदेव काला की पार्टी ने सफाया कर दिया। बलवन्तसिंह बाखासर गिरोह ने 1954 में तत्कालीन मुख्यमंत्री जयनारायण व्यास के समक्ष आत्म समर्पण कर दिया।

जाट बोर्डिंग हाउस, बाड़मेर की स्थापना से जाटों में जोश व साहस का संचार हुआ। पढ़े-लिखे लोगों ने यह समझा कि जागीरदार वर्ग बेवजह ही उनका शोषण कर रहे हैं। जाट साहसी व दिलेर तो होता ही है, उसे मार्गदर्शन एवं नेतृत्व की आवश्यकता रहती है। मालाणी के महामना चौधरी का नेतृत्व मिला तो अमराराम सारण, आईदान भादू, बनाराम जाखड़, खेमाराम बांगड़वा, देवराज बेनीवाल, जोधाराम सारण, देदाराम गोरसिया, केसरीमल चौधरी, गंगाराम चौधरी जैसे कर्मठ, नेक एवं निर्भीक कार्यकर्ता मिले जिन्होंने जाटों को जागीरी के उत्पीड़न, दमन एवं शोषण के नर्क से निकालने का परम पुनीत कार्य किया। किसान केसरी बलदेवराम मिर्धा, नाथूराम मिर्धा, पूनमचन्द विश्नोई, मूलचन्द सियाग, बाबू गुल्लाराम, परमराम मदेरणा जैसे किसान नेताओं ने विधिक सहायता एवं हौसला अफजाई कर किसानों की प्रगति का मार्ग प्रशस्त किया।

## संदर्भ

1. महेश चौधरी : *मालाणी के महामना चौधरी रामदान,* पृ. 8
2. जोगाराम सारण : *बाड़मेर के जाट गौरव,* पृ. 21
3. उपरोक्त, पृ. 22
4. विक्रमादित्य चौधरी, *राजस्थान में किसान आंदोलन,* पृ. 28
5. प्रो. पेमाराम : *उत्तरी राजस्थान में किसान आंदोलन,* पृ. 32
6. जोगाराम सारण : *बाड़मेर के जाट गौरव,* पृ. 33

7. जोगाराम सारण : *बाड़मेर के जाट गौरव*, पृ. 34
8. प्रो. पेमाराम : *जाटों की गौरव गाथा*, पृ. 121
9. महेश चौधरी : *मालाणी के महामना चौधरी रामदान*, पृ. 68
10. महेश चौधरी : *मालाणी के महामना चौधरी रामदान*, पृ. 69
11. विक्रमादित्य चौधरी : *राजस्थान के किसान आंदोलन*, पृ. 137
12. विक्रमादित्य चौधरी : *राजस्थान में किसान आंदोलन*, पृ. 153
13. महेश चौधरी : *मालाणी के महामना चौधरी रामदान*, पृ. 76
14. विक्रमादित्य चौधरी : *राजस्थान में किसान आंदोलन*, पृ. 165
15. *जाट समाज*, पत्रिका आगरा में रूपसिंह लेघा का लेख
16. महेश चौधरी : *मालाणी के महामना चौधरी रामदान*, पृ. 103
17. डॉ. विक्रमादित्य चौधरी : *राजस्थान में किसान आंदोलन*, पृ. 187
18. जोगाराम सारण : *बाड़मेर के जाट गौरव*, पृ. 49
19. रामदानजी के एक सहयोगी
20. महेश चौधरी : *मालाणी के महामना चौधरी रामदान*, पृ. 117
21. अमराराम सारण : *सवाऊ के संस्मरण*
22. जोगाराम सारण : *बाड़मेर के जाट गौरव*, पृ. 53
23. भूरचन्द जैन : *मालाणी के गांधी वृद्धिचन्द जैन*, पृ. 20-21
24. जोगाराम सारण : *बाड़मेर के जाट गौरव*, पृ. 55
25. विक्रमादित्य चौधरी : *राजस्थान में किसान आंदोलन*, पृ. 198-99
26. रूपसिंह लेघा का *जाट समाज*, पत्रिका में लेख
27. जोगाराम सारण : *बाड़मेर के जाट गौरव*, पृ. 60-61

28

# जाट जातीय सुधार सभाओं द्वारा राजपूताना रियासतों में जाटों के सामाजिक, शैक्षणिक एवं कृषकीय जीवन में बदलाव के प्रयास (20वीं सदी के पूर्वार्द्ध में)

सुमेस्ता

बीसवीं शताब्दी के पूर्वार्द्ध में राजस्थान में जाट समाज के सामाजिक विकास, शिक्षा की प्रगति एवं आर्थिक हितों की रक्षा के लिए जातीय सुधार सभाओं की महत्वपूर्ण भूमिका रही है।

इन सभाओं ने शेखावाटी, मारवाड़ (जोधपुर) और बीकानेर के ग्रामीण क्षेत्रों में आन्तरिक जातीय सुधारों और सामंतीय शोषण के खिलाफ जाटों को लामबन्द करके जाट समाज में व्याप्त सामाजिक कुरीतियों तथा बाल-विवाह, बेमेल विवाह (बाल-वृद्ध विवाह), दहेज-प्रथा, नशा इत्यादि के उन्मूलन, तथा जाटों को जागीरदारों (सामंतों) के शोषण से बचाकर आर्थिक हितों की रक्षा पर बल दिया। जाटों के प्रति उपरोक्त कर्त्तव्यों को पूरा करने के लिए विभिन्न जाट सभाओं के कार्य जिनका अध्ययन निम्नवत हैः

**अखिल भारतीय जाट महासभा का अक्तूबर 1925 का पुष्कर अधिवेशन तथा राजस्थान के जाटों में नई चेतना :** सर्वप्रथम अक्तूबर 1925 में अखिल भारतीय जाट महासभा (1911 में स्थापित) के वार्षिक अधिवेशन पर गौर करना अति आवश्यक है। इस अधिवेशन की अध्यक्षता भरतपुर के शासक महाराजा कृष्ण सिंह ने की थी। यहां राजस्थान के प्रत्येक राज से जाट प्रतिनिधि पहुँचे थे। राजस्थान के अतिरिक्त इस आन्दोलन में उत्तर प्रदेश, पंजाब, दिल्ली इत्यादि अन्य प्रान्तों से भी प्रतिनिधि शामिल हुए थे जो राजस्थान के जाटों से अधिक सम्पन्न व शिक्षित थे अतः इससे भी राजस्थान के जाटों को अपनी स्थिति में सुधार करने के लिए प्रेरणा मिली और उन्होंने जाटों में पिछड़ेपन को दूर करने के लिए शिक्षा पर जोर देना अनिवार्य समझा।[1]

इस अधिवेशन में प्रख्यात जाट संतों और आर्य समाजी नेताओं द्वारा[1] जाट समाज में व्यापक सुधार करने, मारवाड़ी समितियों द्वारा शेखावाटी क्षेत्र में सामाजिक व शैक्षणिक सुधार लाने तथा इनसे भी बढ़कर *जाट वीर* (साप्ताहिक समाचार-पत्र)[2] में जाट समाज से सम्बन्धित बेमेल-विवाहों के खिलाफ तथा उम्र में समानता के आधार पर विवाहों पर जोर दिया गया। इन सभी मुद्दों पर चल रही बहस तथा समाज सुधारकों के प्रयासों को 1920 दशक में रचनात्मक सोच वाले जाटों ने समाज सुधार के लिए मार्गदर्शक माना। उपरोक्त सुधारवादी सभा के कार्यों को देखते हुए जाट महासभा के पुष्कर अधिवेशन (1925) में सभा का विस्तार किया गया और खण्डेला जाट पंचायत की स्थापना भी कर दी गई। इस अधिवेशन में सभा के उद्देश्यों में अत्यधिक महत्वपूर्ण रहा जाट समाज में जागृति पैदा करके सामाजिक व आर्थिक सुधारों को लाना।[3]

जाट सभा ने जाटों में विशेष तौर पर प्रचलित कुछ सामाजिक कुरीतियों यथा बाल-विवाह, औसर-मौसर (मृत्युभोज), दहेज-प्रथा, आपसी विवाद के समय मुकदमेबाजी, तम्बाकू, शराब, इत्यादि को दूर करने पर जोर दिया। दूसरी तरफ 'नाता' प्रथा अथवा 'पल्ले' लगाई अथवा पुनर्विवाह (जो सिर्फ जाटों व कुछ अन्य तथाकथित निम्न जातियों में प्रचलित था) को बढ़ावा देते हुए विधवा स्त्रियों के जीवन से अन्धकार को मिटाने पर भी बल दिया।[4]

**राजस्थान जाट महासभा तथा शेखावाटी क्षेत्र में सामाजिक, शैक्षिक तथा आर्थिक जागृति के प्रयास :** 1930 में राजस्थान जाट-क्षत्रिय सभा की स्थापना की गई जो 1932 से ही शेखावाटी क्षेत्र (जाटों का गढ़) में सामाजिक सुधारों के लिए अत्यधिक सक्रिय हुई।[5] राजस्थान जाट महासभा ने जाटों में समाज सुधारों की प्रक्रिया को दो दिशाओं में निर्देशित किया। प्रथम, सभा ने जाट समुदाय के लोगों द्वारा कोर्ट-कचहरियों एवं एक दूसरे के खिलाफ मुकदमेबाजी से समाज में फैलने वाली दुर्भावना व द्वेष से बचाने के लिए तथा उस पर होने वाले अनावश्यक व्यय से बचने के लिए कार्य किया। साथ ही जाटों में आपसी भाईचारा बढ़ाने तथा अपने लड़के व लड़कियों को शिक्षा देने पर बल दिया।[6] दूसरा, जाट सुधार सभा ने जागीरदारों और राज्याधिकारियों को ज्ञापन देने और प्रतिनिधियों को भेजने की नीति के तहत शेखावाटी के जाटों की सामाजिक एवं आर्थिक स्थिति को सुधारने के प्रयास करने का निवेदन किया।[7]

जागीरदारों एवं राज्याधिकारियों द्वारा ऐसा न करने की स्थिति में जाटों ने उन्हें लगान एवं अन्य कर न देने की धमकी दी। उदाहरणतः फरवरी, 1932 मे दो जाट प्रतिनिधिमण्डल, एक तहसील सिंघाणा के गाँवों का व दूसरा तहसील चिड़ावा के गाँवों के प्रतिनिधियों का खेतड़ी (ठिकाना) के सुपरिन्टेन्डेन्ट से मिला तथा उससे कस्टम

ड्यूटीज तथा नये लगाये गये भैंस कर को हटाने का आग्रह किया तथा साथ ही उन्होंने चेतावनी दी कि यदि उनकी मांगों पर ध्यान नहीं दिया जायेगा तो वे कोई भी कर नहीं देंगे।[8] आन्दोलन के इस चरण में जनवरी 1934 में जाट प्रजापति महायज्ञ के सामाजिक व धार्मिक उत्सव के मौके पर सीकर में जाटों ने सीकर ठिकाने के प्रशासनिक अधिकारियों के उस आदेश का खुलेआम उल्लंघन किया जिसमें हाथी पर चढ़कर जाटों को इस उत्सव में भाग लेने की मनाही की गई थी। एक मत से सभी जाटों ने इस प्रकार के आदेशों की अवहेलना की। परिणामस्वरूप सीकर प्रशासन को जाटों को अन्य समुदायों की तरह सामाजिक अधिकार देने पड़े। अतः प्रशासन से सामाजिक सुधारों की लड़ाई में जाट समुदाय की एक बहुत बड़ी विजय थी। इससे उत्साहित होकर खाण्डलवाटी, शेखावाटी, सीकरवाटी, उदयपुरवाटी और तंवरवाटी क्षेत्रों की जाट सभाओं ने सामाजिक एवं आर्थिक सुधारों के क्षेत्र में अपने उद्देश्य समान बनाये और इसके बाद उपरोक्त सभी क्षेत्रों की जाट सभाएँ एक मंच पर आने के लिए तैयार हो गई। 1935 ई. में उपरोक्त सभी शाखाओं ने मिलकर शेखावाटी किसान सभा की स्थापना भी कर दी।

बाद में शेखावाटी किसान सभा ने इस क्षेत्र के किसानों (जाटों) के हितों और उनके अधिकारों के लिये लम्बी लड़ाई लड़ी।[9] परन्तु जाटों में इस प्रकार समाज-सुधारों से कुछ राजपूतों में ईर्ष्या की भावना आने लगी। राजस्थान जाट सभा के प्रयासों से जाटों में तेजी से बदलाव आने लगे जिससे कुछ रूढ़िवादी राजपूतों को ऐसा लग रहा था कि जाट समाज में इस प्रकार के परिवर्तन से वे उनसे आगे निकल रहे थे। जाटों द्वारा सामाजिक व सांस्कृतिक उत्सवों पर ढोल बजवाने, विवाह के अवसर पर दुल्हे के घोड़ी पर चढ़ने का राजपूतों ने इसलिए विरोध करना शुरू किया क्योंकि शानो-शौकत वाले उत्सवों पर वे सिर्फ राजपूतों का अधिकार मानते थे। अतः शेखावाटी में जाट-राजपूत संघर्ष बढ़ने लगे। उदाहरणतः 1935 में ही शेखावाटी के गांव खूरी व कूदना में[10] इस प्रकार के संघर्ष सामने आये। सीकर के खूरी गांव में जाट दुल्हे को घोड़ी पर नहीं बैठने दिये जाने पर संघर्ष बढ़ गया जिसमें राजपूतों द्वारा गोलियां चलाये जाने से कई जाटों की मृत्यु हो गई। कूदना गांव में एक राजपूत रिवेन्यू अधिकारी द्वारा जाटों के प्रति अभद्र-व्यवहार के कारण झगड़ा सामने आया जिसमें जाटों ने उस अधिकारी पर हमला कर दिया था।

फरवरी, 1947 ई. में शेखावाटी क्षेत्र के ही चान्दना गांव में जाट काश्तकारों की एक सभा हो रही थी जिस पर राजपूत समाज के कुछ असामाजिक तत्वों ने हमला कर दिया।[11]

यद्यपि इस शोध-पत्र के उद्देश्यों मे जाट-राजपूत संघर्ष का उल्लेख करना सम्मिलित नहीं है तथापि इस प्रकार के संघर्ष से यह स्पष्ट होता है कि जाट सभाओं के प्रयासों से जाट (कृषक) समाज में निरन्तर परिवर्तन हो रहे थे जो तत्कालीन सामाजिक व राजनीतिक माहौल में कुछ रूढ़िवादी लोगों को पसंद नहीं आ रहे थे।

**मारवाड़ (जोधपुर) जाट कृषक सुधारक सभा तथा जाटों में सामाजिक, शैक्षणिक विकास, सामाजिक कुरीतियों का उन्मूलन तथा किसानों के आर्थिक हितों पर बल :** इस बात को बिलकुल नहीं नकारा जा सकता कि 1938 में मारवाड़ (जोधपुर) जाट कृषक सुधारक सभा की स्थापना से पहले जाट समाज में सुधार के लिये मारवाड़ में बहुत अधिक प्रयास किये गये थे। 1925 में पुष्कर में अखिल भारतीय जाट क्षत्रिय महासभा के अधिवेशन में राजस्थान के अन्य हिस्सों के साथ-साथ मारवाड़ के प्रतिनिधियों ने भी भाग लिया था जिन्होंने इस अधिवेशन से वापिस लौटकर जाटों में अशिक्षा व सामाजिक कुरीतियों को दूर करने के उद्देश्य से जगह-जगह स्कूल खोले तथा दूर-दराज के छात्रों को भी इन स्कूलों में दाखिले के लिये प्रोत्साहित किया। उन्हें छात्रवृत्ति देने की व्यवस्था की गई तथा उनके रहने के लिए चंदा एकत्रित करके छात्रावास बनवाये। उम्मेद स्टेशन, जोधपुर में किसान बच्चों के लिये एक शैक्षणिक संस्था खोली गई। 1927 में जाट बोर्डिंग हाउस जोधपुर की स्थापना की गई।[12] इसी तर्ज पर 1930 में नागौर में जाट किसानों के बच्चों को शिक्षित करने के लिए छात्रावास की स्थापना की गई।[13] बाड़मेर में 1934 में, डीडवाना में 1935 ई. में तथा साथ ही मारोठ, परबतसर, बिलाड़ा इत्यादि में भी जाट बच्चों की शिक्षा व्यवस्था के लिये छात्रावास खोले गये।[14] उपरोक्त छात्रावासों के अतिरिक्त बाप्पा, रोड़ू, भूंडाना, मादलया, कवासरा, डडेसरी, रताऊ, ढींगसरी, इनाड़ा, फिड़ोद, शिलगांव, अमरपुरा इत्यादि में कुछ पाठशालाएँ स्थापित करके जाट समाज में शिक्षा का प्रसार करने व बाल-विवाह, बहु-विवाह (यद्यपि इस प्रकार के उदाहरण एक-आध ही मिलते हैं), दहेज, नशा इत्यादि सामाजिक कुरीतियों के प्रति जन-चेतना लाने के भरसक प्रयास किये।[15] स्पष्टतया मारवाड़ जाट कृषक सुधार सभा से पूर्व मारवाड़ के तरक्की पसंद उदारवादी जाट नेताओं ने राजस्थान जाट क्षत्रिय सभा में भाग लेकर व अन्य क्षेत्रों के जाटों की तरक्की में शिक्षा के योगदान से प्रेरित होकर उपरोक्त शैक्षणिक संस्थाओं की स्थापना की और मारवाड़ के जाटों में जन-जागृति की कोशिश की।

निश्चित रूप से शिक्षा के उपरोक्त प्रयासों से मारवाड़ के जाटों में जागृति आयी। अतः 1938 ई. में इस क्षेत्र के जाट नेताओं ने मारवाड़ जाट कृषक सुधारक सभा की स्थापना की जिसके उद्देश्य थे- शहरों की बजाय देहातों में पाठशालाएं, लड़कियों की

शिक्षा के लिए कन्या पाठशालाएँ एवं छात्रावास स्थापित करना, छात्रवृत्ति की व्यवस्था करना, सरकारी खेती विभाग व पशु-प्रजनन विभागों के लाभों से जाटों को अवगत कराना, महाजनों के चंगुल से जाटों को बचाना, अकाल व दुर्भिक्ष की स्थिति में कृषकों को आर्थिक सहायता की व्यवस्था करना, आपसी झगड़े व मुकदमेबाजी में रुपये बर्बाद करने व वैमनस्य फैलने से बचाने के लिए पंचायती निर्णयों पर जोर देना, बाल-विवाह, बेमेल विवाह, औसर-मौसर (मृत्युभोज), दहेज इत्यादि से जाट समाज को मुक्त करना तथा नशीले व हानिकारक पदार्थों से समाज में उत्पन्न होने वाले व्यभिचार व आर्थिक तंगी से बचाने के लिए लोगों को जागृत करना, इत्यादि।[16]

सुधारक सभा ने विद्यार्थियों की टोलियों को कविताओं, भजनों व उपदेशकों के रूप में तैयार करके उपरोक्त सभी सामाजिक कुरीतियों व अन्य व्यभिचारों से जाट समाज को बचाने तथा जागृत करने के लिए क्षेत्र के गांव-गांव में भेजा। विद्यार्थियों की ये टोलियां न केवल गांवों में बल्कि पशु मेलों में भी (जहां अधिकतम लोग मवेशी खरीदने व बेचने के उद्देश्य से आते थे) जाकर लोगों को जागृत करने का कार्य करती थीं।[17]

यही नहीं मारवाड़ जाट कृषक सभा के प्रयासों से जोधपुर राज्य ने अप्रैल 1946 में मारवाड़ में औसर-मौसर (मृत्युभोज) को कानूनी रूप से बंद करने के आदेश पारित कर दिये और ऐसा करने वालों के खिलाफ कानूनी कार्यवाही करने के आदेश दिये।[18]

समीचीन है कि शेखावाटी क्षेत्र में भी राजस्थान जाट सभा की सुधारवादी गतिविधियां जागीरदारों अथवा रूढ़िवादी राजपूतों को पसंद नहीं आई थी और वे जाट समाज में बढ़ती शिक्षा के प्रभाव व प्रगतिशीलता से खुश नहीं थे। अतः यहां जाट-राजपूत संघर्ष बढ़े। ठीक उसी प्रकार मारवाड़ में जाटों में शिक्षा के प्रसार, समाप्त होती सामाजिक कुरीतियों इत्यादि से जागीरदार बहुत नाराज हुये और उनमें से कुछ ने अपनी जागीरों के गाँवों में जाटों द्वारा पाठशालाएँ खोलने तथा सामाजिक जागृति लाने के जाटों के अन्य कार्यों का विरोध किया।[19] इतना ही नहीं जागीरी गांवों में जागीरदार जाटों (किसानों) से ऊंची लगान, नई व पुरानी लागों तथा बेगार लेने के मामलों में किसानों पर ज्यादतियां करने लगे। परिणामस्वरूप सितम्बर 1941 में मारवाड़ जाट कृषक सुधार सभा ने जोधपुर राज्य से इस प्रकार की समस्याओं का हल निकालने की सिफारिश की।[20] परन्तु कुछ हल निकलने की बजाय जागीरदारों के अत्याचार अधिक बढ़ने लगे और उन्होंने जाटों के कुछ ढाणियों व गांवों पर आक्रमण भी किया।[21]

**मारवाड़ किसान सभा :** जागीरदारों के अत्याचारों से मारवाड़ के किसानों के हितों की रक्षा के लिए ऐसा प्रतीत हुआ कि किसी नये राजनीतिक संगठन की स्थापना की जानी चाहिये। अतः मारवाड़ जाट कृषक सुधारक सभा ने जून, 1941 ई. में

जोधपुर में मारवाड़ किसान सभा की स्थापना की। मारवाड़ लोक परिषद के साथ जाटों को न जुड़ने देने के लिए राज्य सरकार के पास यह एक अच्छा विकल्प था। अतः सरकार ने मारवाड़ किसान सभा को स्वीकार कर लिया।[22] सभा के उद्देश्यों से यह प्रतीत होता है कि सभा की स्थापना जाट (किसानों) के हितों के लिये तो की गई थी, परन्तु साथ ही किसान नेता जोधपुर सरकार के सहयोग व समर्थन से ही किसानों को न्याय दिलवाना चाहते थे एवं किसी भी प्रकार के हिंसक आन्दोलन के पक्षधर नहीं थे।[23] जागीदारों के अत्याचारों की जांच करने के किसान सभा के आग्रह पर राज्य सरकार ने 30 जून 1941 ई. को सेन्ट्रल लाग-बाग कमेटी की स्थापना की।[24] इस समिति ने अपनी रिपोर्ट में जागीरदारों को किसानों से अत्यधिक लगान वसूल करने तथा उन पर अत्याचार के लिये दोषी पाया। राज्य सरकार ने आरम्भ में कार्यवाही नहीं की, परन्तु किसान सभा और जाट कृषक सुधारक सभा ने जाटों से अपील की कि वो लाग-बाग न दें और जरूरत पड़ने पर कुछ समय के लिये कृषि करना बंद कर दें।[25] दूसरी तरफ मारवाड़ लोक परिषद ने भी जाट सभा के साथ मिलकर इस समस्या को गम्भीरता से लिया। परिणामस्वरूप सरकार ने कुछ कदम उठाये। परन्तु मारवाड़ के जागीरदारों की राजपूत एसोसिएशन ने सरकार की लैंड सेटलमैंट की नीति का विरोध किया। इस प्रकार यह संघर्ष चलता रहा। परिणाम यह हुआ कि मारवाड़ किसान सभा ने राज्य सरकार की आशा के विपरीत मारवाड़ लोक परिषद के साथ मिलकर किसानों की मदद करनी आरम्भ कर दी और जाटों ने भी लोक परिषद के राजनीतिक आन्दोलनों में बढ़-चढ़कर भाग लेना आरम्भ कर दिया।

मारवाड़ जाट कृषक सभा व मारवाड़ किसान सभा जाटों के सामाजिक उत्थान, शैक्षिक विकास व आर्थिक हितों के लिये लड़ती रही और 17 जून, 1948 ई. को जयनारायण व्यास के नेतृत्व में बनी सरकार ने जाटों की कृषि सम्बन्धी मांगों को पूरा करते हुए 6 अप्रैल, 1949 ई. को मारवाड़ टेनेन्सी ऐक्ट पारित करके किसानों को खातेदारी के हक दिये।[26]

**रियासत बीकानेर (चुरू) में स्थापित सर्वहितकारिणी सभा तथा जाट समाज में जागृति :** बीकानेर रियासत के चुरू कस्बे में 1907 में ही स्वामी गोपालदास के प्रयासों से उक्त सभा की स्थापना की गई। सभा के मुख्य उद्देश्यों में जाटों में शिक्षा की प्रगति के प्रयास करना, शोषित एवं पीड़ित जाटों की सहायता करना तथा जाटों में प्रचलित सामाजिक कुरीतियों एवं नशे की आदतों को दूर करने के प्रयास करना इत्यादि शामिल थे। सभा ने कुछ धनी-दानी लोगों से चंदा एकत्रित करके सर्वप्रथम रियासत के विभिन्न कस्बों में स्कूल खोलने पर बल दिया और 1912 ई. तक कई जगह स्कूल, पुस्तकालय इत्यादि खोले। परन्तु 1913-14 ई. में राज्य सरकार ने सभा के मुख्य संस्थापक स्वामी

गोपालदास एवं सभा की जांच करने के आदेश दिये तथा सभा गतिविधियों पर अंकुश लगाने के प्रयास किये।[27]

जनवरी 1932 में सर्वहितकारिणी सभा के आम जलसे में स्वामी गोपालदास तथा अन्य जाट नेताओं ने जगात बढ़ाने के लिये सरकार की निंदा की। अतः प्रशासन ने, जो पहले से ही बीकानेर में सभा एवं स्वामी जी की गतिविधियों को पसंद नहीं करता था, जाट नेताओं के खिलाफ दमनचक्र आरम्भ कर दिया।[28]

इसके बाद यद्यपि लम्बे समय तक बीकानेर में जाट बिरादरी के नेता राजनीति से दूर रहे तथापि उन्होंने जाटों में शिक्षा की प्रगति के लिये सराहनीय कार्य किये। उदाहरणतः स्वामी केशवानन्द ने पंजाब (वर्तमान हरियाणा) के कुछ जाट सहयोगियों की मदद से राजगढ़ के आस-पास के गावों गागरवास, कालरी, हैडल, मोटियार व छांगू में जाटों के बच्चों को शिक्षित करने के लिए प्राथमिक पाठशालाएँ स्थापित की।[29] स्वामी कर्मानन्द तथा अन्य नेताओं ने शिक्षा की व्यवस्था का उद्देश्य यह रखा ताकि जाट पढ़-लिखकर सामाजिक बुराइयों से बाहर आयें तथा अपने कृषकीय हितों के लिये जागीरदारों के खिलाफ आवाज बुलंद करें। इसका निश्चित ही प्रभाव पड़ा और क्षेत्र के जाटों ने अपने हितों के लिये जागीरदरों के खिलाफ विद्रोह कर दिया और लाग-बाग देने से इन्कार कर दिया। देखते-देखते यह चिन्गारी रियासत के बहुत से इलाकों में सुलग पड़ी थी।[30] जो देखते ही देखते राजपूताना की अन्य रियासतों की तर्ज पर प्रजामण्डल आन्दोलनों का एक हिस्सा बन गई।

अंत में यह कहा जा सकता है कि राजपूताना में जाटों के सामाजिक उत्थान, शैक्षिक विकास व कृषकीय हितों के लिये उपरोक्त सभी जाट सभाओं ने अहम भूमिका निभाई और लगभग पूरे राजपूताना में इसके सकारात्मक परिणाम देखने को मिले। पढ़-लिखकर जाटों ने सर्वप्रथम अपने समाज में व्याप्त बाल-विवाह, बेमेल विवाह इत्यादि कुरीतियों को दूर करने के प्रयास किये। अपने कृषकीय हितों के लिये जागीरदारों से लड़ाई लड़ी और इसमें बहुत हद तक सफलता भी प्राप्त की। इन जाट सभाओं के आन्दोलनों की समाज में एक बहुत अहम भूमिका रही। इसके द्वारा मारवाड़ लोक परिषद जैसे प्रजामण्डल आन्दोलनों से हाथ मिलाकर राजपूताना में निरंकुश शासकों के शासन को खत्म करके प्रजातन्त्र की तरफ ले जाने में महत्वपूर्ण भूमिका रही।

## संदर्भ

1. पेमाराम : *शेखावाटी किसान आन्दोलन का इतिहास*, पृ. 22

2. *जाट वीर* अखिल भारतीय जाट-क्षत्रिय महासभा द्वारा प्रकाशित साप्ताहिक समाचार-पत्र था, जो 1924 ई. में आगरा से प्रकाशित होना आरम्भ हुआ था। यह पत्र शेखावाटी के जाटों में काफी लोकप्रिय था, क्योंकि शेखावाटी के जाट समाज की सामाजिक समस्याओं को इसमें बहुत जगह मिलती थी।

3. देशराज : *शेखावाटी के जन-जागरण एवं किसान आन्दोलन के चार दशक,* राजस्थान नव-जागरण सोसाइटी, जयपुर (1961), पृ. 9-13

4. वी.के. वशिष्ठ : कास्ट रिफार्म एसोसियेशन्स एण्ड देयर सोशल एंड पोलिटिकल मोबिलाईजेशन इन दि प्रिंसली स्टेट्स ऑफ राजपूताना 1877-1949, इन पी.सी. माथुर (एडिटर), *सोशल एंड इक्नोमिक डॉयनामिक्स ऑफ राजस्थान पोलिटिक्स- बिफोर एण्ड ऑफ्टर 1947,* आलेख पब्लिशर्स, जयपुर (1984), पृ. 98-100

5. *जयपुर रिकाड्र्स,* महकमा खास, फाइल नं. 87, 1934 (कॉनफिडेंशियल रिपोर्ट ऑफ नाजिम शेखावाटी इकराम हसन खान, 25 अक्टूबर 1931, जी 20), राजस्थान राज्य अभिलेखागार (इसके बाद रा.रा.अ.) (ब्रांच), जयपुर।

6. *वही* : देशराज (सचिव, राजस्थान जाट क्षत्रिय महासभा) द्वारा हस्ताक्षरित पर्चा जो 1932 ई. में झुन्झुनु में बांटा गया था; चौधरी रिसाल सिंह (म्यूनिसिपल कमिश्नर तथा ऑनरेरी मजिस्ट्रेट, दिल्ली) का प्रेसीडेन्शियल ऐडरेस जो 11-13 फरवरी, 1932 ई. को अखिल भारतीय जाट क्षत्रिय महासभा के वार्षिक अधिवेशन के समय झुन्झुनु में पढ़ा गया था।

7. 14 फरवरी, 1932 ई. को अ.भा. जाट-क्षत्रिय महासभा के प्रतिनिधियों द्वारा जयपुर के महाराजा को अधिवेशन में पारित प्रस्ताव की नकल (हिन्दी में) भेजी गई। सी.एफ. महकमा खास, फाइल नं. 87, 1934, जी-20, रा.रा.अ. (ब्रांच), जयपुर।

8. *जयपुर रिकाड्र्स,* महकमा खास फाइल नं. 87, ज.ए. कारोल, सुपरिन्टेन्डेन्ट ठिकाना खेतड़ी का पत्र, सी.एल. अलेक्जेन्डर, रिवेन्यू मेम्बर, काउंसिल ऑफ स्टेट, जयपुर, दिनांक 11 फरवरी 1932, रा.रा.अ. (ब्रांच), जयपुर।

9. रिचर्ड शेसन : *दी कांग्रेस पार्टी इन राजस्थान,* ऑक्सफोर्ड यूनिवर्सिटी प्रैस, दिल्ली, पृ. 85-86 (1972)

10. दुल सिंह : *ए स्टडी ऑफ लैंड रिफोर्म्स इन राजस्थान,* प्लानिंग कमीशन, गवर्नमेंट ऑफ इंडिया, नई दिल्ली, पृ. 35 (1964)

11. *जयपुर लेजिस्लेटिव ऐसेम्बली डिबेट्स,* मार्च 1947, वाल्यूम 4, नं. 1, पृ. 59, रा. रा.अ. (ब्रांच), जयपुर।

12. *रिपोर्ट ऑन दी जाट बोर्डिंग हाउस,* जोधपुर, पृ. 1-2, रा.रा.अ. बीकानेर।

13. आचार्य गोपाल प्रसाद कौशिक : *चौधरी मूलचन्द अभिनन्दन ग्रंथ,* पृ. 117-18

14. वही, पृ. 149; लक्ष्मीनारायण बुद्धिसागर मिश्र : *चौधरी गुल्लाराम स्मृति ग्रंथ,* पृ. 24, 821
15. रिपोर्ट ऑन दी मारवाड़ जाट कृषक सुधारक सभा, फरवरी 1942, पृ. 17-18, रा. रा.अ. बीकानेर।
16. वही, पृ. 1-21
17. आचार्य गोपाल प्रसाद कौशिक : पूर्व उद्धृत, पृ. 120-21; *रिपोर्ट ऑन दी मारवाड़ जाट कृषक सुधारक सभा,* पृ. 151
18. जोधपुर रिकाड्र्स, मारवाड़ गजट नोटीफिकेशन नं. 8749, दिनांक 26 अप्रैल, 1946, रा.रा.अ. बीकानेर।
19. *रिपोर्ट ऑन दी मारवाड़ जाट कृषक सुधारक सभा,* पृ. 2-3
20. पेमाराम : *एग्रेरियन मूवमेंट इन राजस्थान,* पृ. 222
21. *रिपोर्ट ऑन दी मारवाड़ जाट कृषक सुधारक सभा,* पृ. 14-16
22. पेमाराम : *पूर्व उद्धृत,* पृ. 220
23. *पूर्व उद्धृत,* पृ. 220
24. *जोधपुर रिकाड्र्स, एडमिनिस्ट्रेशन रिकाड्र्स,* फाइल नं. सी/76, पार्ट 4, 1941, रा. रा.अ. बीकानेर।
25. *जोधपुर रिकाड्र्स, जोधपुर कॉन्फिडेन्शियल रिर्काड्र्स,* रा.रा.अ. बीकानेर, 1942।
26. पेमाराम : *पूर्व उद्धृत,* पृ. 238
27. *बीकानेर रिकॉर्ड्स,* होम डिपार्टमेंट (बीकानेर स्टेट), कॉनफिडेंशियल, फाइल नं. सी-3, 1932, रा.रा.अ. बीकानेर।
28. वही
29. *बीकानेर रिकॉर्ड्स,* होम डिपार्टमेंट (बीकानेर स्टेट) कॉनफिडेंशियल, फाइल नं. सी-1, 1945, रा.रा.अ. बीकानेर।
30. वही।

## 29

# राजस्थान की राजनीति : जाट नेतृत्व की भूमिका (1949-54)

**एफ. के. कपिल**

'अब जब हमने बड़े राज्यों को एक वृहत्तर इकाई में सम्मिलित कर लिया है, अब कोई छोटी सोच नहीं रहनी चाहिये। जयपुर, उदयपुर, जोधपुर, बीकानेर, आदि के प्रति भक्ति अब राजस्थान के प्रति समर्पित होनी चाहिये। मैंने देशी नरेशों को प्यार और आग्रह से प्रभावित किया है, मैं जागीरदारों से भी अनुरोध करूंगा कि वे समय के साथ चलें। यह स्वयं उनके हित में है।' (सरदार पटेल, 30 मार्च 1949)[1]

15 अगस्त 1947 तक अन्य देशी राज्यों की तरह राजपूताना के राज्यों का भी भारतीय संघ में विलय हो चुका था। अब इन राज्यों के एकीकरण की गंभीर समस्या भारत सरकार के सम्मुख थी। छोटे राज्यों का बड़ी इकाईयों में परिवर्तित करना एक चुनौतीपूर्ण कार्य था। उड़ीसा, छत्तीसगढ़, सौराष्ट्र, गुजरात, विंध्यप्रदेश, मध्य भारत, पूर्वी पंजाब आदि में छोटे राज्यों का संघ बना कर बड़े राज्यों का गठन किया गया। राजपूताना में 19 सलामी वाले राज्य, 3 छोटे राज्य और अजमेर-मारवाड़ का ब्रिटिश क्षेत्र था।[2]

राजपूताना के एकीकरण का कार्य छोटे राज्यों से प्रारम्भ किया गया क्योंकि इस बात की संभावना थी कि बड़े राज्य एकीकरण का विरोध करेंगे।[3] देश विभाजन के पश्चात अलवर व भरतपुर में साम्प्रदायिक दंगों और जनवरी 1948 में गांधी जी की हत्या से भारत सरकार इन राज्यों पर दबाव डालने में सफल रही। 18 मार्च 1948 को अलवर, भरतपुर, धौलपुर व करौली मिलाकर मत्स्य संघ का निर्माण किया गया।[4] दूसरे चरण में 25 मार्च 1948 को कोटा, बूंदी, झालावाड़, डूंगरपुर, बांसवाड़ा, प्रतापगढ़, टौंक, किशनगढ़ और शाहपुरा को मिलाकर राजस्थान यूनियन का गठन किया गया।[5] 18 अप्रैल, 1948 को उदयपुर के सम्मिलित हो जाने से तीसरा चरण पूरा हुआ।[6] जयपुर, जोधपुर, बीकानेर और जैसलमेर जैसे राज्य अभी भी अलग अस्तित्व बनाये हुए थे।

1948 के प्रारम्भ में जोधपुर, जयपुर, उदयपुर, बीकानेर आदि राज्यों में प्रजामंडल के नेताओं को मंत्री बनाया गया। मार्च 1948 में हीरालाल शास्त्री जयपुर राज्य के मुख्यमंत्री बनाये गये।[7] इसी समय जयनारायण व्यास जोधपुर राज्य के मुख्यमंत्री बने। मारवाड़ किसान सभा के नाथूराम मिर्धा को भी मंत्री बनाया गया।[8] 18 मार्च, 1948 को बीकानेर में भी एक मिला-जुला मंत्रिमंडल बनाया गया, जिसमें हरदत्त सिंह और कुम्भाराम आर्य किसानों (प्रजा परिषद) के प्रतिनिधि थे।[9] स्वाधीनता से एक वर्ष पूर्व विभिन्न देशी राज्यों के प्रजा मंडल मिल कर राजपूताना प्रांतीय सभा का गठन कर चुके थे। यह सभा अखिल भारतीय देशी राज्य लोक परिषद की क्षेत्रीय इकाई का कार्य कर रही थी। अखिल भारतीय कांग्रेस कमेटी के प्रस्ताव के अनुसार जून 1948 में प्रांतीय सभा ने अपने भरतपुर अधिवेशन में अपने को प्रांतीय कांग्रेस कमेटी बना लिया।[10] प्रान्तीय सभा के अध्यक्ष गोकुलभाई भट्ट अब प्रांतीय कांग्रेस कमेटी के अध्यक्ष बन गये।[11] राजस्थान के एकीकरण का विचार जयपुर के कांग्रेस अधिवेशन में निश्चित योजना का रूप धारण कर गया।[12] जयपुर के नेताओं ने राजपूताना की गरीब जनता की कमाई का 60-70 लाख रुपया सन 1948 में जयपुर में आयोजित कांग्रेस के नेताओं के सम्मान में खर्च किया। इससे जयपुर के राजा को राजस्थान का राज प्रमुख, जयपुर को राज्य की राजधानी और उसी राज्य के हीरालाल शास्त्री को प्रांत का मुख्य (प्रधान) मंत्री बनाने के लिये सहमति प्राप्त की गई। इसी कारण अजमेर-मेरवाड़ा क्षेत्र को राजस्थान में नहीं मिलाया गया।[13] राजपूताना के राज्यों के नरेश अपने-अपने राज्यों का भारतीय संघ में विलय कर चुके थे, लेकिन इन राज्यों के प्रतिगामिनी शक्तियों के षडयंत्र अभी भी चल रहे थे।[14] 19वीं सदी के प्रारम्भ तक जागीरदारों को बाह्य आक्रमण अथवा राज्य के शासक की सेना के लिये अपनी प्रजा की आवश्यकता होती थी लेकिन ब्रिटिश नियंत्रण के पश्चात उनका दृष्टिकोण बदलने लगा। जागीरदारों की नयी पीढ़ी पाश्चात्य जीवन पद्धति से प्रभावित थी और उनमें अकर्मण्यता और विलासता तेजी से बढ़ रही थी। इसके लिये उन्हें धन की जरूरत थी। अतः जागीर क्षेत्रों के कृषकों पर नये कर लगाये गये। 20वीं सदी के प्रारम्भ में राजपूताना में कृषि पर निर्भर लोगों की संख्या बढ़ रही थी। अन्य व्यवस्थाओं के विस्थापित लोग कृषि की ओर आ रहे थे और जागीरदार किसानों का शोषण कर रहे थे।[15] राजपूताना के राज्यों में भूमि खालसा और जागीर क्षेत्रों में बंटी हुई थी। खालसा भूमि पर दरबार का सीधा अधिकार था जबकि जागीर क्षेत्र में महाराजा के अधीनस्थ सामन्त भूमि पर नियन्त्रण करते थे।[16] जोधपुर राज्य में जागीरदारों के अधिकार में सर्वाधिक भूमि थी जो कुल भूमि का 72.5 प्रतिशत और खालसा 27.5 प्रतिशत थी। बीकानेर राज्य में जागीरदारी भूमि 64.3 प्रतिशत और खालसा 35.7 प्रतिशत थी, जयपुर में जागीर क्षेत्र 50.4 प्रतिशत और खालसा भूमि 49.6 प्रतिशत

थी और इस राज्य में भी अधिकांश जागीरें शेखावाटी में थी। उदयपुर में जागीर क्षेत्र 58.6 प्रतिशत और खालसा क्षेत्र 41.4 प्रतिशत था।[17] राजपूताना के दक्षिण-पूर्वी क्षेत्रों में खालसा भूमि का अनुपात अधिक था। भूमि पर अधिकार के कुछ और भी तरीके थे, जैसे-भोम, मोमिचार, दान (धर्मार्थ) और इनाम की भूमि आदि। खालसा क्षेत्रों में भूमि का बन्दोबस्त 20वीं सदी के प्रारम्भ में हो चुका था और कृषकों को निश्चित लगान का पता था। जागीरी क्षेत्रों में कृषकों की दयनीय दशा थी जहाँ लगान की वसूली जिन्स में होती थी और जागीरदार को लगान बढ़ाने का अधिकार था और वे कृषकों से बेगार भी लेते थे।[18] जागीर क्षेत्रों में राजपूत जागीरदार और कृषक जातियों मे टकराव की स्थिति थी। जोधपुर, बीकानेर ओर शेखावाटी में प्रमुख किसान वर्ग में प्रमुख जाति जाटों की थी।[19] 20वीं सदी में इन क्षेत्रों में शिक्षण संस्थाओं, छात्रावास और प्रजामंडल के आन्दोलन से जाटों में जागृति हो चुकी थी और वे अपने अधिकारों के लिये सामन्तों को चुनौती दे रहे थे।[20]

मेवाड़ (उदयपुर) के राजस्थान संघ में विलय के पश्चात शेष राज्य भी अलग नहीं रह सकते थे। जोधपुर, बीकानेर और जैसलमेर को मिलाकर एक सीमावर्ती राज्य बनाने का भी प्रस्ताव था लेकिन भारत सरकार इन राज्यों के शासकों से सम्पर्क कर निर्णय लेना चाहती थी। सरदार पटेल के निर्देश पर वी.पी. मेनन ने इन राज्यों के नरेशों से सम्पर्क किया। जयपुर, जोधपुर व बीकानेर के शासन अपने राज्यों के राजस्थान में एकीकरण के पक्ष में नहीं थे लेकिन भारत सरकार ऐसा चाहती थी। जयपुर के महाराजा मानसिंह की यह शर्त थी कि इस बड़े राज्य की राजधानी जयपुर बने और उन्हें स्थायी वंशानुगत राजप्रमुख बनाया जाए।[21] जोधपुर और बीकानेर के शासक ऐसा नहीं चाहते थे लेकिन भारत सरकार के दबाव से उन्हें झुकना पड़ा।[22] एकीकरण के लिये जितने उत्सुक जयपुर के नेता थे उतने जोधपुर, उदयपुर आदि अन्य राज्यों के नहीं थे। लेकिन उन्हें सरदार पटेल की इच्छा के सम्मुख और पार्टी अनुशासन के नाम पर मनाया गया।[23] 11 व 12 जनवरी 1949 को मेनन ने जयपुर, बीकानेर, जोधपुर और उदयपुर के शासकों से प्रस्तावित संघ व एकीकरण के प्रारूप पर सहमति प्राप्त की। 14 जनवरी को उदयपुर की आम सभा में सरदार पटेल ने यह घोषणा की कि जयपुर, जोधपुर, बीकानेर और जैसलमेर के शासक अपने राज्यों को राजस्थान यूनियन में मिलाने के लिये सहमत हो गये हैं।[24]

3 फरवरी, 1949 को राजपूताना प्रान्तीय कांग्रेस कमेटी के अध्यक्ष गोकुलभाई भट्ट, राजस्थान यूनियन के प्रधानमंत्री माणिक्य लाल वर्मा, जयपुर के प्रधानमंत्री हीरालाल शास्त्री और जोधपुर के प्रधानमंत्री जयनारायण व्यास ने विचार-विमर्श के पश्चात् दिल्ली में एक समझौते पर हस्ताक्षर किये जिसके अनुसार महाराजा जयपुर को प्रांत

को राज-प्रमुख बनाने के प्रस्ताव को मान लिया गया।[25] यह भी मान लिया गया कि राजधानी का निर्णय सरदार पटेल जननेताओं की सलाह से करेंगे, राज्य मंत्रिमंडल में नौ मंत्री होंगे, उनमें एक जागीरदारों का प्रतिनिधि होगा। राजपूताना के नरेशों ने भारत सरकार के साथ सम्पन्न एक समझौते के अनुसार अपने शासन को त्याग दिया। यह भी व्यवस्था की गई कि स्थानीय विधानसभा के गठन तक राजप्रमुख और राजस्थान सरकार पर भारत सरकार का नियंत्रण रहेगा। राजपूताना के नरेशों ने इसे सहर्ष स्वीकार कर लिया।[26] राज्यों के जननेताओं ने इस व्यवस्था का विरोध किया लेकिन काफी बहस के पश्चात् वे भी मान गये।[27] 14 फरवरी 1949 को गोकुल भाई भट्ट और माणिक्य लाल वर्मा ने दिल्ली में सरदार पटेल से भेंट की। इस बैठक में पटेल की सलाह से हीरालाल शास्त्री को राजस्थान का मुख्य (प्रधान) मंत्री बनाने का निश्चय किया गया।[28] यह भी समाचार था कि जयपुर के महाराजा को पटेल ने यह आश्वासन दिया था कि राज्य के नरेशों में उनकी स्थिति प्रमुख होगी तथा राजस्थान का प्रथम मुख्यमंत्री जयपुर का ही होगा।[29]

प्रसिद्ध उद्योगपति घनश्याम दास बिड़ला भी शास्त्री के पक्ष में थे। बिड़ला जयपुर राज्य से थे और हीरालाल शास्त्री बिड़ला के निजी सचिव रह चुके थे।[30] सरदार पटेल से बिड़ला के संबंध स्वाधीनता आंदोलन के काल से थे। पटेल और बिड़ला दोपहर के भोजन और प्रातः की सैर के पुराने मित्र थे। राजस्थान के मामले में पटेल ने बिड़ला से अनौपचारिक रूप से सहयोग लिया।[31] पटेल के स्पष्ट आग्रह के कारण जयनारायण व्यास और माणिक्यलाल वर्मा ने सदाशयता का परिचय देते हुये शास्त्री के चयन पर अपनी सहमति दी। वर्मा ने संस्मरण में लिखा है कि उन्होंने सरदार को यह कहा था कि शास्त्री को सत्ता मत देना, राजस्थान के कार्यकर्ता पसन्द नहीं करेंगे।[32] इस निर्णय पर राजस्थान में सर्वत्र आश्चर्य प्रकट किया गया क्योंकि राजनैतिक क्षेत्रों में ऐसी आशा थी कि जयनारायण व्यास राज्य के मुख्यमंत्री होंगे।[33] व्यास उस समय राजस्थान के सबसे प्रसिद्ध नेता थे, जिन्हें सब लोग जानते थे और जिनका प्रान्त में आदर था।[34] वे अखिल भारतीय देशी राज्य लोकपरिषद के अनेक वर्षों तक महासचिव रहे थे। नेहरू इस परिषद के अध्यक्ष थे। रियासती विषयों में वे नेहरू के निकटतम विश्वासपात्र साथी बन गये थे।[35] हीरालाल शास्त्री के स्वाधीनता से पूर्व जयपुर दरबार से अच्छे संबंध थे और 1942 के भारत छोड़ो आंदोलन के समय शास्त्री ने राज्य प्रशासन को सहयोग दिया जिससे जयपुर प्रजामंडल विभाजित हो गया।[36] हीरालाल शास्त्री ने इस आन्दोलन के काल में वनस्थली में शरण के लिये आने वाले आंदोलनकारियों के बारे में जयपुर के प्रधानमंत्री मिर्जा इस्माइल और ब्रिटिश सरकार को सूचित भी किया था।[37]

15 फरवरी, 1949 को दिल्ली में राजपूताना प्रांतीय कांग्रेस कमेटी की बैठक में गोकुल भाई भट्ट ने नेता पद के लिये हीरालाल शास्त्री के नाम का प्रस्ताव रखा और व्यास ने इसका समर्थन किया।[38] नेताओं में यह समझौता हुआ कि शास्त्री व व्यास मंत्रिमंडल में रहेंगे और भट्ट व वर्मा संगठन का कार्य देखेंगे।[39]

हीरालाल शास्त्री के नेता पद पर चयन की प्रांत भर में आलोचना हुई और कांग्रेसी सदस्यों को यह राय दी गई कि यदि वे चाहें तो अब भी सुधार कर सकते हैं।[40] दिल्ली में उदयपुर हाउस में प्रांत के कांग्रेस नेताओं की बैठक में राजधानी के लिये राय ली गई और इसमें अजमेर को सर्वाधिक मत मिले।[41] शास्त्री का विरोध उस समय और बढ़ गया जब 19 फरवरी 1949 को गवर्नर जनरल राजगोपालाचारी ने जयपुर में यह घोषणा की कि राजस्थान की राजधानी जयपुर ही होगी।[42] अन्य राज्यों में इस निर्णय पर बड़ा रोष था कि जयपुर ने सभी कुछ हथिया लिया है।[43] जयनारायण व्यास को आशा थी कि शास्त्री उनकी सलाह से कार्य करेंगे। 22 फरवरी को पत्रकार सम्मेलन में व्यास ने यह कहा कि हमें अपने को वृहत इकाई का नागरिक मानना है। उनके अनुसार अजमेर के राजस्थान में विलय के पश्चात ही राजधानी का स्थायी समाधान होगा।[44] राजपूताना कांग्रेस कमेटी के 43 सदस्यों ने अनिश्चय को दूर करने के लिये प्रदेश कांग्रेस की बैठक बुलाने की मांग की।[45]

28 व 29 मार्च को किशनगढ़ में यह बैठक हुई। इसमें अजमेर और राजधानी के प्रश्न पर बहुत विवाद हुआ। हीरालाल शास्त्री इस बैठक में मंत्रिमंडल गठन के लिये विश्वास मत प्राप्त नहीं कर सके और 8 मतों से पराजित हुए।[46] जयनारायण व्यास और माणिक्यलाल वर्मा के हस्तक्षेप से विरोधियों को चुप किया गया।[47] शास्त्री को मंत्रिमंडल गठन की अनुमति दी गई।[48]

30 मार्च को वृहत राजस्थान राज्य का उद्घाटन करते हुए सरदार पटेल ने यह अपील की कि प्रांत के लोगों को अब अपने-अपने राज्यों के बारे में न सोचकर सम्पूर्ण राजस्थान के बारे में सोचना चाहिये। कांग्रेसी कार्यकर्त्ताओं को उनकी सलाह थी कि उन्हें सत्ता की अपेक्षा सेवा के बारे में सोचना चाहिए, यदि वे सच्चे हैं तो उन्हें जबरदस्ती सत्ता सौंपी जायेगी।[49] उसी दिन हीरालाल शास्त्री को मुख्यमंत्री पद की शपथ दिलाई गई। अनेक कांग्रेसी नेताओं ने समारोह का बहिष्कार किया क्योंकि उनके बैठने की सम्मानजनक व्यवस्था नहीं थी।[50]

2 अप्रैल, 1949 को पटेल को लिखे पत्र में जयनारायण व्यास ने आरोप लगाया कि उन्होंने जयपुर के महाराजा को प्रसन्न करने के लिये कांग्रेसियों की आलोचना की है। व्यास ने यह भी लिखा कि पटेल, मेनन, बिड़ला या कृष्णामाचारी में से कोई राजधानी के बारे में महाराजा जयपुर को आश्वासन दे चुके हैं।[51]

शास्त्री, व्यास और वर्मा को मंत्री बनाने को तैयार थे लेकिन वे उन दोनों की सलाह को मानने को तैयार नहीं थे। व्यास व वर्मा के सहयोगियों को मंत्री नहीं बनाया गया। शास्त्री ने अपनी पसन्द के मंत्री लिये। जयपुर से सिद्धराज ढढ्ढा, उदयपुर से भूरेलाल बया व प्रेम नारायण माथुर, बीकानेर से रघुवरदयाल गोयल, जोधपुर से नरसिंह कच्छवाहा, फूलचंद बाफना व रावराजा हनवंत सिंह और कोटा से वेदपाल त्यागी को मंत्री पद की शपथ दिलाई गई। प्रसिद्ध नेता बाहर रखे गये। 15 मई, 1949 को मत्स्य संघ का राजस्थान में विलय होने पर शोभाराम को भी मंत्री बनाया गया।[52]

हीरालाल शास्त्री ने अपने मंत्रिमंडल में जोधपुर, बीकानेर और शेखावाटी, किसी भी क्षेत्र से किसी जाट नेता को नहीं लिया। अनुसूचित जाति और जनजाति से भी कोई मंत्री नहीं बनाया गया।[53] शास्त्री का तर्क था कि उन्हें यह अधिकार है कि वे अपनी पसन्द के व्यक्ति नियुक्त करें। उन्हें संदेह था कि कुछ लोगों को लेने पर वे भीतर से गड़बड़ी करेंगे।[54] जयपुर, जोधपुर, बीकानेर, उदयपुर और अन्य जिलों की कांग्रेस समितियों ने शास्त्री मंत्रिमंडल का विरोध किया।[55] 25 अप्रैल, 1949 को सरदार पटेल ने जयनारायण व्यास को चेतावनी दी कि वे उनकी गतिविधियों को देख रहे है और व्यास को शीघ्र यह समझ लेना चाहिये वे गलत रास्ते पर हैं।[56]

30 अप्रैल को जयपुर के कांग्रेसी नेता रामकरण जोशी ने अनेक सदस्यों के हस्ताक्षरयुक्त एक ज्ञापन प्रांतीय कांग्रेस के अध्यक्ष को दिया जिसमें प्रांतीय कमेटी की आपात बैठक बुलाने की मांग की गई जिसमें प्रांतीय कांग्रेस के अध्यक्ष गोकुलभाई भट्ट और हीरालाल शास्त्री मंत्रिमंडल के विरुद्ध अविश्वास पर चर्चा करने की मांग की गई।[57] बीकानेर के कांग्रेस जनों की सहानुभूति व्यास के साथ थी। इस संघर्ष में भट्ट के विरुद्ध अविश्वास प्रस्ताव पहला कदम था।[58] भट्ट द्वारा 21 दिन में बैठक न बुलाने पर जोशी ने बैठक बुलाई जो 9 जून 1949 को आयोजित हुई। इसमें प्रदेश कांग्रेस के 80 सदस्य उपस्थित थे। इसमें शेखावाटी के सरदार हरलाल सिंह चौधरी ने शास्त्री मंत्रिमंडल के विरुद्ध अविश्वास का प्रस्ताव रखा, मेवाड़ में माणिक्य लाल वर्मा के सहयोगी किशनलाल शर्मा ने इसका समर्थन किया। भट्ट के विरुद्ध अविश्वास का प्रस्ताव जयपुर के बंशीलाल लुहाड़िया ने रखा और माणिक्य लाल वर्मा के सहयोगी हरिदेव जोशी ने उसका समर्थन किया। ये दोनों प्रस्ताव बिना किसी विरोध के पारित हुए।[59]

11 जून को प्रांतीय कमेटी की बैठक में गोकुलभाई भट्ट ने अपना त्याग-पत्र दे दिया और कमेटी ने जयनारायण व्यास को नया अध्यक्ष चुन लिया। उसी दिन व्यास ने पटेल को एक तार भेजा-'आज राजस्थान कांग्रेस की विशेष बैठक में भट्ट के त्यागपत्र

को स्वीकार करके मुझे नया अध्यक्ष चुना गया है। कमेटी ने एक प्रस्ताव द्वारा शास्त्री मंत्रिमंडल से त्यागपत्र की मांग की है। 88 सदस्य इस प्रस्ताव के पक्ष में थे, एक ने विरोध किया, कुछ तटस्थ रहे, भट्ट व उनके साथी मतदान के समय चले गये।'[60]

12 जून को पटेल ने व्यास को तार दिया - 'भट्ट का त्यागपत्र और उनकी जगह आपका चयन स्थानीय कांग्रेस का मामला है जिससे मेरा कोई संबध नहीं। लेकिन मुख्यमंत्री के रूप में शास्त्री प्रांतीय कांग्रेस के प्रति उत्तरदायी नहीं हैं। प्रांतीय कांग्रेस विधानसभा का कार्य करने का दावा नहीं कर सकती। शास्त्री प्रांतीय कांग्रेस के आदेश के कारण मुख्यमंत्री नहीं है बल्कि मेरे द्वारा किये गये चयन के कारण हैं। चुनाव होने तक वे पद पर बने रहेंगे, यदि इसी बीच में वे हमारा विश्वास न खो दें। यह सब जानते हुए आपने जो अवांछनीय और हानिकारक रवैया धारण किया है, उसके परिणाम आपको भोगने होंगे।'[61]

जयनारायण व्यास ने अपनी कार्यकारिणी में विभिन्न क्षेत्रों के प्रसिद्ध नेताओं को लिया- उदयपुर से माणिक्यलाल वर्मा और मोहनलाल सुखाड़िया, बीकानेर से कुंभाराम आर्य, अलवर से मास्टर भोलानाथ, भरतपुर से आदित्येन्द्र, जयपुर से टीकाराम पालीवाल, डूंगरपुर से भोगीलाला पण्ड्या, झुंझुनू से चौधरी हरलाल सिंह, शाहपुरा से गोकुललाल असावा, जोधपुर से मीठालाल त्रिवेदी और कोटा से अभिन्न हरि।[62] प्रदेश समिति की आर्थिक स्थिति बहुत चिंताजनक थी। उस पर 11 हजार रुपये का कर्ज था और कार्यालय के नाम पर एक फटी-सटी चटाई व टूटी-फूटी टेबल थी। बीकानेर के कांग्रेसजनों ने व्यास का अभिनन्दन समारोह आयोजित कर 21 हजार रुपये की थैली भेंट की।[63] यह समारोह कुंभाराम आर्य के प्रयत्नों से मेरूदान सेठिया की बगीची में हुआ।[64]

पटेल का तार कांग्रेसजनों के विरोध को नहीं दबा सका। प्रदेश कार्य समिति ने पटेल के तार की शैली पर आपत्ति की और इसे जनतंत्रीय परम्पराओं के विरुद्ध बताया। कार्यसमिति ने यह स्पष्ट किया कि अखिल भारतीय कांग्रेस कमेटी के अध्यक्ष पट्टाभि सीतारामैया ने व्यास को भेजे अपने पत्र में यह माना कि प्रांतीय कमेटी सरकार के नेता के विरुद्ध प्रस्ताव पारित कर सकती है।[65] 16 जून को केन्द्रीय संचार मंत्री रफी अहमद किदवई ने पटेल को लिखे अपने पत्र में उनके द्वारा जयनारायण व्यास को भेजे गये तार पर आश्चर्य और दुःख प्रकट किया और कहा कि पूर्व अध्यक्ष राजेन्द्र बाबू और पट्टाभि अपने निर्देशों में बार-बार इस बात पर जोर दे चुके हैं कि कांग्रेस की सरकार और संगठन में सहयोग रखा जाए। जब मत्रिमंडल में ऐसे व्यक्ति लिये जायें जिनमें संगठन का विश्वास न हो तब यह कैसे संभव है?[66] 19 जून को अपने उत्तर में पटेल ने लिखा कि वे समझ नहीं सके है कि रफी को शिकायत क्या है? पटेल ने यह भी

स्पष्ट किया कि रियासती मंत्रालय को समझौते के अनुसार निर्देशन और नियंत्रण का अधिकार है।[67]

1 जुलाई को जयनारायण व्यास ने प्रांत के सभी कांग्रेसजनों से स्वागत समारोह आदि में मत्रियों का बहिष्कार करने की अपील की।[68] नवम्बर में प्रांतीय कांग्रेस कमेटी का अधिवेशन जोधपुर में हुआ जिसमें शास्त्री ने भाग नहीं लिया। सरदार पटेल इन सबसे बहुत नाराज हुए और उन्होंने जोधपुर राज्य के भूतपूर्व मंत्रियों जयनारायण व्यास, मथुरादास माथुर और द्वारकादास पुरोहित पर उनके कार्यकाल के समय भोजन व यातायात के झूठे बिल बनाने और कीमती कारों को खरीदने के बारे में मुकदमे चलाने के निर्देश दिये।[69]

दिसम्बर 1949 में राजस्थान के राजप्रमुख द्वारा एक अध्यादेश से विशेष अदालत नियुक्त की गई और इन नेताओं पर मुकदमे चलाये गये।[70] उदयपुर के भूतपूर्व मंत्रियों पर मुकदमे नहीं चले क्योंकि माणिक्यलाल वर्मा ने हरिभाऊ उपाध्याय को साथ लेकर सरदार पटेल को 50,000 रुपये का हिसाब देकर अपनी सफाई दे दी थी।[71] जनवरी, 1950 में भारतीय संविधान लागू हो जाने पर इन पूर्व मंत्रियों ने सर्वोच्च न्यायालय में अपील की जिससे मुकदमों को कार्यवाही रोक दी गई।[72] मुकदमों के साथ-साथ व्यास पर राज्य मंत्रिमण्डल में सम्मिलित होने का दबाव भी डाला जा रहा था। मुम्बई के सेठ गजाधर सोमानी के द्वारा घनश्याम दास बिड़ला ने व्यास को यह संदेश भेजा कि वे शास्त्री मंत्रिमंडल में सम्मिलित होने की स्वीकृति दें अन्यथा परिणाम बहुत भयंकर होंगे। व्यास का उत्तर था- 'मैं उनकी तस्वीर में फिट नहीं होता। मैं तो जमीन पर सोता हूँ।'[73]

अनेक व्यक्ति, जिनमें राष्ट्रपति डॉ. राजेन्द्र प्रसाद और वी. पी. मेनन भी थे, व्यास और उनके साथियों पर चलाये गये मुकदमे को ठीक नहीं मानते थे।[74] राजस्थान के जाट नेता इस संघर्ष में व्यास के साथ रहे। सरदार हरलाल सिंह कुछ साथियों के साथ व्यास को लेकर पटेल से मिले लेकिन पटेल ने क्रोध और आवेश में अपमानजनक व्यवहार किया। चौधरी हरलाल सिंह ने फिर प्रयत्न किया और माणिक्य लाल वर्मा और आदित्येन्द्र के साथ मिलकर पटेल को पत्र लिखा और उत्तर देने के लिये जयनारायण व्यास का दिल्ली का पता दिया जहाँ हरलाल सिंह ठहरे हुए थे। पटेल ने इस सबको व्यास के साथ मिलने के लिये बुलाया। व्यास जब जोधपुर से दिल्ली लौटे तो उन्हें पटेल का पत्र मिला और वे क्रोधित हो गये। हरलाल सिंह की काफी देर की मेहनत के पश्चात वे पटेल से मिलने गये। पटेल का रुख बदल चुका था। वे सभी संतुष्ट होकर लौटे।[75] दसरी ओर पटेल के निजी सचिव वी. शंकर से मथरादास माथर का सम्पर्क था। व्यास.

माथुर और द्वारकादास पुरोहित द्वारा आरोपों पर रियासती मंत्रालय को अपने जवाब दिये गये और सरकार ने मुकदमे वापिस लेने का निर्णय किया।[76]

इसी अवधि में जुलाई 1950 में आरोपों व प्रत्यारोपों के मध्य राजस्थान कांग्रेस कमेटी के सदस्यों का चुनाव हुआ जिसमें व्यास के समर्थकों ने 131 में से 103 स्थानों पर विजय प्राप्त की।[77] पटेल पर इसका प्रभाव पड़ा। सितम्बर 1950 में नासिक में कांग्रेस अध्यक्ष पद के लिये पटेल पुरुषोत्तम दास टंडन का समर्थन कर रहे थे जबकि नेहरू आचार्य कृपलानी के पक्ष में थे। पटेल की इच्छा थी कि व्यास का गुट टंडन का समर्थन करे। संघर्ष के काल में व्यास नेहरू से सहयोग की आशा कर रहे थे और राजस्थान के समाचार पत्रों में नेहरू द्वारा हस्तक्षेप करने के समाचार भी छपे। नेहरू ने व्यास को लिखे अपने पत्र में इन पर आपत्ति की और स्पष्ट कर दिया कि वे इस विवाद में नहीं पड़ना चाहते और इस तरह के प्रचार से व्यास राजस्थान व कांग्रेस को हानि पहुंचा रहे हैं।[78] इसी तरह शास्त्री को लिखे अपने पत्र में नेहरू ने राजस्थान के पत्रों में छपे समाचारों का उल्लेख करते हुए यह निर्देश दिया कि शास्त्री सार्वजनिक रूप से ऐसे अपयश वाले प्रचार से अपने को अलग करें।[79]

अब तक व्यास व उनके सहयोगी भी समझ चुके थे कि नेहरू उनकी सहायता नहीं करेंगे और उनके साथ रहने से वे घाटे में रहेंगे।[80] दूसरी ओर सरदार का भाव यह था कि वे स्थानीय स्थिति को समझ चुके हैं और राजस्थान को तो संभालना होगा।[81] व्यास की इच्छा थी कि आचार्य कृपलानी कांग्रेस अध्यक्ष बनें, लेकिन पटेल का यह आग्रह रहा कि व्यास उनको नेता मानें और उनका प्रत्यक्ष प्रमाण भी दिया जाए। पटेल गोकुल भाई भट्ट और शास्त्री को यह निर्देश दे चुके थे कि शास्त्री को त्यागपत्र देना है और व्यास के नेतृत्व में नये मंत्रिमंडल का गठन हो। हीरालाल शास्त्री भी त्यागपत्र देने को तैयार थे।[82] चुनाव में व्यास, वर्मा और उनके समर्थकों का भारी बहुमत टण्डन के पक्ष में गया और वही निर्णायक रहा।[83]

15 दिसम्बर, 1950 को पटेल का देहान्त हो गया। नेहरू ने हीरालाल शास्त्री को त्यागपत्र की सलाह दी। प्रदेश कांग्रेस में बहुमत नहीं होने के आधार पर शास्त्री ने त्यागपत्र दे दिया।[84] जनवरी 1951 में एक आई.सी.एस. अधिकारी वेंकटाचार को मुख्यमंत्री बनाया गया। राजस्थान सरकार ने पूर्व मंत्रियों पर चलाये गये मुकदमे वापिस ले लिये।[85] राजस्थान के कांग्रेसजन एक अधिकारी के मुख्यमंत्री बनने से संतुष्ट नहीं थे। रफी अहमद किदवई नेहरू के विश्वस्त सहयोगी थे। कुंभाराम आर्य, मथुरादास माथुर और मातादीन भगेलिया रफी से मिले और टण्डन के निर्वाचन के पश्चात उनकी गलतफहमी दूर करने का प्रयास किया। नेहरू को भी बताया गया कि जयनारायण व्यास उनसे क्यों

नाराज थे।[85] 26 अप्रैल 1951 को व्यास को मुख्यमंत्री पद की शपथ दिलाई गई।[87] व्यास मंत्रि-मंडल में उदयपुर से मोहनलाल सुखाड़िया व बलवंत सिंह मेहता, जयपुर से टीकाराम पालीवाल, बीकानेर से कुंभाराम आर्य, जोधपुर से मथुरादास माथुर, भरतपुर से युगलकिशोर चतुर्वेदी, झुंझुनू से नरोत्तमलाल जोशी और बूंदी से ब्रजसुंदर शर्मा मंत्री बनाये गये।[88] व्यास ने मुख्यमंत्री बनने के बाद प्रदेश कांग्रेस अध्यक्ष के पद से त्यागपत्र दे दिया। प्रांतीय कांग्रेस कमेटी ने सर्वसम्मति के माणिक्य लाल वर्मा को अध्यक्ष चुना।[89]

राजस्थान के एकीकरण के पश्चात् पुरानी रियासतों के कर्मचारियों में वरिष्ठता और पदस्थापना को लेकर भारी असंतोष था। व्यास मंत्रिमण्डल ने अधिक भू-राजस्व वाली जागीरें समाप्त करने का निर्णय किया था जो राष्ट्रपति के पास स्वीकृति के लिये भेजा गया था। इससे सामन्तवर्ग कांग्रेस के विरुद्ध हो गया। राज्य में 60 प्रतिशत भूमि जागीरदारों के पास थी जो मनचाहा लगान लेते थे। लाग-बाग और बेगार प्रथा के कारण किसानों का शोषण जारी था। राजस्थान क्षत्रिय महासभा सरकार को चुनौती दे रही थी। सरकार को केन्द्र से जागीर विधेयक की स्वीकृति प्रथम आम चुनाव तक नहीं मिली। कांग्रेस भी आंतरिक रूप से विभाजित थी, उसके नेताओं में क्षेत्रीयता की भावना थी।[90] व्यास मंत्रिमंडल में कुंवर जसवंत सिंह को राजपूतों के प्रतिनिधि के रूप में लिया गया था जो बीकानेर के महाराजा गंगासिंह के निजी सचिव और बाद में बीकानेर के प्रधानमंत्री रह चुके थे।[91]

प्रथम चुनाव से पूर्व कांग्रेस के नेताओं ने क्षत्रिय महासभा और राजस्थान किसान सभा (पूर्व में मारवाड़ किसान सभा) से चुनाव में गठबंधन की वार्ता की। मारवाड़ में जोधपुर के युवा महाराजा हनवंत सिंह अधिकांश सीटों पर चुनाव लड़कर अपनी शक्ति प्रदर्शित करना चाहते थे। हीरालाल शास्त्री ने किसान सभा के मंत्री नाथूराम मिर्धा को यह आश्वासन दिया कि यदि किसान सभा कांग्रेस के साथ न मिले और अलग चुनाव लड़े तो वे आर्थिक सहयोग करेंगे। प्रथम किश्त के रूप में मिर्धा को धनराशि भी दी गई। लेकिन मथुरादास माथुर के प्रयास से ब्यावर के समीप बर में जयनारायण व्यास, बलदेव राम मिर्धा (किसान सभा के अध्यक्ष), कुंभाराम आर्य, गोवर्धन चौधरी, लाल सिंह चौधरी और मथुरादास माथुर के बीच विस्तृत चर्चा के पश्चात मारवाड़ किसान सभा ने कांग्रेस में विलय करना मान लिया।[92]

हनवन्त सिंह ने सामन्तों का नेतृत्व किया और उनकी महत्त्वाकांक्षा से कांग्रेस को गंभीर चुनौती मिली। चुनाव में जयनारायण व्यास, बलदेवराम मिर्धा, द्वारकादास पुरोहित आदि पराजित हुए। मारवाड़ में कांग्रेस को 35 में से केवल 4 स्थान मिले।[93] इस चुनाव में चित्तौड़ में माणिक्यलाल वर्मा, सिरोही में गोकुल भाई भट्ट और प्रथम राजस्थान

यूनियन के प्रधानमंत्री गोकुल असावा भी पराजित हुए। चुनाव में 12 जाट विधायक निर्वाचित हुए जिनमें 9 कांग्रेस के थे। 160 के सदन में से 54 राजपूत जीते जिन में 51 सामन्तों के पक्षधर थे। कांग्रेस को विधानसभा में 82 स्थान प्राप्त हुए।[94]

टीकाराम पालीवाल अंतरिम काल के मुख्यमंत्री बनाये गये। इस मंत्रिमंडल में नाथू राम मिर्धा को मंत्री बनाया गया। मेवाड़ व मारवाड़ के कांग्रेसजनों के आग्रह से किशनगढ़ के विधायक से त्यागपत्र ले कर जयनारायण व्यास को वहां से उपचुनाव में विधायक बनाया गया। इस उपचुनाव में बीकानेर के कार्यकर्ताओं ने कुभाराम आर्य के नेतृत्व में स्वयं के खर्चे पर व्यास का प्रचार किया। चौधरी देवीलाल सहित अनेक नेताओं ने स्वामी केशवानंद से भी वहां प्रचार करने का आग्रह किया लेकिन वे व्यास की जीत के बारे में आश्वस्त थे क्योंकि गंगानगर के कार्यकर्ता पूरे उत्साह से वहाँ गये थे।[95]

1 नवम्बर, 1952 को जयनारायण व्यास पुनः मुख्यमंत्री बन गये। नाथूराम मिर्धा भी उनके साथ मंत्री बनाये गये। 1953 में क्षत्रिय महासभा की अपील पर नेहरू ने जागीर पुनर्ग्रहण विधेयक के विवाद में उत्तर प्रदेश के मुख्यमंत्री गोविन्द वल्लभ पंत को मध्यस्थ नियुक्त किया। पंत की मध्यस्थता से सरकार का जागीरदारों में समझौता हो गया। उस समय नेहरू ने कुछ राजपूत नेताओं को कांग्रेस में आने की सलाह दी। राजस्थान में यह सुझाव सर्वप्रथम माणिक्यलाल वर्मा ने दिया लेकिन पार्टी में व्यास के बढ़ते विरोध के कारण वे पीछे हट गये।[97] कांग्रेस दल में मतभेद बढ़ रहे थे। टीकाराम पालीवाल को उपनेता बनाये जाने का कुंभाराम विरोध कर रहे थे और पालीवाल गुट कुंभाराम और मथुरादास माथुर को मंत्री बनाने के पक्ष में नहीं था। जयनारायण व्यास की स्थिति पार्टी में मजबूत नहीं थी। उनके सहयोगी अपनी स्थिति को मजबूत बनाने में लगे हुए थे।[98] 14 अप्रैल, 1953 को टीकाराम पालीवाल, नाथूराम मिर्धा और रामकिशोर व्यास ने मंत्री पद से त्यागपत्र दे दिये। उसी दिन जयनारायण व्यास ने कुंभाराम आर्य को मंत्री बना दिया। आठ माह पश्चात टीकाराम पालीवाल पुनः मंत्री बनाये गये। पार्टी के विधायकों में असंतोष था और वे अनुशासन का पालन नहीं कर रहे थे। मंत्रियों और वरिष्ठ नेताओं में मतभेद बढ़ रहे थे। जयपुर क्षेत्र में रामकरण जोशी और हरलाल सिंह पालीवाल से नाराज थे। जोधपुर क्षेत्र से मथुरादास माथुर व द्वारकादास पुरोहित में मंत्री बनने की होड़ थी। माणिक्यलाल वर्मा नियुक्तियों, स्थानान्तरण, उद्योगधंधों के विकास में मंत्रियों को अधिक अधिकार देने के पक्ष में थे और यह चाहते थे कि व्यास संगठन की सलाह मानें। जबकि व्यास शासन में हस्तक्षेप नहीं चाहते थे।[99]

फरवरी, 1954 में क्षत्रिय महासभा की कार्यसमिति ने यह घोषणा की कि संगठन के सदस्य अपनी पसन्द के किसी भी राजनीतिक दल में सम्मिलित हो सकते हैं।[100] इसी

माह के अंत में 43 जागीरदारों ने, जिनमें 25 विधायक भी थे, एक संयुक्त वक्तव्य में सभी राजस्थानवासियों से कांग्रेस को सहयोग देने की अपील की।[101] 14 अप्रैल, 1954 को व्यास ने कार्यसमिति की बैठक में 23 जागीरदारों द्वारा जागीरें समर्पित करने के प्रस्ताव की सूचना दी जिसे स्वीकृत कर लिया गया।[102]

कुंभाराम आर्य राजपूत जागीरदारों के कांग्रेस में प्रवेश के विरुद्ध थे। उन्होंने यह धमकी भी दी कि जाट कांग्रेस छोड़ सकते हैं। नेहरू के हस्तक्षेप से उन्हें समझाया गया। जाट व्यास मंत्रिमंडल के सदस्य रामकरण जोशी से भी नाराज थे।[103] व्यास विरोधी गुट को यह भय था कि पार्टी में शक्ति बढ़ने से व्यास उनकी उपेक्षा करेंगे। माणिक्यलाल वर्मा, मोहनलाल सुखाड़िया, कुंभाराम और मथुरादास माथुर का यह आरोप था कि जागीरदारों से समझौता कर व्यास अपनी सत्ता बनाये रखना चाहते हैं, इसीलिये पाँच हजार से कम आय की जागीरें अभी समाप्त नहीं करना चाहते। प्रान्तीय कांग्रेस कमेटी की बैठक में व्यास को चुनौती देते हुए वर्मा ने कहा-'आज से आपकी हुकुमत के विरुद्ध विद्रोह करता हूँ। आप भी शास्त्री के रास्ते पर जा रहे हैं, आपका नेतृत्व कांग्रेस की हथेलियों पर है।' व्यास का उत्तर था - 'मैं मुख्यमंत्री हूँ, मैं धमकियों से नहीं डरता और किसी के झुकाने से नहीं झुक सकता।'[104] व्यास बैठक से चले गये।

कुंभाराम आर्य ने कांग्रेस विधायक दल की बैठक बुलाने और उसमें व्यास द्वारा विश्वास प्रस्ताव पारित कराने की मांग की। सुखाड़िया समर्थकों ने भी नेहरू को एक ज्ञापन भेजा।[105] व्यास के विरोध में कुंभाराम, चौधरी हरलाल सिंह, मथुरादास माथुर आदि ने सुखाड़िया को नेता बनाने का निश्चय किया। नेहरू कांग्रेस विधायक दल के नेतृत्व में परिवर्तन के पक्ष में नहीं थे। उनकी राय थी कि व्यास मंत्रिमंडल का पुनर्गठन कर विरोधियों की जगह अपनी पसन्द के व्यक्ति लें और फिर विश्वास मत प्राप्त करें। अखिल भारतीय कांग्रेस कमेटी के महामंत्री बलवंत राय मेहता और लालबहादुर शास्त्री जयपुर आये और सभी को समझाने के प्रयास किये लेकिन असफल रहे। रफी अहमद किदवई ने भी व्यास को समझाने की चेष्टा की लेकिन व्यास प्रस्ताव लेने की बात पर अड़े रहे।[106]

24 अक्तूबर, 1954 को रफी अहमद किदवई के देहान्त से व्यास की स्थिति कमजोर हुई। मतदान से दो दिनपूर्व माथुर का व्यास से यह प्रस्ताव था कि वे यथास्थिति बनाये रखें और सुखाड़िया, कुंभाराम व माथुर को बुला कर उन्हें आश्वस्त कर दें। लेकिन व्यास को यह विश्वास था कि वे संघर्ष में सफल होंगे।[107]

इस विश्वास मत को प्राप्त करने के लिये व्यास कोई सौदेबाजी करने के लिये तैयार नहीं थे। विधायकों को धनराशि देने का प्रस्ताव भी उन्होंने ठुकरा दिया। जयपुर के

विधायक उन्हें समर्थन देने को तैयार थे, यदि वे रामकरण जोशी को मंत्रिमंडल में न रखें। जोशी स्वयं हटने को तैयार थे, लेकिन व्यास नहीं माने।[108] सुखाड़िया और माथुर के प्रयास से कुछ राजपूत विधायक भी उनके साथ हो गये।[109]

13 नवम्बर, 1954 को विधायक दल की बैठक में व्यास अपने विरोधी सुखाड़िया से 8 मतों से पराजित हुए। परिणाम के पश्चात व्यास बैठक से अन्य मित्रों के साथ चले गये जबकि सुखाड़िया, कुंभाराम और माथुर वहीं बैठे रहे, उनकी आँखों से आंसू टपक रहे थे। वहाँ से तीनों वर्मा के निवास पर गये और उन्हें साथ लेकर व्यास के घर पहुँच कर उनके चरण स्पर्श किये ओर क्षमायाचना करते हुए कहा कि उनका स्थान कांग्रेस पार्टी के नेता से कहीं अधिक है। जो कुछ हुआ उसे हम सब भुला दें। वे और वर्मा उनका मार्गदर्शन करें। व्यास की प्रतिक्रिया सहज नहीं थी, उनकी आंखे क्रोध से भरी थी।[110]

त्यागपत्र के पश्चात् व्यास ने एक वक्तव्य में अपने बारे में फैली गलत फहमियां दूर करने के लिये यह स्पष्ट किया कि 'जागीरदारों को विधान सभा कांग्रेस दल में शामिल करने के लिये अखिल भारतीय कांग्रेस के महामंत्री, प्रांतीय कांग्रेस के अध्यक्ष आदित्येन्द्र व माणिक्यलाल वर्मा ने चेष्टा की थी। मैंने केवल इस प्रयत्न का स्वागत किया था। मैं आपसी विचार-विमर्श और शांतिपूर्ण तरीके से सामन्तशाही को समाप्त करना चाहता था।'[111]

कुंभाराम आर्य के अनुसार व्यास एक हठयोगी थे। वे अपनी बात और हठ के धनी रहे। स्थितियां बदल गई, पर वे नहीं बदले। शासन में रहते हुए इसी स्वभाव का उन्होंने परिचय दिया और अन्त में उससे अलग हो गये, झुके नहीं।[112] ठाकुर देशराज के अनुसार 'व्यास में बहुत से गुण थे, किंतु कुछ कमियां भी थी। उन्हें आदमी की परख बहुत कम थी। दूसरे उनमें बांस जैसी लचक नहीं थी, फरास जैसी कड़क थी।'[113] रामनिवास मिर्धा, जिन्हें राजनीति में लाने में व्यास की भूमिका भी थी और नाथूराम मिर्धा, उनकी ईमानदारी, सैद्धान्तिक निष्ठा और कार्यकर्त्ताओं के प्रति स्नेहमय व्यवहार के प्रशंसक थे।[114]

वर्षों से पीड़ित और शोषित किसान वर्ग के प्रतिनिधियों के रूप में जाट नेताओं ने राजनीति में जो महत्त्व प्राप्त किया था, जागीरदारों के कांग्रेस में प्रवेश के कारण वे उसे समाप्त करने को तैयार नहीं थे। अतः राजस्थान में एक नयी पीढ़ी को सत्ता प्राप्त हुई।

## संदर्भ

1. वी. पी. मेनन : *द स्टोरी ऑफ द इंटीग्रेशन आफ इंडियन स्टेट्स*, पृ. 115-18

2. *उपरोक्त*, पृ. 239
3. एफ. के. कपिल का लेख, राजस्थान के निर्माण पर नेतृत्व संघर्ष, राजस्थान इतिहास कांग्रेस, पाली, पृ. 65 (1974)
4. रिचर्ड सिसन : द *कांग्रेस पार्टी इन राजस्थान*, पृ. 107-108
5. मेनन : *पूर्वोक्त*, पृ. 243-45
6. *उपरोक्त*, पृ. 259
7. हीरालाल शास्त्री : *प्रत्यक्ष शास्त्र*, पृ. 75
8. द *जोधपुर गवर्नमेंट गजट*, 3 मार्च 1943, वाल्यूम 83, नं. 43
9. *रियासती*, 23 मार्च 1948, पृ. 4
10. सिसन : *उपरोक्त*, पृ. 97-98
11. के. एल. कमल : *पार्टी पॉलिटिक्स इन इण्डियन स्टेट्स*, पृ. 38
12. मथुरादास माथुर : एस.एन. मनचंदा से 24.10.1982 को भेंटवार्ता, नेहरू मेमोरियल म्यूजियम एवं पुस्तकालय, नई दिल्ली, पृ. 153
13. (i) पृथ्वीसिंह मेहता : *हमारा राजस्थान*, पृ. 509 (ii) शास्त्री : पूर्वोक्त, पृ. 75
14. मेहता : *पूर्वोक्त*, पृ. 500
15. मामराज सिंह जैन : *आधुनिक राजस्थान का इतिहास*, पृ. 281-82
16. सिसन : *पूर्वोक्त*, पृ. 24
17. *राजस्थान-मध्यभारत जागीर इन्क्वायरी कमेटी की रिपोर्ट*, गवर्नमेंट प्रेस 1950
18. जैन : *पूर्वोक्त*, पृ. 285
19. सिसन : *पूर्वोक्त*, पृ. 27
20. पेमाराम : *राजस्थान के जाटों का इतिहास*, पृ. 255-84
21. मेनन : *पूर्वोक्त*
22. दुर्गादास (सं.) : *सरदार पटेल कॉरसपोन्डेस*, खण्ड 8, पृ. 504
23. राजेन्द्रलाल हांडा : *जयनारायण व्यास कामेमोरेशन वॉल्यूम*, पृ. 79
24. मेनन : *पूर्वोक्त*, पृ. 251
25. पटेल : *कॉरसपोन्डेस*, खण्ड 7, पृ. 440-41
26. पटेल : *कॉरसपोन्डेस*, खण्ड 7, पृ. 430, 435, 441

27. मेनन : *पूर्वोक्त*, पृ. 253
28. माइकल वेनर : *स्टेट पॉलिटिक्स इन इण्डिया*, पृ. 345
29. सिसन : *पूर्वोक्त*, पृ. 116
30. कमल : *पूर्वोक्त*, पृ. 52
31. रामनिवास जाजू : *मरूभूमि का वह मेघ*, पृ. 151, 154 व 170
32. (i) कमल : *पूर्वोक्त*, पृ. 52ए (ii) शंकर सहाय सक्सेना : *जो देश के लिये जिये*, पृ. 169-70
33. सत्यदेव विद्यालंकार (सं) : 'धुन के धनी', ब्रजलाल बियानी का लेख (संस्मरण), पृ. 164
34. वेनर : *पूर्वोक्त*, पृ. 332
35. विद्यालंकार : गोकुल भाई भट्ट का लेख, पृ. 151
36. सिंसन : *पूर्वोक्त*, पृ. 116
37. माथुर : *पूर्वोक्त*, पृ. 160
38. कमल : *पूर्वोक्त*, पृ. 52
39. शास्त्री : *पूर्वोक्त*, पृ. 76
40. *रियासती*, 18 फरवरी, 1949, *नव राजस्थान*, 23 फरवरी, 1949, पृ. 160
41. माथुर : *पूर्वोक्त*, पृ. 158
42. *प्रजा सेवक साप्ताहिक*, 25 फरवरी, 1949
43. शास्त्री : *पूर्वोक्त*, पृ. 77
44. *प्रजासेवक* : 25 फरवरी, 1949
45. *उपरोक्त* : 9 मार्च, 1949
46. सिसन : *पूर्वोक्त*, पृ. 116
47. माथुर : *पूर्वोक्त*, पृ. 158
48. शास्त्री : *पूर्वोक्त*, पृ. 76
49. *स्पीचेज ऑफ सरदार पटेल*, सूचना मंत्रालय, भारत सरकार, पृ. 43
50. *शास्त्री : पूर्वोक्त*
51. *सरदार पटेल कोरेसपोंडेंस*, खंड 8, पृ. 503
52. कमल : *पूर्वोक्त*, पृ. 53

53. *उपरोक्त*, पृ. 53
54. शास्त्री : पृ. 53
55. कमल : *पूर्वोक्त*, पृ. 53
56. सरदार पटेल : *कोरेसपोन्डेस*, खण्ड 8, पृ. 505
57. सिसन : *पूर्वोक्त*, पृ. 117
58. विद्यालंकार : *उपरोक्त*, कुम्भाराम आर्य का लेख, पृ. 194
59. प्रांतीय कांग्रेस कमेटी 9 जून की बैठक की कार्यवाही का विवरण, सिसन : पूर्वोक्त से उद्धृत, पृ. 117
60. *सरदार पटेल कोरेसपोन्डेस*, खण्ड 8, पृ. 556
61. *उपरोक्त*, पृ. 557
62. *प्रजा सेवक* (साप्ताहिक), 22 जून, 1949
63. विद्यालंकार : *पूर्वोक्त*, चौधरी कुभाराम आर्य का संस्मरण, पृ. 194
64. *उपरोक्त*, स्वामी केशवानंद का संस्मरण, पृ. 174
65. *अमर ज्योति* (साप्ताहिक), 12 जून, 1949
66. रफी का पत्र दि. 16 जून, 1949, *पटेल कोरेसपोन्डेंस*, खण्ड 8, पृ. 558
67. पटेल का पत्र दि. 19 जून, 1949, *उपरोक्त*, खण्ड 8, पृ. 559
68. पटेल का पत्र दि. 19 जून, 1949, *उपरोक्त*, खण्ड 8, पृ. 565
69. शास्त्री : *पूर्वोक्त*, पृ. 79
70. *राजस्थान लॉ वीकली*, 1951, पृ. 206
71. *प्रजा सेवक*, 8 फरवरी, 1950
72. *राजस्थान लॉ वीकली*, 1951 पृ. 206
73. विद्यालंकार : *पूर्वोक्त*, सीताराम मिश्र का लेख, पृ. 297
74. पटेल : *कॉरेसपोन्डेंस*, खण्ड 9. पृ. 457
75. विद्यालंकार : *पूर्वोक्त*, सरदार हरलाल सिंह चौधरी का लेख. पृ. 456
76. माथुर : *पूर्वोक्त*, पृ. 168-78
77. विद्यालंकार : *पूर्वोक्त*, सीताराम मिश्र का लेख, पृ. 298
78. नेहरू का व्यास को पत्र दि. 16 जुलाई, 1949, शास्त्री : *उपरोक्त*, पृ. 333

79. नेहरू का शास्त्री को पत्र दि. 28 जुलाई, 1949, *उपरोक्त*, पृ. 333

80. *प्रेरणा* (साप्ताहिक), जोधपुर दि. 22 मार्च, 1969

81. विद्यालंकार : *पूर्वोक्त*, सरदार हरलाल सिंह का लेख, पृ . 456

82. (i) *प्रजा सेवक*; दि. 23 अगस्त, 1950 (ii) माथुर : *पूर्वोक्त*, पृ. 176

83. *उपरोक्त*

84. शास्त्री : *पूर्वोक्त*, पृ. 82, 256

85. *राजस्थान लॉ वीकली*, 1951 पृ. 206

86. *प्रेरणा*, 22 मार्च, 1969, मातादीन भगेरिया का लेख, पृ. 12

87. भंडारी : *पूर्वोक्त*, पृ. 36

88. *उपरोक्त*, पृ. 40

89. *उपरोक्त*, पृ. 41

90. *उपरोक्त*, पृ. 47-49

91. सिसन : *पूर्वोक्त*, पृ. 138

92. माथुर : *पूर्वोक्त*, पृ. 185

93. (i) माथुर : *उपरोक्त*, पृ. 190 (ii) नत्थन सिंह : (सं.) *राजस्थान के किसान गांधी : नाथूराम मिर्धा*, ज्ञान प्रकाश पिलानिया का लेख, पृ. 52-54

94. भंडारी : *उपरोक्त*, पृ. 52-54

95. विद्यालंकार : *उपरोक्त* (i) कुम्भाराम आर्य का लेख, पृ. 194 (ii) स्वामी केशवानंद का लेख, पृ. 174

96. सिसन : *पूर्वोक्त*, पृ. 139

97. *उपरोक्त*, पृ. 140

98. कमल : *पूर्वोक्त*, पृ. 57-58

99. शंकर सहाय सक्सेना : *जो देश के लिए*, पृ. 194-200

100. *हिन्दुस्तान टाइम्स*, 11 फरवरी, 1954

101. *उपरोक्त*, 27 फरवरी, 1954

102. सक्सेना : *पूर्वोक्त*, पृ. 198-99

103. कमल : *पूर्वोक्त*, पृ. 60

104. विद्यालंकार : *उपरोक्त,* नागर का लेख, पृ. 94-96

105. कमल : *पूर्वोक्त,* पृ. 61

106. सक्सेना : *पूर्वोक्त,* पृ. 202-203

107. माथुर : *पूर्वोक्त,* पृ. 220-22

108. विद्यालंकार : (i) कृष्णगोपाल गर्ग का लेख, पृ. 212-13, (ii) काशीराम गुप्ता का लेख, पृ. 201

109. विद्यालंकार : *उपरोक्त* (i) खेतसिंह राठौड़ का लेख, पृ. 257, (ii) मदन गोपाल काबरा : *मेरी भूली बिसरी यादें,* पृ. 101

110. माथुर : *उपरोक्त,* पृ. 223-24

111. प्रजासेवक : 17 नवम्बर, 1954, पृ. 11

112. विद्यालंकार : कुंभाराम आर्य का लेख, पृ. 192

113. *उपरोक्त,* देशराज का लेख, पृ. 181

114. *उपरोक्त,* रामनिवास मिर्धा और नाथूराम मिर्धा के लेख, पृ. 146 और पृ. 158

30

# बुन्देलखण्ड के जटवारा भूभाग के कुछ गाँवों का सामाजिक एवं आर्थिक जीवन

डॉ. रामस्वरूप ढेंगुला

बुन्देलखण्ड प्रदेश इतिहास काल में देश के मध्य में स्थित भूभाग को कहते थे। इस प्रदेश की पश्चिमी सीमा पर बुन्देला ठाकुरों का दतिया राज्य स्थित था। दतिया राज्य के उत्तर की ओर इन्दरगढ़ (दतिया जिला) से लेकर गोहद (भिन्ड जिले की तहसील) एवं पश्चिमी की ओर पिछोर (ग्वालियर जिला) के भागों को जटवारा भूभाग के रूप में चिन्हित किया जाता है। यह वह भूभाग था, जिसके अनेक गांव जाट कृषकों एवं जाट सामंतों द्वारा बसाए गये थे। इन भूभागों में अनेक गढ़ियाँ जाट सामंतों-जागीरदारों की बनवाई हुई आज भी अवशेष के रूप में देखी जा सकती हैं। भरतपुर, आगरा, मथुरा, गोहद आदि क्षेत्रों से आकर जाटों ने दतिया जिले के इन्दरगढ़ के आसपास के क्षेत्रों में अपनी राजनैतिक शक्ति को स्थिर किया था और वे सामंत, कृषक-जमीदार के रूप में कृषि के विस्तार एवं सामाजिक स्वरूप में बुन्देली संस्कृति को अपनाकर, उस भूभाग में आम नागरिक के रूप में रम गये थे।[1] इस क्षेत्र में एक प्रसिद्ध कहावत है-

अनपढ़ जाट पढ़ा जैसा और पढ़ा जाट खुदा जैसा।

यह ''जटवारी'' अर्थात् जाट क्षेत्र में प्रचलित बोली-भाव का उदाहरण है, जो इस क्षेत्र में जाट समाज की प्रकृति-स्वभाव को रेखांकित करता है। इसी परिवेश के बीच जाट समाज ने अपना मुकाम बनाकर अपने जीवन को समृद्धस्वरूप में ढालकर, इस क्षेत्र में स्थाई आसन ग्रहण किया था।

अकबरकालीन प्रशासनिक व्यवस्था में, आगरा सूबे की पवाया सरकार के महाल रतनगढ़ के अंतर्गत केवल जाट-समाज की उपस्थिति बताई गई है। *आईने-अकबरी*

के अनुसार इस महाल के दुर्ग में 200 अश्वारोही और 4000 पैदल सैनिक रहते थे, संभवतः इस सेना के अधिकांश सैनिक जाट रहे होंगे या इस क्षेत्र में जाट कृषक अधिक रहे होंगे, यह दो ही संभावनायें यहां देखी जा सकती हैं।

वर्तमान जटवारा क्षेत्र का समस्त भूभाग इन्दरगढ़ सहित रतनगढ़ और सोहंदी अर्थात सेंवढ़ा महाल के अंतर्गत आ जाता था। रतनगढ़ व सेंवढ़ा दोनों ही सिंध नदी के समीपवर्ती और करीब-करीब के स्थान हैं। वर्तमान में इंदरगढ़ परिक्षेत्र, दतिया जिले की इसी सेंवढ़ा तहसील का भाग है। इसी पवाया सरकार के महाल करईया (ग्वालियर जिले की डबरा-भितरवार तहसील में) और कंद एवं कांद (शिवपुरी जिले) में जाटों की उपस्थिति बताई गई है। जाटों की यह उपस्थिति सैनिक एवं कृषक-जागीरदार दोनों रूप में हो सकती है।[2] मुगलकाल में उक्त क्षेत्रों में जंगलों व हिंसक जानवरों की भरमार थी। वनभूमि को कृषिभूमि में परिवर्तित करने की समस्या लगातार इस काल में बनी रही थी। माना जाता है कि इंदरगढ़ परिक्षेत्र पर सन 1758 ई. तक जाटों का राज्य था और उस समय इस स्थान का नाम दद्रगांव था। इंदरगढ़ की यात्रा के समय वहां के जाट समाज से जानकारी मिली कि इंदरगढ़ पर राज्य करने वाले जाट लोग दांदर गोत्र के थे। अतः इस स्थान का नाम दद्रगांव पड़ा था। इन्दरगढ़ से पश्चिम दिशा में तीन किलोमीटर के करीब खड़ऊआ गांव है, माना जाता है कि इस गांव की सत्रहवीं सदी की बावड़ी के समीप एक मंदिर में भरतपुर-डींग के शासक बदनसिंह जाट (1723-1756) की मूर्ति बनी हुई है। यह मूर्ति बैठी अवस्था में है और यह मंदिर सत्रहवीं सदी के मध्य का बना प्रतीत होता है खड़ऊआ की बावड़ी ओरछा के इतिहास प्रसिद्ध लोकनायक हरदौल बुन्देला (मृत्यु 1632-33) की बहन कुंजावती के समय में बनी थीं, इस बावड़ी में कुंजावती की मूर्ति भी बनी हुई है। आज इन सब स्थानों की पूजा पूरे श्रद्धाभाव से की जाती है। उल्लेखनीय है कि बदनसिंह जाट ने जाट राज्य की स्थापना की नींव रखी थी और इतिहास प्रसिद्ध सूरजमल जाट (1756-1763) उसका यशस्वी, प्रतापी पुत्र था। बदनसिंह जाट के मंदिर की पूजा इस अंचल की जनता पूरे आदरभाव के साथ करती है और यहां गोटों के गायन (अर्थात् लोकगीतों का) का आयोजन भी होता है।[3]

**सामाजिक एवं आर्थिक जीवन :**

इन्दरगढ़-भाण्डेर मार्ग पर सोन (मृगा) नदी के पार बसा भलका ग्राम जाटों का एक बड़ा स्थान है। भलका के जाट राजस्थान भरतपुर सिनसिनी[4] (जाटों के प्रसिद्ध स्थान) से पहले ग्वालियर जिले की डबरा तहसील के चीनोर के पास भोली गांव, फिर बाद में यहां आकर बसे थे। इस गांव के 80 वर्षीय कम्मोदसिंह ने बताया कि हमारे पूर्वज बताते थे कि मुगलों के आतंक से तमाम परिवार इन क्षेत्रों में आकर रहने लगे थे। यह भलका ग्राम

भांडेर तहसील का गांव है, यह स्थान अभी कुछ ही वर्ष पूर्व ग्वालियर जिले से दतिया जिले में शामिल हुआ है। भलका से तात्पर्य ताड़ के वृक्ष से माना जाता है, बताया जाता है इस गांव के बसने के पूर्व यहां ताड़ के वृक्ष बहुत थे, अतः उसका नाम यहां आकर बसे जाटों ने भलका रखा और यहां के जंगलों को साफ कर यहां खेती करना प्रारंभ किया। यहां की मिट्टी उपजाऊ और काली है और यहां की जमीन में कुआँ बनाने पर पानी शीघ्र ही निकल आता है। वर्तमान में तो यहां नहर भी है और सोन नदी समीप ही होने के कारण यहां बोरिंग बहुत सफल है। पहले इस क्षेत्र में ज्वार, मूंग, अरहर, रोंसा आदि फसलें अधिक हुआ करती थी। पर अब पिछले लगभग चालीस साल से पानी की अच्छी उपलब्धता के कारण यहां के जाट कृषक धान की भरपूर फसल उत्पन्न कर रहे हैं। इस कारण जाट कृषकों की आमदनी बढ़ गई है और उन्होंने इन्दरगढ़, दतिया शहर एवं ग्वालियर नगर में मकान बनवा लिये हैं। यह परिवर्तन पिछले 70-80 साल से लगातार जारी है। यह जाट कृषकों की मेहनत का फल है, जो इस क्षेत्र में जाटों के बसने से हुआ है। इस क्षेत्र में जाटों के प्रमुख कृषि-स्पर्धी गुर्जर लोग हैं, दोनों के बीच आपसी सद्भाव और प्रेमभाव देखने को मिलता है। इस क्षेत्र में प्रचलित लोकदेवत्व की पूजा को दोनों लोग समानरूप से मान्यता प्रदान करते हैं। इस क्षेत्र के लोक देवताओं में हरदौल बाबा, कुंअरबाबा, ठाकुरबाबा आदि की पूजा प्रचलित है। जाट समाज के लोग अपने पूर्वजों के चबूतरों को पूजते हैं, और शादी-विवाह के अवसर पर उन चबूतरों पर जाकर आदरभाव प्रकट करते हैं। इस समय दतिया जिले में जाटों के भलका, अहरौनी, कर्रा, नौगंवा, मलऊआ, सेंथरी, रिछोरा, पहाड़ी रावत, पिपरौआ, थरेट (कस्बा) कुदारी, जरौली, बरा, पचेरा, पचोखरा, कुलैथ, खड़ऊआ, इन्दरगढ़ (कस्बा) आदि गांव है। सेवढ़ा के पार गोहद की ओर एवं उचाड के उस पार ग्वालियर की ओर जटवारे भूभाग के अन्य स्थान भी हैं। भरौली-भड़ौल, इंदरगढ़ के समीपवर्ती स्थानों में जाटों के बनवाये दुर्ग भी देखे जा सकते हैं। अठारहवीं सदी में जाटों और बुन्देलों के बीच सत्ताई जंग छिड़ी थी, जिसमें गूजरों के सहयोग से बुन्देलों को सफलता मिली थी। बाद में जाट लोग सामंत और बड़े-बड़े कृषक-जमींदार के रूप में इन क्षेत्रों में अपनी उपस्थिति प्रदर्शित करते रहे थे।[5] इन क्षेत्रों में गेंहू-चना, मटर, गन्ना आदि की फसलें एवं दूध का उत्पादन भरपूर होता है। इस क्षेत्र का जाट कृषक महनती है, और जाटों ने कृषि-व्यापार के मामले में भी अब उल्लेखनीय प्रगति की है।

सामाजिक-आर्थिक जीवन की पड़ताल के लिए इस क्षेत्र के जितने भी जाट परिवारों से संपर्क किया, सभी का कहना है कि वे इन क्षेत्रों में आगरा, भरतपुर, मथुरा, गोहद, धौलपुर आदि क्षेत्रों से आए थे। कुंतीबाई नामक 92 वर्षीय बुजुर्ग जाट महिला, जो मूलरूप से धमूरी गांव, तहसील गोहद, जिला भिण्ड की रहने वाली हैं, उसने

समकालीन सामाजिक व्यवस्था में पर्दा प्रथा की चर्चा उठने पर कहा, "बहुत लंबा घूंघट काढ़कर घर में आए, घर का दरवाजा तक नहीं देखा था, मानस (पुरुष) के सामने बात तक नहीं कर सकते थे, अब तो लड़कियां मानसों पर चढ़ी जाती हैं।" यह 20वीं सदी की जाट महिलाओं के सामाजिक जीवन की इस जटवारा भूभाग की कथा है। भलका गांव के युवा कुलदीपसिंह जाट की पत्नी गुड्डो भरतपुर के पास के किसी गांव की रहने वाली हैं, बहुत मनाने पर भी सामने आकर बात करने से कतराती रहीं। परन्तु उन्होंने लिखकर एक लोकगीत की पंक्ति भेजीं जिनमें भरतपुर का नाम आता है-

अबकी जान बचा मेरे अल्ला भरतपुर वाले से,<br>
गोली धीरे से चलाइयो बदनसिंह...<br>
बाहर आई-गई मेवन की फौज तोप चली बन्दूक चली,<br>
चलें फर्सा, चलें कटारें।<br>
गोली धीरे-धीरे से चलाइयो बदनसिंह राजा।

उल्लेखनीय है कि बदनसिंह (1723-1756) ने डीग-भरतपुर आदि क्षेत्रों में जाटों के राज्य की नींव रखी थी और भरतपुर सीमा क्षेत्र के उत्तरी भाग के शक्तिशाली मेवों को पराजित कर, उन पर नियंत्रण स्थापित कर लिया था। इस प्रकार के लोकगीत जटवारा क्षेत्र के गांव में अभी भी प्रचलित हैं, जो जाटों की सामाजिक लोक-संस्कृति के बुन्देलखण्ड भूभाग में फैलाव और प्रसार के स्पष्ट संकेत हैं।[6] इस क्षेत्र के जाट-परिवारों में लड़की की शादी के अवसर पर जो मांगलिक गीत गाये जाते हैं, इनको ''लाड़ी'' कहते हैं, इस शब्द का अर्थ बेटी से होता है। जो लाड़ी बुजुर्ग कुन्तीबाई जाट महिला ने सुनाई थी, वही गीत एक बुन्देला सामंत परिवार की बुजुर्ग महिला ने भी सुनाया था। इस मांगलिक गीत के बोल इस प्रकार हैं-

कोट नवें, परवत नवें, शहरा नवाये न जावें<br>
माथो आजुलजू कौ, जब नवें, जब साजन आवें।

... ... ... ...

ऊंचे अटा चढ़ देखें, आजुल राजा, कितनी आई बरात<br>
भलें एक लख हथिया, सवा लख घुड़ला, पैदल ओड़ न छोड़।

लोक विभाजित नहीं होता, वह तो परम्पराओं का आत्मीयता का और आनंद का सम्वाहक होता है। शादी-विवाह, समारोह-उत्सव ये सब गांवों में, संपूर्ण गावों की लोक संस्कृति का नेतृत्व करते दिखाई देते हैं।[7]

बुन्देलखण्ड के भूभागों में एवं ग्वालियर राज्य के भूभागों में स्थित जटवारा क्षेत्र पूरी तरह ब्रज संस्कृति से ओतप्रोत और प्रभावित रहा है। इन भूभागों के निवासी जाट कृषक भी ब्रज क्षेत्रों से यहां आकर बसे थे। ये सब लोग भी कृष्ण भक्ति की विचारधारा लेकर आए थे। इन्दरगढ़, भलका, खड़ऊआ आदि जटवारा क्षेत्र के गांवों में कृष्णभक्त विचारधारा का प्रवाह स्पष्ट रूप से देखा जा सकता है। दतिया शहर को ''लघु वृन्दावन'' की संज्ञा दी जाती है, बुन्देली सांस्कृतिक विरासत और जाट समुदाय की विरासत मिलेजुले स्वरूप में इन भूभागों में उपस्थित है। भलका ग्राम निवासी 66 वर्षीय गिरवरसिंह जाट सीमेंट, लोहा, प्लास्टर ऑफ पेरिस, कंक्रीट और कॉपर आदि के मिश्रण से बड़ी सुन्दर मूर्तिया बनाते हैं। उन्होंने कृष्ण भगवान, सरस्वती, हनुमानजी आदि की बड़ी ही सुन्दर कलात्मक मूर्तियाँ बनाई हैं। गिरवरसिंह जाट की कलाकृतियों में ब्रजभूमि की झलक दिखाई देती है, यह सामाजिक-सांस्कृतिक इतिहास की जनप्रवृत्ति है।[8] विद्वान प्रभुदयाल मित्तल ने महाराजा सूरजमल (1756-1763) का मूल्यांकन करते समय लिखा है, 'दिल्ली के निकटवर्ती बल्लभगढ़ से लेकर ग्वालियर के समीपवर्ती गोहद तक का जटवारा क्षेत्र उसके प्रभाव में था। जटवारा नाम उस समय के मरहठा राज्य के दरबारी कागज पत्रों में मिलता है।'[9] इस प्रकार जटवारा भू-भाग महाराजा सूरजमल जाट अर्थात अठारहवीं सदी के मध्य से ही इस क्षेत्र में जाटों की सामाजिक-आर्थिक संस्कृति के क्षेत्राधिकार का विषय बन चुका था। इंदरगढ़ के आसपास के जाट प्रभावित गांवों के जाट, हिन्दूवादी संस्कृति के पोषक और भारतीय संस्कृति के रक्षक के रूप में रहे हैं। इन्दरगढ़ के समीप के गांव पिपरऊआ के स्वर्गीय सीताराम जाट सन् 1940-50 के दौर में जाटों के प्रसिद्ध लोकप्रिय नेता के रूप में उभरे थे। सन 1804-1836 के बीच यह क्षेत्र भाण्डेर परगने के अंतर्गत गोहद के जाट शासक कीरतसिंह के अधीन था। उन्होंने सन् 1804 ई. के लगभग पिपरऊआ के जाट तेजसिंह के पुत्र तुलसीदास को यह गांव जागीर में दिया था।[10]

इस क्षेत्र में 'जटवारी' बोली बुन्देली की उपबोली के रूप में प्रचलित और स्थापित हुई थी। इसकी समानार्थी क्षेत्रवाद के रूप में स्थापित और प्रचलित अन्य बोलियां भी हैं। डॉ. सीताकिशोर खरे के अनुसार, 'बुन्देलखण्ड की पूर्व रियासतों वाले भू-भाग में हिन्दी की बुन्देली बोली का व्यवहार है सिकरवारी, तंवरधारी, जटवारी, भदावरी, राजपूतधारी, कछवायधारी, पमारी, रघुवंशी, लोधांती, खटोला, बनाफरी, आदि बुन्देली बोली के रूप में हैं।' यह बोली व्यवहार का उपभाषायी रूप जाट इतिहास के सामाजिक एवं आर्थिक स्वरूप की विवेचना के अंतर्गत आता है।[11]

जटवारा के भूभाग के कुछ गांवों का सर्वेक्षण एवं संपर्क के आधार पर किया गया यह शोध-पत्र जाट इतिहास के सामाजिक एवं आर्थिक पक्ष के स्वरूप को बिन्दुरूप में

उपस्थित करता है। इस समस्त रूप का व्यापक सर्वे एवं संपर्कयात्रा जाट संस्कृति को एक विशाल रूपक दे सकती है। फिर भी उत्तर मध्यकालीन एवं मराठाकालीन 18-20 वीं सदी के बुन्देलखण्ड के जटवारा भू-भाग के सामाजिक-आर्थिक जीवन की झांकी यहां प्रस्तुत करने का यह एक लघु प्रयास है।

## संदर्भ सूची

1. पी. एन. श्रीवास्तव : गजेटियर विभाग, भोपाल, (1977) पृ. 306; *बुन्देलखण्ड की पूर्व रियासतों में पत्र-पाडुलिपियों का सर्वेक्षण* (डॉ. सीताकिशोर खरे) आराधना, कानपुर, (1994) पृ. 23-25।
2. द *आइन-ए-अकबरी*, भाग 2 (अबुलफजल कृत), अनुवाद, एच.एस. जैरिट, डी. के. पब्लिशर, दिल्ली (1994), पृ. 199-200।
3. इंदरगढ़ के शंभू राणा एवं क्षेत्र से संकलित जानकारी।
4. सिनसिनी राजस्थान के भरतपुर जिले से उत्तर-पश्चिम में 22 किमी. के लगभग है।
5. भलका-खडऊआ आदि गांवों का लेखक द्वारा किया गया सर्वेक्षण। भलका के कम्मोदसिंह, गिरिवरसिंह जाट एवं इन्दरगढ़ के लल्ला भइया गुर्जर तथा विनय गुर्जर के सहयोग से।
6. वर्तमान में भलका में निवासरत बुजुर्ग कुंतीबाई एवं कुलदीपसिंह जाट की धर्मपत्नी गुड्डी बाई के सौजन्य से। *महाराजा सूरजमल* (कुंअर नटवरसिंह, राधाकृष्ण प्रकाशन दिल्ली, 1985) पृ. 46-56; *जाट और मुगल साम्राज्य* (डॉ. गिरीशचन्द्र द्विवेदी, सं. वीर सिंह, ओरिजिनल्स, दिल्ली), पृ. 100-298।
7. जटवारा-भूभाग के गांवों से संकलित जानकारी।
8. *ब्रज का सांस्कृतिक इतिहास*, भाग 2 (प्रभुदयाल मित्तल, साहित्य संस्थान, मथुरा, 1966) पृ. 229-243, एवं भलका निवासी गिरवरसिंह जाट के सौजन्य से।
9. *वही*, पृ. 242।
10. *बुन्देलखण्ड की पूर्व रियासतों में पत्र-पाण्डुलिपियों का सर्वेक्षण* (डॉ. सीताकिशोर, आराधना, कानपुर, 1994) पृ. 101।
11. *वही*, पृ. 26।

31

# पंज प्यारों में एक थे भाई धर्मसिंह

तेजपाल सिंह

जब वैदिक धर्म रूपी सिंह पौराणिक धर्म के सामने घुटने टेक गया, सूर्य जगनू के सामने कान्तिहीन हो गया, तब ईश्वर प्रदत्त भेंट के रूप में श्री नानक देव जी महाराज का प्रादुर्भाव सम्वत 1526 विक्रमी में कार्तिक सुदी 15 को हुआ। गुरु नानक गृहस्थ जीवन में रहते हुए संत बने तथा कुप्रथाओं एवं आडम्बरों का विरोध कर समाज का कल्याण किया।

कोई भी समतावादी आंदोलन तत्कालीन परिस्थितियों मे एक राजनैतिक और सैनिक आंदोलन का रूप ग्रहण कर सकता है। सन् 1675 में धर्मांध औरंगजेब ने गुरु तेग बहादुर को मौत के घाट उतार दिया। परिणामस्वरूप सिख आंदोलन धीरे-धीरे 'सैनिक नेतृत्व' का रूप ग्रहण करता चला गया। गुरु गोबिन्द सिंह ने इसमें महत्त्वपूर्ण योगदान दिया और उन्होंने अपनी संगठन क्षमता का भरपूर परिचय दिया। पीड़ित मानवता के उद्धार के लिए उन्हें सम्राट औरंगजेब के विरुद्ध हथियार उठाने पड़े।

धर्मांधता के कारण मुगल वंश की सत्ता का खूँटा औरंगजेब के देखते-देखते ही हिल गया। इसी से लाभ उठाने के लिए रोहतक के माडौठी छारा के दलाल वंशी चार भाई भूवाल सिंह, जठमल सिंह, जगराम सिंह और गुरुवा सिंह युवावस्था, बाहुबल, अदम्य साहस और भाग्य के भरोसे पर महत्त्वाकांक्षाओं की पूर्ति के लिए जत्था बनाकर उत्तर प्रदेश की ओर बढ़ गए तथा कई गांवों को बसाकर रहने लगे तथा आस-पास के इलाकों को अधिकार में कर लिया एवं कालान्तर में इस वंश के लोगों ने कुचेसर राज कायम किया।[1] इन्हीं लोगों में से चौधरी संतराम ने अपने पौरुष से हस्तिनापुर के पास 5 गांवों की जमींदारी हासिल की। संतराम वर्तमान सैफपुर गांव के निकट जो उनकी जमींदारी में आता था, निवास करने लगे। उनकी धर्मपत्नी माता सांभोदेवी की पवित्र कुक्षी से दो पुत्र धर्मदास एवं कर्मचन्द्र उत्पन्न हुए। कर्मचन्द्र के नाम पर गांव का नाम कर्मचन्द्रपुर

पड़ा। कालान्तर में सैफ अली नवाब का कब्जा होने के कारण आज गांव का नाम सैफपुर कर्मचन्द्रपुर पड़ गया। धर्मदास का जन्म 1666 ई. (सम्वत 1724) के लगभग हुआ था।[2] जवान होते-होते यह सिखों के संग रहने लगा तथा सिख धर्म की शिक्षाओं से प्रभावित हो गया। 30 वर्ष की आयु में उसने अपनी ज्ञान पिपासा को शान्त करने के लिए घर त्याग दिया तथा नानक प्याऊ धर्मस्थल पर पहुंच गया। वहां उसे आनन्दपुर साहिब जाकर गुरु गोबिन्द सिंह के दर्शन कर ज्ञान प्राप्त करने की सलाह मिली। 1698 में धर्मदास आनन्दपुर साहिब पहुंच गया क्योंकि ईश्वर उसे भारत के रंगमंच पर अपने जौहर दिखाने की प्रेरणा दे रहा था।

**गुरु गोबिन्द सिंह द्वारा पंच प्यारे तथा खालसा पंथ की घोषणा**

गुरु जी ने तमाम सिख संगतों के नाम संवत 1756 में फरमान जारी किया कि वह चैत्र के अंत में आने वाली बैसाखी को मनाने के लिए आनन्दपुर में एकत्रित हों। भारी संख्या में लोगों ने आनन्दपुर साहिब में शिरकत की। हजारों की संख्या में लोग गुरु दर्शन की उत्कंठा लिए देखते हैं कि यकायक गुरु गोबिन्द सिंह हाथ में नंगी तलवार लिए हुए सभा स्थल पर उपस्थित हो गए। सामने मंच पर खड़ा, आँखों से चिंगारी बखेरता, नंगी चमचमाती तलवार घुमाता हुआ तैंतीस वर्षीय युवा व्यक्ति कह रहा था, "जालिम के अत्याचार की भड़क रही अग्नि को बुझाने तथा धर्म रक्षा की वेदी पर बलिदान करने के लिए मुझे सिर चाहिए.... मुझे सिर चाहिए।"

''मैं अपना सिर देने के लिए तैयार हूँ। मेरा नाम दयाराम है। मैं खत्री हूँ और लाहौर का रहने वाला हूँ!'' वह उठा और हाथ जोड़कर प्रार्थना की कि सतगुरु जी इस दास का शीश आपके चरणों में हाजिर है। फिर वह और लपलपाती तलवार वाला व्यक्ति एक खेमे की ओट में चले जाते है। 'खटाक' और खेमे ने खून की धार वह निकलती है। मंच पर फिर वह तलवार चमचमा रही है, परन्तु वह इस बार अधिक भयावह होकर वातावरण पर फिर से झूल रही है।

"एक सिर और चाहिए।"

सन्नाटा गहरा हो गया। इस हो रही घटना को देखकर लोग कुछ दहल से गए परन्तु जब गुरु जी ने दूसरी बार वही सवाल किया तो किसी कोने से धर्म के परवाने की आवाज आई, "अपना सिर देने को तैयार हूँ। मैं धर्मदास हूँ। गुरु जी, मैं जाट हूँ और हस्तिनापुर का रहने वाला।" और भीड़ की लहरों पर से उठता हुआ वह जाट उस तलवार को चूमने इस तरह से चला जा रहा है जैसे परवाना दीपशिखा की ओर। उसने नम्र विनती की कि सच्चे पादशाह दास हाजिर है। गुरु जी ने कहा कि क्या तुम्हें मृत्यु का भय नहीं। तो भाई धर्मा ने उत्तर दिया-"मृत्यु को तो एक दिन अवश्य आना है उससे

फिर भय कैसा? यदि यह शीश धर्म की वेदी पर न्यौछावर हो जाए तो इससे अच्छी कौन सी बात हो सकती है।"

'खटाक' की आवाज ज्यादा खरतनाक हुई। खेमे से ज्यादा खून बहता हुआ निकला। चमचमाते वाली तलवार खून में और सन गई और सिर मांगने वाले युवक की आँखों की चिनगारियां संकेत की चुभन ज्यादा बांधने लग गई। "एक सिर और चाहिए।" मैं अपना सिर देने को तैयार हूँ। मैं द्वारका निवासी मोहकम चन्द छीपा।" "एक सिर और चाहिए।" जिसके उत्तर में बीदर निवासी भाई साहब चन्द नाई। "फिर एक सिर की और मांग....." जगन्नाथ निवासी भाई हिम्मत कहार ने गुरु के सामने अपना शीश भेंट किया। वे पांचों गुरु के प्यारे बन गए। सबके प्यारे बन गए - पंचप्यारे। अमृत तैयार किया गया पाँचों को एक ही बाँटे (पात्र) में पिलाया गया और वे सब सिंह बन गए। धर्मदास अब भाई धर्मसिंह बन गए।[3]

## आनन्दपुर साहिब का संग्राम

धर्मदास से बने भाई धर्मसिंह ने आनन्दपुर की भयंकर लड़ाई में गुरु जी के साथ युद्ध में भाग लिया। वह युद्ध पंजाब के समस्त मुस्लिम हाकिम व पहाड़ी राजपूत राजाओं के संयुक्त बल के साथ 1761 वि. में लड़ा गया था। गुरुद्वारा आनन्दपुर साहिब को छोड़ते समय भाई धर्मसिंह उन्हीं के साथ रहे तथा सभी सुख-दुःखों में साथ दिया। इसके उपरान्त गुरुजी के साथ वे चमकौर की तरफ बढ़ चले।[4]

## चमकौर का विचित्र युद्ध

चमकौर के विचित्र युद्ध में धर्मसिंह कंधे से कंधा मिलाकर गुरुजी के साथ रहे। शाही सेना और आस-पास के लाखों की संख्या में ग्रामीण लोगों ने छोटे से गांव चमकौर को घेर लिया। गुरु जी के पास केवल 40 सिख योद्धा थे। भयंकर युद्ध हुआ हजारों मुगल धराशायी हुए तथा 20 सिख भी इसमें शहीद हो गए। दोनों साहिबजादे अजीत सिंह तथा जुझारसिंह अपना महान बलिदान देकर चले गए। सर्वसम्मत प्रार्थना पर भविष्य की नीति-निर्धारण के लिए गुरु जी भाई धर्मसिंह, भाई दयासिंह तथा मानसिंह के सुरक्षा घेरे में हवेली को छोड़ सुरक्षित निकल गए।

## जफर नामा

भाई धर्मसिंह तथा भाई दयासिंह गुरु गोबिन्द सिंह का पत्र 'जफर नामा' औरंगजेब को पेश करने के लिए दक्षिण भारत गए। यह कार्य बड़ा दुरुह था क्योंकि यह शेर के जबड़े में हाथ डालने जैसा था।[5]

**राजकुमार मुअज्जम को समर्थन**

20 फरवरी 1707 को औरंगजेब की मृत्यु हो गयी। उसके तीनों पुत्रों मुअज्जम, आजम और कामबख्श में उत्तराधिकार के लिए खींचतान आरम्भ हो गई एवं युद्ध का बिगुल बज गया। शहजादे मुअज्जम ने गुरु गोबिन्द सिंह से सहायता की याचना की। गुरु जी ने अपने विश्वासपात्र सेनानायक भाई धर्मसिंह को 8 जून 1707 को एक छोटी सैनिक टुकड़ी लेकर जजाऊ के युद्ध में मुअज्जम की सहायता के लिए भेजा। फलस्वरूप शहजादे मुअज्जम की जीत हुई और वह बहादुरशाह के नाम से हिन्दुस्तान की गद्दी पर बैठा।[6]

धर्मसिंह आनन्दपुर साहिब से हजूर साहिब (नाँदेड़), महाराष्ट्र की यात्रा तक गुरुजी के साथ रहे और गुरु जी की मृत्यु (7 अक्तूबर 1708) के समय भी उनके साथ थे। इनका अकाल चलाना (देहावसान) सम्वत 1765 को हजूर साहिब में हुआ। नाँदेड़ साहिब में धर्मसिंह की याद को संजोये रखने के लिये एक गुरुद्वारा बना हुआ है।[7]

भाई धर्मसिंह ने सचेत एवं जाग्रत होकर समर्पण भाव से गुरु जी की सेवा की एवं एक महामानव की भांति इस नश्वर संसार को छोड़कर चले गये। इन्हीं के परिवार के एक सदस्य उदयवीर सिंह दलाल ने बताया कि भाई धर्मसिंह बनने के उपरांत फिर वे कभी अपने गांव वापिस नहीं आए। ग्राम सैफपुर कर्मचन्द्रपुर, जनपद मेरठ में पंज प्यारे भाई धर्मसिंह का ऐतिहासिक भव्य गुरुद्वारा बना हुआ है। डेरा कार सेवा बाबा हरवंश सिंह (दिल्ली वाले) लंगर तथा प्रशासनिक प्रबंध को सुचारु रूप से चला रहे हैं। क्षेत्र के सभी लोगों विशेषकर जाट जाति को उनके द्वारा धर्म की रक्षा के कार्य पर गर्व है।

**संदर्भ**


1. योगेन्द्र पाल शास्त्री : *जाट क्षत्रिय इतिहास*, कुचेसर (1944), पृ. 257
2. गुरुद्वारा सैफपुर की दीवार पर बने पट्ट पर लिखा आलेख : पाँच प्यारे भाई धर्मसिंह जी का जन्म गांव सैफपुर मेरठ (हस्तिनापुर) के निवासी भाई संतराम जाट के घर माता साभों की कोख से सम्वत् 1724 को हुआ। सम्वत् 1756 (13 अप्रैल सन् 1699) की बैसाखी के शुभ दिन पर जब भाई धर्मसिंह जी की आयु 32 साल थी। श्री गुरु गोबिन्द सिंह जी की दूसरी बार सिर की मांग करने पर आप जी ने सीस भेंट किया। अमृतपान करके धर्मदास से धर्मसिंह बन गए। अमृतपान करने के बाद भाई धर्मसिंह जी आनंदपुर साहिब से हजूर साहिब (नाँदेड़) महाराष्ट्र की यात्रा तक साथ रहे। इनका अकाल चलाना सम्वत् 1765 की हजूर साहब में हुआ।
3. ठाकुर देशराज : *सिख इतिहास*, ग्रामोत्थान विद्यापीठ, संगरिया (संवत 2011), पृ.

181-200

4. *उपरोक्त*, पृ. 172-73
5. गुरमीत सिंह बेदी : संत सिपाही गुरु गोबिन्द सिंह, *दैनिक जागरण*, 3 जनवरी 2006।
6. विजय कुमार माथुर : गुरु गोबिन्द सिंह एण्ड दि खालसा, *टाइम्स ऑफ इंडिया*, 28 दिसम्बर, 1995।
7. एस.एस. अहलूवालिया : श्री गोबिन्द सिंह जी, *नवभारत टाइम्स*, नई दिल्ली, 28 दिसम्बर 1995

# Contributors

*Dr. Etee Bahadur*
Research Officer, J.N. Memorial Fund, Teen Murti Bhawan, New Delhi-110011

*Dr. Farha Adeeba*
Department of Persian, University of Delhi, Delhi-110007

*Dr. Khajan Singh Sangwan*
Professor, Department of Sociology, M. D. University, Rohtak (Haryana)

*Dr. K.S. Bajwa*
Associate Professor, Punjab Historical Studies, Punjabi University, Patiala

*Dr. Mahender Singh Bagi*
Associate Professor, Department of History, Govt. College, Bapauli (Panipat)

*Mamta Tyagi*
Research Scholar, History Department, Delhi University, B-266, Palam Extension, Part 1, Sector 7, Dwarka, New Delhi-110077

*Manisha Choudhary*
Associate Professor, Deptt. of History, Bharti College, New Delhi

*Manveer Kaur*
Research Scholar, Department of History, Punjab University, Chandigarh

*Dr. M.S. Rana*
D-80, Shastri Nagar, Meerut (U.P.)

*Nirmal Kumar*

Fellow, NMML, Teen Murti Bhawan, New Delhi-110011

*i Singh*

H.N. 206, Sector 28, Noida-201301 (U.P.)

*. Alam*

Archivist, National Archives of India, Janpath, New Delhi-110002

*P.K. Shukla*

Former Member Secretary, ICHR, 16, Uttaranchal Apartments, Plot 5, Patparganj, New Delhi-110092

*Rajesh Kumar*

Assistant Director (Research), Indian Council of Historical Research, New Delhi

*R.K. Kundu*

Faculty Member, Department of Public Administration, M.D. University, Rohtak (Haryana)

*S.L. Kundu*

Project Fellow (UGC), Department of Public Administration, M.D. University, Rohtak (Haryana)

*S.S. Rana*

Former Dean of Colleges, University of Delhi, Delhi; Former Vice-President, Surajmal Memorial Education Society, New Delhi, B-13, IDC Aptts, Plot 8C, Sector 11, Dwarka, New Delhi-110075

*ir Husain*

Archivist, National Archives of India, Janpath, New Delhi-110001

*आरती चौधरी*

हीराकुंज, आलोक सदन, शर्मा कॉलोनी, रानी बाजार, बीकानेर-334001 (राजस्थान)

*एफ. के. कपिल*

निकट रघुनाथ मंदिर, पाकों का वास, पोंगलपुरा मार्ग, जोधपुर, राजस्थान

*डॉ. एस. एल. वरे*

प्रोफेसर एंव विभागाध्यक्ष, इतिहास विभाग एवं शोध केन्द्र, शासकीय माधव स्नातकोत्तर महाविद्यालय, मध्य प्रदेश

*कल्पना चौधरी*

हीराकुंज, आलोक सदन, शर्मा कॉलोनी, रानी बाजार, बीकानेर-334001 (राजस्थान)

*जसवंत सिंह खीचड़*

उप-रजिस्ट्रार, महाराजा गंगासिंह विश्वविद्यालय, बीकानेर, राजस्थान

*जोगाराम सारण*

अशोक पुस्तक भंडार, किसान मार्केट, बाड़मेर, राजस्थान

*तेजपाल सिंह*

डी-2ए/95ए, जनकपुरी, नई दिल्ली-110058

*डॉ. धर्मेन्द्र पारे*

सहायक प्राध्यापक, हिन्दी विभाग, शासकीय कला एवं वाणिज्य स्नातकोत्तर महाविद्यालय, हरदा, मध्य प्रदेश

*डॉ. प्रणव देव*

राजकीय स्नातकोत्तर महाविद्यालय, झालावाड़, राजस्थान

*प्रो. ब्रह्माराम चौधरी*

हीराकुंज, आलोक सदन, शर्मा कॉलोनी, रानी बाजार, बीकानेर-334001 (राजस्थान)

*डॉ. मनोहर सिंह राणावत*

उपनिदेशक, श्री नटनागर शोध संस्थान, सीतामऊ, मध्य प्रदेश

*डॉ. मलिका बोहरा*

व्याख्याता इतिहास, महाराणा प्रताप राजकीय महाविद्यालय, प्रतापनगर, चितौड़गढ़, राजस्थान

*डॉ. महेन्द्र सिंह खड़गावत*

निदेशक, राजस्थान राज्य अभिलेखागार, बीकानेर, राजस्थान

*श्री योगानन्द शास्त्री*

स्पीकर, विधानसभा, दिल्ली प्रदेश

*डॉ. राकेश कुमार शर्मा*

व्याख्याता इतिहास, बा. शा. रा. राजकीय कला महाविद्यालय, अलवर, राजस्थान

*डॉ. रामस्वरुप ढेंगुला*

कुंजनपुरा, दतिया, मध्य प्रदेश

*सुमेस्ता*

शोधार्थी, इतिहास विभाग, गवर्मेन्ट डूंगर कॉलेज, बीकानेर, राजस्थान

*प्रो. शिव कुमार भनोत*

विभागाध्यक्ष इतिहास, एम. जी. एस. विश्वविद्यालय, बीकानेर, राजस्थान